TEACHING WITH

The Bedford Guide for College Writers

THIRD EDITION

VOLUME TWO
BACKGROUND READINGS

TEACHING WITH

The Bedford Guide for College Writers

THIRD EDITION

by

X. J. Kennedy, Dorothy M. Kennedy, and Sylvia A. Holladay

VOLUME TWO
BACKGROUND READINGS

Edited by
Shirley Morahan
Northeast Missouri State University

Bedford Books *of* St. Martin's Press
Boston

7   6   5   4   3   2

f   e   d   c   b   a

For information, write: St. Martin's Press, Inc.
175 Fifth Avenue, New York, NY 10010

Editorial Offices: Bedford Books *of* St. Martin's Press
29 Winchester Street, Boston, MA 02116

ISBN: 0–312–06648–1

Instructors who have adopted *The Bedford Guide for College Writers,* Third Edition, as a textbook for a course are authorized to duplicate portions of this manual for their students.

Acknowledgments

David Bartholomae, "Inventing the University." From *When a Writer Can't Write: Studies in Writer's Block and Other Composing Problems,* edited by Mike Rose. Reprinted by permission of The Guilford Press.

Richard Beach, "Demonstrating Techniques for Assessing Writing in the Writing Conference," *College Composition and Communication,* February 1986. Copyright 1986 by the National Council of Teachers of English. Reprinted with permission.

Patricia Bizzell and Bruce Herzberg, "Research as a Social Act," *The Clearing House* 60 (March 1987): 303–306. Reprinted with permission of the Helen Dwight Reid Educational Foundation. Published by Heldref Publications, 1319 Eighteenth St., N.W., Washington, D.C. 20036-1802. Copyright © 1987. "Writing Across the Curriculum: A Bibliographic Essay." This essay first appeared in *The Territory of Language: Linguistics, Stylistics, and the Teaching of Composition* (Carbondale: Southern Illinois University Press, 1986) and is reprinted with the permission of the authors and the copyright holder, Donald McQuade.

Robert Brooke, "Modeling a Writer's Identity: Reading and Imitation in the Writing Classroom," *College Composition and Communication,* February 1988. Copyright 1988 by the National Council of Teachers of English. Reprinted with permission.

Kenneth A. Bruffe, "The Art of Collaborative Learning: Making the Most of Knowledgeable Peers," *Change* (March/April 1987): 42–47. Reprinted with permission of the Helen Dwight Reid Educational Foundation. Published by Heldref Publications, 1319 Eighteenth Street, N.W., Washington, D.C. 20036-1802. Copyright 1987.

Lisa Ede and Andrea Lunsford, "Audience Addressed/Audience Invoked: The Role of Audience in Composition," *College Composition and Communication,* May 1984. Copyright 1984 by the National Council of Teachers of English. Reprinted with permission.

Peter Elbow, "Closing My Eyes as I Speak: An Argument for Ignoring Audience," *College English,* January 1987. Copyright 1987 by the National Council of Teachers of English. Reprinted with permission. "Embracing Contraries in the Teaching Process," *College English,* April 1983. Copyright 1983 by the National Council of Teachers of English. Reprinted with permission.

Preface

This collection of readings in current composition theory can help you acquire or broaden a theoretical and practical background for *The Bedford Guide for College Writers,* Third Edition. Although I've selected the readings with first-time instructors in mind, I also hope that veteran instructors in community colleges and four-year institutions will find useful ideas and suggestions in them.

Writing theorists and teachers have had lively discussions and spirited debates about the philosophical issues and pedagogical assumptions that inform these readings. From such conversation — public and private — and their own classroom experiences, writing instructors have gained more confidence about their teaching hunches and skills. I hope your own "conversation" with these readings will help you as they have other writing instructors to become a particularly adept and creative teacher of writing.

The readings in this book address the main concerns of *The Bedford Guide for College Writers.* The first part, "Teaching Writing: An Introduction," includes articles describing philosophies and pedagogies of composition and about responding to student writing. Part Two, "The Writing Process," includes articles on the aspects of the writing process discussed in *The Bedford Guide.* Part Three, "Options," provides articles about the connections among reading and writing, collaborative learning, and writing across the curriculum. Finally, the annotated bibliography at the end cites the many fine articles that space would not allow elsewhere. It is, of course, not a comprehensive bibliography, but a good jumping-off point for a more sustained reflection on and research into composition and the artful teaching of composition.

This arrangement of readings reflects the organization of *The Bedford Guide for College Writers.* However, just as the textbook is recursive, you can also jump into these readings at any point and work forward, from that reading on, drop back to read or reread an article earlier in the collection, skip ahead to see how Elbow on audience connects with Elbow's philosophy, or stop and consider how Flower's discussion of purpose resonates against Perl's "felt sense."

You'll find in these readings very practical discussion with specific recommendations about teaching strategies. You'll also find more philosophical discussion of the large assumptions that inform our teaching and thinking about composition. A headnote to each reading focuses on the key assumptions of the piece. Two categories of questions follow each selection: "The Writer's Insights as a Resource for Your Teaching" and "The Writer's Insights as a Resource for the Writing Classroom." I called on my experiences teaching and supervising novice instructors of writers and working with faculty who use writing across the curriculum for the first set of exercises. They're designed to prompt you into reflection and into growth as a writing teacher. The second set suggests applications of the insights of each reading for your writing classroom.

In the accompanying manual, *Teaching with* The Bedford Guide for College Writers, Third Edition: *Practical Suggestions,* you'll find commentary on many of the same issues addressed in this volume and, in particular, descriptions of how I understand the *Bedford*

Guide readings and writing assignments to interconnect with the discussion of the large discourse community that you entered when you began to teach writing and that you find reflected in this sourcebook. I recommend that you use the two volumes together so that you can most imaginatively and effectively mine the mother lode of *The Bedford Guide for College Writers*.

Revising this set of readings and commentary gave me another opportunity to synthesize my own reading in and reflection on the discipline of teaching writing. Often we tell student writers that we discover what we think and feel when we write, formally or informally. As a result of my work for this book, I've clarified further what I think about writing in a community and how that thinking informs my teaching. Several first-year instructors and veteran teachers have reported to Bedford Books that they used the readings and resources both for their own professional development and for the most effective use of *The Bedford Guide for College Writers* in their classrooms. I hope you find these materials equally useful.

Contents

TEACHING WITH

The Bedford Guide for College Writers

THIRD EDITION

VOLUME TWO
BACKGROUND READINGS

PART ONE

TEACHING WRITING: AN INTRODUCTION

In Part One of this ancillary, you will find readings that will, I think, provoke you to reflect about the process of teaching writing and about many of the characteristics of *The Bedford Guide for College Writers*. The readings have been chosen for two reasons: to illuminate some of the major assumptions about why and whom we teach in a writing classroom and to illustrate some of the pedagogic strategies used by writing instructors who organize their courses with various foci such as writing as a recursive process, the writer's resources, writing as critical thinking, and evaluation for revision. I recommend that you begin your research into and reflection on composition theory and pedagogy with these readings and that you return to them when you want to step back and look again at the experiences of the community of writers that you foster.

PHILOSOPHIES AND PEDAGOGIES

Every choice you make as a writing instructor is informed by some philosophy of composition and of teaching composition, even if you're not fully aware of the philosophy you hold. The more aware you become of your assumptions and premises, the more you can look at, rethink, and improve your teaching. To begin this process of reflection, I recommend that before you begin to teach a writing course or early in the semester you sit down and freewrite or brainstorm for about fifteen minutes, listing your "I believes" about writing and about the teaching of writing. Periodically, shape those beliefs into some prose (or poetry) that you can refer to as you plan assignments, structure sequences of assignments, build or redesign a syllabus, ponder a writing curriculum, propose support services for writers across the curriculum, or discuss your pedagogy with teaching colleagues. You might also want to consult the final section of *Teaching with* The Bedford Guide for College Writers: *Practical Suggestions,* which offers a number of essays to help you shape your teaching philosophy. Reading the essays crafted by experienced writing teachers like those whom you meet in this book will also be a resource for your reflecting and your teaching. The essays in this section come from highly esteemed writer-teachers. The writers share their major assumptions with writing teachers in colleges and universities nationwide.

Many first-year instructors keep a "reflective journal" in which they log and reflect on what occurred in class and how students responded to assignments. Those instructors use the journal to describe their own reactions and responses to the class dynamic, to the process of building a writing community, and to the connections they make among what they are reading outside the classroom and actual events within the classroom. Two or three times a semester they read over their entries and chart their own learning and growth as instructors. By the end of the first semester, most new instructors can see some dramatic change in confidence, attitudes about writing communities and student writing, use of teaching strategies, and understanding of how the parts of the syllabus or the course connect.

The reflective journal is a very useful resource for writing about teaching, for developing a final draft of a philosophy for teaching writing, and for designing syllabi for second-semester or second-year courses. It could be an important part of a "teaching portfolio," a collection of products that demonstrate your practice and improvement as an instructor. That portfolio could include assignments given, copies of student responses, syllabi, descriptions of classroom activities, and notes on reading. From that collection, you might on occasion select representative materials for others to view, read, hear, and evaluate. The "teaching portfolio" is particularly useful for self-assessment and teaching evaluation. You might use it when you apply for jobs, fellowships, research grants, tenure, and promotions.

EMBRACING CONTRARIES IN THE TEACHING PROCESS

Peter Elbow

This essay by Peter Elbow expresses clearly and eloquently what most writing teachers — whether novice or experienced — intuit and grapple to name. Elbow focuses on the dialectical process of teaching. He describes a "paradoxical coherence" that is necessary if we are to remain inspirited and effective as teachers. Elbow believes that we can use as a paradigm our conflicting loyalties of commitment to students and of commitment to standards. By taking a "contradictory stance" and by admitting that we will always be involved in the dialectic of students and standards, we will be less likely to confuse ourselves or our students. He anchors his philosophy in practical suggestions about using the dialectical process and argues that good teaching, like good writing, is a recursive process of "embracing contraries."

My argument is that good teaching seems a struggle because it calls on skills or mentalities that are actually contrary to each other and thus tend to interfere with each other. It was my exploration of writing that led me to look for contraries in difficult or complex processes. I concluded that good writing requires on the one hand the ability to conceive copiously of many possibilities, an ability which is enhanced by a spirit of open, accepting generativity; but on the other hand good writing also requires an ability to criticize and reject everything but the best, a very different ability which is enhanced by a tough-minded critical spirit. I end up seeing in good writers the ability somehow to be extremely creative and extremely critical, without letting one mentality prosper at the expense of the other or being halfhearted in both. (For more about this idea see my *Writing with Power* [New York: Oxford UP, 1981], especially Chapter 1.)

In this frame of mind I began to see a paradoxical coherence in teaching where formerly I was perplexed. I think the two conflicting mentalities needed for good teaching stem from the two conflicting obligations inherent in the job: we have an obligation to students but we also have an obligation to knowledge and society. Surely we are incomplete as teachers if we are committed only to what we are teaching but not to our students, or only to our students but not to what we are teaching, or halfhearted in our commitment to both.

We like to think that these two commitments coincide, and often they do. It happens often enough, for example, that our commitment to standards leads us to give a low grade or tough comment, and it is just what the student needs to hear. But just as often we see that a student needs praise and support rather than a tough grade, even for her weak performance, if she is really to prosper as a student and a person — if we are really to nurture her fragile investment in her studies. Perhaps we can finesse this conflict between a "hard" and "soft" stance if it is early in the semester or we are only dealing with a rough draft; for the time being we can give the praise and support we sense is humanly appropriate and hold off strict judgment and standards till later. But what about when it is the end of the course or a final draft needs a grade? It is comforting to take as our paradigm that first situation where the tough grade was just right, and to consider the trickier situation as somehow anomalous, and thus to assume that we always serve students best by serving knowledge, and vice versa. But I now think I can throw more light on the nature of teaching by taking our conflicting loyalties as paradigmatic.

2

Our loyalty to students asks us to be their allies and hosts as we instruct and share: to invite all students to enter in and join us as members of a learning community — even if they have difficulty. Our commitment to students asks us to assume they are all capable of learning, to see things through their eyes, to help bring out their best rather than their worst when it comes to tests and grades. By taking this inviting stance we will help more of them learn.

But our commitment to knowledge and society asks us to be guardians or bouncers: we must discriminate, evaluate, test, grade, certify. We are invited to stay true to the inherent standards of what we teach, whether or not that stance fits the particular students before us. We have a responsibility to society — that is, to our discipline, our college or university, and to other learning communities of which we are members — to see that the students we certify really understand or can do what we teach, to see that the grades and credits and degrees we give really have the meaning or currency they are supposed to have.[1]

A pause for scruples. Can we give up so easily the paradigm of teaching as harmonious? Isn't there something misguided in the very idea that these loyalties are conflicting? After all, if we think we are being loyal to students by being extreme in our solicitude for them, won't we undermine the integrity of the subject matter or the currency of the credit and thereby drain value from the very thing we are supposedly giving them? And if we think we are being loyal to society by being extreme in our ferocity — keeping out *any* student with substantial misunderstanding — won't we deprive subject matter and society of the vitality and reconceptualizations they need to survive and grow? Knowledge and society only exist embodied — that is, flawed.

This sounds plausible. But even if we choose a middle course and go only so far as fairness toward subject matter and society, the very fact that we grade and certify at all — the very fact that we must sometimes flunk students — tempts many of them to behave defensively with us. Our mere fairness to subject matter and society tempts students to try to hide weaknesses from us, "psych us out," or "con us." It is as though we are doctors trying to treat patients who hide their symptoms from us for fear we will put them in the hospital.

Student defensiveness makes our teaching harder. We say, "Don't be afraid to ask questions," or even, "It's a sign of intelligence to be willing to ask naive questions." But when we are testers and graders, students too often fear to ask. Towards examiners they must play it safe, drive defensively, not risk themselves. This stunts learning. When they trust the teacher to be wholly an ally, students are more willing to take risks, connect the self to the material, and experiment. Here is the source not just of learning but also of genuine development or growth.

Let me bring this conflict closer to home. A department chair or dean who talks with us about our teaching and who sits in on our classes is our ally insofar as she is trying to help us teach better; and we can get more help from her to the degree that we openly share with her our fears, difficulties, and failures. Yet insofar as she makes promotion or tenure decisions about us or even participates in those decisions, we will be tempted not to reveal our weaknesses and failures. If we want the best help for our shortcomings, someone who is merely fair is not enough. We need an ally, not a judge.

Thus we can take a merely judicious, compromise position toward our students only if we are willing to settle for being *sort of* committed to students and *sort of* committed to subject matter and society. This middling or fair stance, in fact, is characteristic of many teachers who lack investment in teaching or who have lost it. Most invested teachers, on the other hand, tend to be a bit passionate about supporting students or else passionate about serving and protecting the subject matter they love — and thus they tend to live more on one side or the other of some allegedly golden mean.

But supposing you reply, "Yes, I agree that a compromise is not right. Just middling. Muddling. Not excellence or passion in either direction. But that's not what I'm after. My scruple had to do with your very notion of *two directions*. There is only one direction.

3

Excellence. Quality. The very conception of conflict between loyalties is wrong. An inch of progress in one direction, whether toward knowledge or toward students, is always an inch in the direction of the other. The needs of students and of knowledge or society are in essential harmony."

To assert this harmony is, in a sense, to agree with what I am getting at in this paper. But it is no good just asserting it. It is like asserting, "Someday you'll thank me for this," or "This is going to hurt me worse than it hurts you." I may say to students, "My fierce grading and extreme loyalty to subject matter and society are really in your interests," but students will still tend to experience me as adversary and undermine much of my teaching. I may say to knowledge and society, "My extreme support and loyalty to all students is really in your interests," but society will tend to view me as a soft teacher who lets standards down.

It is the burden of this paper to say that a contradictory stance is possible — not just in theory but in practice — but not by pretending there is no tension or conflict. And certainly not by affirming only one version of the paradox, the "paternal" version, which is to stick up for standards and firmness by insisting that to do so is good for students in the long run, forgetting the "maternal" version, which is to stick up for students by insisting that to do so is good for knowledge and society in the long run. There is a genuine paradox here. The positions are conflicting and they are true.

Let me turn this structural analysis into a narrative about the two basic urges at the root of teaching. We often think best by telling stories. I am reading a novel and I interrupt my wife to say, "Listen to this, isn't this wonderful!" and I read a passage out loud. Or we are walking in the woods and I say to her, "Look at the tree!" I am enacting the pervasive human itch to share. It feels lonely, painful, or incomplete to appreciate something and not share it with others.[2]

But this urge can lead to its contrary. Suppose I say, "Listen to this passage," and my wife yawns or says, "Don't interrupt me." Suppose I say, "Look at that beautiful sunset on the lake," and she laughs at me for being so sentimental and reminds me that Detroit is right there just below the horizon — creating half the beauty with its pollution. Suppose I say, "Listen to this delicate irony," and she can't see it and thinks I am neurotic to enjoy such bloodless stuff. What happens then? I end up *not* wanting to share it with her. I hug it to myself. I become a lone connoisseur. Here is the equally deep human urge to protect what I appreciate from harm. Perhaps I share what I love with a few select others — but only after I find a way somehow to extract from them beforehand assurance that they will understand and appreciate what I appreciate. And with them I can even sneer at worldly ones who lack our taste or intelligence or sensibility.

Many of us went into teaching out of just such an urge to share things with others, but we find students turn us down or ignore us in our efforts to give gifts. Sometimes they even laugh at us for our very enthusiasm in sharing. We try to show them what we understand and love, but they yawn and turn away. They put their feet up on our delicate structures; they chew bubble gum during the slow movement; they listen to hard rock while reading *Lear* and say, "What's so great about Shakespeare?"

Sometimes even success in sharing can be a problem. We manage to share with students what we know and appreciate, and they love it and eagerly grasp it. But their hands are dirty or their fingers are rough. We overhear them saying, "Listen to this neat thing I learned," yet we cringe because they got it all wrong. Best not to share.

I think of the medieval doctrine of poetry that likens it to a nut with a tough husk protecting a sweet kernel. The function of the poem is not to disclose but rather to conceal the kernel from the many, the unworthy, and to disclose it only to the few worthy (D. W. Robertson, *A Preface to Chaucer* [Princeton: Princeton UP, 1963] 61ff.). I have caught myself more than a few times explaining something I know or love in this tricky double-edged way: encoding my meaning with a kind of complexity or irony such that only those who have the right sensibility will hear what I have to say — others will not understand at all. Surely this is the source of much obscurity in learned discourse. We would rather have readers miss entirely what we say or turn away in boredom or frustration than reply, "Oh, I see what you mean. How ridiculous!" or, "How naive!" It is marvelous, actually, that we can make one utterance do so many things: communicate with the right people, stymie the wrong people, and thereby help us decide who *are* the right and the wrong people.

I have drifted into an unflattering portrait of the urge to protect one's subject, a defensive urge that stems from hurt. Surely much bad teaching and academic foolishness derive from this immature reaction to students or colleagues who will not accept a gift we tried generously to give (generously, but sometimes ineffectually or condescendingly or autocratically). Surely I must learn not to pout just because I can't get a bunch of adolescents as excited as I am about late Henry James. Late Henry James may be pearls, but when students yawn, that doesn't make them swine.

But it is not immature to protect the integrity of my subject in a positive way, to uphold standards, to insist that students stretch themselves till they can do justice to the material. Surely these impulses are at the root of much good teaching. And there is nothing wrong with these impulses in themselves — only *by themselves.* That is, there is nothing wrong with the impulse to guard or protect the purity of what we cherish so long as that act is redeemed by the presence of the opposite impulse also to give it away.

In Piaget's terms learning involves both assimilation and accommodation. Part of the job is to get the subject matter to bend and deform so that it fits inside the learner (that is, so it can fit or relate to the learner's experiences). But that's only half the job. Just as important is the necessity for the learner to bend and deform himself so that he can fit himself around the subject without doing violence to it. Good learning is not a matter of finding a happy medium where both parties are transformed as little as possible. Rather both parties must be maximally transformed — in a sense deformed. There is violence in learning. We cannot learn something without eating it, yet we cannot really learn it either without letting it eat us.

Look at Socrates and Christ as archetypal good teachers — archetypal in being so paradoxical. They are extreme on the one hand in their impulse to share with everyone and to support all learners, in their sense that everyone can take and get what they are offering; but they are extreme on the other hand in their fierce high standards for what will pass muster. They did not teach gut courses, they flunked "gentleman C" performances, they insisted that only "too much" was sufficient in their protectiveness toward their "subject matter." I am struck also with how much they both relied on irony, parable, myth, and other forms of subtle utterance that hide while they communicate. These two teachers were willing in some respects to bend and disfigure and in the eyes of many to profane what they taught, yet on the other hand they were equally extreme in their insistence that learners bend or transform themselves in order to become fit receptacles.

It is as though Christ, by stressing the extreme of sharing and being an ally — saying "suffer the little children to come unto me" and praising the widow with her mite — could be more extreme in this sternness: "unless you sell all you have," and "I speak to them in parables, because seeing they do not see and hearing they do not hear, nor do they understand" (saying in effect, "I am making this a tough course *because* so many of you are poor students"). Christ embeds the two themes of giving away and guarding — commitment to "students" and to "subject matter" — in the one wedding feast story: the host invites the guests from the highways and byways, anybody, but then angrily ejects one into outer darkness because he lacks the proper garment.

Let me sum up the conflict in two lists of teaching skills. If on the one hand we want to help more students learn more, I submit we should behave in the following four ways:

5

1. We should see our students as smart and capable. We should assume that they *can* learn what we teach — all of them. We should look through their mistakes or ignorance to the intelligence that lies behind. There is ample documentation that this "teacher expectation" increases student learning (Robert Rosenthal, "Teacher Expectation and Pupil Learning," in R. D. Strom, ed., *Teachers and the Learning Process* [Englewood Cliffs: Prentice, 1971] 33–60).

2. We should show students that we are on their side. This means, for example, showing them that the perplexity or ignorance they reveal to us will not be used against them in tests, grading, or certifying. If they hide their questions or guard against us they undermine our efforts to teach them.

3. Indeed, so far from letting their revelations hurt them in reading, we should be as it were lawyers for the defense, explicitly trying to help students do better against the judge and prosecuting attorney when it comes to the "trial" of testing and grading. ("I may be able to get you off this charge but only if you tell me what you really were doing that night.") If we take this advocate stance students can learn more from us, even if they are guilty of the worst crimes in the book: not having done the homework, not having learned last semester, not *wanting* to learn. And by learning more — even if not learning perfectly — they will perform better, which in turn will usually lead to even better learning in the future.

4. Rather than try to be perfectly fair and perfectly in command of what we teach — as good examiners ought to be — we should reveal our own position, particularly our doubts, ambivalences, and biases. We should show we are still learning, still willing to look at things in new ways, still sometimes uncertain or even stuck, still willing to ask naive questions, still engaged in the interminable process of working out the relationship between what we teach and the rest of our lives. Even though we are not wholly peer with our students, we can still be peer in this crucial sense of also being engaged in learning, seeking, and being incomplete. Significant learning requires change, inner readjustments, willingness to let go. We can increase the chances of our students being willing to undergo the necessary anxiety involved in change if they see we are also willing to undergo it.

Yet if, on the other hand, we want to increase our chances of success in serving knowledge, culture, and institutions I submit that we need skill at behaving in four very different ways:

1. We should insist on standards that are high — in the sense of standards that are absolute. That is, we should take what is almost a kind of Platonic position that there exists a "real world" of truth, of good reasoning, of good writing, of knowledge of biology, whatever — and insist that anything less than the real thing is not good enough.

2. We should be critical-minded and look at students and student performances with a skeptical eye. We should assume that some students cannot learn and others will not, even if they can. This attitude will increase our chances of detecting baloney and surface skill masquerading as competence or understanding.

3. We should not get attached to students or take their part or share their view of things; otherwise we will find it hard to exercise the critical spirit needed to say, "No, you do not pass," "No, you cannot enter in with the rest of us," "Out you go into the weeping and gnashing of teeth."

4. Thus we should identify ourselves primarily with knowledge or subject matter and care more about the survival of culture and institutions than about individual students — even when that means students are rejected who are basically smart or who tried as

hard as they could. We should keep our minds on the harm that can come to knowledge and society if standards break down or if someone is certified who is not competent, rather than on the harm that comes to individual students by hard treatment.

Because of this need for conflicting mentalities I think I see a distinctive distribution of success in teaching. At one extreme we see a few master or genius teachers, but they are striking for how differently they go about it and how variously and sometimes surprisingly they explain what they do. At the other extreme are people who teach very badly, or who have given up trying, or who quit teaching altogether: they are debilitated by the conflict between trying to be an ally as they teach and an adversary as they grade. Between these two extremes teachers find the three natural ways of making peace between contraries: there are "hard" teachers in whom loyalty to knowledge or society has won out; "soft" teachers in whom loyalty to students has won out; and middling, mostly dispirited teachers who are sort of loyal to students and sort of loyal to knowledge or society. (A few of this last group are not dispirited at all but live on a kind of knife edge of almost palpable tension as they insist on trying to be scrupulously fair both to students and to what they teach.)

This need for conflicting mentalities is also reflected in what is actually the most traditional and venerable structure in education: a complete separation between teaching and official assessment. We see it in the Oxford and Cambridge structure that makes the tutor wholly an ally to help the student prepare for exams set and graded by independent examiners. We see something of the same arrangement in many European university lecture-and-exam systems which are sometimes mimicked by American Ph.D. examinations. The separation of teaching and examining is found in many licensing systems and also in some new competence-based programs.

Even in conventional university curricula we see various attempts to strengthen assessment and improve the relationship between teacher and student by making the teacher more of an ally and coach. In large courses with many sections, teachers often give a common exam and grade each other's students. Occasionally, when two teachers teach different courses within each other's field of competence, they divide their roles and act as "outside examiner" for the other's students. (This approach, by the way, tends to help teachers clarify what they are trying to accomplish in a course since they must communicate their goals clearly to the examiner if there is to be any decent fit between the teaching and examining.) In writing centers, tutors commonly help students improve a piece of writing which another teacher will assess. We even see a hint of this separation of roles when teachers stress collaborative learning: they emphasize the students' role as mutual teachers and thereby emphasize their own pedagogic role as examiner and standard setter.

But though the complete separation of teacher and evaluator is hallowed and useful I am interested here in ways for teachers to take on both roles better. It is not just that most teachers are stuck with both; in addition I believe that opposite mentalities or processes can enhance each other rather than interfere with each other if we engage in them in the right spirit.

How can we manage to do contrary things? Christ said, "Be ye perfect," but I don't think it is good advice to try being immensely supportive and fierce in the same instant, as he and Socrates somehow managed to be. In writing, too, it doesn't usually help to try being immensely generative and critical-minded in the same instant as some great writers are — and as the rest of us sometimes are at moments of blessed inspiration. This is the way of transcendence and genius, but for most of us most of the time there is too much interference or paralysis when we try to do opposites at once.

But it is possible to make peace between opposites by alternating between them so that you are never trying to do contrary things at any one moment. One opposite leads naturally to the other; indeed, extremity in one enhances extremity in the other in a positive, reinforcing fashion. In the case of my own writing I find I can generate more and better when I consciously hold off critical-minded revising till later. Not only does it help to go whole hog with one mentality, but I am not afraid to make a fool of myself since I know I will soon be just as wholeheartedly critical. Similarly, I can be more fierce and discriminating in my critical revising because I have more and better material to work with through my earlier surrender to uncensored generating.

What would such an alternating approach look like in teaching? I will give a rough picture, but I do so hesitantly because if I am right about my theory of paradox, there will be widely different ways of putting it into practice.

In teaching we traditionally end with the critical or gatekeeper function: papers, exams, grades, or less institutionalized forms of looking back, taking stock, and evaluating. It is also traditional to start with the gatekeeper role: to begin a course by spelling out all the requirements and criteria as clearly as possible. We often begin a course by carefully explaining exactly what it will take to get an A, B, C, etc.

I used to be reluctant to start off on this foot. It felt so vulgar to start by emphasizing grades, and thus seemingly to reinforce a pragmatic preoccupation I want to squelch. But I have gradually changed my mind, and my present oppositional theory tells me I should exaggerate, or at least take more seriously than I often do, my gatekeeper functions rather than run away from them. The more I try to soft-pedal assessment, the more mysterious it will seem to students and the more likely they will be preoccupied and superstitious about it. The more I can make it clear to myself and to my students that I do have a commitment to knowledge and institutions, and the more I can make it specifically clear how I am going to fulfill that commitment, the easier it is for me to turn around and make a dialectical change of role into being an extreme ally to students.

Thus I start by trying to spell out requirements and criteria as clearly and concretely as possible. If I am going to use a midterm and final exam, it would help to pass out samples of these at the beginning of the course. Perhaps not a copy of precisely the test I will use but something close. And why not the real thing? If it feels as though I will ruin the effectiveness of my exam to "give it away" at the start, that means I must have a pretty poor exam — a simple-minded task that can be crammed for and that does not really test what is important. If the exam gets at the central substance of the course then surely it will help me if students see it right at the start. They will be more likely to learn what I want them to learn. It might be a matter of content: "Summarize the three main theories in this course and discuss their strengths and weaknesses by applying them to material we did not discuss." Or perhaps I am more interested in a process or skill: "Write an argumentative essay on this (new) topic." Or "Show how the formal characteristics of this (new) poem do and do not reinforce the theme." I might want to give room for lots of choice and initiative: "Write a dialogue between the three main people we have studied that illustrates what you think are the most important things about their work." Passing out the exam at the start — and perhaps even samples of strong and weak answers — is an invitation to make a tougher exam that goes more to the heart of what the course is trying to teach. If I don't use an exam, then it is even more crucial that I say how I will determine the grade — even if I base it heavily on slippery factors: e.g., "I will count half your grade on my impression of how well you motivate and invest yourself," or "how well you work collaboratively with your peers." Of course this kind of announcement makes for a tricky situation, but if these are my goals, surely I want my students to wrestle with them all term — in all their slipperiness and even if it means arguments about how unfair it is to grade on such matters — rather than just think about them at the end.

When I assign papers I should similarly start by advertising my gatekeeper role, by clearly communicating standards and criteria. That means not just talking theoretically about what I am looking for in an A paper and what drags a paper down to B or C or F, but rather passing out a couple of samples of each grade and talking concretely about what makes me give each one the grade I give it. Examples help because our actual grading sometimes reflects criteria we do not talk about, perhaps even that we are not aware of. (For example, I have finally come to admit that neatness counts.) Even if our practice fits our preaching, sometimes students do not really understand preaching without examples. Terms like "coherent" and even "specific" are notoriously hard for students to grasp because they do not read stacks of student writing. Students often learn more about well-connected and poorly connected paragraphs or specificity or the lack of it in examples from the writing of each other than they learn from instruction alone, or from examples of published writing.

I suspect there is something particularly valuable here about embodying our commitment to knowledge and society in the form of documents or handouts: words on palpable sheets of paper rather than just spoken words-in-the-air. Documents heighten the sense that I do indeed take responsibility for these standards; writing them forces me to try to make them as concrete, explicit, and objective as possible (if not necessarily fair). But most of all, having put all this on paper I can more easily go on to separate myself from them in some way — leave them standing — and turn around and schizophrenically start being a complete ally of students. I have been wholehearted and enthusiastic in making tough standards, but now I can say, "Those are the specific criteria I will use in grading; that's what you are up against, that's really me. But now we have most of the semester for me to help you attain those standards, do well on those tests and papers. They are high standards but I suspect all of you can attain them if you work hard. I will function as your ally. I'll be a kind of lawyer for the defense, helping you bring out your best in your battles with the other me, the prosecuting-attorney me when he emerges at the end. And if you really think you are too poorly prepared to do well in one semester, I can help you decide whether to trust that negative judgment and decide now whether to drop the course or stay and learn what you can."

What is pleasing about this alternating approach is the way it naturally leads a teacher to higher standards yet greater supportiveness. That is, I feel better about being really tough if I know I am going to turn around and be more on the student's side than usual. And contrarily I do not have to hold back from being an ally of students when I know I have set really high standards. Having done so, there is now no such thing as being "too soft," supportive, helpful, or sympathetic — no reason to hold back from seeing things entirely from their side, worrying about their problems. I can't be "cheated" or taken advantage of.

In addition, the more clearly I can say what I want them to know or be able to do, the better I can figure out what I must provide to help them attain those goals. As I make progress in this cycle, it means I can set my goals even higher — ask for the deep knowledge and skills that are really at the center of the enterprise.

But how, concretely, can we best function as allies? One of the best ways is to be a kind of coach. One has set up the hurdle for practice jumping, one has described the strengths and tactics of the enemy, one has warned them about what the prosecuting attorney will probably do: now the coach can prepare them for these rigors. Being an ally is probably more a matter of stance and relationship than of specific behaviors. Where a professor of jumping might say, in effect, "I will explain the principles of jumping," a jumping coach might say, in effect, "Let's work on learning to jump over those hurdles; in doing so I'll explain the principles of jumping." If we try to make these changes in stance, I sense we will discover some of the resistance, annoyances, and angers that make us indeed reluctant genuinely to be on the student's side. How can we be teachers for long without piling up resentment at having been misunderstood and taken advantage of? But the dialectical need to be in addition an extreme adversary of students will give us a legitimate medium for this hunger to dig in one's heels even in a kind of anger.

This stance provides a refreshingly blunt but supportive way to talk to students about weaknesses. "You're strong here, you're weak there, and over here you are really out of it.

9

We've got to find ways to work on these things so you can succeed on these essays or exams." And this stance helps reward students for volunteering weaknesses. The teacher can ask, "What don't you understand? What skills are hard for you? I need to decide how to spend our time here and I want it to be the most useful for your learning."

One of the best ways to function as ally or coach is to role-play the enemy in a supportive setting. For example, one can give practice tests where the grade doesn't count, or give feedback on papers which the student can revise before they count for credit. This gets us out of the typically counterproductive situation where much of our commentary on papers and exams is really justification for the grade — or is seen that way. Our attempt to help is experienced by students as a slap on the wrist by an adversary for what they have done wrong. No wonder students so often fail to heed or learn from our commentary. But when we comment on practice tests or revisable papers we are not saying, "Here's why you got this grade." We are saying, "Here's how you can get a better grade." When later we read final versions as evaluator we can read faster and not bother with much commentary.[3]

It is the spirit or principle of serving contraries that I want to emphasize here, not any particular fleshing out in practice such as above. For one of the main attractions of this theory is that it helps explain why people are able to be terrific teachers in such diverse ways. If someone is managing to do two things that conflict with each other, he is probably doing something mysterious: it's altogether natural if his success involves slipperiness, irony, or paradox. For example, some good teachers look like they are nothing but fierce gatekeepers, cultural bouncers, and yet in some mysterious way — perhaps ironically or subliminally — they are supportive. I think of the ferocious Marine sergeant who is always cussing out the troops but who somehow shows them he is on their side and believes in their ability. Other good teachers look like creampuffs and yet in some equally subtle way they embody the highest standards of excellence and manage to make students exert and stretch themselves as never before.

For it is one's spirit or stance that is at issue here, not the mechanics of how to organize a course in semester units or how to deal in tests, grading, or credits. I do not mean to suggest that the best way to serve knowledge and society is by having tough exams or hard grading — or even by having exams or grades at all. Some teachers do it just by talking, whether in lectures or discussions or conversation. Even though there is no evaluation or grading, the teacher can still demonstrate her ability to be wholehearted in her commitment to what she teaches and wholehearted also in her commitment to her students. Thus her talk itself might in fact alternate between attention to the needs of students and flights where she forgets entirely about students and talks over their head, to truth, to her wisest colleagues, to herself.[4]

The teacher who is really in love with Yeats or with poetry will push harder, and yet be more tolerant of students' difficulties because his love provides the serenity he needs in teaching: he knows that students cannot hurt Yeats or his relationship with Yeats. It is a different story when we are ambivalent about Yeats or poetry. The piano teacher who meanspiritedly raps the fingers of pupils who play wrong notes usually harbors some inner ambivalence in his love of music or some disappointment about his own talent.

In short, there is obviously no one right way to teach, yet I argue that in order to teach well we must find *some* way to be loyal both to students and to knowledge or society. Any way we can pull it off is fine. But if we are teaching less well than we should, we might be suffering from the natural tendency for these two loyalties to conflict with each other. In such a case we can usually improve matters by making what might seem an artificial separation of focus so as to give each loyalty and its attendant skills and mentality more room in which to flourish. That is, we can spend part of our teaching time saying in some fashion or other, "Now I'm being a tough-minded gatekeeper, standing up for high critical standards in my loyalty to what I teach"; and part of our time giving a contrary message: "Now my attention is wholeheartedly on trying to be your ally to try to help you learn, and I am not worrying about the purity of standards or grades or the need of society or institutions."

It is not that this approach makes things simple. It confuses students at first because they are accustomed to teachers being either "hard" or "soft" or in the middle — not both. The approach does not take away any of the conflict between trying to fulfill two conflicting functions. It merely gives a context and suggests a structure for doing so. Most of all it helps me understand better the demands on me and helps me stop feeling as though there is something wrong with me for feeling pulled in two directions at once.

I have more confidence that this conscious alternation or separation of mentalities makes sense because I think I see the same strategy to be effective with writing. Here too there is obviously no one right way to write, but it seems as though any good writer must find some way to be both abundantly inventive yet tough-mindedly critical. Again, any way we can pull it off is fine, but if we are not writing as well as we should — if our writing is weak in generativity or weak in tough-minded scrutiny (not to mention downright dismal or blocked) — it may well be that we are hampered by a conflict between the accepting mentality needed for abundant invention and the rejecting mentality needed for tough-minded criticism. In such a case too, it helps to move back and forth between sustained stretches of wholehearted, uncensored generating and wholehearted critical revising to allow each mentality and set of skills to flourish unimpeded.

Even though this theory encourages a separation that could be called artificial, it also points to models of the teaching and writing process that are traditional and reinforced by common sense: teaching that begins and ends with attention to standards and assessment and puts lots of student-directed supportive instruction in the middle; writing that begins with exploratory invention and ends with critical revising. But I hope that my train of thought rejuvenates these traditional models by emphasizing the underlying structure of contrasting mentalities which is central rather than merely a mechanical sequence of external stages which is not necessary at all.

In the end, I do not think I am just talking about how to serve students and serve knowledge or society. I am also talking about developing opposite and complementary sides of our character or personality: the supportive and nurturant side and the tough, demanding side. I submit that we all have instincts and needs of both sorts. The gentlest, softest, and most flexible among us really need a chance to stick up for our latent high standards, and the most hawk-eyed, critical-minded bouncers at the bar of civilization among us really need a chance to use our nurturant and supportive muscles instead of always being adversary.

Notes

[1] I lump "knowledge and society" together in one phrase but I acknowledge the importance of the potential conflict. For example, we may feel *society* asking us to adapt our students to it, while we feel *knowledge* — our vision of the truth — asking us to unfit our students for that society. Socrates was convicted of corrupting the youth. To take a more homely example, I may feel institutions asking me to teach students one kind of writing and yet feel impelled by my understanding of writing to teach them another kind. Thus where this paper paints a picture of teachers pulled in two directions, sometimes we may indeed be pulled in three.

[2] Late in life, I realize I must apologize and pay my respects to that form of literary criticism that I learned in college to scorn in callow fashion as the "Ah lovely!" school: criticism which tries frankly to share a perception and appreciation of the work rather than insist that there is some problem to solve or some complexity to analyze.

[3] Since it takes more time for us to read drafts and final versions too, no matter how quickly we read final versions, it is reasonable to conserve time in other ways — indeed I see independent merits. Don't require students to revise every draft. This permits you to grade students on their best work and thus again to have higher standards, and it is easier for students to invest themselves in revising if it is on a piece they care more about. And in giving feedback on drafts, wait till you have two drafts in hand

and thus give feedback only half as often. When I have only one paper in hand I often feel, "Oh dear, everything is weak here; nothing works right; where can I start?" When I have two drafts in hand I can easily say, "This one is better for the following reasons; it's the one I'd choose to revise; see if you can fix the following problems." With two drafts it is easier to find genuine strengths and point to them and help students consolidate or gain control over them. Yet I can make a positive utterance out of talking about what *didn't* work in the better draft and how to improve it.

⁴Though my argument does not imply that we need to use grades at all, surely it implies that if we do use them we should learn to improve the way we do so. I used to think that conventional grading reflected too much concern with standards for knowledge and society, but now I think it reflects too little. Conventional grading reflects such a single-minded hunger to *rank* people along a single scale or dimension that it is willing to forgo any communication of what the student really knows or can do. The competence-based movement, whatever its problems, represents a genuine attempt to make grades and credits do justice to knowledge and society. (See Gerald Grant et al., *On Competence: A Critical Analysis of Competence-Based Reform in Higher Education* [San Francisco: Jossey-Bass, 1979]. See also my "More Accurate Evaluation of Student Performance," *Journal of Higher Education* 40 [1969]: 219–30.)

Elbow's Insights as a Resource for Your Teaching

1. You may have been surprised by some of Elbow's statements because they either confirmed or challenged something you already believe about teaching. Reflect on your current beliefs to determine if some fall into "contraries." I encourage you to imitate Elbow's thinking and writing and engage in some "dialectical reasoning." Begin and maintain a double-entry journal. Focus the journal on your experiences, feelings, insights, and perplexities about the processes of teaching writing. Use one side of the notebook for comments about your teaching that you would categorize as "loyalty to students." Use the other for comments about "loyalty to standards." Leave space in the entries so that you can come back to add anecdotes, insights, and questions.

At the end of the semester, you can review entries and revise them to set the "contraries" — which are parallel in some way — side by side. If your word processing program has a split-screen feature, you can also keep this journal on disk.

This journal, like a continuous drafting of a philosophy of composition, can give you a set of lenses for analyzing and evaluating your own teaching, can become a cumulative record that might prompt a scholarly essay or a research proposal, can motivate a search for additional professional writings that might respond to the questions you set yourself, and can prompt an ongoing dialogue with yourself about the dialectical process of teaching and learning to teach better.

2. Draft and redraft a "philosophy of teaching composition." You'll revise it as you teach and learn more from your students and from your colleagues as well as from your experiences in the classroom. Elbow is clearly offering his philosophy of teaching "mostly writing" and he tells us how he shaped his philosophy and what kind of rethinking informed it. (Elbow is equally specific in discussing his philosophy in *Writing without Teachers, Writing with Power,* and the larger text *Embracing Contraries.*)

If this drafting a philosophy seems too self-conscious to you, think about it pragmatically. A favorite and frequent interview question from members of writing faculties will be "So, what do you believe about teaching writing?" You'll be ready to respond confidently and eloquently because you will have been writing and reflecting through this philosophical essay.

3. Drafting an "attendance and grading policy statement" could be a way for you to embrace the contraries implicit in your teaching. In this statement, which should be shared with your students the first week of class, try to represent each of your important beliefs that you listed in exercise 1.

Elbow's Insights as a Resource for the Writing Classroom

1. First-year writers experience many conflicts of opposing ideas, values, lifestyles, and goals. They need assistance coping with the tension, frustration, anxiety, and even fear that those conflicts create. Being able to "embrace contraries" is a fairly mature activity and a sophisticated cognitive task. To aid your writers in transition as thinkers, writers, and members of the writing community, encourage them to use journal entries to list and describe the conflicts they experience. Initially, those entries might be mostly therapeutic, allowing the students to express perceptions and feelings that might be too risky to express in jam sessions or letters home. Eventually, the entries should allow the writers to begin to see patterns among the examples of "contraries." The journal can become a sourcebook of ideas for writing assignments that call for problem solving (see Chapters 7 and 8 of *The Bedford Guide for College Writers*).

2. Many first-year writers have difficulty moving from personal and expressive writing to the critical writing prompted by Part Two of *The Bedford Guide for College Writers*. Teaching a writer to identify and then to analyze personal or campus-centered conflicts eases the transition. A demonstration of problem solving through dialectical statement taps personal experience and also leads to some objective evaluation. Show students how to write two basic paradigms — Hegelian and Marxist — for a dialectical situation.

Hegelian dialectic describes a *thesis* and then an *antithesis,* a situation opposed to and creating conflict with the thesis. The *synthesis* is a recommendation about resolving the conflict. Often, "compromise" or "golden mean" solutions are created. Here's an example that many of your students will quickly identify from reading psychology. Freud defines the process of ego formation as a dialectical process.

Thesis: The id, the unconscious, spontaneous, and individualistic energy of a person (the yea-saying child).

Antithesis: The superego, the conscious, culturally influenced, and socially directed energy of a person (the nay-saying parent).

Synthesis: The ego, the balancing of energies to accommodate the needs of self and society (the "let's consider this" adult).

With the Marxist dialectic, the *thesis* describes a situation that inevitably gives rise to its *antithesis.* The *synthesis* describes a recommendation for resolving the conflict that is often not a compromise or a balancing of the tension between thesis and antithesis. Unlike the Hegelian synthesis, the Marxist synthesis provokes more dialectic. The synthesis becomes a thesis, which inevitably gives rise to an antithesis. Here are examples.

Thesis: Feudalism met the human needs for stability and security roles.

Antithesis: The human need for individual initiative and freedom came in conflict with the status quo of feudalism.

Synthesis: An economic system developed allowing the individual to compete openly in a free market and to use the means of production and distribution to create capital.

This historical dialectical process gives rise to:

Thesis: Capitalism allows the individual to compete freely and to use the means of production and distribution to create capital.

Antithesis: Large numbers of workers are made the "means of production" and become oppressed and unable to prosper in capitalist society.

Synthesis: In the Soviet Union, the revolution brought a "classless" society and communism. In the United States, the labor union movement brings "safety and protection of economic rights" to the rank and file.

Students will jump in at this point of the demonstration to point out serious problems with Soviet communism and American labor unions; their observations can be described as "antitheses," and the thinking about "syntheses" will proceed.

After the demonstration, ask students to work in small groups to generate a list of conflicts they are experiencing as first-year students. Tell them to select several of those conflicts and to frame them first as Hegelian and then as Marxist dialectics.

3. Follow up the class exercise in writing dialectical paradigms with an essay assignment that calls for use of the dialectical paradigm to generate thought and to structure an essay. Review with your students the discussions of the writing strategy of comparison and contrast (see Chapter 17, "Strategies for Developing," and also the techniques for generating ideas and shaping a draft in Chapter 9, "Evaluating"). Those treatments can help writers work with structuring an essay dialectically.

Have the class brainstorm transition terms and phrases, metaphors, and verbs that dramatize a conflict or a tension between opposites. During peer evaluation sessions, have editors restate the gist of the essay they are editing by abstracting its dialectical paradigm.

Expect the writers to surprise themselves with the new ideas they discover about their personal experiences and their ability to solve conflict. Recommend this process as one thinking strategy to use whenever they're asked to problem-solve in classes.

INVENTING THE UNIVERSITY[1]

David Bartholomae

Notice that from the epigraph forward, David Bartholomae challenges some of the assumptions that educators may hold and argues for alternative assumptions. He challenges the "gatekeepers" of discourse, the tendency of some educators to respond more to the "errors" of basic writers than to the logic of the errors, and the assumption of many readers that a "clean" essay is better than an essay that unevenly attempts the ways of knowing and speaking peculiar to a new discourse community.

What Bartholomae describes as "inventing the university" is a challenge to basic and advanced writers alike. In fact, each time a learner enters a new interpretive community or knowledge community, that student may go back to the basics and may experience difficulty in learning to write with the language of the new community. As Bartholomae frequently reminds us, "inventing the university" is further complicated because the writer is "trying on the discourse even though he doesn't have the knowledge that makes the discourse more than a routine, a set of conventional rituals and gestures."

Bartholomae indicates, following the lead of Mina Shaughnessy in Errors and Expectations, *that as writing instructors we should have profound respect for the students in our classes whom we evaluate as "basic writers." He cites Patricia Bizzell's argument that the problems of basic writers might be understood better if we consider "their unfamiliarity with the academic discourse community, combined, perhaps, with such limited experience outside their native discourse communities that they are unaware that there is such a thing as a discourse community with conventions to be mastered."*

Basic writers have not yet learned all the "codes" that operate within a kind of discourse. Advanced writers may have learned codes of syntax and grammar that give them some facility, but they may be equally unaware of other codes of academic writing. When the advanced writer begins "inventing the university," that writer may lose some of the control of codes of syntax and grammar even as he or she becomes aware of or tries to mimic the new codes of academic discourse. The writer may consequently produce writing that would be evaluated as "basic writing."

Bartholomae suggests that educators can assist novices in the academic community both by "demystifying" the conventions of discourse and by understanding that novices may need to write problematic prose as they grapple with new ideas and new conventions for exploring and exposing those ideas to view.

If you wish to have your students examine and respond to brief examples of writing from various disciplines in the academic community, consult the "Applying What You Learn" sections in the first ten chapters of The Bedford Guide.

Education may well be, as of right, the instrument whereby every individual, in a society like our own, can gain access to any kind of discourse. But we well know that in its distribution, in what it permits and in what it prevents, it follows the well-trodden battle-lines of social conflict. Every educational system is a political means of maintaining or of modifying the appropriation of discourse, with the knowledge and the powers it carries with it.

— Foucault, "The Discourse on Language"

Every time a student sits down to write for us, he has to invent the university for the occasion — invent the university, that is, or a branch of it, like History or Anthropology or Economics or English. He has to learn to speak our language, to speak as we do, to try on the peculiar ways of knowing, selecting, evaluating, reporting, concluding, and arguing that define the discourse of our community. Or perhaps I should say the *various* discourses of our community, since it is in the nature of a liberal arts education that a student, after the first year or two, must learn to try on a variety of voices and interpretive schemes — to write, for example, as a literary critic one day and an experimental psychologist the next, to work within fields where the rules governing the presentation of examples or the development of an argument are both distinct and, even to a professional, mysterious.

The students have to appropriate (or be appropriated by) a specialized discourse, and they have to do this as though they were easily and comfortably one with their audience, as though they were members of the academy, or historians or anthropologists or economists; they have to invent the university by assembling and mimicking its language, finding some compromise between idiosyncrasy, a personal history, and the requirements of convention, the history of a discipline. They must learn to speak our language. Or they must dare to speak it, or to carry off the bluff, since speaking and writing will most certainly be required long before the skill is "learned." And this, understandably, causes problems.

Let me look quickly at an example. Here is an essay written by a college freshman, a basic writer:

In the past time I thought that an incident was creative was when I had to make a clay model of the earth, but not of the classical or your everyday model of the earth which consists of the two cores, the mantle and the crust. I thought of these things in a dimension of which it would be unique, but easy to comprehend. Of course, your materials to work with were basic and limited at the same time, but thought help to put this limit into a right attitude or frame of mind to work with the clay.

In the beginning of the clay model, I had to research and learn the different dimensions of the earth (in magnitude, quantity, state of matter, etc.) After this, I learned how to put this into the clay and come up with something different than any other person in my class at the time. In my opinion, color coordination and shape was the key to my creativity of the clay model of the earth.

Creativity is the venture of the mind at work with the mechanics relay to the limbs from the cranium, which stores and triggers this action. It can be a burst of energy released at a precise time a thought is being transmitted. This can cause a frenzy of the human body, but it depends of the characteristics of the individual and how they can relay the message clearly enough through mechanics of the body to us as an observer. Then we must determine if it is creative or a learned process varied by the individuals thought process. Creativity is indeed a tool which has to exist, or our world will not succeed into the future and progress like it should.

15

I am continually impressed by the patience and good will of our students. This student was writing a placement essay during freshman orientation. (The problem set to him was "Describe a time when you did something you felt to be creative. Then, on the basis of the incident you have described, go on to draw some general conclusions about 'creativity.' ") He knew that university faculty would be reading and evaluating his essay, and so he wrote for them.

In some ways it is a remarkable performance. He is trying on the discourse even though he doesn't have the knowledge that makes the discourse more than a routine, a set of conventional rituals and gestures. And he does this, I think, even though he *knows* he doesn't have the knowledge that makes the discourse more than a routine. He defines himself as a researcher, working systematically, and not as a kid in a high school class: "I thought of these things in a dimension of . . ."; "had to research and learn the different dimensions of the earth (in magnitude, quantity, state of matter, etc.)." He moves quickly into a specialized language (his approximation of our jargon) and draws both a general, textbook-like conclusion ("Creativity is the venture of the mind at work . . .") and a resounding peroration ("Creativity is indeed a tool which has to exist, or our world will not succeed into the future and progress like it should"). The writer has even, with that "indeed" and with the qualifications and the parenthetical expressions of the opening paragraphs, picked up the rhythm of our prose. And through it all he speaks with an impressive air of authority.

There is an elaborate but, I will argue, a necessary and enabling fiction at work here as the student dramatizes his experience in a "setting" — the setting required by the discourse — where he can speak to us as a companion, a fellow researcher. As I read the essay, there is only one moment when the fiction is broken, when we are addressed differently. The student says, "Of course, your materials to work with were basic and limited at the same time, but thought help to put this limit into a right attitude or frame of mind to work with the clay." At this point, I think, we become students and he the teacher, giving us a lesson (as in, "You take your pencil in your right hand and put your paper in front of you"). This is, however, one of the most characteristic slips of basic writers. It is very hard for them to take on the role — the voice, the person — of an authority whose authority is rooted in scholarship, analysis, or research. They slip, then, into the more immediately available and realizable voice of authority, the voice of a teacher giving a lesson or the voice of a parent lecturing at the dinner table. They offer advice or homilies rather than "academic" conclusions. There is a similar break in the final paragraph, where the conclusion that pushes for a definition ("Creativity is the venture of the mind at work with the mechanics relay to the limbs from the cranium . . .") is replaced by a conclusion which speaks in the voice of an Elder ("Creativity is indeed a tool which has to exist, or our world will not succeed into the future and progress like it should").

It is not uncommon, then, to find such breaks in the concluding sections of essays written by basic writers. Here is the concluding section of essay written by a student about his work as a mechanic. He had been asked to generalize about "work" after reviewing an on-the-job experience or incident that "stuck in his mind" as somehow significant: "How could two repairmen miss a leak? Lack of pride? No incentive? Lazy? I don't know." At this point the writer is in a perfect position to speculate, to move from the problem to an analysis of the problem. Here is how the paragraph continues, however (and notice the change in pronoun reference):

> From this point on, I take my time, do it right, and don't let customers get under your skin. If they have a complaint, tell them to call your boss and he'll be more than glad to handle it. Most important, worry about yourself, and keep a clear eye on everyone, for there's always someone trying to take advantage of you, anytime and anyplace.

We get neither a technical discussion nor an "academic" discussion but a Lesson on Life.[2] This is the language he uses to address the general question "How could two repairmen miss a leak?" The other brand of conclusion, the more academic one, would have required him to speak of his experience in our terms; it would, that is, have required a special vocabulary, a special system of presentation, and an interpretive scheme (or a set of commonplaces) he could use to identify and talk about the mystery of human error. The writer certainly had access to the range of acceptable commonplaces for such an explanation: "lack of pride," "no incentive," "lazy." Each would dictate its own set of phrases, examples, and conclusions, and we, his teachers, would know how to write out each argument, just as we would know how to write out more specialized arguments of our own. A "commonplace," then, is a culturally or institutionally authorized concept or statement that carries with it its own necessary elaboration. We all use commonplaces to orient ourselves in the world; they provide a point of reference and a set of "prearticulated" explanations that are readily available to organize and interpret experience. The phrase "lack of pride" carries with it its own account for the repairman's error just as, at another point in time, a reference to "original sin" would provide an explanation, or just as, in a certain university classroom, a reference to "alienation" would enable a writer to continue and complete the discussion. While there is a way in which these terms are interchangeable, they are not all permissible. A student in a composition class would most likely be turned away from a discussion of original sin. Commonplaces are the "controlling ideas" of our composition textbooks, textbooks that not only insist upon a set form for expository writing but a set view of public life.[3]

When the student above says, "I don't know," he is not saying, then, that he has nothing to say. He is saying that he is not in a position to carry on this discussion. And so we are addressed as apprentices rather than as teachers or scholars. To speak to us as a person of status or privilege, the writer can either speak to us in our terms — in the privileged language of university discourse — or, in default (or in defiance), he can speak to us as though we were children, offering us the wisdom of experience.

I think it is possible to say that the language of the "Clay Model" paper has come through the writer and not from the writer. The writer has located himself (he has located the self that is represented by the *I* on the page) in a context that is, finally, beyond him, not his own and not available to his immediate procedures for inventing and arranging text. I would not, that is, call this essay an example of "writer-based" prose. I would not say that it is egocentric or that it represents the "interior monologue of a wrier thinking and talking to himself" (Flower 63). It is, rather, the record of a writer who has lost himself in the discourse of his readers. There is a context beyond the reader that is not the world but a way of talking about the world, a way of talking that determines the use of examples, the possible conclusions, the acceptable commonplaces, and the key words of an essay on the construction of a clay model of the earth. This writer has entered the discourse without successfully approximating it.

Linda Flower has argued that the difficulty inexperienced writers have with writing can be understood as a difficulty in negotiating the transition between writer-based and reader-based prose. Expert writers, in other words, can better imagine how a reader will respond to a text and can transform or restructure what they have to say around a goal shared with a reader. Teaching students to revise for readers, then, will better prepare them to write initially with a reader in mind. The success of this pedagogy depends upon the degree to which a writer can imagine and conform to a reader's goals. The difficulty of this act of imagination, and the burden of such conformity, are so much at the heart of the problem that a teacher must pause and take stock before offering revision as a solution. Students like the student who wrote the "Clay Model" paper are not so much trapped in a private language as they are shut out from one of the privileged languages of public life, a language they are aware of but cannot control.

Our students, I've said, have to appropriate (or be appropriated by) a specialized discourse, and they have to do this as though they were easily or comfortably one with their audience. If you look at the situation this way, suddenly the problem of audience awareness becomes enormously complicated. One of the common assumptions of both composition research and composition teaching is that at some "stage" in the process of composing an essay a writer's ideas or his motives must be tailored to the needs and expectations of his audience. A writer has to "build bridges" between his point of view and his readers. He has to anticipate and acknowledge his readers' assumptions and biases. He must begin with "common points of departure" before introducing new or controversial arguments. There is a version of the pastoral at work here. It is assumed that a person of low status (like a shepherd) can speak to a person of power (like a courtier), but only (at least so far as the language is concerned) if he is not a shepherd at all, but actually a member of the court out in the fields in disguise.

Writers who can successfully manipulate an audience (or, to use a less pointed language, writers who can accommodate their motives to their readers' expectations) are writers who can both imagine and write from a position of privilege. They must, that is, see themselves within a privileged discourse, one that already includes and excludes groups of readers. They must be either equal to or more powerful than those they would address. The writing, then, must somehow transform the political and social relationships between basic writing students and their teachers.

If my students are going to write for me by knowing who I am — and if this means more than knowing my prejudices, psyching me out — it means knowing what I know; it means having the knowledge of a professor of English. They have, then, to know what I know and how I know what I know (the interpretive schemes that define the way I would work out the problems I set for them); they have to learn to write what I would write, or to offer up some approximation of that discourse. The problem of audience awareness, then, is a problem of power and finesse. It cannot be addressed, as it is in most classroom exercises, by giving students privilege and denying the situation of the classroom, by having students write to an outsider, someone excluded from their privileged circle: "Write about 'To His Coy Mistress,' not for your teacher, but for the students in your class"; "Describe Pittsburgh to someone who has never been there"; "Explain to a high school senior how best to prepare for college"; "Describe baseball to a Martian."

Exercises such as these allow students to imagine the needs and goals of a reader and they bring those needs and goals forward as a dominant constraint in the construction of an essay. And they argue, implicitly, what is generally true about writing — that it is an act of aggression disguised as an act of charity. What they fail to address is the central problem of academic writing, where students must assume the right of speaking to someone who knows Pittsburgh or "To His Coy Mistress" better than they do, a reader for whom the general commonplaces and the readily available utterances about a subject are inadequate. It should be clear that when I say that I know Pittsburgh better than my basic writing students I am talking about a way of knowing that is also a way of writing. There may be much that they know that I don't know, but in the setting of the university classroom I have a way of talking about the town that is "better" (and for arbitrary reasons) than theirs.

I think that all writers, in order to write, must imagine for themselves the privilege of being "insiders" — that is, of being both inside an established and powerful discourse, and of being granted a special right to speak. And I think that right to speak is seldom conferred upon us — upon any of us, teachers or students — by virtue of the fact that we have invented or discovered an original idea. Leading students to believe that they are responsible for something new or original, unless they understand what those words mean with regard to writing, is a dangerous and counterproductive practice. We do have the right to expect students to be active and engaged, but that is more a matter of being continually and stylistically working against the inevitable presence of conventional language; it is not a matter of inventing a language that is new.

When students are writing for a teacher, writing becomes more problematic than it is for the students who are describing baseball to a Martian. The students, in effect, have to assume privilege without having any. And since students assume privilege by locating themselves within the discourse of a particular community — within a set of specifically acceptable gestures and commonplaces — learning, at least as it is defined in the liberal arts curriculum, becomes more a matter of imitation or parody than a matter of invention and discovery.

What our beginning students need to learn is to extend themselves into the commonplaces, set phrases, rituals, gestures, habits of mind, tricks of persuasion, obligatory conclusions, and necessary connections that determine the "what might be said" and constitute knowledge within the various branches of our academic community. The course of instruction that would make this possible would be based on a sequence of illustrated assignments and would allow for successive approximations of academic or "disciplinary" discourse. Students will not take on our peculiar ways of reading, writing, speaking, and thinking all at once. Nor will the command of a subject like sociology, at least as that command is represented by the successful completion of a multiple choice exam, enable students to write sociology. Our colleges and universities, by and large, have failed to involve basic writing students in scholarly projects, projects that would allow them to act as though they were colleagues in an academic enterprise. Much of the written work students do is test-taking, report or summary, work that places them outside the working discourse of the academic community, where they are expected to admire and report on what we do, rather than inside that discourse, where they can do its work and participate in a common enterprise.[4] This is a failure of teachers and curriculum designers who, even if they speak of writing as a mode of learning, all too often represent writing as a "tool" to be used by a (hopefully) educated mind.

Pat Bizzell is one of the most important scholars writing now on basic writers and on the special requirements of academic discourse.[5] In a recent essay, "Cognition, Convention, and Certainty: What We Need to Know about Writing," she argues that the problems of basic writers might be

> better understood in terms of their unfamiliarity with the academic discourse community, combined, perhaps, with such limited experience outside their native discourse communities that they are unaware that there is such a thing as a discourse community with conventions to be mastered. What is underdeveloped is their knowledge both of the ways experience is constituted and interpreted in the academic discourse community and of the fact that all discourse communities constitute and interpret experience. (230)

One response to the problems of basic writers, then, would be to determine just what the community's conventions are, so that those conventions can be written out, "demystified," and taught in our classrooms. Teachers, as a result, could be more precise and helpful when they ask students to "think," "argue," "describe," or "define." Another response would be to examine the essays written by basic writers — their approximations of academic discourse — to determine more clearly where the problems lie. If we look at their writing, and if we look at it in the context of other student writing, we can better see the points of discord when students try to write their way into the university.

The purpose of the remainder of this paper will be to examine some of the most striking and characteristic problems as they are presented in the expository essays of basic writers. I will be concerned, then, with university discourse in its most generalized form — that is, as represented by introductory courses — and not with the special conventions required by advanced work in the various disciplines. And I will be concerned with the difficult, and often violent, accommodations that occur when students locate themselves in a discourse that is not "naturally" or immediately theirs.

I have reviewed five hundred essays written in response to the "creativity" question used during one of our placement exams. (The essay cited at the opening of this paper was one of that group.) Some of the essays were written by basic writers (or, more properly, those essays led readers to identify the writers as "basic writers"); some were written by students who "passed" (who were granted immediate access to the community of writers at the university).

As I read these essays, I was looking to determine the stylistic resources that enabled writers to locate themselves within an "academic" discourse. My bias as a reader should be clear by now. I was not looking to see how the writer might represent the skills demanded by a neutral language (a language whose key features were paragraphs, topic sentences, transitions, and the like — features of a clear and orderly mind). I was looking to see what happened when a writer entered into a language to locate himself (a textual self) and his subject, and I was looking to see how once entered, that language made or unmade a writer.

Here is one essay. Its writer was classified as a basic writer. Since the essay is relatively free of sentence level errors, that decision must have been rooted in some perceived failure of the discourse itself.

> I am very interested in music, and I try to be creative in my interpretation of music. While in high school, I was a member of a jazz ensemble. The members of the ensemble were given chances to improvise and be creative in various songs. I feel that this was a great experience for me, as well as the other members. I was proud to know that I could use my imagination and feelings to create music other than what was written.
>
> Creativity to me, means being free to express yourself in a way that is unique to you, not having to conform to certain rules and guidelines. Music is only one of the many areas in which people are given opportunities to show their creativity. Sculpting, carving, building, art, and acting are just a few more areas where people can show their creativity.
>
> Through my music I conveyed feelings and thoughts which were important to me. Music was my means of showing creativity. In whatever form creativity takes, whether it be music, art, or science, it is an important aspect of our lives because it enables us to be individuals.

Notice, in this essay, the key gesture, one that appears in all but a few of the essays I read. The student defines as his own that which is a commonplace. "Creativity, to *me,* means being free to express yourself in a way that is unique to you, not having to conform to certain rules and guidelines." This act of appropriation constitutes his authority; it constitutes his authority as a writer and not just as a musician (that is, as someone with a story to tell). There were many essays in the set that told only a story, where the writer's established presence was as a musician or a skier or someone who painted designs on a van, but not as a person removed from that experience interpreting it, treating it as a metaphor for something else (creativity). Unless those stories were long, detailed, and very well told (unless the writer was doing more than saying, "I am a skier or a musician or a van-painter"), those writers were all given low ratings.

Notice also that the writer of the jazz paper locates himself and his experience in relation to the commonplace (creativity is unique expression; it is not having to conform to rules or guidelines) regardless of whether it is true or not. Anyone who improvises "knows" that improvisation follows rules and guidelines. It is the power of the commonplace (its truth as a recognizable, and, the writer believes, as a final statement) that justifies the example and completes the essay. The example, in other words, has value because it stands within the field of the commonplace. It is not the occasion for what one might call an "objective" analysis or a "close" reading. It could also be said that the essay stops with the articulation of the commonplace. The following sections speak only to the power of that statement. The reference to "sculpting, carving, building, art, and acting" attest to the universal of the commonplace (and it attests to the writer's nervousness with the status he has appropriated for himself — he is saying, "Now, I'm not the only one here who's done something unique"). The commonplace stands by itself. For this writer, it does not need to be elaborated. By virtue of having written it, he has completed the essay and established the contract by which we may be spoken to as equals: "In whatever form creativity takes, whether it be music, art, or science, it is an important aspect of *our lives* because it enables *us* to be individuals." (For me to break that contract, to argue that *my* life is not represented in that essay, is one way for me to begin as a teacher with that student in that essay.)

I said that the writer of the jazz paper offered up a commonplace regardless of whether it was "true" or not, and this, I said, was an example of the power of a commonplace to determine the meaning of an example. A commonplace determines a system of interpretation that can be used to "place" an example within a standard system of belief. You can see a similar process at work in this essay.

> During the football season, the team was supposed to wear the same type of cleats and the same type socks, I figured that I would change this a little by wearing my white shoes instead of black and to cover up the team socks with a pair of my own white ones. I thought that this looked better than what we were wearing, and I told a few of the other people on the team to change too. They agreed that it did look better and they changed there combination to go along with mine. After the game people came up to us and said that it looked very good the way we wore our socks, and they wanted to know why we changed from the rest of the team.
>
> I feel that creativity comes from when a person lets his imagination come up with ideas and he is not afraid to express them. Once you create something to do it will be original and unique because it came about from your own imagination and if any one else tries to copy it, it won't be the same because you thought of it first from your own ideas.

This is not an elegant paper, but it seems seamless, tidy. If the paper on the clay model of the earth showed an ill-fit between the writer and his project, here the discourse seems natural, smooth. You could reproduce this paper and hand it out to a class, and it would take a lot of prompting before the students sense something fishy and one of the more aggressive ones might say, "Sure he came up with the idea of wearing white shoes and white socks. Him and Billy White-shoes Johnson. Come on. He copied the very thing he said was his own idea, 'original and unique.' "

The "I" of this text, the "I" who "figured," "thought," and "felt" is located in a conventional rhetoric of the self that turns imagination into origination (I made it), that argues an ethic of production (I made it and it is mine), and that argues a tight scheme of intention (I made it because I decided to make it). The rhetoric seems invisible because it is so common. This "I" (the maker) is also located in a version of history that dominates classroom accounts of history. It is an example of the "Great Man" theory, where history is rolling along — the English novel is dominated by a central, intrusive narrative presence; America is in the throes of a great depression; during football season the team was supposed to wear the same kind of cleats and socks — until a figure appears, one who can shape history — Henry James, FDR, the writer of the football paper — and everything is changed. In the argument of the football paper, "I figured," "I thought," "I told," "they agreed," and, as a consequence, "I feel that creativity *comes from* when a person lets his imagination come up with ideas and he is not afraid to express them." The story of appropriation becomes a narrative of courage and conquest. The writer was able to write that story when he was able to imagine himself in that discourse. Getting him out of it will be a difficult matter indeed.

There are ways, I think, that a writer can shape history in the very act of writing it. Some students are able to enter into a discourse, but, by stylistic maneuvers, to take possession of it at the same time. They don't originate a discourse, but they locate themselves within it aggressively, self-consciously.

Here is one particularly successful essay. Notice the specialized vocabulary, but also the way in which the text continually refers to its own language and to the language of others.

> Throughout my life, I have been interested and intrigued by music. My mother has often told me of the times, before I went to school, when I would "conduct" the orchestra on her records. I continued to listen to music and eventually started to play the guitar and the clarinet. Finally, at about the age of twelve, I started to sit down and to try to write songs. Even though my instrumental skills were far from my own high standards, I would spend much of my spare time during the day with a guitar around my neck, trying to produce a piece of music.

21

Each of these sessions, as I remember them, had a rather set format. I would sit in my bedroom, strumming different combinations of the five or six chords I could play, until I heard a series which sounded particularly good to me. After this, I set the music to a suitable rhythm, (usually dependent on my mood at the time), and ran through the tune until I could play it fairly easily. Only after this section was complete did I go on to writing lyrics, which generally followed along the lines of the current popular songs on the radio.

At the time of the writing, I felt that my songs were, in themselves, an original creation of my own; that is, I, alone, made them. However, I now see that, in this sense of the word, I was not creative. The songs themselves seem to be an oversimplified form of the music I listened to at the time.

In a more fitting sense, however, I *was* being creative. Since I did not purposely copy my favorite songs, I was, effectively, originating my songs from my own "process of creativity." To achieve my goal, I needed what a composer would call "inspiration" for my piece. In this case the inspiration was the current hit on the radio. Perhaps with my present point of view, I feel that I used too much "inspiration" in my songs, but, at that time, I did not.

Creativity, therefore, is a process which, in my case, involved a certain series of "small creations" if you like. As well, it is something, the appreciation of which varies with one's point of view, that point of view being set by the person's experience, tastes, and his own personal view of creativity. The less experienced tend to allow for less originality, while the more experienced demand real originality to classify something a "creation." Either way, a term as abstract as this is perfectly correct, and open to interpretation.

This writer is consistent and dramatically conscious of herself forming something to say out of what has been said *and* out of what she has been saying in the act of writing this paper. "Creativity" begins, in this paper, as "original creation." What she thought was "creativity," however, she now calls "imitation" and, as she says, "in this sense of the word" she was not "creative." In another sense, however, she says that she *was* creative since she didn't purposefully copy the songs but used them as "inspiration."

The writing in this piece (that is, the work of the writer within the essay) goes on in spite of, or against, the language that keeps pressing to give another name to her experience as a song writer and to bring the discussion to closure. (Think of the quick closure of the football shoes paper in comparison.) Its style is difficult, highly qualified. It relies on quotation marks and parody to set off the language and attitudes that belong to the discourse (or the discourses) it would reject, that it would not take as its own proper location.[6]

In the papers I've examined in this essay, the writers have shown a varied awareness of the codes — or the competing codes — that operate within a discourse. To speak with authority student writers have not only to speak in another's voice but through another's "code"; and they not only have to do this, they have to speak in the voice and through the codes of those of us with power and wisdom; and they not only have to do this, they have to do it before they know what they are doing, before they have a project to participate in and before, at least in terms of our disciplines, they have anything to say. Our students may be able to enter into a conventional discourse and speak, not as themselves, but through the voice of the community. The university, however, is the place where "common" wisdom is only of negative value; it is something to work against. The movement toward a more specialized discourse begins (or perhaps, best begins) when a student can both define a position of privilege, a position that sets him against a "common" discourse, and when he can work self-consciously, critically, against not only the "common" code but his own.

The stages of development that I've suggested are not necessarily marked by corresponding levels in the type or frequency of error, at least not by the type or frequency of sentence level errors. I am arguing, then, that a basic writer is not necessarily a writer who makes a lot of mistakes. In fact, one of the problems with curricula designed to aid basic writers is that they too often begin with the assumption that the key distinguishing feature of a basic writer is the presence of sentence level error. Students are placed in courses because their placement essays show a high frequency of such errors and those courses are designed with the goal of making those errors go away. This approach to the problems of the basic writer ignores the degree to which error is not a constant feature but a marker in the development of a writer. Students who can write reasonably correct narratives may fall to pieces when faced with more unfamiliar assignments. More importantly, however, such courses fail to serve the rest of the curriculum. On every campus there is a significant number of college freshmen who require a course to introduce them to the kinds of writing that are required for a university education. Some of these students can write correct sentences and some cannot, but as a group they lack the facility other freshmen possess when they are faced with an academic writing task.

The "White Shoes" essay, for example, shows fewer sentence level errors than the "Clay Model" paper. This may well be due to the fact, however, that the writer of that paper stayed well within the safety of familiar territory. He kept himself out of trouble by doing what he could easily do. The tortuous syntax of the more advanced papers on my list is a syntax that represents a writer's struggle with a difficult and unfamiliar language, and it is a syntax that can quickly lead an inexperienced writer into trouble. The syntax and punctuation of the "Composing Songs" essay, for example, shows the effort that is required when a writer works against the pressure of conventional discourse. If the prose is inelegant (although I'll confess I admire those dense sentences), it is still correct. This writer has a command of the linguistic and stylistic resources (the highly embedded sentences, the use of parentheses and quotation marks) required to complete the act of writing. It is easy to imagine the possible pitfalls for a writer working without this facility.

There was no camera trained on the "Clay Model" writer while he was writing, and I have no protocol of what was going through his mind, but it is possible to speculate that the syntactic difficulties of sentences like the following are the result of an attempt to use an unusual vocabulary and to extend his sentences beyond the boundaries that would be "normal" in his speech or writing:

> In past time I thought that an incident was creative was when I had to make a clay model of the earth, but not of the classic or your everyday model of the earth which consists of the two cores, the mantle and the crust. I thought of these things in a dimension of which it would be unique, but easy to comprehend.

There is reason to believe, that is, that the problem is with this kind of sentence, in this context. If the problem of the last sentence is a problem of holding together these units — "I thought," "dimension," "unique," and "easy to comprehend" — then the linguistic problem is not a simple matter of sentence construction.

I am arguing, then, that such sentences fall apart not because the writer lacks the necessary syntax to glue the pieces together but because he lacks the full statement within which these key words are already operating. While writing, and in the thrust of his need to complete the sentence, he has the key words but not the utterance. (And to recover the utterance, I suspect, he will need to do more than revise the sentence.) The invisible conventions, the prepared phrases remain too distant for the statement to be completed. The writer must get inside of a discourse he can only partially imagine. The act of constructing a sentence, then, becomes something like an act of transcription, where the voice on the tape unexpectedly fades away and becomes inaudible.

Mina Shaughnessy speaks of the advanced writer as a writer with a more facile but still incomplete possession of this prior discourse. In the case of the advanced writer, the evidence of a problem is the presence of dissonant, redundant, or precise language, as in a sentence such as this: "No education can be *total,* it must be *continuous.*" Such a student, Shaughnessy says, could be said to hear the "melody of formal English" while still unable to make precise or exact distinctions. And, she says, the pre-packaging feature of language, the possibility of

23

taking over phrases and whole sentences without much thought about them, threatens the writer now as before. The writer, as we have said, inherits the language out of which he must fabricate his own messages. He is therefore in a constant tangle with the language, obliged to recognize its public, communal nature and yet driven to invent out of this language his own statements (19).

For the unskilled writer, the problem is different in degree and not in kind. The inexperienced writer is left with a more fragmentary record of the comings and goings of academic discourse. Or, as I said above, he often has the key words without the complete statements within which they are already operating.

It may very well be that some students will need to learn to crudely mimic the "distinctive register" of academic discourse before they are prepared to actually and legitimately do the work of the discourse, and before they are sophisticated enough with the refinements of tone and texture to do it with grace or elegance. To say this, however, is to say that our students must be our students. Their initial progress will be marked by their abilities to take on the role of privilege, by their abilities to establish authority. From this point of view, the student who wrote about constructing the clay model of the earth is better prepared for his education than the student who wrote about playing football in white shoes, even though the "White Shoes" paper was relatively error-free and the "Clay Model" paper was not. It will be hard to pry the writer of the "White Shoes" paper loose from the tidy, pat discourse that allows him to dispose of the question of creativity in a such a quick and efficient manner. He will have to be convinced that it is better to write sentences he might not so easily control, and he will have to be convinced that it is better to write muddier and more confusing prose (in order that it may sound like ours), and this will be harder than convincing the "Clay Model" writer to continue what he has begun.[7]

Notes

[1]This article represents an abridged version of a chapter in *When a Writer Can't Write: Studies in Writer's Block and Other Composing Problems*, ed. Mike Rose (New York: Guilford, 1985).

[2]David Olson has made a similar observation about school-related problems of language learning in younger children. Here is his conclusion: "Depending upon whether children assumed language was primarily suitable for making assertions and conjectures or primarily for making direct or indirect commands, they will either find school texts easy or difficult" (107).

[3]For Aristotle there were both general and specific commonplaces. A speaker, says Aristotle, has a "stock of arguments to which he may turn for a particular need."

If he knows the *topic* (regions, places, lines of argument) — and a skilled speaker will know them — he will know where to find what he wants for a special case. The general topics, or *common*places, are regions containing arguments that are common to all branches of knowledge. . . . But there are also special topics (regions, places, *loci*) in which one looks for arguments appertaining to particular branches of knowledge, special sciences, such as ethics or politics. (154–55)

And, he says "The topics or places, then, may be indifferently thought of as in the science that is concerned, or in the mind of the speaker." But the question of location is "indifferent" *only* if the mind of the speaker is in line with set opinion, general assumption. For the speaker (or writer) who is not situated so comfortably in the privileged public realm, this is indeed not an indifferent matter at all. If he does not have the commonplace at hand, he will not, in Aristotle's terms, know where to go at all.

[4]See especially Bartholomae and Rose for articles on curricula designed to move students into university discourse. The movement to extend writing "across the curriculum" is evidence of a general concern for locating students within the work of the university: see especially Bizzell or Maimon et al. For longer works directed specifically at basic writing, see Ponsot and Deen, and Shaughnessy. For a book describing a course for more advanced students, see Coles.

[5]See especially Bizzell, and Bizzell and Herzberg. My debt to Bizzell's work should be evident everywhere in this essay.

[6]In support of my argument that this is the kind of writing that does the work of the academy, let me offer the following excerpt from a recent essay by Wayne Booth ("The Company We Keep: Self-Making in Imaginative Art, Old and New"):

> I can remember making up songs of my own, no doubt borrowed from favorites like "Hello, Central, Give Me Heaven," "You Can't Holler Down My Rain Barrel," and one about the ancient story of a sweet little "babe in the woods" who lay down and died, with her brother.
>
> I asked my mother, in a burst of creative egotism, why nobody ever learned to sing my songs, since after all I was more than willing to learn *theirs*. I can't remember her answer, and I can barely remember snatches of two of "my" songs. But I can remember dozens of theirs, and when I sing them, even now, I sometimes feel again the emotions, and see the images, that they aroused then. Thus who I am now — the very shape of my soul — was to a surprising degree molded by the works of "art" that came my way.
>
> I set "art" in quotation marks, because much that I experienced in those early books and songs would not be classed as art according to most definitions. But for the purposes of appraising the effects of "art" on "life" or "culture," and especially for the purposes of thinking about the effects of the "media," we surely must include every kind of artificial experience that we provide for one another. . . .
>
> In this sense of the word, all of us are from the earliest years fed a steady diet of art. . . . (58–59)

While there are similarities in the paraphrasable content of Booth's arguments and my student's, what I am interested in is each writer's method. Both appropriate terms from a common discourse (about *art* and *inspiration*) in order to push against an established way of talking (about tradition and the individual). This effort of opposition clears a space for each writer's argument and enables the writers to establish their own "sense" of the key words in the discourse.

[7]Preparation of this manuscript was supported by the Learning Research and Development Center of the University of Pittsburgh, which is supported in part by the National Institute of Education. I am grateful also to Mike Rose, who pushed and pulled at this paper at a time when it needed it.

Works Cited

Aristotle. *The Rhetoric of Aristotle*. Trans. L. Cooper. Englewood Cliffs: Prentice, 1932.

Bartholomae, D. "Writing Assignments: Where Writing Begins." *Forum* Ed. P. Stock. Montclair: Boynton/Cook, 1983. 300–312.

Bizzell, P. "The ethos of academic discourse." *College Composition and Communication* 29 (1978): 351–355.

————. "Cognition, Convention, and Certainty: What We Need to Know about Writing." *Pre/text* 3 (1982): 213–244.

————. "College Composition: Initiation into the Academic Discourse Community." *Curriculum Inquiry* 12 (1982): 191–207.

Bizzell, P., and B. Herzberg. "'Inherent' Ideology, 'Universal' History, 'Empirical' Evidence, and 'Context-Free' Writing: Some Problems with E. D. Hirsch's *The Philosophy of Composition*." *Modern Language Notes* 95 (1980): 1181–1202.

Coles, W. E., Jr. *The Plural I*. New York: Holt, 1978.

Flower, Linda S. "Revising Writer-Based Prose." *Journal of Basic Writing* 3 (1981): 62–74.

Maimon, E. P., G. L. Belcher, G. W. Hearn, B. F. Nodine, and F. X. O'Connor. *Writing in the Arts and Sciences*. Cambridge: Winthrop, 1981.

Olson, D. R. "Writing: The Divorce of the Author from the Text." *Exploring Speaking-Writing Relationships: Connections and Contrasts*. Ed. B. M. Kroll and R. J. Vann. Urbana: National Council of Teachers of English, 1981.

Ponsot, M., and R. Deen. *Beat Not the Poor Desk*. Montclair: Boynton/Cook, 1982.

Rose, M. "Remedial Writing Courses: A Critique and a Proposal." *College English* 45 (1983): 109–128.

Shaughnessy, Mina. *Errors and Expectations*. New York: Oxford UP, 1977.

Bartholomae's Insights as a Resource for Your Teaching

1. Think about your own experience of moving from undergraduate to graduate study. Write a description of any difficulties you had writing for an "advanced" community. Analyze the processes you used to "invent the university." Describe and analyze this process of "initiation" that you observed in some colleagues. Use your insights about moving from novice to a member of the academic community to help the writers in your course realize that their "problems" are growth pains and that "you often get worse before you get better."

2. Shaughnessy and Bartholomae both indicate that muddled prose and syntax are often the results of learning new kinds of discourse. This understanding of "writing problems" will affect the kinds of comments you make on early drafts of student writing. Keep this article in mind when you read Sommers, "Responding to Student Writing" (the next selection) and as you practice "contextualizing" your responses to student writing.

Bartholomae's Insights as a Resource for the Writing Classroom

1. One important topic for discussion and drafting in a writing classroom should be the very process of becoming aware of and learning the diverse codes of academic discourse. Ask your students to read the "Keeping a Journal" section of Chapter 14 and to write journal entries describing what they read in their introductory courses. Ask them to describe any patterns of logic, structure, syntax, and word choice that they find repeated in the readings for a course. Use their observations to prompt a discussion of "the way they talk in college" (or history or business management or drama).

2. Peer editors are often sensitive to "the way it should sound" in academic writing. Ask them to highlight instances where the writer seems to be talking with a special vocabulary or system of presentation. Ask them to list the insights or ideas of the paper and to make a judgment about whether the "speaking their language" sections aid or hinder their understanding as they read the paper. Then confer with the writer about peer commentary (discussed in depth in Chapter 19) and about revision.

3. Frequently, writing across the curriculum programs encourage a collegial discussion of conventions and codes of discourse within disciplines. If your campus has a WAC initiative, invite faculty from other disciplines who are willing to talk with your students about the "secret language" of their disciplines. This could be a particularly interesting activity when the class members are working with conversation as a resource.

RESPONDING TO STUDENT WRITING

Some responses to student writing facilitate growth; others impede growth. The readings here focus on the effects of commentary and conferences on the drafting and revision experiences of student writers. Both readings recommend pedagogic behaviors that should foster writing improvement. In addition to these two readings, you might want to consult "Responding to Student Writing" in the final section of *Teaching with* The Bedford Guide for College Writers: *Practical Suggestions.*

RESPONDING TO STUDENT WRITING

Nancy Sommers

Nancy Sommers describes our responsibility as writing instructors in her concluding paragraph: "to show [student writers] through our comments why new choices would positively change their texts, and thus to show them the potential for development implicit in their own writing." Her definition of the "experienced adult writer" also informs her essay "Revision Strategies of Student Writers and Experienced Adult Writers," on page 55. In that essay she reports research findings on the comments that teachers use to motivate revision.

All our responses to student writing should constitute "thoughtful commentary" and help students become more effective writers. The research finding that an instructor's comments can have the effect of "appropriating the text" would not surprise the students in a first-year writing course who remark on course evaluation forms, "I did what the teacher asked but it still wasn't right" and "I learned what the teacher wanted me to write and how the teacher thinks I should write. I didn't learn enough about my own ideas or making my own style." Sommers offers good advice about how to avoid confusing students with the comments we make about revision.

Student writers will agree with the research finding that many teachers' comments are not "text-specific and could be interchanged, rubber-stamped, from text to text." When they come to conferences about their work-in-progress or wait after class for a quick discussion of a manuscript they have received back, they ask, politely, "Could you explain to me where I'm not being attentive to you as a reader?" or "Well, I don't exactly know why these phrases you marked are imprecise." Too often our comments to students model the abstract, vague, and general writing that we want our students to avoid. Sommers explains how these vague directives about revision unaccompanied by strategies for revising fail to motivate students to revise because the instructors who wrote those comments confused the product with the process.

These styles of comments also show up in the comments instructors write when they evaluate finished drafts and grade final products. Such comments fail to motivate students to use their experiences with drafting and revising as resources for future writing or to provide them with clear criteria that they might use when they assess their own writing for other courses.

More than any other enterprise in the teaching of writing, responding to and commenting on student writing consumes the largest proportion of our time. Most teachers estimate that it takes them at least 20 to 40 minutes to comment on an individual student paper, and those 20 to 40 minutes times 20 students per class, times 8 papers, more or less, during the course of a semester add up to an enormous amount of time. With so much time and energy directed to a single activity, it is important for us to understand the nature of the enterprise. For it seems, paradoxically enough, that although commenting on student writing is the most widely used method for responding to student writing, it is the least understood. We do not know in any definitive way what constitutes thoughtful commentary or what effect, if any, our comments have on helping our students become more effective writers.

Theoretically, at least, we know that we comment on our students' writing for the same reasons professional editors comment on the work of professional writers or for the same reasons we ask our colleagues to read and respond to our own writing. As writers we need and want thoughtful commentary to show us when we have communicated our ideas and when not, raising questions from a reader's point of view that may not have occurred to us as writers. We want to know if our writing has communicated our intended meaning and, if not, what questions or discrepancies our reader sees that we, as writers, are blind to.

27

In commenting on our students' writing, however, we have an additional pedagogical purpose. As teachers, we know that most students find it difficult to imagine a reader's response in advance, and to use such responses as a guide in composing. Thus, we comment on student writing to dramatize the presence of a reader, to help our students to become that questioning reader themselves, because, ultimately, we believe that becoming such a reader will help them to evaluate what they have written and develop control over their writing.[1]

Even more specifically, however, we comment on student writing because we believe that it is necessary for us to offer assistance to student writers when they are in the process of composing a text, rather than after the text has been completed. Comments create the motive for revising. Without comments from their teachers or from their peers, student writers will revise in a consistently narrow and predictable way. Without comments from readers, students assume that their writing has communicated their meaning and perceive no need for revising the substance of their text.[2]

Yes as much as we as informed professionals believe in the soundness of this approach to responding to student writing, we also realize that we don't know how our theory squares with teachers' actual practice — do teachers comment and students revise as the theory predicts they should? For the past year my colleagues, Lil Brannon, Cyril Knoblach, and I have been researching this problem, attempting to discover not only what messages teachers give their students through their comments, but also what determines which of these comments the students choose to use or to ignore when revising. Our research has been entirely focused on comments teachers write to motivate revisions. We have studied the commenting styles of thirty-five teachers at New York University and the University of Oklahoma, studying the comments these teachers wrote on first and second drafts, and interviewing a representative number of these teachers and their students. All teachers also commented on the same set of three student essays. As an additional reference point, one of the student essays was typed into the computer that had been programmed with the "Writer's Workbench," a package of twenty-three programs developed by Bell Laboratories to help computers and writers work together to improve a text rapidly. Within a few minutes, the computer delivered editorial comments on the student's text, identifying all spelling and punctuation errors, isolating problems with wordy or misused phrases, and suggesting alternatives, offering a stylistic analysis of sentence types, sentence beginnings, and sentence lengths, and finally, giving our freshman essay a Kincaid readability score of 8th grade which, as the computer program informed us, "is a low score for this type of document." The sharp contrast between the teachers' comments and those of the computer highlighted how arbitrary and idiosyncratic most of our teachers' comments are. Besides, the calm, reasonable language of the computer provided quite a contrast to the hostility and mean-spiritedness of most of the teachers' comments.

The first finding from our research on styles of commenting is that *teachers' comments can take students' attention away from their own purposes in writing a particular text and focus that attention on the teachers' purpose in commenting*. The teacher appropriates the text from the student by confusing the student's purpose in writing the text with her own purpose in commenting. Students make the changes the teacher wants rather than those that the student perceives are necessary, since the teachers' concerns imposed on the text create the reasons for the subsequent changes. We have all heard our perplexed students say to us when confused by our comments: "I don't understand how *you* want me to change this" or "Tell me what *you* want me to do." In the beginning of the process there was the writer, her words, and her desire to communicate her ideas. But after the comments of the teacher are imposed on the first or second draft, the student's attention dramatically shifts from "This is what I want to say," to "This is what *you* the teacher are asking me to do."

This appropriation of the text by the teacher happens particularly when teachers identify errors in usage, diction, and style in a first draft and ask students to correct these errors when they revise; such comments give the student an impression of the importance of these errors that is all out of proportion to how they should view these errors at this point in the process. The comments create the concern that these "accidents of discourse" need to be attended to before the meaning of the text is attended to.

It would not be so bad if students were only commanded to correct errors, but, more often than not, students are given contradictory messages; they are commanded to edit a sentence to avoid an error or to condense a sentence to achieve greater brevity of style, and then told in the margins that the particular paragraph needs to be more specific or to be developed more. An example of this problem can be seen in the following student paragraph:

wordy; be precise — which Sunday?   comma needed   word choice

Every year [on one Sunday in the middle of January] tens of millions of people cancel all

wordy

events, plans or work to watch the Super Bowl. This audience includes [little boys and girls,

be specific — what reasons?

old people, and housewives and men.] Many reasons have been given to explain why the Super

and why   what spots?)   awkward

Bowl has become so popular that commercial [spots cost up to $100,000.00. One explanation is

another what?   spelling

that people like to take sides and root for a team. Another is that some people like the pageritry

too colloquial

and excitement of the event. These reasons alone, however, do not explain a happening as big

you need to do more research.

This paragraph needs to be expanded in order to be more interesting to a reader.

as the Super Bowl.

In commenting on this draft, the teacher has shown the student how to edit the sentences, but then commands the student to expand the paragraph in order to make it more interesting to a reader. The interlinear comments and the marginal comments represent two separate tasks for this student; the interlinear comments encourage the student to see the text as a fixed piece, frozen in time, that just needs some editing. The marginal comments, however, suggest that the meaning of the text is not fixed, but rather that the student still needs to develop the meaning by doing some more research. Students are commanded to edit and develop at the same time; the remarkable contradiction of developing a paragraph after editing the sentences in it represents the confusion we encountered in our teachers' commenting styles. These different signals given to students, to edit and develop, to condense and elaborate, represent also the failure of teachers' comments to direct genuine revision of the text as a whole.

Moreover, the comments are worded in such a way that it is difficult for students to know what is the most important problem in the text and what problems are of lesser importance. No scale of concerns is offered to a student, with the result that a comment about spelling or a comment about an awkward sentence is given weight equal to a comment about organization or logic. The comment that seemed to represent this problem best was one teacher's command to his student: "Check your commas and semicolons and think more about what you are thinking about." The language of the comments makes it difficult for a student to sort out and decide what is most important and what is least important.

When the teacher appropriates the text for the student in this way, students are encouraged to see their writing as a series of parts — words, sentences, paragraphs — and not as a whole discourse. The comments encourage students to believe that their first drafts are finished drafts, not invention drafts, and that all they need to do is patch and polish their writing. That is, teachers' comments do not provide their students with an inherent reason for revising the structure and meaning of their texts, since the comments suggest to students that the meaning of their text is already there, finished, produced, and all that is necessary is a better word or phrase. The processes of revising, editing, and proofreading are collapsed and reduced to a single trivial activity, and the students' misunderstanding of the revision process as a rewording activity is reinforced by their teachers' comments.

It is possible, and it quite often happens, that students follow every comment and fix their texts appropriately as requested, but their texts are not improved substantially, or, even worse, their revised drafts are inferior to their previous drafts. Since the teachers' comments take the students' attention away from their own original purposes, students concentrate more, as I have noted, on what the teachers commanded them to do than on what they are trying to say. Sometimes students do not understand the purpose behind their teachers' comments and take these comments very literally. At other times students understand the comments, but the teacher has misread the text and the comments, unfortunately, are not applicable. For instance, we repeatedly saw comments in which teachers commanded students to reduce and condense what was written, when in fact what the text really needed at this stage was to be expanded in conception and scope.

The process of revising always involves a risk. But, too often revision becomes a balancing act for students in which they make the changes that are requested but do not take the risk of changing anything that was not commented on, even if the students sense that other changes are needed. A more effective text does not often evolve from such changes alone, yet the student does not want to take the chance of reducing a finished, albeit inadequate, paragraph to chaos — to fragments — in order to rebuild it, if such changes have not been requested by the teacher.

The second finding from our study is that *most teachers' comments are not text-specific and could be interchanged, rubber-stamped, from text to text.* The comments are not anchored in the particulars of the students' texts, but rather are a series of vague directives that are not text-specific. Students are commanded to "Think more about [their] audience, avoid colloquial language, avoid the passive, avoid prepositions at the end of sentences or conjunctions at the beginning of sentences, be clear, be specific, be precise, but above all, think more about what [they] are thinking about." The comments on the following student paragraph illustrate this problem:

> *Begin by telling your reader what you are going to write about.*
> In the sixties it was drugs, in the seventies it was rock and roll. Now in the eighties, one of the *avoid "one of the"*
>
> *elaborate*
> most controversial subjects is nuclear power. The United States is in great need of its own
>
> source of power. Because of environmentalists, coal is not an acceptable source of energy.
> *be specific* *avoid "it seems"*
> [Solar and wind power have not yet received the technology necessary to use them.] It seems
>
> that nuclear power is the only feasible means right now for obtaining self-sufficient power.
>
> However, too large a percentage of the population are against nuclear power claiming it is
>
> *be precise*
> unsafe. With as many problems as the United States is having concerning energy, it seems a
>
> shame that the public is so quick to "can" a very feasible means of power. Nuclear energy
>
> should not be given up on, but rather, more nuclear plants should be built.

Think more about your reader.

Thesis sentence needed.

One could easily remove all the comments from this paragraph and rubber-stamp them on another student text, and they would make as much or as little sense on the second text as they do here.

We have observed an overwhelming similarity in the generalities and abstract commands given to students. There seems to be among teachers an accepted, albeit unwritten canon for commenting on student texts. This uniform code of commands, requests, and pleadings demonstrates that the teacher holds license for vagueness while the student is commanded to be specific. The students we interviewed admitted to having great difficulty with these vague directives. The students stated that when a teacher writes in the margins or as an end comment, "choose precise language," or "think more about your audience," revising becomes a guessing game. In effect, the teacher is saying to the student, "Somewhere in this paper is imprecise language or lack of awareness of an audience and you must find it." The problem presented by these vague commands is compounded for the students when they are not offered any strategies for carrying out these commands. Students are told that they have done something wrong and that there is something in their text that needs to be fixed before the text is acceptable. But to tell students that they have done something wrong is not to tell them what to do about it. In order to offer a useful revision strategy to a student, the teacher must anchor that strategy in the specifics of the student's text. For instance, to tell our student, the author of the above paragraph, "to be specific," or "to elaborate," does not show our student what questions the reader has about the meaning of the text, or what breaks in logic exist, that could be resolved if the writer supplied specific information; nor is the student shown how to achieve the desired specificity.

Instead of offering strategies, the teachers offer what is interpreted by students as rules for composing; the comments suggest to students that writing is just a matter of following the rules. Indeed, the teachers seem to impose a series of abstract rules about written products even when some of them are not appropriate for the specific text the student is creating.[3] For instance, the student author of our sample paragraph presented above is commanded to follow the conventional rules for writing a five-paragraph essay — to begin the introductory paragraph by telling his reader what he is going to say and to end the paragraph with a thesis sentence. Somehow these abstract rules about what five-paragraph products should look like do not seem applicable to the problems this student must confront when revising, nor are the rules specific strategies he could use when revising. There are many inchoate ideas ready to be exploited in this paragraph, but the rules do not help the student to take stock of his (or her) ideas and use the opportunity he has, during revision, to develop those ideas.

The problem here is a confusion of process and product; what one has to say about the process is different from what one has to say about the product. Teachers who use this method of commenting are formulating their comments as if these drafts were finished drafts and were not going to be revised. Their commenting vocabularies have not been adapted to revision and they comment on first drafts as if they were justifying a grade or as if the first draft were the final draft.

Our summary finding, therefore, from this research on styles of commenting is that the news from the classroom is not good. For the most part, teachers do not respond to student writing with the kind of thoughtful commentary which will help students to engage with the issues they are writing about or which will help them think about their purposes and goals in writing a specific text. In defense of our teachers, however, they told us that responding to student writing was rarely stressed in their teacher-training or in writing workshops; they had been trained in various prewriting techniques, in constructing assignments, and in evaluating papers for grades, but rarely in the process of reading a student text for meaning or in offering commentary to motivate revision. The problem is that most of us as teachers of writing have been trained to read and interpret literary texts for meaning, but, unfortunately, we have not been trained to act upon the same set of assumptions in reading student texts as we follow in reading literary texts.[4] Thus, we read student texts with biases about what the writer should have said or about what he or she should have written, and our biases determine how we will comprehend the text. We read with our preconceptions and preoccupations, expecting to find errors, and the result is that we find errors and misread our students' texts.[5] We find what we look for; instead of reading and responding to the meaning of a text, we correct our students' writing. We need to reverse this approach. Instead of finding errors or showing students how to patch up parts of their texts, we need to sabotage our students' conviction that the drafts they have written are complete and coherent. Our comments need to offer students revision tasks of a different order of complexity and sophistication from the ones that they themselves identify, by forcing students back into the chaos, back to the point where they are shaping and restructuring their meaning.[6]

For if the content of a student text is lacking in substance and meaning, if the order of the parts must be rearranged significantly in the next draft, if paragraphs must be restructured for logic and clarity, then many sentences are likely to be changed or deleted anyway. There seems to be no point in having students correct usage errors or condense sentences that are likely to disappear before the next draft is completed. In fact, to identify such problems in a text at this early first draft stage, when such problems are likely to abound, can give a student a disproportionate sense of their importance at this stage in the writing process.[7] In responding to our students' writing, we should be guided by the recognition that it is not spelling or usage problems that we as writers first worry about when drafting and revising our texts.

We need to develop an appropriate level of response for commenting on a first draft, and to differentiate that from the level suitable to a second or third draft. Our comments need to be suited to the draft we are reading. In a first or second draft, we need to respond as any reader would, registering questions, reflecting befuddlement, and noting places where we are puzzled about the meaning of the text. Comments should point to breaks in logic, disruptions in meaning, or missing information. Our goal in commenting on early drafts should be to engage students with the issues they are considering and help them clarify their purposes and reasons in writing their specific text.

For instance, the major rhetorical problem of the essay written by the student who wrote the first paragraph (the paragraph on nuclear power) quoted above was that the student had two principal arguments running through his text, each of which brought the other into question. On the one hand, he argued that we must use nuclear power, unpleasant as it is, because we have nothing else to use; though nuclear energy is a problematic source of energy, it is the best of a bad lot. On the other hand, he also argued that nuclear energy is really quite safe and therefore should be our primary resource. Comments on this student's first draft need to point out this break in logic and show the student that if we accept his first argument, then his second argument sounds fishy. But if we accept his second argument, his first argument sounds contradictory. The teacher's comments need to engage this student writer with this basic rhetorical and conceptual problem in his first draft rather than impose a series of abstract commands and rules upon his text.

Written comments need to be viewed not as an end in themselves — a way for teachers to satisfy themselves that they have done their jobs — but rather as a means for helping students to become more effective writers. As a means for helping students, they have limitations; they are, in fact, disembodied remarks — one absent writer responding to another absent writer. The key to successful commenting is to have what is said in the comments and what is done in the classroom mutually reinforce and enrich each other. Commenting on papers assists the writing course in achieving its purpose; classroom activities and the comments we write to our students need to be connected. Written comments need to be an extension of the teacher's voice — an extension of the teacher as reader. Exercises in such activities as revising a whole text or individual paragraphs together in class, noting how the sense of the whole dictates the smaller changes, looking at options, evaluating actual choices, and then discussing the effect of these changes on revised drafts — such exercises need to be designed to take students through the cycles of revising and to help them overcome their anxiety about revising: that anxiety we all feel at reducing what looks like a finished draft into fragments and chaos.

The challenge we face as teachers is to develop comments which will provide an inherent reason for students to revise; it is a sense of revision as discovery, as a repeated process of beginning again, as starting out new, that our students have not learned. We need to show our students how to seek, in the possibility of revision, the dissonances of discovery — to show them through our comments why new choices would positively change their texts, and thus to show them the potential for development implicit in their own writing.

Notes

[1]C. H. Knoblach and Lil Brannon, "Teacher Commentary on Student Writing: The State of the Art," *Freshman English News* 10 (Fall 1981): 1–3.

[2]For an extended discussion of revision strategies of student writers see Nancy Sommers, "Revision Strategies of Student Writers and Experienced Adult Writers," *College Composition and Communication* 31 (Dec. 1980): 378–88. [Reprinted in this book, pages 55–62.]

[3]Nancy Sommers and Ronald Schleifer, "Means and Ends: Some Assumptions of Student Writers," *Composition and Teaching* 2 (Dec. 1980): 69–76.

[4]Janet Emig and Robert P. Parker, Jr., "Responding to Student Writing: Building a Theory of the Evaluating Process," unpublished paper, Rutgers University.

[5]For an extended discussion of this problem see Joseph Williams, "The Phenomenology of Error," *College Composition and Communication* 32 (May 1981): 152–68.

[6]Ann Berthoff, *The Making of Meaning* (Upper Montclair: Boynton/Cook, 1981).

[7]W. U. McDonald, "The Revising Process and the Marking of Student Papers," *College Composition and Communication* 24 (May 1978): 167–70.

Sommers's Insights as a Resource for Your Teaching

1. Sommers clearly advises multiple readings of student writing. She indicates that reading a student text to understand its meaning and to provide commentary that can motivate revision is critical to students' growth as writers. Don't be daunted by the paper load. If you focus your commentary on what happens as you read and respond to the meaning of a text, you'll find that what may have distracted you at the lexical level has disappeared from or changed substantively in the draft submitted for evaluation and grading. You may be spending the same amount of time or even less time overall when you read early and late drafts.

Revision conferences also provide opportunities for you to offer thoughtful commentary. They force you to make text-specific comments. Advise your students to take advantage of the discovery checklists and rewriting checklists in *The Bedford Guide for College Writers* to supplement your specific conversation about revision.

2. Ask a colleague teaching the same course to work with you reading some early drafts. Trade a set of drafts. Write your comments about revision on a separate sheet of paper; exchange and compare your comments, paying particular attention to the specificity of each comment and to precision of language. You'll both profit from the discussion and may find your reading of the text enhanced by this "external assessor."

You might also use this technique when you evaluate late drafts. The ensuing conversation about your evaluative comments and criteria for evaluation will certainly give you both perspective on and confidence about your process of evaluating and grading.

Sommers's Insights as a Resource for the Writing Classroom

1. Ask students to write from recall about the commentary they received or receive outside your writing classroom on their writing (this would be a good exercise for Chapter 1, "Writing from Recall"). Ask them to explain, in journal entries or in fifteen-minute writing sessions, how a comment prompted or inhibited deep-level revising. One caution: because such an assignment can trigger painful or angry memories, advise the students not to name the person who wrote comments that obstructed revision. Explain that the "text" of the comment can be analyzed for its effect without your having to know the author. If the students want to

laud the instructor whose comments motivated them to revise for wholeness, suggest they write that instructor a fan letter.

2. Peer editors might fall into these same styles of commentary. Bring in a sampler of peer editing comments and ask the class as a whole or in small groups to analyze how well they prompt revision. Direct their attention to the peer commentary incorporated in *The Bedford Guide for College Writers* on pages 404–412.

3. Use one of the peer editing checklists from *The Bedford Guide for College Writers* or one that your class has constructed in response to a shared writing task for an in-class evaluation session. Ask students to write sentence-length, specific comments about issues of meaning and attention to the readers' concerns. Move from writer to writer and read the comments. Tell each peer editor if his or her comments would motivate you to revise.

4. Ask class members to identify commentary that has assisted them in deep revision when they write a self-assessment to accompany a submitted draft. Ask a question like "What advice did your peer readers give and what did you do with the advice?"

DEMONSTRATING TECHNIQUES FOR ASSESSING WRITING IN THE WRITING CONFERENCE

Richard Beach

Richard Beach reports on a variety of techniques that he uses to assist student writers to assess their writing and to detect "dissonance" between their goals and their texts. Like Sommers, he believes that the "dissonances of discovery" will motivate revision.

The article describes ways to demonstrate to students how to assess their own drafts and to use that self-assessment for revision. Beach models techniques for describing a draft, judging its success, and selecting appropriate revisions. He emphasizes that the writing instructor must be a careful listener, implying that the instructor must guard against "appropriating" the writer's work when demonstrating how he or she, acting as the writer, would pose self-assessment questions. You'll find many useful and specific questions that you would be likely to ask in a conference. In the conclusion of the essay, Beach explains that he only uses two or three of the conferencing techniques he describes in any one conference with a student.

Beach recommends that you begin conferences by asking the writers to tell you their reactions to their difficulties with a draft. The "guided assessing form" that the writers prepare before conferences is a particularly effective way to make them take responsibility for the conferences.

Notice how Beach has worked to shift the focus of the conference from the teacher describing the writing and its success to the writer assessing his or her own work. Beach indicates that such self-assessment is a new experience that must often be demonstrated so that the writer can practice it.

For further advice on handling the writing conference, see "Individualizing Instruction with the Writing Conference," on page 233 of Teaching with The Bedford Guide for College Writers: *Practical Suggestions.*

In a conference, I ask a student to tell me how she feels about her draft. "Oh, I feel pretty good about it" is her response; "maybe it needs a few more details." Having read the draft, I know that it's riddled with more serious problems than lack of details.

How can this student be taught to critically assess her writing? As experienced teachers know, simply telling the students what their problems are and what to do about those problems doesn't help them learn to become their own best readers. It teaches them only how to follow instructions.

Moreover, in giving students "reader-based feedback" — how I respond as a reader — which presumably implies to students that certain problems exist, I must assume that they are capable of defining the implied problem, which is often not the case. The majority of students who have difficulty assessing their own writing need some instruction in how to assess. Teachers typically demonstrate techniques for assessing writing by discussing rhetorical or logical problems in published and/or students' texts. Unfortunately, students often have difficulty applying this instruction to assessment of problems in their own texts. For these students, a teacher may then need to augment classroom instruction in assessing techniques by demonstrating these techniques in writing conferences — showing them how to assess their own unique problems — and then having them practice this assessing in the conference.

This more individualized approach to teaching assessing in conferences involves the following steps:

1. determining a student's own particular difficulty by analyzing his or her use of certain assessing techniques;
2. demonstrating the stages of assessing: describing, judging, and selecting appropriate revisions;
3. describing the different components of the rhetorical context — purpose, rhetorical strategies, organization, and audience, showing students how each component implies criteria for judging drafts and selecting appropriate revisions;
4. having students practice the technique that was just demonstrated.

Techniques of Assessing

In order to discuss ways of demonstrating different assessing techniques, I propose a model of assessing. As illustrated in the chart [Figure 1], assessing involves three basic stages: describing, judging, and selecting/testing out revisions. I will briefly define each of these stages and then, for the remainder of this paper, discuss how I demonstrate these techniques in a conference.

As depicted in this chart, each of the first two stages implies a subsequent stage. By *describing* their goals, strategies, or audience, writers have some basis for making judgments about their drafts. For example, a writer describes his strategy — that in the beginning of his story, he is "setting the scene in order to show what a small-town world is like." He describes his audience — noting that the audience probably knows little about that particular setting. Now he can infer appropriate criteria for judging his setting — whether he has included enough information to convey the sense of a "small-town world" to his reader. This judgment, in turn, helps him in the final stage, *selecting appropriate revisions* — in this case, adding more information about the setting.

In demonstrating assessing techniques, I am therefore showing students more than how to use a specific technique. I am also showing them that describing audience implies criteria for judging or that defining a problem implies criteria for selecting revisions. These demonstrations help students appreciate the value of describing and judging in helping them make revisions.

One benefit of a conference is that it provides a forum for students to practice their assessing with a teacher. The teacher can then note instances in which a student is having difficulty and, instead of simply telling the student how to improve her assessing, demonstrate how to assess. The student then has a concrete guide for trying out a certain assessing technique.

35

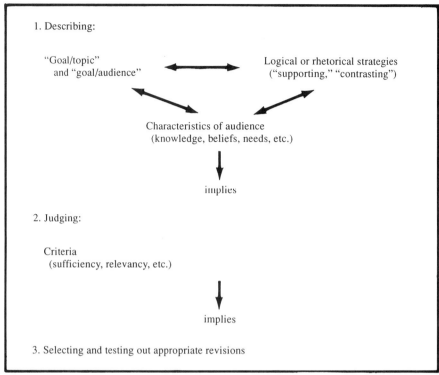

1. Describing:

"Goal/topic"   Logical or rhetorical strategies
and "goal/audience"   ("supporting," "contrasting")

Characteristics of audience
(knowledge, beliefs, needs, etc.)

implies

2. Judging:

Criteria
(sufficiency, relevancy, etc.)

implies

3. Selecting and testing out appropriate revisions

Figure 1. Stages of the Assessing Process

Determining Difficulties in Assessing

In order to know which technique to demonstrate, I try to pinpoint a student's difficulty in using a particular technique. I therefore have students begin the conference by giving me their reactions to and sense of the difficulties in describing, judging, or selecting revisions. However, given the brevity of many conferences, I often can't diagnose students' difficulties by relying solely on their comments in the conference. I therefore use guided assessing forms, which students complete prior to the conference.

The questions on these forms are based on the three assessing stages, as listed below:

The Guided Assessing Form

Describing

1. What are you trying to say or show in this section?

2. What are you trying to do in this section?

3. What are some specific characteristics of your audience?

4. What are you trying to get your audience to do or think?

Judging

5. What are some problems you perceive in achieving 1, 2, and 4?

Selecting Appropriate Revisions

6. What are some changes you can make to deal with these problems?

In using the forms, students divide their draft into sections, answering the questions on the form for each section. The students don't necessarily need to begin with the "describing" questions; they may begin by noting problems and then working back to the describing stage.

By reading over the form in the beginning of the conference and by listening to their reactions to the draft I try to determine a student's particular difficulty in assessing her draft. If, for example, for each of three sections in her draft a student has difficulty describing what she is "trying to say or show," I might conclude that she has difficulty defining her intentions. The fact that she's also had difficulty answering my questions about goals further suggests that inferring intentions is a problem for her.

I then demonstrate how I would identify intentions. Rather than using my own writing, which the student isn't familiar with, I use the student's writing. I adopt the student's role or persona, demonstrating how I, from her perspective, would infer intentions. I stress to the student that while I am showing her how *I* would infer intentions, I am not implying that my approach is the "one correct way." I also *avoid* telling the students what they ought to be saying, for example, by telling them what I think they are "really trying to say." Rather, I am showing students how to do something rather than telling them what to say.

After I demonstrate a certain technique, I then ask the student to make her own inferences. If she continues to have difficulty, I demonstrate that technique further.

All of this requires careful attention to clues suggesting difficulties, as well as a conceptual framework for sorting out and isolating certain strategies. Based on my own experience and research on assessing, I will now discuss how I demonstrate each of the stages of the assessing process — describing, judging, and selecting revisions.

The Describing Stage

The describing stage consists of describing goals for content (What am I trying to say?), audience (What do I want my audience to do or think?), logical or rhetorical strategies (What am I trying to do: supporting, contrasting, shifting to a different point?), and audience characteristics (knowledge, traits, needs, etc.). Writers obviously use goals as criteria for judging whether their text says or does what they want it to say or do. Once they identify their goals, they can detect dissonance between their goals and their text, dissonance that leads to judgments about problems in achieving their goals.

This is not to imply that writers must always articulate their goals in order to assess their writing. Writers often have only a "felt sense" of their intentions without ever articulating them, but they know how to use their unarticulated intentions to determine that something is amiss and to decide what to do about their problems.

In a conference, it is often useful to have students articulate their goals because those goals are necessary for judging, for determining the extent to which those goals have or have not been fulfilled. If students are to be able to make these judgments, they may need help articulating goals.

Difficulties in describing goal/topic and goal/audience. In my research on use of the guided assessing forms, I asked students to describe what they were trying to say or show ("goal/topic") or what they wanted their audience to do or think ("goal/audience") in each of several sections of their draft.[1] Many students in these studies have difficulty stating what it is that they are trying to say or show. They often simply restate their text *verbatim* rather than stating their intended topic or idea. For example, in writing an analysis of citizen participation in the government of her hometown, a student described her draft section as saying that "a lot of citizens in the town don't vote and there often aren't enough candidates to run for local offices," almost a verbatim restatement of what she was saying in the draft. She did not go beyond that restatement to recognize a point of that section, her "goal/topic" — that citizens aren't involved in town government. She also had difficulty identifying her "goal/audience," what she wanted her audience to do or think having read her essay. Because she had difficulty identifying these goals, she had difficulty judging her draft.

To some degree, identifying these goals is difficult, particularly if students don't perceive the purpose for defining goals — to further assess their draft. I therefore try to show students that clearly defining goals helps them in judging their draft.

In demonstrating definitions of goal/topic, I demonstrate the difference between simply restating the content of a section of their draft and recognizing the goal or purpose of that section. In working with the student writing about her local government, I first take her restatement of the text, "that citizens don't vote and there aren't enough candidates" and, playing the role of the "dumb reader," to use Walker Gibson's term, ask the question "what's the point?" I then infer a goal statement — that the citizens aren't involved — and show her that, in contrast to her restatement, I can use this goal statement to pinpoint disparities between goal and text.

Another problem with students' identifications of goal/topic is that they are often so global that they are not very useful for perceiving disparities between goals and text.[2] For example, in writing an autobiographical narrative about a series of shoplifting incidents, a student states that he was "trying to show what I was like when I was a teenager." This description is too global for assessing what it is he wants to show about this past self. The student needs to identify what the incidents show about his past self.

Having diagnosed the student's goals as too global, I then propose, using his other comments in the conference, a more precise goal statement: "in portraying my shoplifting, I'm trying to show that I was so lonely that I would do anything to be popular with my peers." I then use this inferred goal to review the shoplifting episodes, judging whether or not the descriptions of the student's behavior in each episode convey his need for friendship. Again, I am demonstrating the value of goal statements, particularly precise goal statements.

Difficulties in describing rhetorical or logical strategies. In describing rhetorical or logical strategies, writers are defining what they are doing in their texts — supporting, defining, stating, requesting, contrasting, describing, evaluating, specifying, etc. In naming these strategies, writers go beyond simply summarizing what they are trying to say, to identifying what they are trying to do, conceiving of their text from a functional or pragmatic perspective.

Each of these strategies implies certain criteria for assessing the success or failure of that strategy. By describing these strategies, writers evoke the particular criteria necessary for judging the use of that strategy. Writers then narrow down the criteria in light of their particular goals and the characteristics of their audience. For example, the strategy, supporting, implies the criteria, *sufficiency, relevancy,* or *specificity of support:* do I have enough support? is my support relevant to my thesis? is my support specific enough? Given an audience which the writer assumes knows little about the topic, the writer is particularly concerned about the sufficiency of information — is there enough supportive information for that audience to understand a point? Or, in requesting, as suggested by speech-act theorists, I am concerned about my power, right, or ability to make a request; my reader's ability to fulfill my request; and my reader's perception of my sincerity in making a request. Given a reader who may doubt my right to make a request, I'm particularly concerned that my request implies that I have the right to make such a request.

For example, the administration at my university has decided to reduce my program, but without giving any clear rationale for the proposed reduction. In writing to the administration requesting some clarification of their rationale, I somewhat cynically anticipate their response — that I have no right to make such a request. I argue that I have the right to ask for clarification because further reductions would jeopardize my program and my job. I therefore clearly define my affiliation with the program in order to imply my right to make such a request.

Describing strategies and inferring implied criteria is a complicated process that requires a pragmatic perspective on writing — conceiving of writing as doing things rather than simply conveying information. It also requires tacit knowledge of the conditions governing the use of these strategies. It is therefore not surprising that, as our analysis of the assessing forms indicated, many students had difficulty describing their strategies and inferring implied criteria.[3] When asked to describe their strategies, students often had difficulty going beyond describing what they were trying to "say" to inferring what it is they were trying to "do." They frequently restated content — "I am writing about my high school and college courses," rather than inferring strategy — "I am contrasting my high school and college courses." These students, with only a restatement of content, then had difficulty making judgments about their text. Those students who identified a strategy were more likely to make a judgment because they were able to successfully contrast high school and college courses.

In demonstrating the difference between a summary of content and a description of strategy I again demonstrate how descriptions of strategies can be used to imply criteria. For example, having inferred that the student is contrasting high school and college classes, I then note that "contrasting" implies, among other criteria, the importance of information relevant to the contrast and the validity of the contrast — whether or not the information constitutes valid evidence for a contrast.

Difficulties in describing characteristics of audience. Making inferences about characteristics of audience is also a complex process. There is much debate regarding the conflicting evidence about how much writers actually think about their audience.[4]

I would argue that, rather than conceiving of audience as a unified global construct, writers infer or create specific prototypical characteristics such as what and how much members of an audience know about a topic, what they believe about a topic, and their needs, status, power, attitudes, or expectations. For example, in writing a set of directions for windsurfing, a writer may conceive of her audience as "someone who knows little about windsurfing." Or, in arguing the case for nationalizing the steel industry, a writer conceives of his audience as "someone who is opposed to my belief about nationalization." These conceptions are prototypical because writers often never know, even with familiar audiences, exactly what their audience knows, believes, needs, etc. They must therefore rely on prototypical constructs derived from approximations of their audience.

Writers also derive these characteristics from their defined goals and strategies. In giving a set of directions for windsurfing, a writer knows that she needs to consider what her audience may or may not know about windsurfing, because that characteristic is particularly useful for judging the relevancy and sufficiency of information in her directions. Writers therefore infer these prototypical constructs because, as with decisions about goals and strategies, the constructs imply relevant criteria for judging their writing.

Inferring these characteristics of audience also allows writers to adopt a reader's schema, as they must in order to distance themselves from their text. Having created the construct, "someone who is opposed to nationalizing the steel industry," they can then assess the text from that perspective.

When, in our research, Sarah Eaton and I asked students to infer characteristics of their audience on their assessing form, most of the students made few if any references to specific audience characteristics.[5] Most of their inferences consisted of anticipated emotional responses such as "my reader should like this beginning" or "my audience will be bothered by this section," inferences reflecting an egocentric orientation. They were more concerned with how their audience would react to their writing than with how to adapt their text to their audience.

When I sense that students are having difficulty inferring characteristics of audience, I demonstrate how I infer these characteristics from my description of strategies or goals. For example, in writing her paper about the lack of citizen participation in affairs of her hometown, the student previously cited began her paper by describing the town's government, noting that she's trying to "provide background information in order to set the scene." However, she has difficulty judging her use of this defined strategy — setting the scene — because she has difficulty inferring audience.

Using her description of her "backgrounding" strategy, I note that in giving background information, I need to determine how much her audience may know about her hometown. Once I've isolated the appropriate attribute — knowledge — I create the construct, "someone who knows little about the town." I then use that construct to judge her descriptions of the town.

The Judging Stage

Sensing dissonance. Having described these components of the rhetorical context, writers then judge their text. In judging, a writer needs to sense dissonance between goals and the text, dissonance that serves as an incentive to revise. However, many students in our research had difficulty sensing dissonance because they had difficulty adopting a reader's perspective. In order to demonstrate ways of sensing dissonance, I go back and describe goals, strategies, characteristics, for example, "someone who knows little about book publishing." I, as instructor, then cite instances in which I, as a reader, didn't have enough background information to understand the draft. Given my goal, as the writer, of informing my reader about book publishing, I know that, from the reader's perspective, something is amiss.

Applying criteria. Once writers sense the dissonance, they need to specify the reason for the problem, why something is amiss.

Students often have difficulty specifying reasons for their problems. They may say that "this is awkward" or "this doesn't flow"; but these judgments often don't point towards any predicted solutions, because they are too vague. In contrast, judgments such as, "I don't have enough examples to support my thesis," imply some specific directions: add more examples.

One reason students aren't able to specify their reasons is that they simply don't know or don't know how to apply criteria such as sufficiency, relevancy, validity, clarity, appropriateness, or coherence. For example, a student thinks that there is a problem with her extended illustration of an ineffective teaching technique, but she can't define the reason for the problem. I then show her how to define a reason for her problem. Having defined her strategy, *giving examples,* I infer implied criteria — relevancy, sufficiency, or clarity of the information in terms of illustrating the point. I then ask the question — given the goals and characteristics of audience, is this a problem of relevancy, sufficiency, or clarity? I then note that, from my perspective as reader, the illustration is too long. This suggests that sufficiency of information serves as a useful criterion for selecting and testing out appropriate revisions. One can hope that the student will then recognize the value of specifying criteria in order to make revisions.

Selecting and Testing Out Appropriate Revisions

Once writers have defined their problem, they select and test out those revisions that will best solve the problem. A writer may select a certain revision strategy — adding, deleting, modifying, rewording, etc. — and/or formulate the content involved in using that revision strategy ("I will add more information about the appearance of the house").

Difficulties in selecting revisions. Just as writers' descriptions imply judgments, their judgments imply appropriate revisions. If their information is irrelevant, then they need to delete that information or make it more relevant. However, when students in our study were asked to answer the question on the form, "What are you going to do about your problem?" many had difficulty identifying possible revisions because they hadn't clearly defined their problem or the reasons for their problem.[6]

In these instances, I go back to the judging stage and demonstrate how specifying problems and reasons for problems implies revisions.

Difficulties in testing out optional revisions. Once students select a revision, they often assume that that revision will do the job, failing to consider why or how that revision works according to their goals, strategies, and characteristics of audience. For example, in writing about police corruption, a student notes that he wants to add some more examples of police corruption, but he doesn't know why he's adding the examples. I then show him how to review his revisions in terms of his goals, strategies, or audience characteristics. The student then realizes that the additional examples help bolster his charge — his central point — that the police corruption exists in all areas of society. Having reaffirmed his goal, he can test out whether each additional example supports his contention that "corruption is everywhere."

In showing students how to justify their revisions by considering their goals, strategies, or audience characteristics, I am illustrating that in assessing, it is essential to constantly cycle back to conceptions of the rhetorical context in order to reaffirm, clarify, or modify those conceptions in light of their advancing comprehension of that context as they write.

Diagnosing Students' Response to Modeling: Comprehending and Applying

These, then, are some of the techniques of assessing that I demonstrate in the conference. In most cases, I demonstrate no more than one or two of these techniques in any one conference. Otherwise, I end up dominating the conference rather than having the students practice their own assessing. After I complete my demonstration, I ask the students whether or not they understood the technique I was demonstrating. If a student didn't understand the technique, I repeat the demonstration until I am confident that the student not only understood the technique but also could actually employ that technique.

In subsequent conferences, I often find that my demonstrations have benefitted students in that they are able to use these techniques on their own, either in the conferences or on the guided assessing forms. In an attempt to determine the influence of the demonstrations, I conducted a study of one teacher's use of demonstration with a group of eight college freshman students enrolled in a remedial composition course.[7] I analyzed (1) the transcripts of conferences and the students' assessing forms for evidence of students' use of assessing techniques, and (2) the students' revisions from the beginning to the end of the course. Over time, most of the students demonstrated marked changes, particularly in their ability to describe goals and strategies and to use those descriptions to judge their drafts and make revisions that improved their writing.

If learning to assess drafts is central to learning to revise and improve writing quality, then demonstrating these assessing techniques assumes a central role in composition instruction.

Notes

[1] Richard Beach and Sarah Eaton, "Factors Influencing Self-assessing and Revising of College Freshmen," *New Directions in Composition Research,* ed. Richard Beach and Lillian Bridwell (New York: Guilford, 1984) 149-70.

41

²Beach and Eaton.

³Beach and Eaton.

⁴Donald Rubin, Gene Piché, Michael Michlin, and Fern Johnson, "Social-Cognitive Ability as a Predictor of the Quality of Fourth-Graders' Written Narratives," *New Directions;* Brant Burleson and Katherine Rowan, "Are Social-Cognitive Ability and Narrative Writing Skill Related?" *Written Communication* 2 (Jan. 1985): 25–43.

⁵Beach and Eaton.

⁶Beach and Eaton.

⁷Richard Beach, "The Self-assessing Strategies of Remedial College Students," paper presented at the annual meeting of the American Educational Research Association, New York, 1977.

Beach's Insights as a Resource for Your Teaching

1. Preparing for revision conferences is critical to your success with them. Before you hold your first set of conferences, role-play with a colleague. Use a sample of your own writing and Beach's "Guided Assessing Form" to prepare. Practice the roles both of apprehensive and "silent" student and nondirective reader. Discuss with your colleague the insights you gained from playing each role.

2. Tape-record or videotape a series of conferences with writers. Analyze them in terms of questions that prompt the writer to self-assess and of demonstrations of assessing techniques that show the writer a process but not "how I would rewrite this draft."

Beach's Insights as a Resource for the Writing Classroom

1. Hold mini-conferences (two or three minutes long) during in-class drafting. Ask each student one or two of the describing questions Beach uses. Most students will be able to answer specifically and return to drafting. The student who is uncertain could use some "intervention" and assistance with generating purpose or thinking about audience.

2. Help students design self-assessment questionnaires for each of the major assignments. Many of the discovery and revision checklists in *The Bedford Guide* provide excellent questions for such a questionnaire. Require each student to reflect on his or her draft and to complete the questionnaire. Often that process prompts the writer to additional revision and redrafting before submitting the manuscript. Often it "primes" the conversation you have in a conference. Some students can recognize difficulties in their draft through a self-assessment questionnaire but need to converse with a more practiced reader-writer to talk through options or to find direction for selecting revisions.

3. Workshops can also prompt self-assessment that leads to revision. Help groups generate assessment questions that they ask each other during a workshop. Often, group members can assist the writer by describing what they understood as his or her purpose and how they reacted as readers. This generates "data" that the writer needs to judge the draft.

PART TWO

THE WRITING PROCESS

The issues of beginning to write, generating ideas, sustaining a draft, rewriting, reflecting on audience and purpose, thinking critically, and investigating are all parts of the complex process of decision making prompted when writers approach writing tasks. In this section, you'll find theoretical stances and practical advice about pedagogic strategies.

GETTING STARTED

The literature about invention and about prewriting is extensive, beginning with Aristotle's *Rhetoric* and continuing with the most recent description of a prewriting strategy in one of the professional journals focused on writing and teaching writing. *The Bedford Guide* discusses "getting started" and gives examples and recommendations with the writing assignment for each chapter. Chapter 14, "Strategies for Generating Ideas," offers an abundance of strategies culled from the experiences of practicing writers (the authors included), from the reports of writing teachers, and from articles in writing journals. The readings in this book deal with a wider range of methods that writers use to begin a draft.

IT WAS A DARK AND NASTY NIGHT IT WAS A DARK AND YOU WOULD NOT BELIEVE HOW DARK IT WAS A HARD BEGINNING

Betsy S. Hilbert

Betsy S. Hilbert speaks with the authority gained from twenty-seven years in community college writing classrooms in her "meditation" on the task of getting started with a piece of writing. Her respect for the students she meets and their "continually new" voices resonates in the careful analysis of why many writers have a "hard beginning."

Hilbert makes clear that although beginning writers may seem the most anxious and worried about starting to write, all writers experience such fear. She insists that, whatever strategies might work for experienced writers as they get started, every writer must learn to "trust the sense of the work and . . . must believe that it can be written." Hilbert echoes Sondra Perl's description of the writing resource of "a felt sense." (See "Understanding Composing," the next selection.)

The essay offers some implicit advice to writing teachers. Hilbert's "beginning," with its optimism about possibilities, has a counterpart in her concluding warning that writing teachers grow too confident about what they have "taught" about writing because writers as they begin a new work meet new choices and struggle with new variants of old problems. When she quotes John Gregory Dunne's description of the writer's life, Hilbert implies an analogy to the writing teacher's life. Like students who find new problems to solve and new ways to speak in the very process of writing, we discover new vantages on writing and new ways to speak with writers even as we teach. We all start. We finish. We keep starting over again.

One of the nicest things about college teaching is that periodically everything ends, and then there is a new beginning. One semester finishes with a thud, and another starts in a bright new batch of everything, including my intentions. On opening day, I write my name on the blackboard: Call me Professor. I do my practiced song-and-dance routine (with a few jokes thrown in, to lighten things up) to another group of new same faces, telling them about the rules, the possibilities of the course, and about the things we will do together. September again; there are empty spaces once more in the grade book.

Now I am alone with the first writing samples, opening another composition in the midnight silence of paper-grading that is an English teacher's consistent meditation. This is, approximately, essay number fifty-eight thousand, three hundred and twenty-one that I have graded — twenty-seven years of teaching community college composition, twelve classes a year, thirty students a class, six major papers per student, on average. Oh, I have measured out my life with comma splices. But each new opening paragraph is another beginning. If the work repeats itself endlessly, at least the students' voices are continually new.

The opening sentences of those beginning samples speak, as usual, more eloquently of their authors than about their subjects:

It is to be said that reading for pleasure expands the horizon of a person's way of thinking.

In High school I had attended many, so-called, Honors classes. One of which happened to be English.

I consider English an essential subject in the advancement of human growth.

I am an English professor's nightmare.

Worse nightmares I have had. It is clear, from the first day, that these students are trying to decide how to address both me and their writing. The forms and formalities, elude them. Introductions trouble them. Some sign the top of the page and then announce again in the first sentence "Hello, my name is _____." Some address me directly, as in "Teacher, I've been out of school for fifteen years." Some dispense with any introduction whatever, using their titles as the first lines of their essays. They are all trying to trust the promise of the course, that they will learn not only how to write their beginnings, but how to begin writing. The two activities are separate but interconnected.

"How do we start?" my students ask. I hand them the old saw about rolling a piece of paper into a typewriter and staring at it until drops of blood appear on your forehead. I tell them about hook openings and funnels, about set-the-stage openings, contrasts, and apt quotations. We pass around the only generally workable piece of advice about writing an opening: there is no requirement for writing the first paragraph first. Unfortunately, however, the "don't write the opening first" advice is an overgeneralization too, because for many professional writers having an opening sentence means having a start. John Gregory Dunne reports how an opening sentence can usefully drive the work:

On June 6, 1982, the *New York Times Book Review* asked a number of writers to describe their work in progress. I did not have a work in progress, only a contract for a work in progress, but no matter: if a writer is asked to describe a work in progress, perhaps the work in progress might actually progress. And so for the *Times* I wrote: "This summer I am going to Central America and will be working on a novel called *The Red, White and Blue*. The trip and the novel are not related, but who knows? . . . All I know about *The Red, White and Blue* is that Scott Fitzgerald considered a similar title for *The Great Gatsby*. What will it be about? About 600 pages, I hope."

The result of this fabrication was that my publisher invited me to lunch at The Four Seasons to discuss the work in progress, and the progress I was making on it. The night before the lunch, I sat down at my typewriter in a suite at the Carlyle Hotel that a movie company was picking up the tab for in the misplaced hope that I was paying more attention to the screenplay I was allegedly writing than I was to the novel the producers did not know I allegedly had in progress. In a spasm of fear, I wrote the following sentence: "When the trial began, we left the country." An hour or so later I had reached the point where I could note in my diary the next day, "Lunch w/JE [my publisher] — showed her 1st 3–4 pp RWB." And thus began four years at the factory. (51)

Dunne's final version ran close to his prediction: 710 pages. Professional writers can judge how long a finished piece will be, within a certain range, and within that range they are willing to let a piece take its own shape and distance. But learning to trust one's creation is a problematic procedure. (Even God, from all reports, had difficulties with that one — justifiably so, as it turned out.) Students want to know at the beginning, at the moment of assignment which is really the beginning of a student essay, exactly how many words I require. Are 478 words enough for a 500-word essay? (Exactly what is a 500-word essay, anyway? Textbooks seem to refer to "the 500-word essay" — there is even a composition text by that name — as some kind of special literary genre. Is the 500-word essay anything like the one-minute waltz?) Students are terribly worried about how long the assignment has to be well before they begin writing, and my telling them not to consider length is a lie. The truth is that I am decidedly anticipating more than three sentences per composition, and the students have a right to know approximately what I'm expecting.

Expectations establish the beginnings of literary texts in crucial ways. The opening creates an immediate relationship among reader, writer, and text, setting the parameters of the experience to follow. An opening that has not established tone or mood, vague distant thunder of storms approaching, a sense of style and of scene, has not fulfilled its purpose. (Or, in the case of some modernist prose, fulfilled its purpose only too well in playing with the reader's expectations of what openings should be.) The gun must be brought on stage in Act I, or it can never be fired later.

"Write an opening paragraph that makes me want to read the rest of your essay," I plead with my students. "How?" they whimper.

That worrisome sense of expectations, extraordinarily similar to the sense of being a participant at an extremely formal occasion, harries beginning writers into severe self-consciousness. Writing, after all, is an act of public performance. The writer puts on a mask with the face of a narrator, or the essay-voice, and steps from behind the curtains to face the audience. But even while the *writer*-mask is on, there is still the awful suspicion that the *person's* fly is open. Behind the performer's make-up is the agony that accompanies all self-presentation, experienced or new; no wonder that stage fright and writer's block bear remarkable similarities. Any writer who has ever faced a blank sheet of paper can empathize immediately with the basic writing student in Mina Shaughnessy's *Errors and Expectations,* who writes ten successive opening sentences, carefully crossing out each one and trying again, disintegrating (in Shaughnessy's terminology) slowly from the first fresh, interesting — albeit incorrect — sentence, into a painful paralysis of halting diction and failing spirit (8).

It is hard to remember, in the fullness of a teaching career which practices endless reading and writing, how strange and unnatural both of those activities are, and how much they require a psychic relinquishment of everyday existence. Writers must give themselves to the text; readers, to a world in which they have no control, a world they never made. Both enter the dreamlike state of telling and listening. Practiced readers or writers can trust that they will come back — different, perhaps, but at least back. College students, however, though they well understand stories, sleep, and television (which is a kind of sleep), may still have trouble with the release of emotional or ideological self that written text requires. They have been through so few deaths and rebirths of their own that they often cannot release their holds on selfhood enough to trust they will return, whole and undissolved, in time for supper. Writing, like reading, is a great act of letting go.

So much depends on first impressions. If a student's first impression of his/her own work engenders nothing but a deep mistrust of any ability to go further, the process is inclined to failure. We know that professional writers are often helped by using journals to develop material, but the journal is not successful only because it enables writing in a relaxed manner.

A journal works partly because the writer *owns* the journal — has control over it, and sometimes even a lock to keep out other members of the family. The journal assigned in writing class — a journal that is therefore the teacher's, not the student's — doesn't always work as well as textbooks promise, because its ownership has shifted from student to teacher. One has to be secure on one's own ground, to have the psychological equivalent of Virginia Woolf's room of one's own, to write with any kind of confidence. Moreover, because any act of writing, fiction or nonfiction, as well as any kind of reading, is a venture into unknown territory, a solid opening both increases curiosity and assuages uncertainty.

Experienced writers use preliminary notes as methods of seeking guidance, discovering what they're going to say as they see what they write. Insecure composition students cling to their thesis statements and sentence outlines as itineraries, like AAA Triptiks, from which they cannot deviate. Fear of the unknown is a major reason why composition teachers find the techniques of prewriting so difficult to teach, and why the rigid, five-paragraph, thesis-directed format seems such a treasure to developmental writing students. They seize that solid, inarguable form, that preconceptualized structure, like Dumbo the baby elephant clutching his crow's feather, never conceiving that without the talisman he could truly fly. External structure is always a great comfort in a doubtful situation.

There is, besides the fear of finding out what one really thinks, another major difficulty in beginning writing: the certain knowledge that the words on the page will never be as wonderful as the words in the writer's head. This, of course, is the way of the world; each new beginning betrays possibility. Before a work is begun, it exists in the realm of the imagined, with all its splendor unsullied; it is a perfect, magnificent fantasy. But the moment something takes existence, it becomes part of the messy material world — never quite what it was in its creator's preconceptions. Babies that were never born are angels still; the real ones are a lot more difficult to live with. An essay on paper is never quite as marvelous as when it was first conceived. For that reason, there is a strong tendency never to begin — it is one of the major sources of procrastination — not so much to avoid work but to avoid facing the truth of what happens to our ideas when they take real form. Never committing, never engaging, is the safest position.

Folk wisdom is not much help in the specific situation of helping beginning writers, because there are as many sayings about how a bad beginning makes a good ending as there are about how a good beginning leads to a good ending. Essential folk wisdom actually seems to advise one to wait and see how things turn out, then construct an epigram appropriate to the situation. The only workable direct advice about beginnings seems to be that it is generally best to stop worrying about whether the start will be good or bad, and simply start. Stan Vanderbeek, a wonderful filmmaker of beloved memory, once listened patiently as I subjected him to an hour of my moaning about how the writing wasn't progressing, how editors didn't understand me, how I was blocked, constipated, wrung-out, strung-out, and no longer capable of putting two words together in any meaningful way. At the end of it all, Stan smiled. "Get off your ass," he said.

When does writing begin? Edward Said insists that a novel begins in intention, for "beginning is not only a kind of action; it is also a frame of mind, a kind of work, an attitude, a consciousness" (xv). He reminds us that our attitudes toward acts of creation, toward writing as we understand it, are decidedly culture-bound: "the desire to create an alternative world, to modify or augment the real world through the act of writing (which is one motive underlying the novelistic tradition in the West) is inimical to the Islamic world-view. The Prophet is he who has *completed* a world-view; thus the world *heresy* in Arabic is synonymous with the verb 'to innovate' or 'to begin' " (Said 81).

How does writing begin? In P. D. James's mystery novel *A Taste for Death,* there is an opening moment between two characters, the poet/detective Adam Dalgliesh and an aged grand dame whose son has just had his throat cut:

46

There was a paperback on the round table to the right of her chair. Dalgliesh saw that it was Philip Larkin's *Required Writing*. She put out her hand and laid it on the book, then said:

"Mr. Larkin writes here that it is always true that the idea for a poem and a snatch or line of it come simultaneously. Do you agree, Commander?"

"Yes, Lady Ursula, I think I do. A poem begins with poetry, not with an idea for poetry."

He betrayed no surprise at the question. He knew that shock, grief, trauma took people in different ways, and if this bizarre opening was helping her, he could conceal his impatience. (96)

My students worry over their openings. So-Han firmly laminates a funnel opening onto her three-part thesis sentence, a pattern she learned some years back and clings to as a bit of order among my distressing urgings that she "be creative." Miguel, from Venezuela, begins each essay with his central point, every time; he is studying engineering and doesn't believe in wasting material. Sandra attempts a hook opening, and slips:

On that occasion I lost the battle. I remember it well. It was a summer, warm and lazy. Marge and I were sitting on a step talking.

But Bob succeeds, in a great, wonderful leap:

The more I have thought about college and where to go and what to do, the more I like my dog better.

At the beginning, a writer must trust the sense of the work. He or she must believe that it can be written. He or she must be secure, above all, that no one will laugh or sneer, or at least that when the critical red-pen voices come, they will strike without slicing. The writer must understand, also, that not everything devolves on this one piece now under construction: the conclusion *will* arrive; there will be other openings yet to come. When those conditions are met, it is possible — most of the time — to pick up a pencil.

But a teacher of writing must never get too confident. A few years back, my friend Susan Fawcett was teaching a basic writing class about transitions, and the students, many of whom were not native speakers of Edited American English, were listening intently, absorbing the differences between "therefore" and "however." The class took extensive notes. Susan was pleased with their diligence. A few days later, when the next batch of assignments arrived, she discovered that one student had very carefully begun the first sentence of his composition with a perfect opening phrase: "On the other hand . . ."

"But that is the writer's life," says Dunne. "You write. You finish. You start over again" (57).

Works Cited

Dunne, John Gregory. "On Writing a Novel." *The Best American Essays 1987*. Ed. Gay Talese. New York: Ticknor, 1987. 52–57.
James, P. D. *A Taste for Death*. New York: Knopf, 1986.
Said, Edward W. *Beginnings: Intention and Method*. New York: Columbia UP, 1985.
Shaughnessy, Mina P. *Errors and Expectations*. New York: Oxford UP, 1977.

Hilbert's Insights as a Resource for Your Teaching

1. This essay clearly synthesizes personal writing experience, recreational reading, and professional reading. Think about your most recent experience with "writer's block" and write a description of how it felt and how you finally got started. Collect such personal narratives from "novices" — graduate students in new writing situations, instructors new to

an institution or to a classroom, professionals with their first "real" writing challenge. Add examples from your reading. Use the liveliest anecdotes in class to assure students that all writers find themselves in situations where they feel like beginners.

2. Ask for journal entries about getting started and about fears and fantasies a writer has about beginning a work. Often, venting feelings about getting started frees a writer to just plain start.

3. Play the "dark and stormy night" game. Have small groups of two or three students draw up a list of clichéd openings. Then ask each group to collaborate and draft a paragraph that uses a cliché. Have groups share their beginning paragraphs and vote on "most original" and "most effective" use of overused openings.

Hilbert's Insights as a Resource for the Writing Classroom

1. Each chapter of the textbook has advice for getting started. When you begin the course, encourage students to first write for ten minutes about "hard" and "easy" beginnings and then to share some experience with or useful strategy for getting started. Fears lessen as individual writers discover that they aren't alone in having difficulty starting a piece of writing.

2. Ask for one-minute writings on each day given to working with an assignment. Each writing should answer the question "What today do you think will be your opening sentence?" Return the series of one-minute writings after the peer editing workshop and before the writer begins a final revision. Many writers will appreciate the "structure" of having to write something and also will appreciate the emphasis that no writer has to be wed to an opening statement.

3. For a self-assessment exercise to accompany a submitted draft, ask the writer to talk about how he or she came to the final version of the opening and whether and why the writer is satisfied with the opening.

UNDERSTANDING COMPOSING

Sondra Perl

Sondra Perl's assumption that writing is a recursive process is shared by many researchers and teachers. It informs every chapter of The Bedford Guide for College Writers. *And look at the description of recursiveness in "To the Student." Perl uses her own observations of the composing processes of a variety of writers to analyze the significance of those processes. She defines a "felt sense" that may be a very rich and necessary resource for the writer even as it may be one that the writer (and his or her audience) has difficulty describing and consciously triggering.*

Perl believes that "skilled writers" rely on a felt sense even when they don't know it. She implies that "unskilled writers" might come to use this felt sense and to engage in "retrospective structuring" more productively. She theorizes that writers who have internalized a model of writing as a recursive process rather than a linear process may have an easier time attending to their inner reflections.

I anticipate that you will find "new thoughts" about composing as you read Perl's conjectures about "felt sense." You'll be interested in the link of "felt sense" with "projective structuring," Perl's name for the process in which writers make what they intend to say intelligible to others.

Any psychological process, whether the development of thought or voluntary behavior, is a process undergoing changes right before one's eyes. . . . Under certain conditions it becomes possible to trace this development.[1]

— L. S. Vygotsky

It's hard to begin this case study of myself as a writer because even as I'm searching for a beginning, a pattern of organization, I'm watching myself, trying to understand my behavior. As I sit here in silence, I can see lots of things happening that never made it onto my tapes. My mind leaps from the task at hand to what I need at the vegetable stand for tonight's soup to the threatening rain outside to ideas voiced in my writing group this morning, but in between "distractions" I hear myself trying out words I might use. It's as if the extraneous thoughts are a counterpoint to the more steady attention I'm giving to composing. This is all to point out that the process is more complex than I'm aware of, but I think my tapes reveal certain basic patterns that I tend to follow.

— Anne, New York City teacher

Anne is a teacher of writing. In 1979, she was among a group of twenty teachers who were taking a course in research and basic writing at New York University.[2] One of the assignments in the course was for the teachers to tape their thoughts while composing aloud on the topic "My Most Anxious Moment as a Writer." Everyone in the group was given the topic in the morning during class and told to compose later on that day in a place where they would be comfortable and relatively free from distractions. The result was a tape of composing aloud and a written product that formed the basis for class discussion over the next few days.

One of the purposes of this assignment was to provide teachers with an opportunity to see their own composing processes at work. From the start of the course, we recognized that we were controlling the situation by assigning a topic and that we might be altering the process by asking writers to compose aloud. Nonetheless we viewed the task as a way of capturing some of the flow of composing and, as Anne later observed in her analysis of her tape, she was able to detect certain basic patterns. This observation, made not only by Anne, then leads me to ask "What basic patterns seem to occur during composing?" and "What does this type of research have to tell us about the nature of the composing process?"

Perhaps the most challenging part of the answer is the recognition of recursiveness in writing. In recent years, many researchers including myself have questioned the traditional notion that writing is a linear process with a strict plan-write-revise sequence.[3] In its stead, we have advocated the idea that writing is a recursive process, that throughout the process of writing, writers return to substrands of the overall process, or subroutines (short successions of steps that yield results on which the writer draws in taking the next set of steps); writers use these to keep the process moving forward. In other words, recursiveness in writing implies that there is a forward-moving action that exists by virtue of a backward-moving action. The questions that then need to be answered are "To what do writers move back?" "What exactly is being repeated?" "What recurs?"

To answer these questions, it is important to look at what writers do while writing and what an analysis of their processes reveals. The descriptions that follow are based on my own observations of the composing processes of many types of writers including college students, graduate students, and English teachers like Anne.

Writing does appear to be recursive, yet the parts that recur seem to vary from writer to writer and from topic to topic. Furthermore, some recursive elements are easy to spot while others are not.

1. The most visible recurring feature or backward movement involves rereading little bits of discourse. Few writers I have seen write for long periods of time without returning briefly to what is already down on the page.

49

For some, like Anne, rereading occurs after every few phrases; for others, it occurs after every sentence; more frequently, it occurs after a "chunk" of information has been written. Thus, the unit that is reread is not necessarily a syntactic one, but rather a semantic one as defined by the writer.

2. The second recurring feature is some key word or item called up by the topic. Writers consistently return to their notion of the topic throughout the process of writing. Particularly when they are stuck, writers seem to use the topic or a key word in it as a way to get going again. Thus many times it is possible to see writers "going back," rereading the topic they were given, changing it to suit what they have been writing or changing what they have written to suit their notion of the topic.

3. There is also a third backward movement in writing, one that is not so easy to document. It is not easy because the move, itself, cannot immediately be identified with words. In fact, the move is not to any words on the page nor to the topic but to feelings or nonverbalized perceptions that *surround* the words, or to what the words already present *evoke* in the writer. The move draws on sense experience, and it can be observed if one pays close attention to what happens when writers pause and seem to listen or otherwise react to what is inside of them. The move occurs inside the writer, to what is physically felt. The term used to describe this focus of writers' attention is *felt sense*. The term "felt sense" has been coined and described by Eugene Gendlin, a philosopher at the University of Chicago. In his words, felt sense is

> the soft underbelly of thought . . . a kind of bodily awareness that . . . can be used as a tool . . . a bodily awareness that . . . encompasses everything you feel and know about a given subject at a given time. . . . It is felt in the body, yet it has meanings. It is body *and* mind before they are split apart.[4]

This felt sense is always there, within us. It is unifying, and yet, when we bring words to it, it can break apart, shift, unravel, and become something else. Gendlin has spent many years showing people how to work with their felt sense. Here I am making connections between what he has done and what I have seen happen as people write.

When writers are given a topic, the topic itself evokes a felt sense in them. This topic calls forth images, words, ideas, and vague fuzzy feelings that are anchored in the writer's body. What is elicited, then, is not solely the product of a mind but of a mind alive in a living, sensing body.

When writers pause, when they go back and repeat key words, what they seem to be doing is waiting, paying attention to what is still vague and unclear. They are looking to their felt experience, and waiting for an image, a word, or a phrase to emerge that captures the sense they embody.

Usually, when they make the decision to write, it is after they have a dawning awareness that something has clicked, that they have enough of a sense that if they begin with a few words heading in a certain direction, words will continue to come which will allow them to flesh out the sense they have.

The process of using what is sensed directly about a topic is a natural one. Many writers do it without any conscious awareness that that is what they are doing. For example, Anne repeats the words "anxious moments," using these key words as a way of allowing her sense of the topic to deepen. She asks herself, "Why are exams so anxiety provoking?" and waits until she has enough of a sense within her that she can go in a certain direction. She does not yet have the words, only the sense that she is able to begin. Once she writes, she stops to see what is there. She maintains a highly recursive composing style throughout and she seems unable to go forward without first going back to see and to listen to what she has already created. In her own words, she says:

My disjointed style of composing is very striking to me. I almost never move from the writing of one sentence directly to the next. After each sentence I pause to read what I've written, assess, sometimes edit and think about what will come next. I often have to read the several preceding sentences a few times as if to gain momentum to carry me to the next sentence. I seem to depend a lot on the sound of my words and . . . while I'm hanging in the middle of this uncompleted thought, I may also start editing a previous sentence or get an inspiration for something which I want to include later in the paper.

What tells Anne that she is ready to write? What is the feeling of "momentum" like for her? What is she hearing as she listens to the "sound" of her words? When she experiences "inspiration," how does she recognize it?

In the approach I am presenting, the ability to recognize what one needs to do or where one needs to go is informed by calling on felt sense. This is the internal criterion writers seem to use to guide them when they are planning, drafting, and revising.

The recursive move, then, that is hardest to document but is probably the most important to be aware of is the move to felt sense, to what is not yet *in words* but out of which images, words, and concepts emerge.

The continuing presence of this felt sense, waiting for us to discover it and see where it leads, raises a number of questions.

Is "felt sense" another term for what professional writers call their "inner voice" or their feeling of "inspiration"?

Do skilled writers call on their capacity to sense more readily than unskilled writers?

Rather than merely reducing the complex act of writing to a neat formulation, can the term "felt sense" point us to an area of our experience from which we can evolve even richer and more accurate descriptions of composing?

Can learning how to work with felt sense teach us about creativity and release us from stultifyingly repetitive patterns?

My observations lead me to answer "yes" to all four questions. There seems to be a basic step in the process of composing that skilled writers rely on even when they are unaware of it and that less skilled writers can be taught. This process seems to rely on very careful attention to one's inner reflections and is often accompanied with bodily sensations.

When it's working, this process allows us to say or write what we've never said before, to create something new and fresh, and occasionally it provides us with the experience of "newness" or "freshness," even when "old words" or images are used.

The basic process begins with paying attention. If we are given a topic, it begins with taking the topic in and attending to what it evokes in us. There is less "figuring out" an answer and more "waiting" to see what forms. Even without a predetermined topic, the process remains the same. We can ask ourselves, "What's on my mind?" or "Of all the things I know about, what would I most like to write about now?" and wait to see what comes. What we pay attention to is the part of our bodies where we experience ourselves directly. For many people, it's the area of their stomachs; for others, there is a more generalized response and they maintain a hovering attention to what they experience throughout their bodies.

Once a felt sense forms, we match words to it. As we begin to describe it, we get to see what is there for us. We get to see what we think, what we know. If we are writing about something that truly interests us, the felt sense deepens. We know that we are writing out of a "centered" place.

If the process is working, we begin to move along, sometimes quickly. Other times, we need to return to the beginning, to reread, to see if we captured what we meant to say.

Sometimes after rereading we move on again, picking up speed. Other times by rereading we realize we've gone off the track, that what we've written doesn't quite "say it," and we need to reassess. Sometimes the words are wrong and we need to change them. Other times we need to go back to the topic, to call up the sense it initially evoked to see where and how our words led us astray. Sometimes in rereading we discover that the topic is "wrong," that the direction we discovered in writing is where we really want to go. It is important here to clarify that the terms "right" and "wrong" are not necessarily meant to refer to grammatical structures or to correctness.

What is "right" or "wrong" corresponds to our sense of our intention. We intend to write something, words come, and now we assess if those words adequately capture our intended meaning. Thus, the first question we ask ourselves is "Are these words right for me?" "Do they capture what I'm trying to say?" "If not, what's missing?"

Once we ask "what's missing?" we need once again to wait, to let a felt sense of what is missing form, and then to write out of that sense.

I have labeled this process of attending, of calling up a felt sense, and of writing out of that place, the process of *retrospective structuring*. It is retrospective in that it begins with what is already there, inchoately, and brings whatever is there forward by using language in structured form.

It seems as though a felt sense has within it many possible structures or forms. As we shape what we intend to say, we are further structuring our sense while correspondingly shaping our piece of writing.

It is also important to note that what is there implicitly, without words, is not equivalent to what finally emerges. In the process of writing, we begin with what is inchoate and end with something that is tangible. In order to do so, we both discover and construct what we mean. Yet the term "discovery" ought not lead us to think that meaning exists fully formed inside of us and that all we need do is dig deep enough to release it. In writing, meaning cannot be discovered the way we discover an object on an archeological dig. In writing, meaning is crafted and constructed. It involves us in a process of coming-into-being. Once we have worked at shaping, through language, what is there inchoately, we can look at what we have written to see if it adequately captures what we intended. Often at this moment discovery occurs. We see something new in our writing that comes upon us as a surprise. We see in our words a further structuring of the sense we began with and we recognize that in those words we have discovered something new about ourselves and our topic. Thus when we are successful at this process, we end up with a product that teaches us something, that clarifies what we know (or what we knew at one point only implicitly), and that lifts out or explicates or enlarges our experience. In this way, writing leads to discovery.

All the writers I have observed, skilled and unskilled alike, use the process of retrospective structuring while writing. Yet the degree to which they do so varies and seems, in fact, to depend upon the model of the writing process that they have internalized. Those who realize that writing can be a recursive process have an easier time with waiting, looking, and discovering. Those who subscribe to the linear model find themselves easily frustrated when what they write does not immediately correspond to what they planned or when what they produce leaves them with little sense of accomplishment. Since they have relied on a formulaic approach, they often produce writing that is formulaic as well, thereby cutting themselves off from the possibility of discovering something new.

Such a result seems linked to another feature of the composing process, to what I call *projective structuring,* or the ability to craft what one intends to say so that it is intelligible to others.

A number of concerns arise in regard to projective structuring; I will mention only a few that have been raised for me as I have watched different writers at work.

1. Although projective structuring is only one important part of the composing process, many writers act as if it is the whole process. These writers focus on what they think others want them to write rather than looking to see what it is they want to write. As result, they often ignore their felt sense and they do not establish a living connection between themselves and their topic.

2. Many writers reduce projective structuring to a series of rules or criteria for evaluating finished discourse. These writers ask, "Is what I'm writing correct?" and "Does it conform to the rules I've been taught?" While these concerns are important, they often overshadow all others and lock the writer in the position of writing solely or primarily for the approval of readers.

Projective structuring, as I see it, involves much more than imagining a strict audience and maintaining a strict focus on correctness. It is true that to handle this part of the process well, writers need to know certain grammatical rules and evaluative criteria, but they also need to know how to call up a sense of their reader's needs and expectations.

For projective structuring to function fully, writers need to draw on their capacity to move away from their own words, to decenter from the page, and to project themselves into the role of the reader. In other words, projective structuring asks writers to attempt to become readers and to imagine what someone other than themselves will need before the writer's particular piece of writing can become intelligible and compelling. To do so, writers must have the experience of being readers. They cannot call up a felt sense of a reader unless they themselves have experienced what it means to be lost in a piece of writing or to be excited by it. When writers do not have such experiences, it is easy for them to accept that readers merely require correctness.

In closing, I would like to suggest that retrospective and projective structuring are two parts of the same basic process. Together they form the alternating mental postures writers assume as they move through the act of composing. The former relies on the ability to go inside, to attend to what is there, from that attending to place words upon a page, and then to assess if those words adequately capture one's meaning. The latter relies on the ability to assess how the words on that page will affect someone other than the writer, the reader. We rarely do one without the other entering in; in fact, again in these postures we can see the shuttling back-and-forth movements of the composing process, the move from sense to words and from words to sense, from inner experience to outer judgment and from judgment back to experience. As we move through this cycle, we are continually composing and recomposing our meanings and what we mean. And in doing so, we display some of the basic recursive patterns that writers who observe themselves closely seem to see in their own work. After observing the process for a long time we may, like Anne, conclude that at any given moment the process is more complex than anything we are aware of; yet such insights, I believe, are important. They show us the fallacy of reducing the composing process to a simple linear scheme and they leave us with the potential for creating even more powerful ways of understanding composing.

Notes

[1] L. S. Vygotsky, *Mind in Society,* trans. M. Cole, V. John-Steiner, S. Scribner, and E. Souberman (Cambridge: Harvard UP, 1978)61.

[2] This course was team-taught by myself and Gordon Pradl, Associate Professor of English Education at New York University.

[3] See Janet Emig, *The Composing Processes of Twelfth-Graders,* NCTE Research Report No. 13 (Urbana: National Council of Teachers of English, 1971); Linda Flower and J. R. Hayes, "The Cognition of Discovery," *CCC* 31 (Feb. 1980): 21–32; Nancy Sommers, "The Need for Theory in Composition Research," *CCC* 30 (Feb. 1979): 46–49.

[4] Eugene Gendlin, *Focusing* (New York: Everest, 1978) 35, 165.

Perl's Insights as a Resource for Your Teaching

1. Perl models a "holistic perspective" on the composing process and pays careful attention to the composing processes of the students she teaches. As you read this article and reflect on it, jot down your own memories of this experience of a "felt sense" as well as statements your students have made about such experiences. Save those notes for use in your discussions of getting started with a writing task.

2. Many of the "generating" strategies described in Chapter 14 — those used by individual writers as well as the more formally described heuristics like freewriting, brainstorming, and the reporter's questions — help students start paying attention to inner reflections and to accompanying physical sensations. After they have practiced with several formal heuristics, ask your students to tell you, either in journal entries or in fifteen-minute writing sessions, about what they can notice about their "getting started" and their "beginning again."

3. Journal entries that ask writers simply to list "what I'm thinking now about this assignment" or "things I feel I need to say sometime this year" often provoke students to "listen in" on their inner reflections. The writing assignment for Chapter 5, "Writing from Imagination," gives students license to work from "retrospective structuring"; some students will surprise themselves with their composing for this assignment.

4. Be sure to ask students periodically, particularly at the end of the term, to tell you about times they surprised themselves by composing from "inspiration." Let students know, because you discuss it, that composing often has this basic process of calling on "felt sense." Be careful to respect the comments writers make in conferences about "It isn't right yet" and not to appropriate their texts with your judgment about their drafts.

Perl's Insights as a Resource for the Writing Classroom

1. Perl insists, as does Linda Flower in "Writer-Based Prose: A Cognitive Basis for Problems in Writing" (p. 64), that to craft a writing to be accessible and intelligible to others, writers have to project themselves as readers of the work. They must anticipate the needs of readers even before and while the writing is in process. This sort of "decentering" is difficult for many students. Perl recommends reading as a major resource for such projective structuring. To assist students to call up a felt sense of their readers, ask them to discuss, in journals or in small groups, experiences they have had of being excited by something they read.

Organize a class discussion of a "difficult" reading in *The Bedford Guide* (see "Guide to the Readings" on page 259 of *Teaching with* The Bedford Guide for College Writers: *Practical Suggestions*). Ask students to discuss any experiences of feeling lost or overwhelmed or puzzled by the reading or parts of it. Ask them to use sensory description, if appropriate to their experience.

This discussion assists students to improve as critical readers and to think about readers' needs that they may have anticipated in the essays they are currently drafting.

2. Ask students to write for five minutes listing moments when they felt exhilarated by "inspiration" while reading, writing, or participating in class discussion. Then ask each student to choose one event and to describe it to the class, ending the description with some explanation of "effect." If students say they can't recall such events, tell them to listen carefully to other class members; someone will describe an event that will jar their memories. This exercise could prompt responses to the writing assignment in Chapter 1 that might surprise the students who had never considered their creative lives or learning experiences as topics for discussion, writing, and reading.

REWRITING

We know that the strongest writing comes from the process of multiple drafting and serious rethinking, reordering, and rewriting. Many students have difficulty looking critically at their writing and beginning again to generate ideas, to shape a draft, and to edit. Learning to revise and to rewrite a draft may be the most dramatic experience some of your students have this semester.

REVISION STRATEGIES OF STUDENT WRITERS AND EXPERIENCED ADULT WRITERS

Nancy Sommers

In this landmark study of the revision strategies used by students and by "adult" writers, Sommers concludes that student writers do not work from a holistic perspective on writing nor do they perceive revision as a recursive process. Her categories of "student" and "experienced adult" writers can be borrowed and applied to members of a first-year composition course. Many class members already understand revising as "discovery — a repeated process of beginning over again, starting out new." They are ready to work with the rewriting strategies, the discovery checklists, and the peer editing checklists of The Bedford Guide for College Writers. *Some writers need to acquire this "new" perspective on revision.*

Sommers cites or implies several reasons that students see revision only as a linear process attending to surface features of a manuscript: previous writing experiences, infrequent practice, traditional dicta about the nature of revising, and cognitive readiness. She asserts that writing teachers can assist student writers to mature and to acquire a perspective on writing as discovery and development. She indicates that writing teachers can assist student writers to become comfortable with the same insight she gleaned from her own experience and from her research with adult, experienced writers: "Good writing disturbs; it creates dissonance."

(After you read this article, you may want to reread "Responding to Student Writing" by Nancy Sommers on page 27 in this book so that you can reflect on the interconnections of what we say to writers about their writing and how they use our comments when they revise.)

Although various aspects of the writing process have been studied extensively of late, research on revision has been notably absent. The reason for this, I suspect, is that current models of the writing process have directed attention away from revision. With few exceptions, these models are linear; they separate the writing process into discrete stages. Two representative models are Gordon Rohman's suggestion that the composing process moves from prewriting to writing to rewriting and James Britton's model of the writing process as a series of stages described in metaphors of linear growth, conception — incubation — production.[1] What is striking about these theories of writing is that they model themselves on speech: Rohman defines the writer in a way that cannot distinguish him from a speaker ("A writer is a man who . . . puts [his] experience into words in his own mind" [15]); and Britton backs his theory of writing on what he calls (following Jakobson) the "expressiveness" of speech.[2] Moreover, Britton's study itself follows the "linear model" of the relation of thought and language in speech proposed by Vygotsky, a relationship embodied in the linear movement "from the motive which engenders a thought to the shaping of the thought, *first* in inner speech, *then* in meanings of words, and *finally* in words" (qtd. in Britton 40). What this movement fails to take into account in its linear structure — "first . . . then . . . finally" — is the recursive shaping of thought by language; what it fails to take into account is *revision*. In these linear conceptions of the writing process revision is understood as a separate stage at the end of the process — a stage that comes after the completion of a first or second draft and one that is temporally distinct from the prewriting and writing stages of the process.[3]

The linear model bases itself on speech in two specific ways. First of all, it is based on traditional rhetorical models, models that were created to serve the spoken art of oratory. In whatever ways the parts of classical rhetoric are described, they offer "stages" of composition that are repeated in contemporary models of the writing process. Edward Corbett, for instance, describes the "five parts of a discourse" — *inventio, dispositio, elocutio, memoria, pronuntiatio* — and, disregarding the last two parts since "after rhetoric came to be concerned mainly with written discourse, there was no further need to deal with them,"[4] he produces a model very close to Britton's conception [*inventio*], incubation [*dispositio*], production [*elocutio*]. Other rhetorics also follow this procedure, and they do so not simply because of historical accident. Rather, the process represented in the linear model is based on the irreversibility of speech. Speech, Roland Barthes says, "is irreversible":

> A word cannot be retracted, except precisely by saying that one retracts it. To cross out here is to add: if I want to erase what I have just said, I cannot do it without showing the eraser itself (I must say: "*or rather . . .*" "*I expressed myself badly . . .*"); paradoxically, it is ephemeral speech which is indelible, not monumental writing. All that one can do in the case of a spoken utterance is to tack on another utterance.[5]

What is impossible in speech is *revision:* like the example Barthes gives, revision in speech is an afterthought. In the same way, each stage of the linear model must be exclusive (distinct from the other stages) or else it becomes trivial and counterproductive to refer to these junctures as "stages."

By staging revision after enunciation, the linear models reduce revision in writing, as in speech, to no more than an afterthought. In this way such models make the study of revision impossible. Revision, in Rohman's model, is simply the repetition of writing; or to pursue Britton's organic metaphor, revision is simply the further growth of what is already there, the "preconceived" product. The absence of research on revision, then, is a function of a theory of writing which makes revision both superfluous and redundant, a theory which does not distinguish between writing and speech.

What the linear models do produce is a parody of writing. Isolating revision and then disregarding it plays havoc with the experiences composition teachers have of the actual writing and rewriting of experienced writers. Why should the linear model be preferred? Why should revision be forgotten, superfluous? Why do teachers offer the linear model and students accept it? One reason, Barthes suggests, is that "there is a fundamental tie between teaching and speech," while "writing begins at the point where speech becomes *impossible*."[6] The spoken word cannot be revised. The possibility of revision distinguishes the written text from speech. In fact, according to Barthes, this is the essential difference between writing and speaking. When we must revise, when the very idea is subject to recursive shaping by language, then speech becomes inadequate. This is a matter to which I will return, but first we should examine, theoretically, a detailed exploration of what student writers as distinguished from experienced adult writers *do* when they write and rewrite their work. Dissatisfied with both the linear model of writing and the lack of attention to the process of revision, I conducted a series of studies over the past three years which examined the revision processes of student writers and experienced writers to see what role revision played in their writing processes. In the course of my work the revision process was redefined as *a sequence of changes in a composition — changes which are initiated by cues and occur continually throughout the writing of a work.*

Methodology

I used a case study approach. The student writers were twenty freshmen at Boston University and the University of Oklahoma with SAT verbal scores ranging from 450–600 in their first semester of composition. The twenty experienced adult writers from Boston and Oklahoma City included journalists, editors, and academics. To refer to the two groups, I use the terms *student writers* and *experienced writers* because the principal difference between these two groups is the amount of experience they have had in writing.

Each writer wrote three essays, expressive, explanatory, and persuasive, and rewrote each essay twice, producing nine written products in draft and final form. Each writer was interviewed three times after the final revision of each essay. And each writer suggested revisions for a composition written by an anonymous author. Thus extensive written and spoken documents were obtained from each writer.

The essays were analyzed by counting and categorizing the changes made. Four revision operations were identified: deletion, substitution, addition, and reordering. And four levels of changes were identified: word, phrase, sentence, theme (the extended statement of one idea). A coding system was developed for identifying the frequency of revision by level and operation. In addition, transcripts of the interviews in which the writers interpreted their revisions were used to develop what was called a *scale of concerns* for each writer. This scale enabled me to codify what were the writer's primary concerns, secondary concerns, tertiary concerns, and whether the writers used the same scale of concerns when revising the second or third drafts as they used in revising the first draft.

Revision Strategies of Student Writers

Most of the students I studied did not use the terms *revision* or *rewriting*. In fact, they did not seem comfortable using the word *revision* and explained that revision was not a word they used, but the word their teachers used. Instead, most of the students had developed various functional terms to describe the type of changes they made. The following are samples of these definitions:

Scratch Out and Do Over Again: "I say scratch out and do over, and that means what it says. Scratching out and cutting out. I read what I have written and I cross out a word and put another word in; a more decent word or a better word. Then if there is somewhere to use a sentence that I have crossed out, I will put it there."

Reviewing: "Reviewing means just using better words and eliminating words that are not needed. I go over and change words around."

Reviewing: "I just review every word and make sure that everything is worded right. I see if I am rambling; I see if I can put a better word in or leave one out. Usually when I read what I have written, I say to myself, 'that word is so bland or so trite,' and then I go and get my thesaurus."

Redoing: "Redoing means cleaning up the paper and crossing out. It is looking at something and saying, no that has to go, or no, that is not right."

Marking Out: "I don't use the word rewriting because I only write one draft and the changes that I make are made on top of the draft. The changes that I make are usually just marking out words and putting different ones in."

Slashing and Throwing Out: "I throw things out and say they are not good. I like to write like Fitzgerald did by inspiration, and if I feel inspired then I don't need to slash and throw much out."

The predominant concern in these definitions is vocabulary. The students understand the revision process as a rewording activity. They do so because they perceive words as the unit of written discourse. That is, they concentrate on particular words apart from their role in the text. Thus one student quoted above thinks in terms of dictionaries, and, following the eighteenth century theory of words parodied in *Gulliver's Travels,* he imagines a load of things carried about to be exchanged. Lexical changes are the major revision activities of the students because economy is their goal. They are governed, like the linear model itself, by the Law of Occam's razor that prohibits logically needless repetition: redundancy and superfluity. Nothing governs speech more than such superfluities; speech constantly repeats itself precisely because spoken words, as Barthes writes, are expendable in the cause of communication. The aim of revision according to the students' own description is therefore to clean up speech; the redundancy of speech is unnecessary in writing, their logic suggests, because writing, unlike speech, can be reread. Thus one student said, "Redoing means cleaning up the paper and crossing out." The remarkable contradiction of cleaning by marking might, indeed, stand for student revision as I have encountered it.

The students place a symbolic importance on their selection and rejection of words as the determiners of success or failure for their compositions. When revising, they primarily ask themselves: can I find a better word or phrase? A more impressive, not so clichéd, or less humdrum word? Am I repeating the same word or phrase too often? They approach the revision process with what could be labeled as a "thesaurus philosophy of writing"; the students consider the thesaurus a harvest of lexical substitutions and believe that most problems in their essays can be solved by rewording. What is revealed in the students' use of the thesaurus is a governing attitude toward their writing: that the meaning to be communicated is already there, already finished, already produced, ready to be communicated, and all that is necessary is a better word "rightly worded." One student defined revision as "redoing"; "redoing" meant "just using better words and eliminating words that are not needed." For the students, writing is translating: the thought to the page, the language of speech to the more formal language of prose, the word to its synonym. Whatever is translated, an original text already exists for students, one which need not be discovered or acted upon, but simply communicated.[7]

The students list repetition as one of the elements they most worry about. This cue signals to them that they need to eliminate the repetition either by substituting or deleting words or phrases. Repetition occurs, in large part, because student writing imitates — transcribes — speech: attention to repetitious words is a manner of cleaning speech. Without a sense of the developmental possibilities of revision (and writing in general) students seek, on the authority of many textbooks, simply to clean up their language and prepare to type. What is curious, however, is that students are aware of lexical repetition, but not conceptual repetition. They only notice the repetition if they can "hear" it; they do not diagnose lexical repetition as symptomatic of problems on a deeper level. By rewording their sentences to avoid the lexical repetition, the students solve the immediate problem, but blind themselves to problems on a textual level; although they are using different words, they are sometimes merely restating the same idea with different words. Such blindness, as I discovered with student writers, is the inability to "see" revision as a process: the inability to "re-view" their work again, as it were, with different eyes, and to start over.

The revision strategies described above are consistent with the students' understanding of the revision process as requiring lexical changes but not semantic changes. For the students, the extent to which they revise is a function of their level of inspiration. In fact, they use the word *inspiration* to describe the ease or difficulty with which their essay is written, and the extent to which the essay needs to be revised. If students feel inspired, if the writing comes easily, and if they don't get stuck on individual words or phrases, then they say that they cannot see any reason to revise. Because students do not see revision as an activity in which they modify and develop perspectives and ideas, they feel that if they know what they want to say, then there is little reason for making revisions.

The only modification of ideas in the students' essays occurred when they tried out two or three introductory paragraphs. This results, in part, because the students have been taught in another version of the linear model of composing to use a thesis statement as a controlling device in their introductory paragraphs. Since they write their introductions and their thesis statements even before they have really discovered what they want to say, their early close attention to the thesis statement, and more generally the linear model, function to restrict and circumscribe not only the development of their ideas, but also their ability to change the direction of these ideas.

Too often as composition teachers we conclude that students do not willingly revise. The evidence from my research suggests that it is not that students are unwilling to revise, but rather than they do what they have been taught to do in a consistently narrow and predictable way. On every occasion when I asked students why they hadn't made any more changes, they essentially replied, "I knew something larger was wrong, but I didn't think it would help to move words around." The students have strategies for handling words and phrases and their strategies helped them on a word or sentence level. What they lack, however, is a set of strategies to help them identify the "something larger" that they sensed was wrong and work from there. The students do not have strategies for handling the whole essay. They lack procedures or heuristics to help them reorder lines of reasoning or ask questions about their purposes and readers. The students view their compositions in a linear way as a series of parts. Even such potentially useful concepts as "unity" or "form" are reduced to the rule that a composition, if it is to have form, must have an introduction, a body, and a conclusion, or the sum total of the necessary parts.

The students decide to stop revising when they decide that they have not violated any of the rules for revising. These rules, such as "Never begin a sentence with a conjunction" or "Never end a sentence with a preposition," are lexically cued and rigidly applied. In general, students will subordinate the demands of the specific problems of their text to the demands of the rules. Changes are made in compliance with abstract rules about the product, rules that quite often do not apply to the specific problems in the text. These revision strategies are teacher-based, directed towards a teacher-reader who expects compliance with rules — with pre-existing "conceptions" — and who will only examine parts of the composition (writing comments about those parts in the margins of their essays) and will cite any violations of rules in those parts. At best the students see their writing altogether passively through the eyes of former teachers or their surrogates, the textbooks, and are bound to the rules which they have been taught.

Revision Strategies of Experienced Writers

One aim of my research has been to contrast how student writers define revision with how a group of experienced writers define their revision processes. Here is a sampling of the definitions from the experienced writers:

Rewriting: "It is a matter of looking at the kernel of what I have written, the content, and then thinking about it, responding to it, making decisions, and actually restructuring it."

Rewriting: "I rewrite as I write. It is hard to tell what is a first draft because it is not determined by time. In one draft, I might cross out three pages, write two, cross out a fourth, rewrite it, and call it a draft. I am constantly writing and rewriting. I can only conceptualize so much in my first draft — only so much information can be held in my head at one time; my rewriting efforts are a reflection of how much information I can encompass at one time. There are levels and agenda which I have to attend to in each draft."

Rewriting: "Rewriting means on one level, finding the argument, and on another level, language changes to make the argument more effective. Most of the time I feel as if I can go on rewriting forever. There is always one part of a piece that I could keep working on. It is always difficult to know at what point to abandon a piece of writing. I like this idea that a piece of writing is never finished, just abandoned."

59

Rewriting: "My first draft is usually very scattered. In rewriting, I find the line of argument. After the argument is resolved, I am much more interested in word choice and phrasing."

Revising: "My cardinal rule in revising is never to fall in love with what I have written in a first or second draft. An idea, sentence, or even a phrase that looks catchy, I don't trust. Part of this idea is to wait a while. I am much more in love with something after I have written it than I am a day or two later. It is much easier to change anything with time."

Revising: "It means taking apart what I have written and putting it back together again. I ask major theoretical questions of my ideas, respond to those questions, and think of proportion and structure, and try to find a controlling metaphor. I find out which ideas can be developed and which should be dropped. I am constantly chiseling and changing as I revise."

The experienced writers describe their primary objective when revising as finding the form or shape of their argument. Although the metaphors vary, the experienced writers often use structural expressions such as "finding a framework," "a pattern," or "a design" for their argument. When questioned about this emphasis, the experienced writers responded that since their first drafts are usually scattered attempts to define their territory, their objective in the second draft is to begin observing general patterns of development and deciding what should be included and what excluded. One writer explained, "I have learned from experience that I need to keep writing a first draft until I figure out what I want to say. Then in a second draft, I begin to see the structure of an argument and how all the various sub-arguments which are buried beneath the surface of all those sentences are related." What is described here is a process in which the writer is both agent and vehicle. "Writing," says Barthes, unlike speech, "develops like a seed, not a line,"[8] and like a seed it confuses beginning and end, conception and production. Thus, the experienced writers say their drafts are "not determined by time," that rewriting is a "constant process," that they feel as if they "can go on forever." Revising confuses the beginning and end, the agent and vehicle; it confuses, *in order to find,* the line of argument.

After a concern for form, the experienced writers have a second objective: a concern for their readership. In this way, "production" precedes "conception." The experienced writers imagine a reader (reading their product) whose existence and whose expectations influence their revision process. They have abstracted the standards of a reader and this reader seems to be partially a reflection of themselves and functions as a critical and productive collaborator — a collaborator who has yet to love their work. The anticipation of a reader's judgment causes a feeling of dissonance when the writer recognizes incongruities between intention and execution, and requires these writers to make revisions on all levels. Such a reader gives them just what the students lacked: new eyes to "re-view" their work. The experienced writers believe that they have learned the causes and conditions, the product, which will influence their reader, and their revision strategies are geared towards creating these causes and conditions. They demonstrate a complex understanding of which examples, sentences, or phrases should be included or excluded. For example, one experienced writer decided to delete public examples and add private examples when writing about the energy crisis because "private examples would be less controversial and thus more persuasive." Another writer revised his transitional sentences because "some kinds of transitions are more easily recognized as transitions than others." These examples represent the type of strategic attempts these experienced writers use to manipulate the conventions of discourse in order to communicate to their reader.

But these revision strategies are a process of more than communication; they are part of the process of *discovering meaning* altogether. Here we can see the importance of dissonance; at the heart of revision is the process by which writers recognize and resolve the dissonance they sense in their writing. Ferdinand de Saussure has argued that meaning is differential or "diacritical," based on differences between terms rather than "essential" or inherent qualities of terms. "Phonemes," he said, "are characterized not, as one might think, by their own positive quality but simply by the fact that they are distinct."⁹ In fact, Saussure bases his entire *Course in General Linguistics* on these differences, and such differences are dissonant; like musical dissonances which gain their significance from their relationship to the "key" of the composition which itself is determined by the whole language, specific language (parole) gains its meaning from the system of language (langue) of which it is a manifestation and part. The musical composition — a "composition" of parts — creates its "key" as in an overall structure which determines the value (meaning) of its parts. The analogy with music is readily seen in the compositions of experienced writers: both sorts of composition are based precisely on those structures experienced writers seek in their writing. It is this complicated relationship between the parts and the whole in the work of experienced writers which destroys the linear model; writing cannot develop "like a line" because each addition or deletion is a reordering of the whole. Explicating Saussure, Jonathan Culler asserts that "meaning depends on difference of meaning."¹⁰ But student writers constantly struggle to bring their essays into congruence with a predefined meaning. The experienced writers do the opposite: they seek to discover (to create) meaning in the engagement with their writing, in revision. They seek to emphasize and exploit the lack of clarity, the differences of meaning, the dissonance, that writing as opposed to speech allows in the possibility of revision. Writing has spatial and temporal features not apparent in speech — words are recorded in space and fixed in time — which is why writing is susceptible to reordering and later addition. Such features make possible the dissonance that both provokes revision and promises, from itself, new meaning.

For the experienced writers the heaviest concentration of changes is on the sentence level, and the changes are predominantly by addition and deletion. But, unlike the students, experienced writers make changes on all levels and use all revision operations. Moreover, the operations the students fail to use — reordering and addition — seem to require a theory of the revision process as a totality — a theory which, in fact, encompasses the *whole* of the composition. Unlike the students, the experienced writers possess a nonlinear theory in which a sense of the whole writing both precedes and grows out of an examination of the parts. As we saw, one writer said he needed "a first draft to figure out what to say," and "a second draft to see the structure of an argument buried beneath the surface." Such a "theory" is both theoretical and strategical; once again, strategy and theory are conflated in ways that are literally impossible for the linear model. Writing appears to be more like a seed than a line.

Two elements of the experienced writers' theory of the revision process are the adoption of a holistic perspective and the perception that revision is a recursive process. The writers ask: what does my essay as a *whole* need for form, balance, rhythm, or communication. Details are added, dropped, substituted, or reordered according to their sense of what the essay needs for emphasis and proportion. This sense, however, is constantly in flux as ideas are developed and modified; it is constantly "re-viewed" in relation to the parts. As their ideas change, revision becomes an attempt to make their writing consonant with that changing vision.

The experienced writers see their revision process as a recursive process — a process with significant recurring activities — with different levels of attention and different agenda for each cycle. During the first revision cycle their attention is primarily directed towards narrowing the topic and delimiting their ideas. At this point, they are not as concerned as they are later about vocabulary and style. The experienced writers explained that they get closer to their meaning by not limiting themselves too early to lexical concerns. As one writer commented to explain her revision process, a comment inspired by the summer 1977 New York power failure: "I feel like Con Edison cutting off certain states to keep the generators going. In first and second drafts, I try to cut off as much as I can of my editing generator, and in a third draft, I try to cut off some of my idea generators, so I can make sure that I will actually finish the essay." Although the experienced writers describe their revision process as a series of different levels or cycles, it is inaccurate to assume that they have only one objective. The

61

same objectives and sub-processes are present in each cycle, but in different proportions. Even though these experienced writers place the predominant weight upon finding the form of their argument during the first cycle, other concerns exist as well. Conversely, during the later cycles, when the experienced writers' primary attention is focused upon stylistic concerns, they are still attuned, although in a reduced way, to the form of the argument. Since writers are limited in what they can attend to during each cycle (understandings are temporal), revision strategies help balance competing demands on attention. Thus, writers can concentrate on more than one objective at a time by developing strategies to sort out and organize their different concerns in successive cycles of revision.

It is a sense of writing as discovery — a repeated process of beginning over again, starting out new — that the students failed to have. I have used the notion of dissonance because such dissonance, the incongruities between intention and execution, governs both writing and meaning. Students do not see the incongruities. They need to rely on their own internalized sense of good writing and to see their writing with their "own" eyes. Seeing in revision — seeing beyond hearing — is at the root of the word *revision* and the process itself; current dicta on revising blind our students to what is actually involved in revision. In fact, they blind them to what constitutes good writing altogether. Good writing disturbs: it creates dissonance. Students need to seek the dissonance of discovery, utilizing in their writing, as the experienced writers do, the very difference between writing and speech — the possibility of revision.

Notes

[1]D. Gordon Rohman and Albert O. Wlecke, "Pre-writing: The Construction and Application of Models for Concept Formation in Writing," Cooperative Research Project No. 2174, U.S. Office of Education, Department of Health, Education, and Welfare; James Britton, Anthony Burgess, Nancy Martin, Alex McLeod, Harold Rosen, *The Development of Writing Abilities (11–18)* (London: Macmillan Education, 1975).
[2]Britton is following Roman Jakobson, "Linguistics and Poetics," *Style in Language,* ed. T. A. Sebeok (Cambridge: MIT 1960).
[3]For an extended discussion of this issue see Nancy Sommers, "The Need for Theory in Composition Research," *College Composition and Communication* 30 (Feb. 1979): 46–49.
[4]*Classical Rhetoric for the Modern Student* (New York: Oxford UP, 1965), 27.
[5]Roland Barthes, "Writers, Intellectuals, Teachers," *Image-Music-Text,* trans. Stephen Heath (New York: Hill and Wang, 1977) 190–91.
[6]Bathes 190.
[7]Nancy Sommers and Ronald Schleifer, "Means and Ends: Some Assumptions of Student Writers," *Composition and Teaching* II (1980): 69–76.
[8]*Writing Degree Zero,* in *Writing Degree Zero and Elements of Semiology,* trans. Annette Lavers and Colin Smith (New York: Hill and Wang, 1968) 20.
[9]*Course in General Linguistics,* trans. Wade Baskin (New York, 1966) 119.
[10]Jonathan Culler, *Saussure,* Penguin Modern Masters Series (London: Penguin, 1976) 70.

Acknowledgment: The author wishes to express her gratitude to Professor William Smith, University of Pittsburgh, for his vital assistance with the research reported in this article and to Patrick Hays, her husband, for extensive discussions and critical help.

Sommers's Insights as a Resource for Your Teaching

1. Reflect on the experiences that influenced you to use the possibility of revision in your own writing. List the experiences that helped you mature as a writer who uses revision; list those that may have hindered you. Classify them and compare them to the experiences Sommers describes. Then set yourself two goals for assisting students to rethink "revision" —

one for something you will do in the classroom and one for something you will do when you respond to student writing.

2. When you work with a writer who engages in "deep revision," ask whether that writer will give you permission to use excerpts from his or her multiple drafts. With these drafts, you can demonstrate to future students what can happen when a writer moves beyond surface revision. (Any time you want to use student writing — for teaching or research or published writing — you must receive permission.)

Sommers's Insights as a Resource for the Writing Classroom

1. Ask your students to reflect — in journal entries or in fifteen-minute writing sessions — on their definitions of "revision." Have them write before their first experience with peer evaluation in the course and before you hand back their first writing with your comments about revision. Ask them to reflect again on their definitions of "revision" midway through the term and as they near completion of the course. (If this is your students' first assignment involving journal writing, suggest that they consult "Keeping a Journal" in Chapter 14, "Strategies for Generating Ideas."

2. Use the categories Sommers sets up to prompt small-group discussion about revision. Ask the groups to list what they view as characteristics of good revising. Then introduce the concept of "student" and "mature or experienced student" and ask them to classify the characteristics they described as representative of one or the other. Often students will volunteer descriptions that echo those that Sommers lists. If they don't, you should feel free to cite the "research" you read and ask the students to consider Sommers's list as categories by which they can look at their own revising strategies. If you establish with your students that a "mature" college writer views revision as a recursive process, you give them one criterion by which to assess their growth as writers.

3. Prepare a sampler of revision comments from completed peer editing sheets. (Borrow those comments from a colleague if you feel that any students would be embarrassed by seeing their comments used anonymously.) Ask small groups to evaluate the comments and decide which encourage revising for finding or improving the form or shape of the writer's argument, which encourage revising to assist the reader, and which encourage revising for lexical concerns. Ask each group to list the comments they would like to receive on peer editing sheets and to explain what makes other comments less useful or less accessible to them. The exercise asks readers and writers to reflect on their critical thinking; don't be surprised if some class members find it difficult. Remind them that peer evaluation activities provide a second criterion by which they can assess their growth as readers and writers. (You may want to have your students look over the samples of peer editing by Pamela Kong and Jennifer Balsavias in Chapter 19 of *The Bedford Guide for College Writers*.)

AUDIENCE

From Aristotle on, teachers have questioned how best they might assist apprentice writers to recognize audience as a critical part of any communication process. The authors of *The Bedford Guide* have defined "the reader" in "To the Student" as "yourself," "your instructors," "your classmates," and "your own first reader." They indicate that some of the assignments in the text, particularly those in Chapters 7 and 8, and "assignments" in the academic community and the professional world will require the writer to consider his or her audience.

The decision to identify the audience, beginning with the self, is pragmatic; writers must write to and from the self to be authentic, whether in public or private discourse. Fellow writers can provide immediate response to the success of a draft and can tell a writer what needs they still have as readers and "decoders" of the communication. The writing instructor can role-play other kinds of readers in addition to clearly describing his or her reader's response to a draft. Through the support of this writing community, individual writers increase their awareness of the reader-writer relationship. They become more confident about considering the nature and needs of the reader in writing situations that are new to them.

Throughout *The Bedford Guide for College Writers*, the authors ask questions to help focus the writers' attention — most often during revision — on anticipating and meeting the needs of the audience. The literature on audience is extensive. The readings here provide an overview of the discussion of audience in contemporary composition theory and pedagogy along with practical recommendations for how and when to assist student writers to consider the reader.

WRITER-BASED PROSE: A COGNITIVE BASIS FOR PROBLEMS IN WRITING

Linda Flower

This article and the many that Linda Flower has researched and written — frequently with colleagues — expanded the ways that writing instructors thought about both student writing and the processes of student writers. It's a useful article for thinking about and talking to students about audience. It also provides a strong and positive motivation for encouraging multiple drafting and serious revision to aid the reader.

Like Mina Shaughnessy, whom she frequently cites, Flower looks behind "writing problems" and "error" to the cognitive and linguistic strategies that produced them. Her definitions for writer-based and reader-based prose have helped writing instructors reflect on the interconnections of thinking and writing as expressed thought. They have shown writing teachers practical ways to assist writers in the process of "transforming" expressed thought into prose that effectively communicates the writer's expression.

Flower uses the insights of Jean Piaget and Lev Vygotsky to analyze the nature of writer-based prose. She describes this prose as a "major and familiar mode of expression which we all use from time to time" and as "a major, functional stage in the composing process and a powerful strategy well fitted to a part of the job of writing." She explains that writing teachers can motivate student writers to persist with "the task of transforming the groundwork laid in the first stage of the process" by regarding writer-based prose as content that has an interior if uncommunicated coherence and wholeness.

If writing is simply the act of "expressing what you think" or "saying what you mean," why is writing often such a difficult thing to do? And why do papers that do express what the writer meant (to his or her own satisfaction) often fail to communicate the same meaning to a reader? Although we often equate writing with the straightforward act of "saying what we mean," the mental struggles writers go through and the misinterpretations readers still make suggest that we need a better model of this process. Modern communication theory and practical experience agree; writing prose that actually communicates what we mean to another person demands more than a simple act of self-expression. What communication theory does not tell us is how writers do it.

An alternative to the "think it/say it" model is to say that effective writers do not simply *express* thought but *transform* it in certain complex but describable ways for the needs of a reader. Conversely, we may find that ineffective writers are indeed merely "expressing" themselves by offering up an unretouched and underprocessed version of their own thought. Writer-Based prose, the subject of this paper, is a description of this undertransformed mode of verbal expression.

As both a style of writing and a style of thought, Writer-Based prose is natural and adequate for a writer writing to himself or herself. However, it is the source of some of the most common and pervasive problems in academic and professional writing. The symptoms can range from a mere missing referent or an underdeveloped idea to an unfocused and apparently pointless discussion. The symptoms are diverse but the source can often be traced to the writer's underlying strategy for composing and to his or her failure to transform thought into a public, reader-based expression.

In *function,* Writer-Based prose is a verbal expression written by a writer to himself and for himself. It is the record and the working of his own verbal thought. In its *structure,* Writer-Based prose reflects the associative, narrative path of the writer's own confrontation with her subject. In its *language,* it reveals her use of privately loaded terms and shifting but unexpressed contexts for her statements.

In contrast, Reader-Based prose is a deliberate attempt to communicate something to a reader. To do that it creates a shared language and shared context between writer and reader. It also offers the reader an issue-centered rhetorical structure rather than a replay of the writer's discovery process. In its language and structure, Reader-Based prose reflects the *purpose* of the writer's thought; Writer-Based prose tends to reflect its *process.* Good writing, therefore, is often the cognitively demanding transformation of the natural but private expressions of Writer-Based thought into a structure and style adapted to a reader.

This analysis of Writer-Based prose style and the transformations that create Reader-Based prose will explore two hypotheses:

1. Writer-Based prose represents a major and familiar mode of expression which we all use from time to time. While no piece of writing is a pure example, Writer-Based prose can be identified by features of structure, function, and style. Furthermore, it shares many of these features with the modes of inner and egocentric speech described by Vygotsky and Piaget. This paper will explore that relationship and look at newer research in an effort to describe Writer-Based prose as a verbal style which in turn reflects an underlying cognitive process.

2. Writer-Based prose is a workable concept which can help us teach writing. As a way to intervene in the thinking process, it taps intuitive communication strategies writers already have, but are not adequately using. As a teaching technique, the notion of transforming one's own Writer-Based style has proved to be a powerful idea with a built-in method. It helps writers attack this demanding cognitive task with some of the thoroughness and confidence that comes from an increased and self-conscious control of the process.

My plan for this paper is to explore Writer-Based prose from a number of perspectives. Therefore, the next section, which considers the psychological theory of egocentrism and inner speech, is followed by a case study of Writer-Based prose. I will then pull these practical and theoretical issues together to define the critical features of Writer-Based prose. The final section will look ahead to the implications of this description of Writer-Based prose for writers and teachers.

Inner Speech and Egocentrism

In studying the developing thought of the child, Jean Piaget and Lev Vygotsky both observed a mode of speech which seemed to have little social or communicative function. Absorbed in play, children would carry on spirited elliptical monologues which they seemed to assume others understood, but which in fact made no concessions to the needs of the listener. According to Piaget, in Vygotsky's synopsis. "In egocentric speech, the child talks only about himself, takes no interest in his interlocutor, does not try to communicate, expects no answers, and often does not even care whether anyone listens to him. It is similar to a monologue in a play: The child is thinking aloud, keeping up a running accompaniment, as it were, to whatever he may be doing."[1] In the seven-year olds Piaget studied, nearly fifty percent of their recorded talk was egocentric in nature[2] According to Piaget, the child's "non-communicative" or egocentric speech is a reflection, not of selfishness, but of the child's limited ability to "assume the point of view of the listener: [the child] talks of himself, to himself, and by himself."[3] In a sense, the child's cognitive capacity has locked her in her own monologue.

When Vygotsky observed a similar phenomenon in children he called it "inner speech" because he saw it as a forerunner of the private verbal thought adults carry on. Furthermore, Vygotsky argued, this speech is not simply a by-product of play, it is the tool children use to plan, organize, and control their activities. He put the case quite strongly: "We have seen that egocentric speech is not suspended in a void but is directly related to the child's practical dealings with the real world . . . it enters as a constituent part into the process of rational activity" (22).

The egocentric talk of the child and the mental, inner speech of the adult share three important features in common. First, they are highly elliptical. In talking to oneself the psychological subject of discourse (the old information to which we are adding new predicates) is always known. Therefore, explicit subjects and referents disappear. Five people straining to glimpse the bus need only say, "Coming!" Secondly, inner speech frequently deals in the sense of words, not their more specific or limited public meanings. Words become "saturated with sense" in much the way a key word in a poem can come to represent its entire, complex web of meaning. But unlike the word in the poem, the accrued sense of the word in inner speech may be quite personal, even idiosyncratic; it is, as Vygotsky writes, "the sum of all the psychological events aroused in our consciousness by the word" (146).

Finally, a third feature of egocentric/inner speech is the absence of logical and causal relations. In experiments with children's use of logical-causal connectives such as *because, therefore,* and *although,* Piaget found that children have difficulty managing such relationships and in spontaneous speech will substitute a non-logical, non-causal connective such as *then.* Piaget described this strategy for relating things as *juxtaposition:* "the cognitive tendency simply to link (juxtapose) one thought element to another, rather than to tie them together by some causal or logical relation."[4]

One way to diagnose this problem with sophisticated relationships is to say, as Vygotsky did, that young children often think in *complexes* instead of concepts.[5] When people think in complexes they unite objects into families that really do share common bonds, but the bonds are concrete and factual rather than abstract or logical. For example, the notion of "college student" would be a complex if it were based, for the thinker, on facts such as college students live in dorms, go to classes, and do homework.

Complexes are very functional formations, and it may be that many people do most of their day-to-day thinking without feeling the need to form more demanding complex concepts. *Complexes* collect related objects; *concepts,* however, must express abstract, logical relations. And it is just this sort of abstract, synthetic thinking that writing typically demands. In a child's early years the ability to form complex concepts may depend mostly on developing cognitive capacity. In adults this ability appears also to be a skill developed by training and a tendency fostered by one's background and intellectual experience. But whatever its source, the ability to move from the complexes of egocentric speech to the more formal relations of conceptual thought is critical to most expository writing.

Piaget and Vygotsky disagreed on the source, exact function, and teleology of egocentric speech, but they did agree on the features of this distinctive phenomenon, which they felt revealed the underlying logic of the child's thought. For our case, that may be enough. The hypothesis on which this paper rests is not a developmental one. Egocentric speech, or rather its adult written analogue, Writer-Based prose, is not necessarily a stage through which a writer must develop or one at which some writers are arrested. But for adults it does represent an available mode of expression on which to fall back. If Vygotsky is right, it may even be closely related to normal verbal thought. It is clearly a natural, less cognitively demanding mode of thought and one which explains why people, who can express themselves in complex and highly intelligible modes, are often obscure. Egocentric expression happens to the best of us; it comes naturally.

The work of Piaget and Vygotsky, then, suggests a source for the cognitive patterns that underlie Writer-Based prose, and it points to some of the major features such a prose style would possess. Let us now turn to a more detailed analysis of such writing as a verbal style inadequately suited for the needs of the reader.

Writer-Based Prose: A Case Study of a Transformation

As an introduction to the main features of Writer-Based prose and its transformations, let us look at two drafts of a progress report written by students in an organizational psychology class. Working as consulting analysts to a local organization, the writers needed to show progress to their instructor and to present an analysis with causes and conclusions to the client. Both readers — academic and professional — were less concerned with what the students did or saw than with *why* they did it and *what* they made of their observations.

To gauge the Reader-Based effectiveness of this report, skim quickly over Draft 1 and imagine the response of the instructor of the course, who needed to answer these questions: As analysts, what assumptions and decisions did my students make? Why did they make them? At what stage in the project are they now? Or, play the role of the client-reader who wants to know: How did they define my problem, and what did they conclude? As either reader, can you quickly extract the information the report should be giving you? Next, try the same test on Draft 2.

Draft 1:
Group Report

(1) Work began on our project with the initial group decision to evaluate the Oskaloosa Brewing Company. Oskaloosa Brewing Company is a regionally located brewery manufacturing several different types of beer, notably River City and Brough Cream Ale. This beer is marketed under various names in Pennsylvania and other neighboring states. As a group, we decided to analyze this organization because two of our group members had had frequent customer contact with the sales department. Also, we were aware that Oskaloosa Brewing had been losing money for the past five years and we felt we might be able to find some obvious problems in their organizational structure.

(2) Our first meeting, held February 17th, was with the head of the sales department, Jim Tucker. Generally, he gave us an outline of the organization from president to worker, and discussed the various departments that we might ultimately decide to analyze. The two that seemed the most promising and most applicable to the project were the sales and production departments. After a few group meetings and discussions with the personnel manager, Susan Harris, and our advisor Professor Charns, we felt it best suited our needs and the Oskaloosa Brewing's to evaluate their bottling department.

(3) During the next week we had a discussion with the superintendent of production, Henry Holt, and made plans for interviewing the supervisors and line workers. Also, we had a tour of the bottling department which gave us a first hand look into the production process. Before beginning our interviewing, our group met several times to formulate appropriate questions to use in interviewing, for both the supervisors and workers. We also had a meeting with Professor Charns to discuss this matter.

(3a) The next step was the actual interviewing process. During the weeks of March 14–18 and March 21–25, our group met several times at Oskaloosa Brewing and interviewed ten supervisors and twelve workers. Finally during this past week, we have had several group meetings to discuss our findings and the potential problem areas within the bottling department. Also, we have spent time organizing the writing of our progress report.

(4) The bottling and packaging division is located in a separate building, adjacent to the brewery, where the beer is actually manufactured. From the brewery the beer is piped into one of five lines (four bottling lines and one canning line), in the bottling house where the bottles are filled, crowned, pasteurized, labeled, packaged in cases, and either shipped out or stored in the warehouse. The head of this operation, and others, is production manager, Phil Smith. Next in line under him in direct control of the bottling house is the superintendent of bottling and packaging, Henry Holt. In addition, there are a total of ten supervisors who report directly to Henry Holt and who oversee the daily operations and coordinate and direct the twenty to thirty union workers who operate the lines.

(5) During production, each supervisor fills out a data sheet to explain what was actually produced during each hour. This form also includes the exact time when a breakdown occurred, what it was caused by, and when production was resumed. Some supervisors' positions are production staff oriented. One takes care of supplying the raw material (bottles, caps, labels, and boxes) for production. Another is responsible for the union workers assignment each day.

These workers are not all permanently assigned to a production line position. Men called "floaters" are used filling in for a sick worker, or helping out after a breakdown.

(6) The union employees are generally older than 35, some in their late fifties. Most have been with the company many years and are accustomed to having more workers per a slower moving line. They are resentful to what they declare "unnecessary" production changes. Oskaloosa Brewery also employs mechanics who normally work on the production line, and assume a mechanics job only when a breakdown occurs. Most of these men are not skilled

Draft 2:
Memorandum

TO: Professor Martin Chams

FROM: Nancy Lowenberg, Todd Scott, Rosemary Nisson, Larry Vollen

DATE: March 31, 1977

RE: Progress Report: The Oskaloosa Brewing Company

Why Oskaloosa Brewing?

(1) Oskaloosa Brewing Company is a regionally located brewery manufacturing several different types of beer, notably River City and Brough Cream Ale. As a group, we decided to analyze this organization because two of our group members have frequent contact with the sales department. Also, we were aware that Oskaloosa Brewing had been losing money for the past five years and we felt we might be able to find some obvious problems in their organizational structure.

Initial Steps: Where to Concentrate?

(2) Through several interviews with top management and group discussion, we felt it best suited our needs, and Oskaloosa Brewing's, to evaluate the production department. Our first meeting, held February 17, was with the head of the sales department, Jim Tucker. He gave us an outline of the organization and described the two major departments, sales and production. He indicated that there were more obvious problems in the production department, a belief also implied by Susan Harris, personnel manager.

68

Next Step

(3) The next step involved a familiarization of the plant and its employees. First, we toured the plant to gain an understanding of the brewing and bottling process. Next, during the weeks of March 14–18 and March 21–25, we interviewed ten supervisors and twelve workers. Finally, during the past week we had group meetings to exchange information and discuss potential problems.

The Production Process

(4) Knowledge of the actual production process is imperative in understanding the effects of various problems on efficient production; therefore, we have included a brief summary of this process.

The bottling and packaging division is located in a separate building, adjacent to the brewery, where the beer is actually manufactured. From the brewery the beer is piped into one of five lines (four bottling lines and one canning line) in the bottling house where the bottles are filled, crowned, pasteurized, labeled, packaged in cases, and either shipped out or stored in the warehouse.

People Behind the Process

(5) The head of this operation is production manager, Phil Smith. Next in line under him in direct control of the bottling house is the superintendent of bottling and packaging, Henry Holt. He has authority over ten supervisors who each have two major responsibilities: (1) to fill out production data sheets that show the amount produced/hour, and information about any breakdowns — time, cause, etc., and (2) to oversee the daily operations and coordinate and direct the twenty to thirty union workers who operate the lines. These workers are not all permanently assigned to a production line position. Men called "floaters" are used to fill in for a sick worker or to help out after a breakdown.

(6) The union employees are a highly diversified group in both age and experience. They are generally older than 35, some in their late fifties. Most have been with the company many years and are accustomed to having more workers per a slower moving line. They are resentful to what they feel are unnecessary production changes. Oskaloosa Brewing also employs mechanics who normally work on the production line, and assume a mechanics job only when a breakdown occurs. Most of these men are not skilled.

Problems

Through extensive interviews with supervisors and union employees, we have recognized four apparent problems within the bottle house operations. First, the employees' goals do not match those of the company. This is especially apparent in the union employees whose loyalty lies with the union instead of the company. This attitude is well-founded as the union ensures them of job security and benefits. . . .

In its tedious misdirection, Draft 1 is typical of Writer-Based prose in student papers and professional reports. The reader is forced to do most of the thinking, sorting the wheat from the chaff and drawing ideas out of details. And yet, although this presentation fails to fulfill our needs, it does have an inner logic of its own. The logic which organizes Writer-Based prose often rests on three principles: its underlying focus is egocentric, and it uses either a narrative framework or a survey form to order ideas.

The *narrative framework* of this discussion is established by the opening announcement: "Work began. . . ." In paragraphs 1–3 facts and ideas are presented in terms of when they were discovered, rather than in terms of their implications or logical connections. The writers recount what happened when; the reader, on the other hand, asks, "Why?" and "So what?" Whether he or she likes it or not the reader is in for a blow-by-blow account of the writers' discovery process.

Although a rudimentary chronology is reasonable for a progress report, a narrative framework is often a substitute for analytic thinking. By burying ideas within the events that precipitated them, a narrative obscures the more important logical and hierarchical relations between ideas. Of course, such a narrative could read like an intellectual detective story, because, like other forms of drama, it creates interest by withholding closure. Unfortunately, most academic and professional readers seem unwilling to sit through these home movies of the writer's mind at work. Narratives can also operate as a cognitive "frame" which itself generates ideas.[6] The temporal pattern, once invoked, opens up a series of empty slots waiting to be filled with the details of what happened next, even though those details may be irrelevant. As the revision of Draft 2 shows, our writers' initial narrative framework led them to generate a shaggy project story, instead of a streamlined logical analysis.

The second salient feature of this prose is its focus on the discovery process of the writers: the "I did / I thought / I felt" focus. Of the fourteen sentences in the first three paragraphs, ten are grammatically focused on the writers' thoughts and actions rather than on issues: "Work began," "We decided," "Also we were aware . . . and we felt. . . ."

In the fourth paragraph the writers shift attention from their discovery process to the facts discovered. In doing so they illustrate a third feature of Writer-Based prose: its idea structure simply copies the structure of the perceived information. A problem arises when the internal structure of the data is not already adapted to the needs of the reader or the intentions of the writer. Paragraph five, for example, appears to be a free-floating description of "What happens during production." Yet the client-reader already knows this and the instructor probably does not care. Lured by the fascination of facts, these writer-based writers recite a litany of perceived information under the illusion they have produced a rhetorical structure. The resulting structure could as well be a neat hierarchy as a list. The point is that the writers' organizing principle is dictated by their information, not by their intention.

The second version of this report is not so much a "rewrite" (i.e., a new report) as it is a transformation of the old one. The writers had to step back from their experience and information in order to turn facts into concepts. Pinpointing the telling details was not enough: they had to articulate the meaning they saw in the data. Secondly, the writers had to build a rhetorical structure which acknowledged the function these ideas had for their reader. In the second version, the headings, topic sentences, and even some of the subjects and verbs reflect a new functional structure focused on Process, People, and Problems. The report offers a hierarchical organization of the facts in which the hierarchy itself is based on issues both writer and reader agree are important. I think it likely that such transformations frequently go on in the early stages of the composing process for skilled writers. But for some writers the under-transformed Writer-Based prose of Draft 1 is also the final product and the starting point for our work as teachers.

In the remainder of this paper I will look at the features of Writer-Based prose and the ways it functions for the writer. Clearly, we need to know about Reader-Based prose in order to teach it. But it is also clear that writers already possess a great deal of intuitive knowledge about writing for audiences when they are stimulated to use it. As the case study shows, the concept of trying to transform Writer-Based prose for a reader is by itself a powerful tool. It helps writers identify the lineaments of a problem many can start to solve once they recognize it as a definable problem.

Writer-Based Prose: Function, Structure, and Style

While Writer-Based prose may be inadequately structured for a reader, it does possess a logic and structure of its own. Furthermore, that structure serves some important functions for the writer in his or her effort to think about a subject. It represents a practical strategy for dealing with information. If we could see Writer-Based prose as a *functional system* — not a set of random errors known only to English teachers — we would be better able to teach writing as a part of any discipline that asks people to express complex ideas.

According to Vygotsky, "the inner speech of the adult represents his 'thinking for himself' rather than social adaptation [communication to others]: i.e., it has the same function that egocentric speech has in the child" (18). It helps him solve problems. Vygotsky found that when a child who is trying to draw encounters an obstacle (no pencils) or a problem (what shall I call it?), the incidence of egocentric speech can double.

If we look at an analogous situation — an adult caught up in the complex mental process of composing — we can see that much of the adult's output is not well adapted for public consumption either. In studies of cognitive processes of writers as they composed, J. R. Hayes and I observed much of the writer's verbal output to be an attempt to manipulate stored information into some acceptable pattern of meaning.[7] To do that, the writer generates a variety of alternative relationships and trial formulations of the information she has in mind. Many of these trial networks will be discarded; most will be significantly altered through recombination and elaboration during the composing process. In those cases in which the writer's first pass at articulating knowledge was also the final draft — when she wrote it just as she thought it — the result was often a series of semi-independent, juxtaposed networks, each with its own focus.

Whether such expression occurs in an experimental protocol or a written draft, it reflects the working of the writer's mind upon his material. Because dealing with one's material is a formidable enough task in itself, a writer may allow himself to ignore the additional problem of accommodating a reader. Writer-Based prose, then, functions as a medium for thinking. It offers the writer the luxury of one less constraint. As we shall see, its typical structure and style are simply paths left by the movement of the writer's mind.

The *structure* of Writer-Based prose reflects an economical strategy we have for coping with information. Readers generally expect writers to produce complex concepts — to collect data and details under larger guiding ideas and place those ideas in an integrated network. But as both Vygotsky and Piaget observed, forming such complex concepts is a demanding cognitive task; if no one minds, it is a lot easier to just list the parts. Nor is it surprising that in children two of the hallmarks of egocentric speech are the absence of expressed causal relations and the tendency to express ideas without proof or development. Adults too avoid the task of building complex concepts buttressed by development and proof, by structuring their information in two distinctive ways: as a narrative of their own discovery process or as a survey of the data before them.

As we saw in the Oskaloosa Brewing Case Study, a *narrative* structured around one's own discovery process may seem the most natural way to write. For this reason it can sometimes be the best way as well, if a writer is trying to express a complex network of information but is not yet sure how all the parts are related. For example, my notes show that early fragments of this paper started out with a narrative, list-like structure focused on my own experience: "Writer-Based prose is a working hypothesis because it works in the classroom. In fact, when I first started teaching the concept. . . . In fact, it was my students' intuitive recognition of the difference between Writer-Based and Reader-Based style in their own thought and writing. . . . It was their ability to use even a sketchy version of the distinction to transform their own writing that led me to pursue the idea more thoroughly."

The final version of this sketch (the paragraph numbered 2 on p. 65) keeps the reference to teaching experience, but subordinates it to the more central issue of why the concept works. This transformation illustrates how a writer's major propositions can, on first appearance, emerge embedded in a narrative of the events or thoughts which spawned the proposition. In this example, the Writer-Based early version recorded the raw material of observations; the final draft formed them into concepts and conclusions.

This transformation process may take place regularly when a writer is trying to express complicated information which is not yet fully conceptualized. Although much of this mental work normally precedes actual writing, a first draft may simply reflect the writer's current place in the process. When this happens rewriting and editing are vital operations. Far from being a simple matter of correcting errors, editing a first draft is often the act of transforming a narrative network of information into a more fully hierarchical set of propositions.

A second source of pre-fabricated structure for writers is the internal structure of the information itself. Writers use a *survey* strategy to compose because it is a powerful procedure for retrieving and organizing information. Unfortunately, the original organization of the data itself (e.g., the production process at Oskaloosa Brewing) rarely fits the most effective plan for any given piece of focused analytical writing.

The prose that results from such a survey can, of course, take as many forms as the data. It can range from a highly structured piece of discourse (the writer repeats a textbook exposition) to an unfocused printout of the writer's memories and thoughts on the subject. The form is merely a symptom, because the governing force is the writer's mental strategy: namely, to compose by surveying the available contents of memory without adapting them to a current purpose. The internal structure of the data dictates the rhetorical structure of the discourse, much as the proceedings of Congress organize the *Congressional Record*. As an information processor, the writer is performing what computer scientists would call a "memory dump": dutifully printing out memory in exactly the form in which it is stored.

A survey strategy offers the writer a useful way into the composing process in two ways. First, it eliminates many of the constraints normally imposed by a speech act, particularly the contract between reader and writer for mutually useful discourse. Secondly, a survey of one's own stored knowledge, marching along like a textbook or flowing with the tide of association, is far easier to write than a fresh or refocused conceptualization would be.

But clearly most of the advantages here accrue to the writer. One of the tacit assumptions of the Writer-Based writer is that, once the relevant information is presented, the reader will then do the work of abstracting the essential features, building a conceptual hierarchy, and transforming the whole discussion into a functional network of ideas.

Although Writer-Based prose often fails for readers and tends to preclude further concept formation, it may be a useful road into the creative process for some writers. The structures which fail to work for readers may be powerful strategies for retrieving information from memory and for exploring one's own knowledge network. This is illustrated in Linde and Labov's well-known New York apartment tour experiment.[8] Interested in the strategies people use for retrieving information from memory and planning a discourse, Linde and Labov asked one hundred New Yorkers to "tell me the layout of your apartment" as a part of a "sociological survey." Only 3% of the subjects responded with a map which gave an overview and then filled in the details; for example, "I'd say it's laid out in a huge square pattern, broken down into 4 units." The overwhelming majority (97%) all solved the problem by describing a tour: "You walk in the front door. There was a narrow hallway. To the left, etc." Furthermore, they had a common set of rules for how to conduct the tour (e.g., you don't "walk into" a small room with no outlet, such as a pantry; you just say, "on the left is . . ."). Clearly the tour structure is so widely used because it is a remarkably efficient strategy for recovering all of the relevant information about one's apartment, yet without repeating any of it. For example, one rule for "touring" is that when you dead-end after walking through two rooms, you don't "walk" back but suddenly appear back in the hall.

For us, the revealing sidenote to this experiment is that although the tour strategy was intuitively selected by the overwhelming majority of the speakers, the resulting description was generally very difficult for the listener to follow and almost impossible to reproduce. The tour strategy—like the narrative and textbook structure in prose—is a masterful method for searching memory but a dud for communicating that information to anyone else.

Finally, the *style* of Writer-Based prose also has its own logic. Its two main stylistic features grow out of the private nature of interior monologue, that is, of writing which is primarily a record or expression of the writer's flow of thought. The first feature is that in such monologues the organization of sentences and paragraphs reflects the shifting focus of the writer's attention. However, the psychological subject on which the writer is focused may not be reflected in the grammatical subject of the sentence or made explicit in the discussion at all. Secondly, the writer may depend on code words to carry his or her meaning. That is, the language may be "saturated with sense" and able to evoke — for the writer — a complex but unexpressed context.

Writers of formal written discourse have two goals for style which we can usefully distinguish from one another. One goal might be described as stylistic control, that is, the ability to choose a more embedded or more elegant transformation from variations which are roughly equivalent in meaning. The second goal is to create a completely autonomous text, that is, a text that does not need context, gestures, or audible effects to convey its meaning.

It is easy to see how the limits of short-term memory can affect a writer's stylistic control. For an inexperienced writer, the complex transformation of a periodic sentence — which would require remembering and relating a variety of elements and optional structures such as this sentence contains — can be a difficult juggling act. After all, the ability to form parallel constructions is not innate. Yet with practice many of these skills can become more automatic and require less conscious attention.

The second goal of formal written discourse — the complete autonomy of the text — leads to even more complex problems. According to David Olson the history of written language has been the progressive creation of an instrument which could convey complete and explicit meanings in a text. The history of writing is the transformation of language from utterance to text — from oral meaning created within a shared context of a speaker and listener to a written meaning fully represented in an autonomous text.[9]

In contrast to this goal of autonomy, Writer-Based prose is writing whose meaning is still to an important degree in the writer's head. The culprit here is often the unstated psychological subject. The work of the "remedial" student is a good place to examine the phenomenon because it often reveals first thoughts more clearly than the reworked prose of a more experienced writer who edits as he or she writes. In the most imaginative, comprehensive and practical book to be written on the basic writer, Mina Shaughnessy has studied the linguistic strategies which lie behind the "errors" of many otherwise able young adults who have failed to master the written code. As we might predict, the ambiguous referent is ubiquitous in basic writing: *he*'s, *she*'s and *it*'s are sprinkled through the prose without visible means of support. *It* frequently works as a code word for the subject the writer had in mind but not on the page. As Professor Shaughnessy says, *it* "frequently becomes a free-floating substitute for thoughts that the writer neglects to articulate and that the reader must usually strain to reach if he can."[10]

With all the jobs available, he will have to know more of *it* because thire is a great demand for *it*.

For the writer of the above sentence, the pronoun was probably not ambiguous at all; *it* no doubt referred to the psychological subject of his sentence. Psychologically, the subject of an utterance is the old information, the object you are looking at, the idea on which your attention has been focused. The predicate is the new information you are adding. This means that the psychological subject and grammatical subject of a sentence may not be the same at all. In our example, "college knowledge" was the writer's psychological subject — the topic he had been thinking about. The sentence itself is simply a psychological predicate. The pronoun *it* refers quite reasonably to the unstated but obvious subject in the writer's mind.

The subject is even more likely to be missing when a sentence refers to the writer herself or to "one" in her position. In the following examples, again from *Errors and Expectations,* the "unnecessary" subject is a person (like the writer) who has a chance to go to college.

73

Even if a person graduated from high school who is going on to college to obtain a specific position in his career [ ] should first know how much in demand his possible future job really is.

[he]

If he doesn't because the U.S. Labor Department say's their wouldn't be enough jobs opened, [ ] is a waste to society and a "cop-out" to humanity.

[he]

Unstated subjects can produce a variety of minor problems from ambiguous referents to amusing dangling modifiers (e.g., "driving around the mountain, a bear came into view"). Although prescriptive stylists are quite hard on such "errors," they are often cleared up by context or common sense. However, the controlling but unstated presence of a psychological subject can lead to some stylistic "errors" that do seriously disrupt communication. Sentence fragments are a good example.

One feature of an explicit, fully autonomous text is that the grammatical subject is usually a precise entity, often a word. By contrast, the psychological subject to which a writer wished to refer may be a complex event or entire network of information. Here written language is often rather intransigent; it is hard to refer to an entire clause or discussion unless one can produce a summary noun. Grammar, for example, normally forces us to select a specific referent for a pronoun or modifier: it wants referents and relations spelled out.[11] This specificity is, of course, its strength as a vehicle for precise reasoning and abstract thought. Errors arise when a writer uses one clause to announce his topic or psychological subject and a second clause to record a psychological predicate, a response to that old information. For example:

The jobs that are listed in the paper, I feel you need a college degree.

The job that my mother has, I know I could never be satisfied with it.

The preceding sentences are in error because they have failed to specify the grammatical relationship between their two elements. However, for anyone from the Bronx, each statement would be perfectly effective because it fits a familiar formula. It is an example of topicalization or Y-movement and fits a conventionalized, Yiddish influenced, intonation pattern much like the one in "Spinach — you can have it!" The sentences depend heavily on certain conventions of oral speech, and insofar as they invoke those patterns for the reader, they communicate effectively.[12]

However, most fragments do not succeed for the reader. And they fail, ironically enough, for the same reason — they too invoke intonation patterns in the reader which turn out to be misleading. The lack of punctuation gives off incorrect cues about how to segment the sentence. Set off on an incorrect intonation pattern, the thwarted reader must stop, reread and reinterpret the sentence. The following examples are from Maxine Hairston's *A Contemporary Rhetoric* (Boston: Houghton, 1974):

The authorities did not approve of their acts. These acts being considered detrimental to society. (society, they . . .)

Young people need to be on their own. To show their parents that they are reliable. (reliable, young people . . .) (322)

Fragments are easy to avoid; they require only minimal tinkering to correct. Then why is the error so persistent? One possible reason is that for the writer the fragment is a fresh predicate intended to modify the entire preceding psychological subject. The writer wants to carry out a verbal trick easily managed in speech. For the reader, however, this minor grammatical oversight is significant. It sets up and violates both intonation patterns and strong structural expectations, such as those in the last example where we expect a pause and a noun phrase to follow "reliable." The fragment, which actually refers backward, is posing as an introductory clause.

The problem with fragments is that they are perfectly adequate for the writer. In speech they may even be an effective way to express a new idea which is predicated on the entire preceding unit thought. But in a written text, fragments are errors because they do not take the needs of the reader into consideration. Looked at this way, the "goodness" of a stylistic technique or grammatical rule such as parallelism, clear antecedents, or agreement is that it is geared to the habits, expectations, and needs of the reader as well as to the demands of textual autonomy.

Vygotsky noticed how the language of children and inner speech was often "saturated with sense." Similarly, the words a writer chooses can also operate as code words, condensing a wealth of meaning in an apparently innocuous word. The following examples come from an exercise which asks writers to identify and transform some of their own pieces of mental shorthand.

The students were asked to circle any code words or loaded expressions they found in their first drafts of a summer internship application. That is, they tried to identify those expressions that might convey only a general or vague meaning to a reader, but which represented a large body of facts, experiences, or ideas for them. They then treated this code word as one would any intuition — pushing it for its buried connections and turning those into a communicable idea. The results are not unlike those brilliant explications one often hears from students who tell you what their paper really meant. This example also shows how much detailed and perceptive thought can be lying behind a vague and conventional word:

First Draft: "By having these two jobs, I was able to see the business in an entirely different perspective." (Circle indicates a loaded expression marked by the writer.)

Second Draft with explanation of what she actually had in mind in using the circled phrase: "By having these two jobs, I was able to see the true relationship and relative importance of the various departments in the company. I could see their mutual dependence and how an event in one part of the firm can have an important effect on another."

The tendency to think in code words is a fact of life for the writer. Yet the following example shows how much work can go into exploring our own saturated language. Like any intuition, such language is only a source of potential meanings, much as Aristotle's topics are places for finding potential arguments. In this extended example, the writer first explores her expression itself, laying out all the thoughts which were loosely connected under its name. This process of pushing our own language to give up its buried meanings forces us to make these loose connections explicit and, in the process, allows us to examine them critically. For the writer in our example, pushing her own key words leads to an important set of new ideas in the paper.

Excerpt from an application for the
National Institute of Health Internship Program

First Draft: "I want a career that will help other people while at the same time be challenging scientifically. I had the opportunity to do a biochemical assay for a neuropsychophamocologist at X——— Clinic in Chicago. Besides learning the scientific procedures and techniques that are used, I realized some of the organizational, financial and people problems which are encountered in research. This internship program would let me pursue further my interest in research, while concurrently exposing me to relevant and diverse areas of bioengineering."

Excerpt from Writer's Notes Working on the Circled Phrases

Brainstorm

How did research of Sleep Center tie into overall program of X——— Clinic? Not everyone within dept. knew what the others were doing, could not see overall picture of efforts.

Dr. O. — dept. head — trained for lab yet did 38–40 hrs. paperwork. Couldn't set up test assay in Sleep Center because needed equip. from biochem.

Difficulties in getting equipment

1. Politics between administrators
   Photometer at U. of ——— even though Clinic had bought it.
2. Ordering time, not sufficient inventory, had to hunt through boxes for chemicals.
3. Had to schedule use by personal contact on borrowing equipment — done at time of use and no previous planning.

No definite guidelines had been given to biochem. people as to what was "going on" with assay. Partner who was supposed to learn assay was on vacation. Two people were learning, one was on vac.

No money from state for equipment or research grants.
Departments stealing from each other.
Lobbying, politics, included.

My supervisor from India, felt prejudices on job. Couldn't advance, told me life story and difficulties in obtaining jobs at Univ. Not interested in research at Clinic per se, looking for better opportunities, studying for Vet boards.

Revision (additions in italics)

"As a biomedical researcher, I would fulfill my goal of a career that will help other people while at the same time be challenging scientifically. I had exposure to research while doing a biochemical assay for a neuropsychopharmocologist at X——— Clinic in Chicago. Besides learning the scientific procedures and techniques that are used, I realized some of the organizational, financial and people problems which are encountered in research. *These problems included a lack of funds and equipment, disagreements among research staff, and the extensive amounts of time, paperwork and steps required for testing a hypothesis which was only one very small but necessary part of the overall project. But besides knowing some of the frustrations, I also know that many medical advancements, such as the cardiac pacemaker, artificial limbs and cures for diseases, exist and benefit many people because of the efforts of researchers.* Therefore I would like to pursue my interest in research by participating in the NIH Internship Program. The exposure to many *diverse projects, designed to better understand and improve the body's functioning, would help me to decide which areas of biomedical engineering to pursue.*"

We could sum up this analysis of style by noting two points. At times a Writer-Based prose style is simply an interior monologue in which some necessary information (such as intonation pattern or a psychological subject) is not expressed in the text. The solution to the reader's problem is relatively trivial in that it involves adding information that the writer already possesses. At other times, a style may be Writer-Based because the writer is thinking in code words at the level of intuited but unarticulated connections. Turning such saturated language into communicable ideas can require the writer to bring the entire composing process into play.

Implications for Writers and Teachers

From an educational perspective, Writer-Based prose is one of the "problems" composition courses are designed to correct. It is a major cause of that notorious "breakdown" of communication between writer and reader. However, if we step back and look at it in the broader context of cognitive operations involved, we see that it represents a major, functional stage in the composing process and a powerful strategy well fitted to a part of the job of writing.

In the best of all possible worlds, good writers strive for Reader-Based prose from the very beginning: they retrieve and organize information within the framework of a reader/writer contract. Their top goal or initial question is not, "What do I know about physics, and in particular the physics of wind resistance?" but, "What does a model plane builder need to know?" Many times a writer can do this. For a physics teacher this particular writing problem would be a trivial one. However, for a person ten years out of Physics 101, simply retrieving any relevant information would be a full-time processing job. The reader would simply have to wait. For the inexperienced writer, trying to put complex thought into written language may also be task enough. In that case, the reader is an extra constraint that must wait its turn. A Reader-Based strategy which includes the reader in the entire thinking process is clearly the best way to write, but it is not always possible. When it is very difficult or impossible to write for a reader from the beginning, writing and then transforming Writer-Based prose is a practical alternative which breaks this complex process down into manageable parts. When transforming is a practiced skill, it enters naturally into the pulse of the composing process as a writer's constant, steady effort to test and adapt his or her thought to a reader's needs. Transforming Writer-Based prose is, then, not only a necessary procedure for all writers at times, but a useful place to start teaching intellectually significant writing skills.

In this final section I will try to account for the peculiar virtues of Writer-Based prose and suggest ways that teachers of writing — in any field — can take advantage of them. Seen in the context of memory retrieval, Writer-Based thinking appears to be a tapline to the rich sources of episodic memory. In the context of the composing process, Writer-Based prose is a way to deal with the overload that writing often imposes on short term memory. By teaching writers to use this transformation process we can foster the peculiar strengths of writer-based thought and still alert writers to the next transformation that many may simply fail to attempt.

One way to account for why Writer-Based prose seems to "come naturally" to most of us from time to time is to recognize its ties to our episodic as opposed to semantic memory. As Tulving describes it, "episodic memory is a more or less faithful record of a person's experiences." A statement drawn from episodic memory "refers to a personal experience that is remembered in its temporal-spatial relation to other such experiences. The remembered episodes are . . . autobiographical events, describable in terms of their perceptible dimensions or attributes."[13]

Semantic memory, by contrast, "is the memory necessary for the use of language. It is a mental thesaurus, organized knowledge a person possesses about words and other verbal symbols, their meaning and referents, about relations among them, and about rules, formulas, and algorithms for the manipulation of these symbols, concepts, and relations." Although we know that table salt is NaCl and that motivation is a mental state, we probably do not remember learning the fact or the first time we thought of that concept. In semantic memory facts and concepts stand as the nexus for other words and symbols, but shorn of their temporal and autobiographical roots. If we explored the notion of "writing" in the semantic memory of someone we might produce a network such as this:

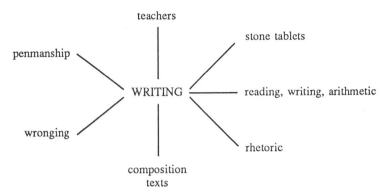

In an effort to retrieve what she or he knew about stone tablets, for example, this same person might turn to episodic memory: "I once heard a lecture on the Rosetta stone, over in Maynard Hall. The woman, as I recall, said that . . . and I remember wondering if. . . ."

Writers obviously use both kinds of memory. The problem only arises when they confuse a fertile source of ideas in episodic memory with a final product. In fact, a study by Russo and Wisher argues that we sometimes store our ideas or images (the symbols of thought) with the mental operations we performed to produce these symbols.[14] Furthermore, it is easier to recall the symbols (that fleeting idea, perhaps) when we bring back the original operation. In other words, our own thinking acts can serve as memory cues, and the easiest way to recover some item from memory may be to *reprocess* it, to reconstruct the original thought process in which it appeared. Much Writer-Based prose appears to be doing just this — reprocessing an earlier thinking experience as a way to recover what one knows.

Writing is one of those activities that places an enormous burden on short-term or working memory. As George Miller put it, "The most glaring result [of numerous experiments] has been to highlight man's inadequacy as a communication channel. As the amount of input information is increased, the amount of information that the man transmits increases at first but then runs into a ceiling. . . . That ceiling is always very low. Indeed, it is an act of charity to call man a channel at all. Compared to telephone or television channels, man is better characterized as a bottleneck."[15]

The short-term memory is the active central processor of the mind, that is, it is the sum of all the information we can hold in conscious attention at one time. We notice its capacity most acutely when we try to learn a new task, such as driving a car or playing bridge. Its limited capacity means that when faced with a complex problem — such as writing a college paper — we can hold and compare only a few alternative relationships in mind at once.

Trying to evaluate, elaborate, and relate all that we know on a given topic can easily overload the capacity of our working memory. Trying to compose even a single sentence can have the same effect, as we try to juggle grammatical and syntactic alternatives plus all the possibilities of tone, nuance, and rhythm even a simple sentence offers. Composing, then, is a cognitive activity that constantly threatens to overload short-term memory. For two reasons Writer-Based prose is a highly effective strategy for dealing with this problem.

1. Because the characteristic structure of Writer-Based prose is often a list (either of mental events or the features of the topic) it temporarily suspends the additional problem of forming complex concepts. If that task is suspended indefinitely, the result will fail to be good analytical writing or serious thought, but as a first stage in the process the list-structure has real value. It allows the writer freedom to generate a breadth of information and a variety of alternative relationships before locking himself or herself into a premature formulation. Furthermore, by allowing the writer to temporarily separate the two complex but somewhat

different tasks of generating information and forming networks, each task may be performed more consciously and effectively.

2. Taking the perspective of another mind is also a demanding cognitive operation. It means holding not only your own knowledge network but someone else's in conscious attention and comparing them. Young children simply can't do it.[16] Adults choose not to do it when their central processing is already overloaded with the effort to generate and structure their own ideas. Writer-Based prose simply eliminates this constraint by temporarily dropping the reader out of the writer's deliberations.[17]

My own research suggests that good writers take advantage of these strategies in their composing process. They use scenarios, generate lists, and ignore the reader, but only for a while. Their composing process, unlike that of less effective writers, is marked by constant re-examination of their growing product and an attempt to refine, elaborate, or test its relationships, plus an attempt to anticipate the response of a reader. Everyone uses the strategies of Writer-Based prose; good writers go a step further to transform the writing these strategies produce.

But what about the writers who fail to make this transformation or (like all of us) fail to do it adequately in places? This is the problem faced by all teachers who assign papers. I think this study has two main and quite happy implications for us as teachers and writers.

The first is that Writer-Based prose is not a composite of errors or a mistake that should be scrapped. Instead, it is a half-way place for many writers and often represents the results of an extensive search and selection process. As a stage in the composing process it may be a rich compilation of significant thoughts which cohere *for the writer* into a network she or he has not yet fully articulated. Writer-Based prose is the writer's homework, and so long as the writer is also the audience, it may even be a well-thought-out communication.

The second happy implication is that writing Reader-Based prose is often simply the task of transforming the groundwork laid in the first stage of the process.[18] Good analytical writing is not different in kind from the writer-based thought that seems to come naturally. It is an extension of our communication with ourselves transformed in certain predictable ways to meet the needs of the reader. The most general transformation is simply to try to take into account the reader's purpose in reading. Most people have well-developed strategies for doing this when they talk. For a variety of reasons — from cognitive effort to the illusion of the omniscient teacher/reader — many people simply do not consider the reader when they write.

More specifically, the transformations that produce Reader-Based writing include these:

Selecting a focus of mutual interest to both reader and writer (e.g., moving from the writer-based focus of "How did I go about my research or reading of the assignment and what did I see?" to a focus on "What significant conclusions can be drawn and why?").

Moving from facts, scenarios, and details to concepts.

Transforming a narrative or textbook structure into a rhetorical structure built on the logical and hierarchical relationships between ideas and organized around the purpose for writing, rather than the writer's process.

Teaching writers to recognize their own Writer-Based writing and transform it has a number of advantages. It places a strong positive value on writing that represents an effort and achievement for the writer even though it fails to communicate to the reader. This legitimate recognition of the uncommunicated content of Writer-Based prose can give anyone, but especially inexperienced writers, the confidence and motivation to go on. By defining writing as a multistage process (instead of a holistic act of "expression") we provide a rationale for editing and alert many writers to a problem they could handle once it is set apart from other problems and they deliberately set out to tackle it. By recognizing transformation as a special skill and task, we give writers a greater degree of self-conscious control over the abilities they already have and a more precise introduction to some skills they may yet develop.

Notes

[1] Lev Vygotsky, *Thought and Language,* ed. and trans. Eugenia Hanfmann and Gertrude Vakar (Cambridge: MIT P, 1962) 15.

[2] Jean Piaget, *The Language and Thought of the Child,* trans. Majorie Gabin (New York: Harcourt, 1932) 49.

[3] Herbert Ginsberg and Sylvia Opper, *Piaget's Theory of Intellectual Development* (Englewood Cliffs: Prentice, 1969) 89.

[4] John Flavell, *The Developmental Psychology of Jean Piaget* (New York: Van Nostrand, 1963) 275. For these studies see the last chapter of Piaget's *Language and Thought of the Child* and *Judgment and Reasoning in the Child,* trans. M. Warden (New York: Harcourt, 1926).

[5] Vygotsky, 75. See also the paper by Gary Woditsch which places this question in the context of curriculum design, "Developing Generic Skills: A Model for a Competency-Based General Education," available from CUE Center, Bowling Green State University.

[6] The seminal paper on frames is M. Minsky's "A Framework for Representing Knowledge," *The Psychology of Computer Vision,* ed. P. Winston (New York: McGraw, 1973). For a more recent discussion of how they work see B. Kuipers, "A Frame for Frames," *Representation and Understanding: Studies in Cognitive Science,* ed. D. Bowbow and A. Collins (New York: Academic, 1975) 151–84.

[7] L. Flower and J. Hayes, "Plans That Guide the Composing Process," *Writing: The Nature, Development and Teaching of Written Communication,* ed. C. Frederikson, M. Whiteman, and J. Dominic (Hillsdale: Erlbaum, in press).

[8] C. Linde and W. Labov, "Spatial Networks as a Site for the Study of Language and Thought," *Language* 51 (1975): 924–39.

[9] David R. Olson, "From Utterance to Text: The Bias of Language in Speech and Writing," *Harvard Educational Review* 47 (1977): 257–81.

[10] Mina Shaughnessy, *Errors and Expectations* (New York: Oxford UP, 1977) 69.

[11] "Pronouns like *this, that, which* and *it* should not vaguely refer to an entire sentence or clause," and "Make a pronoun refer clearly to one antecedent, not uncertainly to two." Floyd Watkins et al., *Practical English Handbook* (Boston: Houghton, 1974) 30.

[12] I am greatly indebted here to Thomas Huckin for his insightful comments on style and to his work in linguistics on how intonation patterns affect writers and readers.

[13] Edel Tulving, "Episodic and Semantic Memory," *Organization of Memory,* ed. Edel Tulving and Wayne Donaldson (New York: Academic, 1972) 387.

[14] J. Russo and R. Wisher, "Reprocessing as a Recognition Cue," *Memory and Cognition* 4 (1976): 683–89.

[15] George Miller, *The Psychology of Communication* (New York: Basic, 1967) 48.

[16] Marlene Scardamalia, "How Children Cope with the Cognitive Demands of Writing," *Writing: The Nature, Development and Teaching of Written Communication,* ed. C. Frederikson, M. Whiteman, and J. Dominic.

[17] Linda Flower and John R. Hayes, "The Dynamics of Composing: Making Plans and Juggling Constraints," *Cognitive Processes in Writing: An Interdisciplinary Approach,* ed. Lee Gregg and Irwin Steinberg (Hillsdale: Erlbaum, 1979).

[18] For a study of heuristics and teaching techniques for this transformation process see L. Flower and J. Hayes, "Problem-Solving Strategies and the Writing Process," *College English* 39 (1977): 449–61.

Flower's Insights as a Resource for Your Teaching

1. The "code words" that represent meaning to the writer but not to the reader are used by writers at every level. Basic writers may overuse ambiguous references, sentence fragments, and imprecise punctuation. Writers who consider themselves prepared for college writing may stay at one level of abstraction, overuse abstract terms and nominalizations, and write lengthy, convoluted compound sentences.

You can help a writer practice "transformation" by identifying and highlighting patterns of writing that impede, obstruct, confuse, or just don't communicate to you. In conferences or in very specific comments, explain what you need as a reader. A writer can scan future drafts for instances of the pattern and revise them so they communicate fully to the reader. Often, writers can add some of those patterns to the style or grammar checks built into their software.

2. Flower cites "those brilliant explications one often hears from students who tell you what their paper really meant." You will hear those explications when you hold individual conferences with writers to discuss their manuscripts. You'll see writers' faces light up with the realization that they haven't made what's clear to them clear to their audience.

It's more effective for the writer and for you as a writing coach or editor to hold those conferences before a draft is submitted for evaluation. Clear, specific comments and questions that you as a reader present to the writer at the drafting stage do much more to prompt "deep revision" or "transformation" than do clear, specific evaluative statements on a graded essay.

3. Flower expects that effective writers will produce multiple drafts and in their "constant re-examination of their growing product" will anticipate the needs and responses of a reader. To assist writers in this process, peer reading sessions are critical. You will need to teach students strategies for providing clear, specific responses to their fellow writers.

Flower's Insights as a Resource for the Writing Classroom

1. Bring in examples of writer-based prose and have small groups list needs and questions they have as readers. When each group reports, write down the range and frequency of reported needs. Make a handout of "generic" needs and questions of readers for writers to consult before they submit a draft for peer review.

2. Imitate Flower and bring in examples of a writing in which you wrote initially for yourself and then revised to reader-based prose. Explain to the students how you became alert to what readers needed while you worked on drafts.

3. Ask writers to look in their journals and bring in a passage of writer-based prose to share. Let them spend ten minutes in class revising the passage to reader-based prose. Have writers exchange those drafts and peer-read them, listing or asking any questions they have. Let them spend ten more minutes revising and have them submit a "finished draft" along with the interim drafts. Ask for a journal entry reflecting on the class activity and the process of revising for a reader.

AUDIENCE ADDRESSED/AUDIENCE INVOKED: THE ROLE OF AUDIENCE IN COMPOSITION THEORY AND PEDAGOGY

Lisa Ede and Andrea Lunsford

Lisa Ede and Andrea Lunsford skillfully demonstrate two major, and seemingly opposed, perspectives on whether and how to emphasize audience in writing courses. They characterize as "audience addressed" the assumptions of many writing teachers and theorists that writers must know — or learn about — the attitudes, beliefs, and expectations of their readers. The authors focus on the theory of Ruth Mitchell and Mary Taylor, who base a writing pedagogy on the concept of addressing the "real" reader. The classification could also include other theorists like Linda Flower, who discusses "reader-based prose" and presents planning strategies for deciding how to address the reader.

Ede and Lunsford contrast the concept of audience addressed with that of "audience invoked." This theory states that the writer invokes an audience by providing "cues" that tell the reader what role the writer wants the reader to play. The authors discuss Walter Ong's "The Writer's Audience Is Always a Fiction," but your students may invoke their audience most clearly in papers they write in response to Chapter 7, "Taking a Stand," and Chapter 8, "Proposing a Solution." In each type of persuasive writing, the successful student not only shapes a persona that readers will trust or respect. The writer also creates a character or role for the reader — perhaps that of being altruistic and humane or of being rational yet cautiously sympathetic.

Through their analysis of the two perspectives on audience, Ede and Lunsford demonstrate that writers need to have skills to anticipate and address readers for some rhetorical situations and skills in invoking readers for others. They remind us how writers redefine audience during revision and cite their own processes of writing the article. They conclude that a "fully elaborated view of audience . . . must balance the creativity of the writer with the different, but equally important, creativity of the reader."

One important controversy currently engaging scholars and teachers of writing involves the role of audience in composition theory and pedagogy. How can we best define the audience of a written discourse? What does it mean to address an audience? To what degree should teachers stress audience in their assignments and discussions? What *is* the best way to help students recognize the significance of this critical element in any rhetorical situation?

Teachers of writing may find recent efforts to answer these questions more confusing than illuminating. Should they agree with Ruth Mitchell and Mary Taylor, who so emphasize the significance of the audience that they argue for abandoning conventional composition courses and instituting a "cooperative effort by writing and subject instructors in adjunct courses. The cooperation and courses take two main forms. Either writing instructors can be attached to subject courses where writing is required, an organization which disperses the instructors throughout the departments participating; or the composition courses can teach students how to write the papers assigned in other concurrent courses, thus centralizing instruction but diversifying topics."[1] Or should teachers side with Russell Long, who asserts that those advocating greater attention to audience overemphasize the role of "observable physical or occupational characteristics" while ignoring the fact that most writers actually create their audiences. Long argues against the usefulness of such methods as developing hypothetical rhetorical situations as writing assignments, urging instead a more traditional emphasis on "the analysis of texts in the classroom with a very detailed examination given to the signals provided by the writer for his audience."[2]

To many teachers, the choice seems limited to a single option — to be for or against an emphasis on audience in composition courses. In the following essay, we wish to expand our understanding of the role audience plays in composition theory and pedagogy by demonstrating that the arguments advocated by each side of the current debate oversimplify the act of making meaning through written discourse. Each side, we will argue, has failed adequately to recognize (1) the fluid, dynamic character of rhetorical situations and (2) the integrated, interdependent nature of reading and writing. After discussing the strengths and weaknesses of the two central perspectives on audience in composition — which we group under the rubrics of *audience addressed* and *audience invoked*[3] — we will propose an alternative formulation, one which we believe more accurately reflects the richness of "audience" as a concept.[4]

Audience Addressed

Those who envision audience as addressed emphasize the concrete reality of the writer's audience; they also share the assumption that knowledge of this audience's attitudes, beliefs, and expectations is not only possible (via observation and analysis) but essential. Questions concerning the degree to which this audience is "real" or imagined, and the ways it differs from the speaker's audience, are generally either ignored or subordinated to a sense of the audience's powerfulness. In their discussion of "A Heuristic Model for Creating a Writer's Audience," for example, Fred Pfister and Joanne Petrik attempt to recognize the ontological complexity of the writer-audience relationship by noting that "students, like all writers, must fictionalize their audience."[5] Even so, by encouraging students to "construct in their imagination an audience that is as nearly a replica as is possible of *those many readers who actually exist in the world of reality*," Pfister and Petrik implicitly privilege the concept of audience as addressed.[6]

Many of those who envision audience as addressed have been influenced by the strong tradition of audience analysis in speech communication and by current research in cognitive psychology on the composing process.[7] They often see themselves as reacting against the current-traditional paradigm of composition, with its a-rhetorical, product-oriented emphasis.[8] And they also frequently encourage what is called "real-world" writing.[9]

Our purpose here is not to draw up a list of those who share this view of audience but to suggest the general outline of what most readers will recognize as a central tendency in the teaching of writing today. We would, however, like to focus on one particularly ambitious attempt to formulate a theory and pedagogy for composition based on the concept of audience as addressed: Ruth Mitchell and Mary Taylor's "The Integrating Perspective: An Audience-Response Model for Writing." We choose Mitchell and Taylor's work because of its theoretical richness and practical specificity. Despite these strengths, we wish to note several potentially significant limitations in their approach, limitations which obtain to varying degrees in much of the current work of those who envision audience as addressed.

In their article, Mitchell and Taylor analyze what they consider to be the two major existing composition models: one focusing on the writer and the other on the written product. Their evaluation of these two models seems essentially accurate. The "writer" model is limited because it defines writing as either self-expression or "fidelity to fact" (255) — epistemologically naive assumptions which result in troubling pedagogical inconsistencies. And the "written product" model, which is characterized by an emphasis on "certain intrinsic features [such as a] lack of comma splices and fragments" (258), is challenged by the continued inability of teachers of writing (not to mention those in other professions) to agree upon the precise intrinsic features which characterize "good" writing.

Most interesting, however, is what Mitchell and Taylor *omit* in their criticism of these models. Neither the writer model nor the written product model pays serious attention to invention, the term used to describe those "methods designed to aid in retrieving information, forming concepts, analyzing complex events, and solving certain kinds of problems."[10] Mitchell and Taylor's lapse in not noting this omission is understandable, however, for the same can be said of their own model. When these authors discuss the writing process, they stress that "our first priority for writing instruction at every level ought to be certain major tactics for structuring material because these structures are the most important in guiding the reader's comprehension and memory" (271). They do not concern themselves with where "the material" comes from — its sophistication, complexity, accuracy, or rigor.

Mitchell and Taylor also fail to note another omission, one which might be best described in reference to their own model (Figure 1). This model has four components. Mitchell and Taylor use two of these, "writer" and "written product," as labels for the models they condemn. The third and fourth components, "audience" and "response," provide the title for their own "audience-response model for writing" (249).

Mitchell and Taylor stress that the components in their model interact. Yet, despite their emphasis on interaction, it never seems to occur to them to note that the two other models may fail in large part because they overemphasize and isolate one of the four elements — wrenching it too greatly from its context and thus inevitably distorting the composing process.

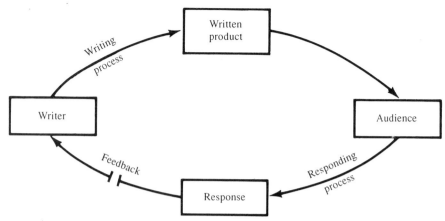

Figure 1. Mitchell and Taylor's "general model of writing" (250)

Mitchell and Taylor do not consider this possibility, we suggest, because their own model has the same weakness.

Mitchell and Taylor argue that a major limitation of the "writer" model is its emphasis on the self, the person writing, as the only potential judge of effective discourse. Ironically, however, their own emphasis on audience leads to a similar distortion. In their model, the audience has the sole power of evaluating writing, the success of which "will be judged by the audience's reaction: 'good' translates into 'effective,' 'bad' into 'ineffective.' " Mitchell and Taylor go on to note that "the audience not only judges writing; it also motivates it" (p. 250),[11] thus suggesting that the writer has less control than the audience over both evaluation and motivation.

Despite the fact that Mitchell and Taylor describe writing as "an interaction, a dynamic relationship" (250), their model puts far more emphasis on the role of the audience than on that of the writer. One way to pinpoint the source of imbalance in Mitchell and Taylor's formulation is to note that they are right in emphasizing the creative role of readers who, they observe, "actively contribute to the meaning of what they read and will respond according to a complex set of expectations, preconceptions, and provocations" (251), but wrong in failing to recognize the equally essential role writers play throughout the composing process not only as creators but also as *readers* of their own writing.

As Susan Wall observes in "In the Writer's Eye: Learning to Teach the Rereading/Revising Process," when writers read their own writing, as they do continuously while they compose, "there are really not one but two contexts for rereading: there is the writer-as-reader's sense of what the established text is actually saying, as of this reading; and there is the reader-as-writer's judgment of what the text might say or should say. . . ."[12] What is missing from Mitchell and Taylor's model, and from much work done from the perspective of audience as addressed, is a recognition of the crucial importance of this internal dialogue, through which writers analyze inventional problems and conceptualize patterns of discourse. Also missing is an adequate awareness that, no matter how much feedback writers may receive after they have written something (or in breaks while they write), as they compose writers must rely in large part upon their own vision of the reader, which they create, as readers do their vision of writers, according to their own experiences and expectations.

Another major problem with Mitchell and Taylor's analysis is their apparent lack of concern for the ethics of language use. At one point, the authors ask the following important question: "Have we painted ourselves into a corner, so that the audience-response model must defend sociologese and its related styles?" (265). Note first the ambiguity of their answer, which seems to us to say no and yes at the same time, and the way they try to deflect its impact:

> No. We defend only the right of audiences to set their own standards and we repudiate the ambitions of English departments to monopolize that standard-setting. If bureaucrats and scientists are happy with the way they write, then no one should interfere.
> But evidence is accumulating that they are not happy. (265)

Here Mitchell and Taylor surely underestimate the relationship between style and substance. As those concerned with Doublespeak can attest, for example, the problem with sociologese is not simply its (to our ears) awkward, convoluted, highly nominalized style, but the way writers have in certain instances used this style to make statements otherwise unacceptable to lay persons, to "gloss over" potentially controversial facts about programs and their consequences, and thus violate the ethics of language use. Hence, although we support Mitchell and Taylor when they insist that we must better understand and respect the linguistic traditions of other disciplines and professions, we object to their assumption that style is somehow value free.

As we noted earlier, an analysis of Mitchell and Taylor's discussion clarifies weaknesses inherent in much of the theoretical and pedagogical research based on the concept of audience as addressed. One major weakness of this research lies in its narrow focus on helping students learn how to "continually modify their work with reference to their audience" (251). Such a focus, which in its extreme form becomes pandering to the crowd, tends to undervalue the responsibility a writer has to a subject and to what Wayne Booth in *Modern Dogma and the Rhetoric of Assent* calls "the art of discovering good reasons."[13] The resulting imbalance has clear ethical consequences, for rhetoric has traditionally been concerned not only with the effectiveness of a discourse, but with truthfulness as well. Much of our difficulty with the language of advertising, for example, arises out of the ad writer's powerful concept of audience as addressed divorced from a corollary ethical concept. The toothpaste ad that promises improved personality, for instance, knows too well how to address the audience. But such ads ignore ethical questions completely.

Another weakness in research done by those who envision audience as addressed suggests an oversimplified view of language. As Paul Kameen observes in "Rewording the Rhetoric of Composition," "discourse is not grounded in forms or experience or audience; it engages all of these elements simultaneously."[14] Ann Berthoff has persistently criticized our obsession with one or another of the elements of discourse, insisting that meaning arises out of their synthesis. Writing is more, then, than "a means of acting upon a receiver" (Mitchell and Taylor 250); it is a means of making meaning for writer *and* reader.[15] Without such a unifying, balanced understanding of language use, it is easy to overemphasize one aspect of discourse, such as audience. It is also easy to forget, as Anthony Petrosky cautions us, that "reading, responding, and composing are aspects of understanding, and theories that attempt to account for them outside of their interaction with each other run the serious risk of building reductive models of human understanding."[16]

Audience Invoked

Those who envision audience as invoked stress that the audience of a written discourse is a construction of the writer, a "created fiction" (Long 225). They do not, of course, deny the physical reality of readers, but they argue that writers simply cannot know this reality in the way that speakers can. The central task of the writer, then, is not to analyze an audience and adapt discourse to meet its needs. Rather, the writer uses the semantic and syntactic resources of language to provide cues for the reader — cues which help to define the role or roles the writer wishes the reader to adopt in responding to the text. Little scholarship in composition takes this perspective; only Russell Long's article and Walter Ong's "The Writer's Audience Is Always a Fiction" focus centrally on this issue.[17] If recent conferences are any indication, however, a growing number of teachers and scholars are becoming concerned with what they see as the possible distortions and oversimplifications of the approach typified by Mitchell and Taylor's model.[18]

Russell Long's response to current efforts to teach students analysis of audience and adaptation of text to audience is typical: "I have become increasingly disturbed not only about the superficiality of the advice itself, but about the philosophy which seems to lie beneath it" (221). Rather than detailing Long's argument, we wish to turn to Walter Ong's well-known study. Published in *PMLA* in 1975, "The Writer's Audience Is Always a Fiction" has had a significant impact on composition studies, despite the fact that its major emphasis is on fictional narrative rather than expository writing. An analysis of Ong's argument suggests that teachers of writing may err if they uncritically accept Ong's statement that "what has been said about fictional narrative applies ceteris paribus to all writing" (17).

Ong's thesis includes two central assertions: "What do we mean by saying the audience is a fiction? Two things at least. First, that the writer must construct in his imagination, clearly or vaguely, an audience cast in some sort of role. . . . Second, we mean that the audience must correspondingly fictionalize itself" (12). Ong emphasizes the creative power of the adept writer, who can both project and alter audiences, as well as the complexity of the reader's role. Readers, Ong observes, must learn or "know how to play the game of being a member of an audience that 'really' does not exist" (12).

On the most abstract and general level, Ong is accurate. For a writer, the audience is not *there* in the sense that the speaker's audience, whether a single person or a large group, is present. But Ong's representative situations — the orator addressing a mass audience versus a writer alone in a room — oversimplify the potential range and diversity of both oral and written communication situations.

Ong's model of the paradigmatic act of speech communication derives from traditional rhetoric. In distinguishing the terms audience and reader, he notes that "the orator has before him an audience which is a true audience, a collectivity. . . . Readers do not form a collectivity, acting here and now on one another and on the speaker as members of an audience do" (11). As this quotation indicates, Ong also stresses the potential for interaction among members of an audience, and between an audience and a speaker.

But how many audiences are actually collectives, with ample opportunity for interaction? In *Persuasion: Understanding, Practice, and Analysis,* Herbert Simons establishes a continuum of audiences based on opportunities for interaction.[19] Simons contrasts commercial mass media publics, which "have little or no contact with each other and certainly have no reciprocal awareness of each other as members of the same audience" with "face-to-face work groups that meet and interact continuously over an extended period of time." He goes on to note that: "Between these two extremes are such groups as the following: (1) the *pedestrian audience,* persons who happen to pass a soap box orator . . . ; (2) the *passive, occasional audience,* persons who come to hear a noted lecturer in a large auditorium . . . ; (3) the *active, occasional audience,* persons who meet only on specific occasions but actively interact when they do meet" (97–98).

Simons's discussions, in effect, questions the rigidity of Ong's distinctions between a speaker's and a writer's audience. Indeed, when one surveys a broad range of situations inviting oral communication, Ong's paradigmatic situation, in which the speaker's audience constitutes a "collectivity, acting here and now on one another and on the speaker" (11), seems somewhat atypical. It is certainly possible, at any rate, to think of a number of instances where speakers confront a problem very similar to that of writers: lacking intimate knowledge of their audience, which comprises not a collectivity but a disparate, and possibly even divided, group of individuals, speakers, like writers, must construct in their imaginations "an audience cast in some sort of role."[20] When President Carter announced to Americans during a speech broadcast on television, for instance, that his program against inflation was "the moral equivalent of warfare," he was doing more than merely characterizing his economic policies. He was providing an important cue to his audience concerning the role he wished them to adopt as listeners — that of a people braced for a painful but necessary and justifiable battle. Were we to examine his speech in detail, we would find other more subtle, but equally important, semantic and syntactic signals to the audience.

We do not wish here to collapse all distinctions between oral and written communication, but rather to emphasize that speaking and writing are, after all, both rhetorical acts. There are important differences between speech and writing. And the broad distinction between speech and writing that Ong makes is both commonsensical and particularly relevant to his subject, fictional narrative. As our illustration demonstrates, however, when one turns to precise, concrete situations, the relationship between speech and writing can become far more complex than even Ong represents.

Just as Ong's distinction between speech and writing is accurate on a highly general level but breaks down (or at least becomes less clear-cut) when examined closely, so too does his dictum about writers and their audiences. Every writer must indeed create a role for the reader, but the constraints on the writer and the potential sources of and possibilities for the reader's role are both more complex and diverse than Ong suggests. Ong stresses the importance of literary tradition in the creation of audience: "If the writer succeeds in writing, it is generally because he can fictionalize in his imagination an audience he has learned to know not from daily life but from earlier writers who were fictionalizing in their imagination audiences they had learned to know in still earlier writers, and so on back to the dawn of written narrative" (11). And he cites a particularly (for us) germane example, a student "asked to write on the subject to which schoolteachers, jaded by summer, return compulsively every autumn: 'How I Spent My Summer Vacation' " (11). In order to negotiate such an assignment successfully, the student must turn his real audience, the teacher, into someone else. He or she must, for instance, "make like Samuel Clemens and write for whomever Samuel Clemens was writing for" (11).

Ong's example is, for his purposes, well chosen. For such an assignment does indeed require the successful student to "fictionalize" his or her audience. But why is the student's decision to turn to a literary model in this instance particularly appropriate? Could one reason be that the student knows (consciously or unconsciously) that his English teacher, who is still the literal audience of his essay, appreciates literature and hence would be entertained (and here the student may intuit the assignment's actual aim as well) by such a strategy? In Ong's example the audience — the "jaded" schoolteacher — is not only willing to accept another role but, perhaps, actually yearns for it. How else to escape the tedium of reading 25, 50, 75 student papers on the same topic? As Walter Minot notes, however, not all readers are so malleable:

> In reading a work of fiction or poetry, a reader is far more willing to suspend his beliefs and values than in a rhetorical work dealing with some current social, moral, or economic issue. The effectiveness of the created audience in a rhetorical situation is likely to depend on such constraints as the actual identity of the reader, the subject of the discourse, the identity and purpose of the writer, and many other factors in the real world.[21]

An example might help make Minot's point concrete.

Imagine another composition student faced, like Ong's, with an assignment. This student, who has been given considerably more latitude in her choice of topic, has decided to write on an issue of concern to her at the moment, the possibility that a home for mentally retarded adults will be built in her neighborhood. She is alarmed by the strongly negative, highly emotional reaction of most of her neighbors and wishes in her essay to persuade them that such a residence might not be the disaster they anticipate.

This student faces a different task from that described by Ong. If she is to succeed, she must think seriously about her actual readers, the neighbors to whom she wishes to send her letter. She knows the obvious demographic factors — age, race, class — so well that she probably hardly needs to consider them consciously. But other issues are more complex. How much do her neighbors know about mental retardation, intellectually or experientially? What is their image of a retarded adult? What fears does this project raise in them? What civic and religious values do they most respect? Based on this analysis — and the process may be much less sequential than we describe here — she must, of course, define a role for her audience, one congruent with her persona, arguments, the facts as she knows them, etc. She must, as Minot argues, *both* analyze and invent an audience.[22] In this instance, after detailed analysis of her audience and her arguments, the student decided to begin her essay by emphasizing what she felt to be the genuinely admirable qualities of her neighbors, particularly their kindness, understanding, and concern for others. In so doing, she invited her audience to see themselves as *she* saw them: as thoughtful, intelligent people who, if they were adequately informed, would certainly not act in a harsh manner to those less fortunate than they. In accepting this role, her readers did not have to "play the game of being a member of an audience that 'really' does not exist" (Ong 12). But they did have to recognize in themselves the strengths the student described and to accept her implicit linking of these strengths to what she hoped would be their response to the proposed "home."

When this student enters her history class to write an examination she faces a different set of constraints. Unlike the historian who does indeed have a broad range of options in establishing the reader's role, our student has much less freedom. This is because her reader's role has already been established and formalized in a series of related academic conventions. If she is a successful student, she has so effectively internalized these conventions that she can subordinate a concern for her complex and multiple audiences to focus on the material on which she is being tested and on the single audience, the teacher, who will respond to her performance on the test.[23]

We could multiply examples. In each instance the student writing — to friend, employer, neighbor, teacher, fellow readers of her daily newspaper — would need, as one of the many conscious and unconscious decisions required in composing, to envision and define a role for the reader. But *how* she defines that role — whether she relies mainly upon academic or technical writing conventions, literary models, intimate knowledge of friends or neighbors, analysis of a particular group, or some combination thereof — will vary tremendously. At times the writer may establish a role for the reader which indeed does not "coincide with his role in the rest of actual life" (Ong 12). At other times, however, one of the writer's primary tasks may be that of analyzing the "real life" audience and adapting the discourse to it. One of the factors that makes writing so difficult, as we know, is that we have no recipes: each rhetorical situation is unique and thus requires the writer, catalyzed and guided by a strong sense of purpose, to reanalyze and reinvent solutions.

Despite their helpful corrective approach, then, theories which assert that the audience of a written discourse is a construction of the writer present their own dangers.[24] One of these is the tendency to overemphasize the distinction between speech and writing while undervaluing the insights of discourse theorists, such as James Moffett and James Britton, who remind us of the importance of such additional factors as distance between speaker or writer and audience and levels of abstraction in the subject. In *Teaching the Universe of Discourse,* Moffett establishes the following spectrum of discourse: recording ("the drama of what is happening"), reporting ("the narrative of what happened"), generalizing ("the exposition of what happens") and theorizing ("the argumentation of what will, may happen").[25] In an extended example, Moffett demonstrates the important points of connection between communication acts at any one level of the spectrum, whether oral or written:

88

Suppose next that I tell the cafeteria experience to a friend some time later in conversation. . . . Of course, instead of recounting the cafeteria scene to my friend in person I could write it in a letter to an audience more removed in time and space. Informal writing is usually still rather spontaneous, directed at an audience known to the writer, and reflects the transient mood and circumstances in which the writing occurs. Feedback and audience influence, however, are delayed and weakened. . . . *Compare in turn now the changes that must occur all down the line when I write about this cafeteria experience in a discourse destined for publication and distribution to a mass, anonymous audience of present and perhaps unborn people.* I cannot allude to things and ideas that only my friends know about. I must use a vocabulary, style, logic, and rhetoric that anybody in that mass audience can understand and respond to. I must name and organize what happened during those moments in the cafeteria that day in such a way that this mythical average reader can relate what I say to some primary moments of experience of his own. (37–38; our emphasis)

Though Moffett does not say so, many of these same constraints would obtain if he decided to describe his experience in a speech to a mass audience — the viewers of a television show, for example, or the members of a graduating class. As Moffett's example illustrates, the distinction between speech and writing is important; it is, however, only one of several constraints influencing any particular discourse.

Another weakness of research based on the concept of audience as invoked is that it distorts the processes of writing and reading by overemphasizing the power of the writer and undervaluing that of the reader. Unlike Mitchell and Taylor, Ong recognizes the creative role the writer plays as reader of his or her own writing, the way the writer uses language to provide cues for the reader and tests the effectiveness of these cues during his or her own rereading of the text. But Ong fails adequately to recognize the constraints placed on the writer, in certain situations, by the audience. He fails, in other words, to acknowledge that readers' own experiences, expectations, and beliefs do play a central role in their reading of a text, and that the writer who does not consider the needs and interests of his audience risks losing that audience. To argue that the audience is a "created fiction" (Long 225), to stress that the reader's role "seldom coincides with his role in the rest of actual life" (Ong 12), is just as much an oversimplification, then, as to insist, as Mitchell and Taylor do, that "the audience not only judges writing, it also motivates it" (250). The former view overemphasizes the writer's independence and power; the latter, that of the reader.

Rhetoric and Its Situations [26]

If the perspectives we have described as audience addressed and audience invoked represent incomplete conceptions of the role of audience in written discourse, do we have an alternative? How can we most accurately conceive of this essential rhetorical element? In what follows we will sketch a tentative model and present several defining or constraining statements about this apparently slippery concept, "audience." The result will, we hope, move us closer to a full understanding of the role audience plays in written discourse.

Figure 2 represents our attempt to indicate the complex series of obligations, resources, needs, and constraints embodied in the writer's concept of audience. (We emphasize that our goal here is *not* to depict the writing process as a whole — a much more complex task — but to focus on the writer's relation to audience.) As our model indicates, we do not see the two perspectives on audience described earlier as necessarily dichotomous or contradictory. Except for past and anomalous audiences, special cases which we describe paragraphs hence, all of the audience roles we specify — self, friend, colleague, critic, mass audience, and future audience — may be invoked or addressed.[27] It is the writer who, as writer and reader of his or her own text, one guided by a sense of purpose and by the particularities of a specific rhetorical situation, establishes the range of potential roles an audience may play. (Readers may, of course, accept or reject the role or roles the writer wishes them to adopt in responding to a text.)

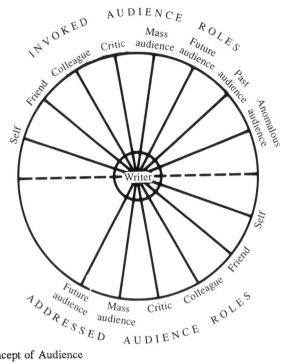

Figure 2. The Concept of Audience

Writers who wish to be read must often adapt their discourse to meet the needs and expectations of an addressed audience. They may rely on past experience in addressing audiences to guide their writing, or they may engage a representative of that audience in the writing process. The latter occurs, for instance, when we ask a colleague to read an article intended for scholarly publication. Writers may also be required to respond to the intervention of others — a teacher's comments on an essay, a supervisor's suggestions for improving a report, or the insistent, catalyzing questions of an editor. Such intervention may in certain cases represent a powerful stimulus to the writer, but it is the writer who interprets the suggestions — or even commands — of others, choosing what to accept or reject. Even the conscious decision to accede to the expectations of a particular addressed audience may not always be carried out; unconscious psychological resistance, incomplete understanding, or inadequately developed ability may prevent the writer from following through with the decision — a reality confirmed by composition teachers with each new set of essays.

The addressed audience, the actual or intended readers of a discourse, exists outside of the text. Writers may analyze these readers' needs, anticipate their biases, even defer to their wishes. But it is only through the text, through language, that writers embody or give life to their conception of the reader. In so doing, they do not so much create a role for the reader — a phrase which implies that the writer somehow creates a mold to which the reader adapts — as invoke it. Rather than relying on incantations, however, writers conjure their vision — a vision which they hope readers will actively come to share as they read the text — by using all the resources of language available to them to establish a broad, and ideally coherent, range of cues for the reader. Technical writing conventions, for instance, quickly formalize any of several writer-reader relationships, such as colleague to colleague or expert to lay reader. But even comparatively local semantic decisions may play an equally essential role. In "The Writer's Audience Is Always a Fiction," Ong demonstrates how Hemingway's use of definite articles in *A Farewell to Arms* subtly cues readers that their role is to be that of a "companion in arms . . . a confidant" (13).

Any of the roles of the addressed audience cited in our model may be invoked via the text. Writers may also invoke a past audience, as did, for instance, Ong's student writing to those Mark Twain would have been writing for. And writers can also invoke anomalous audiences, such as a fictional character — Hercule Poirot perhaps. Our model, then, confirms Douglas Park's observation that the meanings of audience, though multiple and complex, "tend to diverge in two general directions: one toward actual people external to the text, the audience whom the writer must accommodate; the other toward the text itself and the audience implied there: a set of suggested or evoked attitudes, interests, reactions, conditions of knowledge which may or may not fit with the qualities of actual readers or listeners."[28] The most complete understanding of audience thus involves a synthesis of the perspectives we have termed audience addressed, with its focus on the reader, and audience invoked, with its focus on the writer.

One illustration of this constantly shifting complex of meanings for "audience" lies in our own experiences writing this essay. One of us became interested in the concept of audience during an NEH Seminar, and her first audience was a small, close-knit seminar group to whom she addressed her work. The other came to contemplate a multiplicity of audiences while working on a textbook; the first audience in this case was herself, as she debated the ideas she was struggling to present to a group of invoked students. Following a lengthy series of conversations, our interests began to merge: we shared notes and discussed articles written by others on audience, and eventually one of us began a draft. Our long distance telephone bills and the miles we travelled up and down I-5 from Oregon to British Columbia attest most concretely to the power of a co-author's expectations and criticisms and also illustrate that one person can take on the role of several different audiences: friend, colleague, and critic.

As we began to write and rewrite the essay, now for a particular scholarly journal, the change in purpose and medium (no longer a seminar paper or a textbook) led us to new audiences. For us, the major "invoked audience" during this period was Richard Larson, editor of this journal, whose questions and criticisms we imagined and tried to anticipate. (Once this essay was accepted by *CCC,* Richard Larson became for us an addressed audience: he responded in writing with questions, criticisms, and suggestions, some of which we had, of course, failed to anticipate.) We also thought of the readers of *CCC* and those who attend the annual CCCC, most often picturing you as members of our own departments, a diverse group of individuals with widely varying degrees of interest in and knowledge of composition. Because of the generic constraints of academic writing, which limit the range of roles we may define for our readers, the audience represented by the readers of *CCC* seemed most vivid to us in two situations: (1) when we were concerned about the degree to which we needed to explain concepts or terms and (2) when we considered central organizational decisions, such as the most effective way to introduce a discussion. Another, and for us extremely potent, audience was the authors — Mitchell and Taylor, Long, Ong, Park, and others — with whom we have seen ourselves in silent dialogue. As we read and reread their analyses and developed our responses to them, we felt a responsibility to try to understand their formulations as fully as possible, to play fair with their ideas, to make our own efforts continue to meet their high standards.

Our experience provides just one example, and even it is far from complete. (Once we finished a rough draft one particular colleague became a potent but demanding addressed audience, listening to revision upon revision and challenging us with harder and harder questions. And after this essay is published, we may revise our understanding of audiences we thought we knew or recognize the existence of an entirely new audience. The latter would happen, for instance, if teachers of speech communication for some reason found our discussion useful.) But even this single case demonstrates that the term *audience* refers not just to the intended, actual, or eventual readers of a discourse, but to *all* those whose image, ideas, or actions influence a writer during the process of composition. One way to conceive of "audience," then, is as an overdetermined or unusually rich concept, one which may perhaps be best specified through the analysis of precise, concrete situations.

We hope that this partial example of our own experience will illustrate how the elements represented in Figure 2 will shift and merge, depending on the particular rhetorical situation, the writer's aim, and the genre chosen. Such an understanding is critical: because of the complex reality to which the term audience refers and because of its fluid, shifting role in the composing process, any discussion of audience which isolates it from the rest of the rhetorical situation or which radically overemphasizes or underemphasizes its function in relation to other rhetorical constraints is likely to oversimplify. Note the unilateral direction of Mitchell and Taylor's model (5), which is unable to represent the diverse and complex role(s) audience(s) can play in the actual writing process — in the creation of meaning. In contrast, consider the model used by Edward P. J. Corbett in his *Little Rhetoric and Handbook* [see Figure 3].[29] This representation, which allows for interaction among all the elements of rhetoric, may at first appear less elegant and predictive than Mitchell and Taylor's. But it is finally more useful since it accurately represents the diverse range of potential interrelationships in any written discourse.

We hope that our model also suggests the integrated, interdependent nature of reading and writing. Two assertions emerge from this relationship. One involves the writer as reader of his or her own work. As Donald Murray notes in "Teaching the Other Self: The Writer's First Reader," this role is critical, for "the reading writer — the map-maker and map-reader — reads the word, the line, the sentence, the paragraph, the page, the entire text. This constant back-and-forth reading monitors the multiple complex relationships between all the elements in writing."[30] To ignore or devalue such a central function is to risk distorting the writing process as a whole. But unless the writer is composing a diary or journal entry, intended only for the writer's own eyes, the writing process is not complete unless another person, someone other than the writer, reads the text also. The second assertion thus emphasizes the creative, dynamic duality of the process of reading and writing, whereby writers create readers and readers create writers. In the meeting of these two lies meaning, lies communication.

A fully elaborated view of audience, then, must balance the creativity of the writer with the different, but equally important, creativity of the reader. It must account for a wide and shifting range of roles for both addressed and invoked audiences. And, finally, it must relate the matrix created by the intricate relationship of writer and audience to all elements in the rhetorical situation. Such an enriched conception of audience can help us better understand the complex act we call composing.

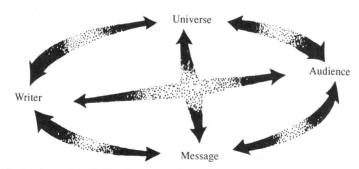

Figure 3. Corbett's model of "The Rhetorical Interrelationships" (5)

Notes

[1]Ruth Mitchell and Mary Taylor, "The Integrating Perspective: An Audience-Response Model for Writing," *CE* 41 (Nov. 1979): 267. Subsequent references to this article will be cited in the text.

[2]Russell C. Long, "Writer-Audience Relationships: Analysis or Invention," *CCC* 31 (May 1980): 223, 225. Subsequent references to this article will be cited in the text.

[3]For these terms we are indebted to Henry W. Johnstone, Jr., who refers to them in his analysis of Chaim Perelman's universal audience in *Validity and Rhetoric in Philosophical Argument: An Outlook in Transition* (University Park, PA: The Dialogue of Man & World, 1978) 105.

[4]A number of terms might be used to characterize the two approaches to audience which dominate current theory and practice. Such pairs as identified/envisaged, "real"/fictional, or analyzed/created all point to the same general distinction as do our terms. We chose "addressed/invoked" because the terms most precisely represent our intended meaning. Our discussion will, we hope, clarify their significance; for the present, the following definitions must serve. The "addressed" audience refers to those actual or real-life people who read a discourse, while the "invoked" audience refers to the audience called up or imagined by the writer.

[5]Fred R. Pfister and Joanne F. Petrik, "A Heuristic Model for Creating a Writer's Audience," *CCC* 31 (May 1980): 213.

[6]Pfister and Petrik 214; our emphasis.

[7]See, for example, Lisa S. Ede, "On Audience and Composition," *CCC* 30 (Oct. 1979): 291–95.

[8]See, for example, David Tedlock, "The Case Approach to Composition," *CCC* 32 (Oct. 1981): 253–61.

[9]See, for example, Linda Flower's *Problem-Solving Strategies for Writers* (New York: Harcourt, 1981) and John P. Field and Robert H. Weiss's *Cases for Composition* (Boston: Little, 1979).

[10]Richard E. Young, "Paradigms and Problems: Needed Research in Rhetorical Invention," *Research on Composing: Points of Departure,* ed. Charles R. Cooper and Lee Odell (Urbana: National Council of Teachers of English, 1978) 32n3.

[11]Mitchell and Taylor do recognize that internal psychological needs ("unconscious challenges") may play a role in the writing process, but they cite such instances as an "extreme case (often that of the creative writer)" (251). For a discussion of the importance of self-evaluation in the composing process see Susan Miller, "How Writers Evaluate Their Own Writing," *CCC* 33 (May 1982): 176–83.

[12]Susan Wall, "In the Writer's Eye: Learning to Teach the Rereading/Revising Process," *English Education* 14 (Feb. 1982): 12.

[13]Wayne Booth, *Modern Dogma and the Rhetoric of Assent* (Chicago: U of Chicago P, 1974) xiv.

[14]Paul Kameen, "Rewording the Rhetoric of Composition," *Pre/Text* 1 (Spring–Fall 1980): 82.

[15]Mitchell and Taylor's arguments in favor of adjunct classes seem to indicate that they see writing instruction, wherever it occurs, as a skills course, one instructing students in the proper use of a tool.

[16]Anthony R. Petrosky, "From Story to Essay: Reading and Writing," *CCC* 33 (Feb. 1982): 20.

[17]Walter J. Ong, S.J., "The Writer's Audience Is Always a Fiction," *PMLA* 90 (Jan. 1975): 9–21. Subsequent references to this article will be cited in the text.

[18]See, for example, William Irmscher, "Sense of Audience: An Intuitive Concept," unpublished paper delivered at the CCCC in 1981; Douglas B. Park, "The Meanings of Audience: Pedagogical Implications," unpublished paper delivered at the CCCC in 1981; and Luke M. Reinsma, "Writing to an Audience: Scheme or Strategy?" unpublished paper delivered at the CCCC in 1982.

[19]Herbert W. Simons, *Persuasion: Understanding, Practice, and Analysis* (Reading: Addison, 1976).

[20]Ong 12. Ong recognizes that oral communication also involves role-playing, but he stresses that it "has within it a momentum that works for the removal of masks" (20). This may be true in certain instances, such as dialogue, but does not, we believe, obtain broadly.

[21]Walter S. Minot, "Response to Russell C. Long," *CCC* 32 (Oct. 1981): 337.

[22]We are aware that the student actually has two audiences, her neighbors and her teacher, and that this situation poses an extra constraint for the writer. Not all students can manage such a complex series of audience constraints, but it is important to note that writers in a variety of situations often write for more than a single audience.

[23]In their paper on "Student and Professional Syntax in Four Disciplines" (unpublished paper delivered at the CCCC in 1981), Ian Pringle and Aviva Freedman provide a good example of what can happen when a student creates an aberrant role for an academic reader. They cite an excerpt from a third year history assignment, the tone of which "is essentially the tone of the opening of a television travelogue commentary" and which thus asks the reader, a history professor, to assume the role of the viewer of such a show. The result is as might be expected: "Although the content of the paper does not

seem significantly more abysmal than other papers in the same set, this one was awarded a dispropor-
tionately low grade" (2).

²⁴One danger which should be noted is a tendency to foster a questionable image of classical
rhetoric. The agnostic speaker-audience relationship which Long cites as an essential characteristic of
classical rhetoric is actually a central point of debate among those involved in historical and theoretical
research in rhetoric. For further discussion, see: Lisa Ede and Andrea Lunsford, "On Distinctions
Between Classical and Modern Rhetoric," *Classical Rhetoric and Modern Discourse: Essays in Honor
of Edward P. J. Corbett,* ed. Robert Connors, Lisa Ede, and Andrea Lunsford (Carbondale: Southern
Illinois UP, 1984).

²⁵James Moffett, *Teaching the Universe of Discourse* (Boston: Houghton, 1968) 47. Subsequent
references will be mentioned in the text.

²⁶We have taken the title of this section from Scott Consigny's article of the same title, *Philosophy
and Rhetoric* 7 (Summer 1974): 175–86. Consigny's effort to mediate between two opposing views of
rhetoric provided a stimulating model for our own efforts.

²⁷Although we believe that the range of audience roles cited in our model covers the general
spectrum of options, we do not claim to have specified all possibilities. This is particularly the case
since, in certain instances, these roles may merge and blend — shifting subtly in character. We might
also note that other terms for the same roles might be used. In a business setting, for instance, colleague
might be better termed co-worker; critic, supervisor.

²⁸ Douglas B. Park, "The Meanings of 'Audience,'" *CE* 44 (Mar. 1982): 249.

²⁹Edward P. J. Corbett, *The Little Rhetoric & Handbook,* 2nd ed. (Glenview: Scott, 1982) 5.

³⁰Donald M. Murray, "Teaching the Other Self: The Writer's First Reader," *CCC* 33 (May 1982):
142.

Ede and Lunsford's Insights as a Resource for Your Teaching

1. Review the introductory handouts and assignment sheets that you gave your students.
To what extent do your materials influence student writers to shape a draft for "audience
addressed" or "audience invoked"? Prompt a class discussion about responses to an assignment; ask writers to explain how they decided who would be the audience. If you find all the
writers focused on only one concept of audience, you might want to analyze your materials to
determine whether you might be unconsciously limiting their understanding of audience.

2. If you have access to a videocamera, arrange to have several of your classes taped.
Watch them until you get past "ego shock" and can see patterns in the way that you speak to
your audience of students. List the assumptions that you have about your students as evidenced by your speaking and nonverbal performance. Then go back to your early handouts
and assignments and list the assumptions you have about your students as evidenced by your
writing. Use the insights from this exercise to analyze how effectively you "model" attention
to the needs of your audience, whether addressed or invoked.

Ede and Lunsford's Insights as a Resource for the Writing Classroom

1. When students keep a reading journal to generate topics for the writing assignment in
Chapter 3, "Writing from Reading," ask them to record their responses to "how the writer
talked to me." Have them read a short essay in class and record their responses to "how the
writer considered me as the reader." Use the entries to initiate a discussion of audience from
their understanding as readers of ways that writers consider audience. Ask them to "imitate"
one of the writers they read in a twenty-minute writing session and to focus on "writing to the
reader" in the same way that the original writer chose to write. In this exercise, content is less
important than rhetorical flexibility with audience.

2. Writing instructors often ask students to write at the top of the manuscript the "audience" whom they were conscious they wrote for. Ask your students to go one step further and
to analyze in a short self-assessment whether they were addressing or invoking an audience.

In your comments on the draft, describe your reader's response as a member of the audience addressed, as a member of the audience invoked, and as the guide in the writing classroom. Ask peer editors who respond to the writings in response to Chapters 7 and 8 to also write comments from the roles of audience addressed, audience invoked, and fellow writer.

CLOSING MY EYES AS I SPEAK:
AN ARGUMENT FOR IGNORING AUDIENCE

Peter Elbow

Peter Elbow argues that writers often need simply to ignore audience. Even though he credits several arguments for audience awareness and agrees that some audiences invite and enable the writer to generate thought and feeling, he cautions that some audiences inhibit and even block writing. In particular, audience awareness in the earliest stages of writing may confuse and inhibit the writer while audience awareness during revision may enlighten and liberate the writer. (Notice how the authors of The Bedford Guide for College Writers *prompt more awareness of the reader through the revision checklists and peer editing checklists than during the "getting started" discussion of each chapter.)*

Elbow both agrees with and extends Linda Flower's theory that students produce "writer-based prose" when they experience "cognitive overload" (see Flower's "Writer-Based Prose: A Cognitive Basis for Problems in Writing" in this section). Although some writing instructors have used this explanation to label writers as "basic" or foundering, Elbow insists that a correct reading of Flower discovers her celebrating the "developmentally enabling" response of writer-based prose. Elbow extends Flower's discussion by asserting that when attention to audience complicates thinking so much that writers short out, we should suggest that the writers ignore the audience and pay attention to their own thinking. Once the writers work out through drafts and "internal conversation" what they think, they can turn their attention back to audience. Elbow insists that "ignoring audience can lead to worse drafts but better revisions."

Elbow quarrels with an interpretation of Piaget's model of cognitive development that leads some writing theorists to look at "writer-based prose," writing that ignores audience, as an indication that the writer is necessarily immature. He disagrees that writers who shape "reader-based prose" are ipso facto more cognitively mature. He insists that the ability to turn off audience awareness when it is distracting or confusing is a higher skill. Writers who can switch off audience awareness and sustain quiet, thoughtful reflection, who can in private reflection make meaning for themselves and shape a discourse from such thinking alone, are independent and mature thinkers. Elbow offers Vygotsky's cognitive model that "development in thinking is not from the individual to the socialized, but from the social to the individual" as support for his assertion that ignoring audience can lead to dialogue with self.

Elbow insists that "private writing" that turns off and away from audience is as important to humans as public writing that addresses and invokes the audience. Writing instructors need to assist their students to discover public writing as a way of "taking part in a community of discourse" and private writing as a means for writing better reflectively. Elbow shows a symbiosis of the two kinds of discourse; each sustains the other.

Elbow concludes with very sound and practical suggestions for how teachers can help students discover the values of both kinds of discourse. He suggests that we must counteract the reality that most schools offer little privacy for writing and little social dimension for writing by heightening both the public and private dimensions of writing. I recommend the discussion of freewriting and of keeping a journal in Chapter 14, "Strategies for Generating Ideas," and the discussion of the personal strategies of a variety of writers for getting started in Chapter 16, "Strategies for Drafting." They show students how critical personal discourse is for developing the private dimension of their mental and emotional lives. Chapter 19,

"Strategies for Working with Other Writers: Collaborative Learning," and the many exercises for group learning throughout the text emphasize how critical public discourse is to growth as thoughtful and creative persons.

Very often people don't listen to you when you speak to them. It's only when you talk to yourself that they prick up their ears.

— John Ashbery

When I am talking to a person or a group and struggling to find words or thoughts, I often find myself involuntarily closing my eyes as I speak. I realize now that this behavior is an instinctive attempt to blot out awareness of audience when I need all my concentration for just trying to figure out or express what I want to say. Because the audience is so imperiously *present* in a speaking situation, my instinct reacts with this active attempt to avoid audience awareness. This behavior — in a sense impolite or antisocial — is not so uncommon. Even when we write, alone in a room to an absent audience, there are occasions when we are struggling to figure something out and need to push aside awareness of those absent readers. As Donald Murray puts it, "My sense of audience is so strong that I have to suppress my conscious awareness of audience to hear what the text demands" (Berkenkotter and Murray 171). In recognition of how pervasive the role of audience is in writing, I write to celebrate the benefits of ignoring audience.[1]

It will be clear that my argument for writing without audience awareness is not meant to undermine the many good reasons for writing *with* audience awareness some of the time. (For example, that we are liable to neglect audience because we write in solitude; that young people often need more practice in taking into account points of view different from their own; and that students often have an impoverished sense of writing as communication because they have only written in a school setting to teachers.) Indeed I would claim some part in these arguments for audience awareness — which now seem to be getting out of hand.

I start with a limited claim: even though ignoring audience will usually lead to weak writing at first — to what Linda Flower calls "writer-based prose," this weak writing can help us in the end to better writing than we would have written if we'd kept readers in mind from the start. Then I will make a more ambitious claim: writer-based prose is sometimes better than reader-based prose. Finally I will explore some of the theory underlying these issues of audience.

A Limited Claim

It's not that writers should never think about their audience. It's a question of when. An audience is a field of force. The closer we come — the more we think about these readers — the stronger the pull they exert on the contents of our minds. The practical question, then, is always whether a particular audience functions as a helpful field of force or one that confuses or inhibits us.

Some audiences, for example, are *inviting* or *enabling*. When we think about them as we write, we think of more and better things to say — and what we think somehow arrives more coherently structured than usual. It's like talking to the perfect listener: we feel smart and come up with ideas we didn't know we had. Such audiences are helpful to keep in mind right from the start.

Other audiences, however, are powerfully *inhibiting* — so much so, in certain cases, that awareness of them as we write blocks writing altogether. There are certain people who always make us feel dumb when we try to speak to them: we can't find words or thoughts. As soon as we get out of their presence, all the things we want to say pop back into our minds. Here is a student telling what happens when she tries to follow the traditional advice about audience:

> You know _____ [author of a text] tells us to pay attention to the audience that will be reading our papers, and I gave that a try. I ended up without putting a word on paper until I decided the hell with _____; I'm going to write to who I damn well want to; otherwise I can hardly write at all.

Admittedly, there are some occasions when we benefit from keeping a threatening audience in mind from the start. We've been putting off writing that letter to that person who intimidates us. When we finally sit down and write *to* them — walk right up to them, as it were, and look them in the eye — we may manage to stand up to the threat and grasp the nettle and thereby find just what we need to write.

Most commonly, however, the effect of audience awareness is somewhere between the two extremes: the awareness disturbs or disrupts our writing and thinking without completely blocking it. For example, when we have to write to someone we find intimidating (and of course students often perceive teachers as intimidating), we often start thinking wholly defensively. As we write down each thought or sentence, our mind fills with thoughts of how the intended reader will criticize or object to it. So we try to qualify or soften what we've just written — or write out some answer to a possible objection. Our writing becomes tangled. Sometimes we get so tied in knots that we cannot even figure out what we *think*. We may not realize how often audience awareness has this effect on our students when we don't see the writing process behind their papers: we just see texts that are either tangled or empty.

Another example. When we have to write to readers with whom we have an awkward relationship, we often start beating around the bush and feeling shy or scared, or start to write in a stilted, overly careful style or voice. (Think about the cute, too-clever style of many memos we get in our departmental mailboxes — the awkward self-consciousness academics experience when writing to other academics.) When students are asked to write to readers they have not met or cannot imagine, such as "the general reader" or "the educated public," they often find nothing to say except clichés they know *they* don't even quite believe.

When we realize that an audience is somehow confusing or inhibiting us, the solution is fairly obvious. We can ignore that audience altogether during the *early* stages of writing and direct our words only to ourselves or to no one in particular — or even to the "wrong" audience, that is, to an *inviting* audience of trusted friends or allies. This strategy often dissipates the confusion; the clenched, defensive discourse starts to run clear. Putting audience out of mind is of course a traditional practice: serious writers have long used private journals for early explorations of feeling, thinking, or language. But many writing teachers seem to think that students can get along without the private writing serious writers find so crucial — or even that students will *benefit* from keeping their audience in mind for the whole time. Things often don't work out that way.

After we have figured out our thinking in copious exploratory or draft writing — perhaps finding the right voice or stance as well — *then* we can follow the traditional rhetorical advice: think about readers and revise carefully to adjust our words and thoughts to our intended audience. For a particular audience it may even turn out that we need to *disguise* our point of view. But it's hard to disguise something while engaged in trying to figure it out. As writers, then, we need to learn when to think about audience and when to put readers out of mind.

Many people are too quick to see Flower's "writer-based prose" as an analysis of what's wrong with this type of writing and miss the substantial degree to which she was celebrating a natural, and indeed developmentally enabling, response to cognitive overload. What she doesn't say, however, despite her emphasis on planning and conscious control in the writing process, is that we can *teach* students to notice when audience awareness is getting in their way — and when this happens, consciously to put aside the needs of readers for a while. She seems to assume that when an overload occurs, the writer-based gear will, as it were, automatically kick into action to relieve it. In truth, of course, writers often persist in using a malfunctioning *reader*-based gear despite the overload — thereby mangling their language or thinking. Though Flower likes to rap the knuckles of people who suggest a "correct" or "natural" order for steps in the writing process, she implies such an order here: when attention to audience causes an overload, start out by ignoring them while you attend to your thinking; after you work out your thinking, turn your attention to audience.

Thus if we ignore audience while writing on a topic about which we are not expert or about which our thinking is still evolving, we are likely to produce exploratory writing that is unclear to anyone else — perhaps even inconsistent or a complete mess. Yet by doing this exploratory "swamp work" in conditions of safety, we can often coax our thinking through a process of new discovery and development. In this way we can end up with something better than we could have produced if we'd tried to write to our audience all along. In short, ignoring audience can lead to worse drafts but better revisions. (Because we are professionals and adults, we often write in the role of expert: we may know what we think without new exploratory writing; we may even be able to speak confidently to critical readers. But students seldom experience this confident professional stance in their writing. And think how much richer *our* writing would be if we defined ourselves as *in*expert and allowed ourselves private writing for new explorations of those views we are allegedly sure of.)

Notice then that two pieties of composition theory are often in conflict:

1. Think about audience as you write (this stemming from the classical rhetorical tradition).

2. Use writing for *making new meaning,* not just transmitting old meanings already worked out (this stemming from the newer epistemic tradition I associate with Ann Berthoff's classic explorations).

It's often difficult to work out new meaning while thinking about readers.

A More Ambitious Claim

I go further now and argue that ignoring audience can lead to better writing — immediately. In effect, writer-based prose can be *better* than reader-based prose. This might seem a more controversial claim, but is there a teacher who has not had the experience of struggling and struggling to no avail to help a student untangle his writing, only to discover that the student's casual journal writing or freewriting is untangled and strong? Sometimes freewriting is stronger than the essays we get only because it is expressive, narrative, or descriptive writing and the student was not constrained by a topic. But teachers who collect drafts with completed assignments often see passages of freewriting that are strikingly stronger *even* when they are expository and constrained by the assigned topic. In some of these passages we can sense that the strength derives from the student's unawareness of readers.

It's not just unskilled, tangled writers, though, who sometimes write better by forgetting about readers. Many competent and even professional writers produce mediocre pieces *because* they are thinking too much about how their readers will receive their words. They are acting too much like a salesman trained to look the customer in the eye and to think at all times about the characteristics of the "target audience." There is something too staged or planned or self-aware about such writing. We see this quality in much second-rate newspaper or magazine or business writing: "good-student writing" in the awful sense of the term. Writing produced this way reminds us of the ineffective actor whose consciousness of self distracts us: he makes us too aware of his own awareness of us. When we read such prose, we wish the writer would stop thinking about us — would stop trying to "adjust" or "fit" what he is saying to our frame of reference. "Damn it, put all your attention on what you are saying," we want to say, "and forget about us and how we are reacting."

When we examine really good student or professional writing, we can often see that its goodness comes from the writer's having gotten sufficiently wrapped up in her meaning and her language as to forget all about audience needs: the writer manages to "break through." The Earl of Shaftesbury talked about writers needing to escape their audience in order to find their own ideas (Cooper 1:109; see also Griffin). It is characteristic of much truly good writing to be, as it were, on fire with its meaning. Consciousness of readers is burned away; involvement in subject determines all. Such writing is analogous to the performance of the actor who has managed to stop attracting attention to her awareness of the audience watching her.

The arresting power in some writing by small children comes from their obliviousness to audience. As readers, we are somehow sucked into a more-than-usual connection with the meaning itself because of the child's gift for more-than-usual concentration on what she is saying. In short, we can feel some pieces of children's writing as being very writer-based. Yet it's precisely that quality which makes it powerful for us as readers. After all, why should we settle for a writer's entering our point of view, if we can have the more powerful experience of being sucked out of our point of view and into her world? This is just the experience that children are peculiarly capable of giving because they are so expert at total absorption in their world as they are writing. It's not just a matter of whether the writer "decenters," but of whether the writer has a sufficiently strong focus of attention to make the *reader* decenter. This quality of concentration is what D. H. Lawrence so admires in Melville:

> [Melville] was a real American in that he always felt his audience in front of him. But when he ceases to be American, when he forgets all audience, and gives us his sheer apprehension of the world, then he is wonderful, his book [*Moby Dick*] commands a stillness in the soul, an awe. (158)

What most readers value in really excellent writing is not prose that is right for readers but prose that is right for thinking, right for language, or right for the subject being written about. If, in addition, it is clear and well suited to readers, we appreciate that. Indeed we feel insulted if the writer did not somehow try to make the writing *available* to us before delivering it. But if it succeeds at being really true to language and thinking and "things," we are willing to put up with much difficulty as readers:

> [Good writing is not always or necessarily an adaptation to communal norms (in the Fish/Bruffee sense) but may be an attempt to construct (and instruct) a reader capable of reading the text in question. The literary history of the "difficult" work — from Mallarmé to Pound, Zukofsky, Olson, etc. — seems to say that much of what we value in writing we've had to learn to value by learning how to read it. (Trimbur)

The effect of audience awareness on *voice* is particularly striking — if paradoxical. Even though we often develop our voice by finally "speaking up" to an audience or "speaking out" to others, and even though much dead student writing comes from students' not really treating their writing as a communication with real readers, nevertheless, the opposite effect is also common: we often do not really develop a strong, authentic voice in our writing till we find important occasions for *ignoring* audience — saying, in effect, "To hell with whether they like it or not. I've got to say this the way *I* want to say it." Admittedly, the voice that emerges when we ignore audience is sometimes odd or idiosyncratic in some way, but usually it is stronger. Indeed, teachers sometimes complain that student writing is "writer-based" when the problem is simply the idiosyncrasy — and sometimes in fact the *power* — of the voice. They would value this odd but resonant voice if they found it in a published writer (see Elbow, "Real Voice," *Writing with Power*). Usually we cannot *trust* a voice unless it is unaware of us and our needs and speaks out in its own terms (see the Ashbery epigraph). To celebrate writer-based prose is to risk the charge of *romanticism:* just warbling one's woodnotes wild. But my position also contains the austere *classic* view that we must nevertheless *revise* with conscious awareness of audience in order to figure out which pieces of writer-based prose are good as they are — and how to discard or revise the rest.

To point out that writer-based prose can be *better* for readers than reader-based prose is to reveal problems in these two terms. Does *writer-based* mean:

1. That the text doesn't work for readers because it is too much oriented to the writer's point of view?

2. Or that the writer was not thinking about readers as she wrote, although the text *may* work for readers?

Does *reader-based* mean:

3. That the text works for readers — meets their needs?

4. Or that the writer was attending to readers as she wrote although her text may *not* work for readers?

In order to do justice to the reality and complexity of what actually happens in both writers and readers, I was going to suggest four terms for the four conditions listed above, but I gradually realized that things are even too complex for that. We really need to ask about what's going on in three dimensions — in the *writer,* in the *reader,* and in the *text* — and realize that the answers can occur in virtually any combination:

Was the *writer* thinking about readers or oblivious to them?

Is the *text* oriented toward the writer's frame of reference or point of view, or oriented toward that of readers? (A writer may be thinking about readers and still write a text that is largely oriented toward her own frame of reference.)

Are the readers' needs being met? (The text may meet the needs of readers whether the writer was thinking about them or not, and whether the text is oriented toward them or not.)

Two Models of Cognitive Development

Some of the current emphasis on audience awareness probably derives from a model of cognitive development that needs to be questioned. According to this model, if you keep your readers in mind as you write, you are operating at a higher level of psychological development than if you ignore readers. Directing words to readers is "more mature" than directing them to no one in particular or to yourself. Flower relates writer-based prose to the inability to "decenter" which is characteristic of Piaget's early stages of development, and she relates reader-based prose to later more mature stages of development.

On the one hand, of course this view must be right. Children do decenter as they develop. As they mature they get better at suiting their discourse to the needs of listeners, particularly to listeners very different from themselves. Especially, they get better at doing so *consciously* — thinking *awarely* about how things appear to people with different viewpoints. Thus much unskilled writing is unclear or awkward *because* the writer was doing what it is so easy to do — unthinkingly taking her own frame of reference for granted and not attending to the needs of readers who might have a different frame of reference. And of course this failure is more common in younger, immature, "egocentric" students (and also more common in writing than in speaking since we have no audience present when we write).

But on the other hand, we need the contrary model that affirms what is also obvious once we reflect on it, namely that the ability to *turn off* audience awareness — especially when it confuses thinking or blocks discourse — is also a "higher" skill. I am talking about an ability to use language in "the desert island mode," an ability that tends to require learning, growth, and psychological development. Children, and even adults who have not learned the art of quiet, thoughtful, inner reflection, are often unable to get much cognitive action going in their heads unless there are other people present to have action *with*. They are dependent on live audience and the social dimension to get their discourse rolling or to get their thinking off the ground.

For in contrast to a roughly Piagetian model of cognitive development that says we start out as private, egocentric little monads and grow up to be public and social, it is important to invoke the opposite model that derives variously from Vygotsky, Bakhtin, and Meade. According to this model, we *start out* social and plugged into others and only gradually, through learning and development, come to "unplug" to any significant degree so as to function in a more private, individual and differentiated fashion: "Development in thinking is not from the individual to the socialized, but from the social to the individual" (Vygotsky 20). The important general principle in this model is that we tend to *develop* our important cognitive capacities by means of social interaction with others, and having done so we gradually learn to perform them alone. We fold the "simple" back-and-forth of dialogue into the "complexity" (literally, "foldedness") of individual, private reflection.

Where the Piagetian (individual psychology) model calls our attention to the obvious need to learn to enter into viewpoints other than our own, the Vygotskian (social psychology) model calls our attention to the equally important need to learn to produce good thinking and discourse *while alone*. A rich and enfolded mental life is something that people achieve only gradually through growth, learning, and practice. We tend to associate this achievement with the fruits of higher education.

Thus we see plenty of students who lack this skill, who have nothing to say when asked to freewrite or to write in a journal. They can dutifully "reply" to a question or a topic, but they cannot seem to *initiate* or *sustain* a train of thought on their own. Because so many adolescent students have this difficulty, many teachers chime in: "Adolescents have nothing to write about. They are too young. They haven't had significant experience." In truth, adolescents don't lack experience or material, no matter how "sheltered" their lives. What they lack is practice and help. Desert island discourse is a learned cognitive process. It's a mistake to think of private writing (journal writing and freewriting) as merely "easy" — merely a relief from trying to write right. It's also hard. Some exercises and strategies that help are Ira Progoff's "Intensive Journal" process, Sondra Perl's "Composing Guidelines," or Elbow's "Loop Writing" and "Open Ended Writing" processes (*Writing with Power* 50–77).

The Piagetian and Vygotskian developmental models (language-begins-as-private vs. language-begins-as-social) give us two different lenses through which to look at a common weakness in student writing, a certain kind of "thin" writing where the thought is insufficiently developed or where the language doesn't really explain what the writing implies or gestures toward. Using the Piagetian model, as Flower does, one can specify the problem as a weakness in audience orientation. Perhaps the writer has immaturely taken too much for granted and unthinkingly assumed that her limited explanations carry as much meaning for readers as they do for herself. The cure or treatment is for the writer to think more about readers.

Through the Vygotskian lens, however, the problem and the "immaturity" look altogether different. Yes, the writing isn't particularly clear or satisfying for readers, but this alternative diagnosis suggests a failure of the private desert island dimension: the writer's explanation is too thin because she didn't work out her train of thought fully enough *for herself*. The suggested cure or treatment is *not* to think more about readers but to think more for herself, to practice exploratory writing in order to learn to engage in that reflective discourse so central to mastery of the writing process. How can she engage readers more till she has engaged herself more?

The current emphasis on audience awareness may be particularly strong now for being fueled by *both* psychological models. From one side, the Piagetians say, in effect, "The egocentric little critters, we've got to *socialize* 'em! Ergo, make them think about audience when they write!" From the other side, the Vygotskians say, in effect, "No wonder they're having trouble writing. They've been bamboozled by the Piagetian heresy. They think they're solitary individuals with private selves when really they're just congeries of voices that derive from their discourse community. Ergo, let's intensify the social context — use peer groups and publication: make them think about audience when they write! (And while we're at it, let's hook them up with a better class of discourse community.)" To advocate ignoring audience is to risk getting caught in the crossfire from two opposed camps.

Two Models of Discourse: Discourse as Communication and Discourse as Poesis or Play

We cannot talk about writing without at least implying a psychological or developmental model. But we'd better make sure it's a complex, paradoxical, or spiral model. Better yet, we should be deft enough to use two contrary models or lenses. (Bruner pictures the developmental process as a complex movement in an upward reiterative spiral — not a simple movement in one direction.)

According to one model, it is characteristic of the youngest children to direct their discourse to an audience. They learn discourse *because* they have an audience; without an audience they remain mute, like "the wild child." Language is social from the start. But we need the other model to show us what is also true, namely that it is characteristic of the youngest children to use language in a *nonsocial* way. They use language not only because people talk to them but also because they have such a strong propensity to play and to build — often in a *nonsocial* or non-audience-oriented fashion. Thus although one paradigm for discourse is social communication, another is private exploration or solitary play. Babies and toddlers tend to babble in an exploratory and reflective way — to themselves and not to an audience — often even with no one else near. This archetypally private use of discourse is strikingly illustrated when we see a pair of toddlers in "parallel play" alongside each other — each busily talking but not at all trying to communicate with the other.

Therefore, when we choose paradigms for discourse, we should think not only about children using language to communicate, but also about children building sandcastles or drawing pictures. Though children characteristically show their castles or pictures to others, they just as characteristically trample or crumple them before anyone else can see them. Of course sculptures and pictures are different from words. Yet discourse implies more media than words; and even if you restrict discourse to words, one of our most mature uses of language is for building verbal pictures and structures for their own sake — not just for communicating with others.

Consider this same kind of behavior at the other end of the life cycle: Brahms staggering from his deathbed to his study to rip up a dozen or more completed but unpublished and unheard string quartets that dissatisfied him. How was he relating to audience here — worrying too much about audience or not giving a damn? It's not easy to say. Consider Glenn Gould deciding to renounce performances before an audience. He used his private studio to produce recorded performances for an audience, but to produce ones that satisfied *himself* he clearly needed to suppress audience awareness. Consider the more extreme example of Kerouac typing page after page — burning each as soon as he completed it. The language behavior of humans is slippery. Surely we are well advised to avoid positions that say it is "always X" or "essentially Y."

James Britton makes a powerful argument that the "making" or poesis function of language grows out of the expressive function. Expressive language is often for the sake of communication with an audience, but just as often it is only for the sake of the speaker — working something out for herself (66–67, 74ff). Note also that "writing to learn," which writing-across-the-curriculum programs are discovering to be so important, tends to be writing for the self or even for no one at all rather than for an outside reader. You throw away the writing, often unread, and keep the mental changes it has engendered.

I hope this emphasis on the complexity of the developmental process — the limits of our models and of our understanding of it — will serve as a rebuke to the tendency to label students as being at a lower stage of cognitive development just because they don't yet write well. (Occasionally they *do* write well — in a way — but not in the way that the labeler finds appropriate.) Obviously the psychologistic labeling impulse started out charitably. Shaughnessy was fighting those who called basic writers *stupid* by saying they weren't dumb, just at an earlier developmental stage. Flower was arguing that writer-based prose is a natural response to a cognitive overload and indeed developmentally enabling. But this kind of talk can be dangerous since it labels students as literally "retarded" and makes teachers and administrators start to think of them as such. Instead of calling poor writers *either* dumb or slow (two forms of blaming the victim), why not simply call them poor writers? If years of schooling haven't yet made them good writers, perhaps they haven't gotten the kind of teaching and support they need. Poor students are often deprived of the very thing they need most to write well (which is given to good students): lots of extended and adventuresome writing for self and for audience. Poor students are often asked to write *only* answers to fill-in exercises.

As children get older, the developmental story remains complex or spiral. Though the first model makes us notice that babies start out with a natural gift for using language in a social and communicative fashion, the second model makes us notice that children and adolescents must continually learn to relate their discourse better to an audience — must struggle to decenter better. And though the second model makes us notice that babies also start out with a natural gift for using language in a *private,* exploratory and playful way, the first model makes us notice that children and adolescents must continually learn to master this solitary, desert island, poesis mode better. Thus we mustn't think of language only as communication — nor allow communication to claim dominance either as the earliest or as the most "mature" form of discourse. It's true that language is inherently communicative (and without communication we don't develop language), yet language is just as inherently the stringing together of exploratory discourse for the self — or for the creation of objects (play, poesis, making) for their own sake.

In considering this important poesis function of language, we need not discount (as Berkenkotter does) the striking testimony of so many witnesses who think and care most about language: professional poets, writers, and philosophers. Many of them maintain that their most serious work is *making,* not *communicating,* and that their commitment is to language, reality, logic, experience, not to readers. Only in their willingness to cut loose from the demands or needs of readers, they insist, can they do their best work. Here is William Stafford on this matter:

> I don't want to overstate this . . . but . . . my impulse is to say I don't think of an audience at all. When I'm writing, the satisfactions in the process of writing are my satisfactions in dealing with the language, in being surprised by phrasings that occur to me, in finding that this miraculous kind of convergent focus begins to happen. That's my satisfaction, and to think about an audience would be a distraction. I try to keep from thinking about an audience. (Cicotello 176)

And Chomsky:

> I can be using language in the strictest sense with no intention of communicating. . . . As a graduate student, I spent two years writing a lengthy manuscript, assuming throughout that it would never be published or read by anyone. I meant everything I wrote, intending nothing as to what anyone would [understand], in fact taking it for granted that there would be no audience. . . . [Communication is only one function of language, and by no means an essential one. (Qtd. in Feldman 5–6)

It's interesting to see how poets come together with philosophers on this point — and even with mathematicians. All are emphasizing the "poetic" function of language in its literal sense — "poesis" as "making." They describe their writing process as more like "getting something right" or even "solving a problem" for its own sake than as communicating with readers or addressing an audience. The task is not to satisfy readers but to satisfy the rules of the system: "[T]he writer is not thinking of a reader at all; he makes it 'clear' as a contract with *language*" (Goodman 164).

Shall we conclude, then, that solving an equation or working out a piece of symbolic logic is at the opposite end of the spectrum from communicating with readers or addressing an audience? No. To draw that conclusion would be a fall again into a one-sided position. Sometimes people write mathematics *for* an audience, sometimes not. The central point in this essay is that we cannot answer audience questions in an *a priori* fashion based on the "nature" of discourse or of language or of cognition — only in terms of the different *uses* or *purposes* to which humans put discourse, language, or cognition on different occasions. If most people have a restricted repertoire of uses for writing — if most people use writing only to send messages to readers, that's no argument for constricting the *definition* of writing. It's an argument for helping people expand their repertoire of uses.

The value of learning to ignore audience while writing, then, is the value of learning to cultivate the private dimension: the value of writing in order to make meaning to oneself, not just to others. This involves learning to free oneself (to some extent, anyway) from the enormous power exerted by society and others, to unhook oneself from external prompts and social stimuli. We've grown accustomed to theorists and writing teachers puritanically stressing the *problem* of writing: the tendency to neglect the needs of readers because we usually write in solitude. But let's also celebrate this same feature of writing as one of its glories: writing *invites* disengagement too, the inward turn of mind, and the dialogue with self. Though writing is deeply social and though we usually help things by enhancing its social dimension, writing is also the mode of discourse best suited to helping us develop the reflective and private dimension of our mental lives.

"But Wait a Minute, ALL Discourse Is Social"

Some readers who see *all* discourse as social will object to my opposition between public and private writing (the "trap of oppositional thinking") and insist that *there is no such thing as private discourse*. What looks like private, solitary mental work, they would say, is really social. Even on the desert island I am in a crowd.

> By ignoring audience in the conventional sense, we return to it in another sense. What I get from Vygotsky and Bakhtin is the notion that audience is not really out there at all but is in fact "always already" (to use that poststructuralist mannerism . . .) inside, interiorized in the conflicting languages of others — parents, former teachers, peers, prospective readers, whomever — that writers have to negotiate to write, and that we do negotiate when we write whether we're aware of it or not. The audience we've got to satisfy in order to feel good about our writing is as much in the past as in the present or future. But we experience it (it's so internalized) as *ourselves*. (Trimbur)

(Ken Bruffee likes to quote from Frost: " 'Men work together, . . . / Whether they work together or apart' " ['The Tuft of Flowers']). Or — putting it slightly differently — when I engage in what seems like private non-audience-directed writing, I am really engaged in communication with the "audience of self." For the self is multiple, not single, and discourse to self is communication from one entity to another. As Feldman argues, "The self functions as audience in much the same way that others do" (290).

Suppose I accept this theory that all discourse is really social — including what I've been calling "private writing" or writing I don't intend to show to any reader. Suppose I agree that all language is essentially communication directed toward an audience — whether some past internalized voice or (what may be the same thing) some aspect of the self. What would this theory say to my interest in "private writing"?

The theory would seem to destroy my main argument. It would tell me that there's no such thing as "private writing"; it's impossible *not* to address audience; there are no vacations from audience. But the theory might try to console me by saying not to worry, because we don't *need* vacations from audience. Addressing audience is as easy, natural, and unaware as breathing — and we've been at it since the cradle. Even young, unskilled writers are already expert at addressing audiences.

But if we look closely we can see that in fact this theory doesn't touch my central practical argument. For even if all discourse is naturally addressed to *some* audience, it's not naturally addressed to the *right* audience — the living readers we are actually trying to reach. Indeed the pervasiveness of past audiences in our heads is one more reason for the difficulty of reaching present audiences with our texts. Thus even if I concede the theoretical point, there still remains an enormous practical and phenomenological difference between writing "public" words for others to read and writing "private" words for no one to read.

Even if "private writing" is "deep down" social, the fact remains that, as we engage in it, we don't have to worry about whether it works on readers or even makes sense. We can refrain from doing all the things that audience-awareness advocates advise us to do ("keeping our audience in mind as we write" and trying to "decenter"). Therefore this social-discourse theory doesn't undermine the benefits of "private writing" and thus provides no support at all for the traditional rhetorical advice that we should "always try to think about (intended) audience as we write."

In fact this social-discourse theory reinforces two subsidiary arguments I have been making. First, even if there is no getting away from *some* audience, we can get relief from an inhibiting audience by writing to a more inviting one. Second, audience problems don't come only from *actual* audiences but also from phantom "audiences in the head" (Elbow, *Writing with Power* 186ff). Once we learn how to be more aware of the effects of both external and internal readers and how to direct our words elsewhere, we can get out of the shadow even of a troublesome phantom reader.

And even if all our discourse is *directed to* or *shaped by* past audiences or voices, it doesn't follow that our discourse is *well directed to* or *successfully shaped for* those audiences or voices. Small children *direct* much talk to others, but that doesn't mean they always *suit* their talk to others. They often fail. When adults discover that a piece of their writing has been "heavily shaped" by some audience, this is bad news as much as good: often the writing is crippled by defensive moves that try to fend off criticism from this reader.

As teachers, particularly, we need to distinguish and emphasize "private writing" in order to teach it, to teach that crucial cognitive capacity to engage in extended and productive thinking that doesn't depend on audience prompts or social stimuli. It's sad to see so many students who can reply to live voices but cannot engage in productive dialogue with voices in their heads. Such students often lose interest in an issue that had intrigued them — just because they don't find other people who are interested in talking about it and haven't learned to talk reflectively to *themselves* about it.

For these reasons, then, I believe my main argument holds force even if I accept the theory that all discourse is social. But, perhaps more tentatively, I resist this theory. I don't know all the data from developmental linguistics, but I cannot help suspecting that babies engage in *some* private poesis — or "play-language" — some private babbling in addition to social babbling. Of course Vygotsky must be right when he points to so much social language in children, but can we really trust him when he denies *all* private or nonsocial language (which Piaget and Chomsky see)? I am always suspicious when someone argues for the total nonexistence of a certain kind of behavior or event. Such an argument is almost invariably an act of definitional aggrandizement, not empirical searching. To say that *all* language is social is to flop over into the opposite one-sidedness that we need Vygotsky's model to save us from.

And even if all language is *originally* social, Vygotsky himself emphasizes how "inner speech" becomes more individuated and private as the child matures. "[Egocentric speech is relatively accessible in three-year-olds but quite inscrutable in seven-year-olds: the older the child, the more thoroughly has his thought become inner speech" (Emerson 254; see also Vygotsky 134). "The inner speech of the adult represents his 'thinking for himself' rather than social adaptation. . . . Out of context, it would be incomprehensible to others because it omits to mention what is obvious to the 'speaker' " (Vygotsky 18).

I also resist the theory that all private writing is really communication with the "*audience of self*." ("When we represent the objects of our thought in language, we intend to make use of these representations at a later time. . . . [T]he speaker-self must have audience directed intentions toward a listener-self" [Feldman 289].) Of course private language often *is* a communication with the audience of self:

- When we make a shopping list. (It's obvious when we can't decipher that third item that we're confronting *failed* communication with the self.)

- When we make a rough draft for ourselves but not for others' eyes. Here we are seeking to clarify our thinking with the leverage that comes from standing outside and reading our own utterance as audience — experiencing our discourse as receiver instead of as sender.

- When we experience ourselves as slightly split. Sometimes we experience ourselves as witness to ourselves and hear our own words from the outside — sometimes with great detachment, as on some occasions of pressure or stress.

But there are other times when private language is *not* communication with audience of self:

- Freewriting to no one: for the *sake* of self but not *to* the self. The goal is not to communicate but to follow a train of thinking or feeling to see where it leads. In doing this kind of freewriting (and many people have not learned it), you don't particularly plan to come back and read what you've written. You just write along and the written product falls away to be ignored, while only the "real product" — any new perceptions, thoughts, or feelings produced in the mind by the freewriting — is saved and looked at again. (It's not that you don't experience your words *at all* but you experience them only as speaker, sender, or emitter — not as receiver or audience. To say that's the same as being audience is denying the very distinction between "speaker" and "audience.")

  As this kind of freewriting actually works, it often *leads* to writing we look at. That is, we freewrite along to no one, following discourse in hopes of getting somewhere, and then at a certain point we often sense that we have *gotten* somewhere: we can tell (but not because we stop and read) that what we are now writing seems new or intriguing or important. At this point we may stop writing; or we may keep on writing, but in a new audience-relationship, realizing that we *will* come back to this passage and read it as audience. Or we may take a new sheet (symbolizing the new audience-relationship) and try to write out for ourselves what's interesting.

- Writing as exorcism is a more extreme example of private writing *not* for the audience of self. Some people have learned to write in order to get rid of thoughts or feelings. By freewriting what's obsessively going round and round in our head we can finally let it go and move on.

I am suggesting that some people (and especially poets and freewriters) engage in a kind of discourse that Feldman, defending what she calls a "communication-intention" view, has never learned and thus has a hard time imagining and understanding. Instead of always using language in an audience-directed fashion for the sake of communication, these writers unleash language for its own sake and let *it* function a bit on its own, without much *intention* and without much need for *communication,* to see where it leads — and thereby end up with some intentions and potential communications they didn't have before.

It's hard to turn off the audience-of-self in writing — and thus hard to imagine writing to no one (just as it's hard to turn off the audience of *outside* readers when writing an audience-directed piece). Consider "invisible writing" as an intriguing technique that helps you become less of an audience-of-self for your writing. Invisible writing prevents you from seeing what you have written: you write on a computer with the screen turned down, or you write with a spent ballpoint pen on paper with carbon paper and another sheet underneath. Invisible writing tend to get people not only to write faster than they normally do, but often better (see Blau). I mean to be tentative about this slippery issue of whether we can really stop being audience to our own discourse, but I cannot help drawing the following conclusion: just as in freewriting, suppressing the *other* as audience tends to enhance quantity and sometimes even quality of writing; so in invisible writing, suppressing the *self* as audience tends to enhance quantity and sometimes even quality.

Contraries in Teaching

So what does all this mean for teaching? It means that we are stuck with two contrary tasks. On the one hand, we need to help our students enhance the social dimension of writing: to learn to be *more* aware of audience, to decenter better and learn to fit their discourse better to the needs of readers. Yet it is every bit as important to help them learn the private dimension of writing: to learn to be *less* aware of audience, to put audience needs aside, to use discourse in the desert island mode. And if we are trying to advance contraries, we must be prepared for paradoxes.

For instance if we emphasize the social dimension in our teaching (for example, by getting students to write to each other, to read and comment on each other's writing in pairs and groups, and by staging public discussions and even debates on the topics they are to write about), we will obviously help the social, public, communicative dimension of writing — help students experience writing not just as jumping through hoops for a grade but rather as taking part in the life of a community of discourse. But "social discourse" can also help private writing by getting students sufficiently involved or invested in an issue so that they finally want to carry on producing discourse alone and in private — and for themselves.

Correlatively, if we emphasize the private dimension in our teaching (for example, by using lots of private exploratory writing, freewriting, and journal writing and by helping students realize that of course they may need practice with this "easy" mode of discourse before they can use it fruitfully), we will obviously help students learn to write better reflectively for themselves without the need for others to interact with. Yet this private discourse can also help public, social writing — help students finally feel full enough of their *own* thoughts to have some genuine desire to *tell* them to others. Students often feel they "don't have anything to say" until they finally succeed in engaging themselves in private desert island writing for themselves alone.

Another paradox: whether we want to teach greater audience awareness or the ability to ignore audience, we must help students learn not only to "try harder" but also to "just relax." That is, sometimes students fail to produce reader-based prose because they don't *try* hard enough to think about audience needs. But sometimes the problem is cured if they just relax and write *to* people — as though in a letter or in talking to a trusted adult. By unclenching, they effortlessly call on social discourse skills of immense sophistication. Sometimes, indeed, the problem is cured if the student simply writes in a more social *setting* — in a classroom where it is habitual to share lots of writing. Similarly, sometimes students can't produce sustained private discourse because they don't try hard enough to keep the pen moving and forget about readers. They must persist and doggedly push aside those feelings of, "My head is empty, I have run out of anything to say." But sometimes what they need to learn through all that persistence is how to relax and let go — to unclench.

As teachers, we need to think about what it means to *be an audience* rather than just be a teacher, critic, assessor, or editor. If our only response is to tell students what's strong, what's weak, and how to improve it (diagnosis, assessment, and advice), we actually *undermine* their sense of writing as a social act. We reinforce their sense that writing means doing school exercises, producing for authorities what they already know — *not* actually trying to say things to readers. To help students experience us as *audience* rather than as assessment machines, it helps to respond by "replying" (as in a letter) rather than always "giving feedback."

Paradoxically enough, one of the best ways teachers can help students learn to turn off audience awareness and write in the desert island mode — to turn off the babble of outside voices in the head and listen better to quiet inner voices — is to be a special kind of private audience to them, to be a reader who nurtures by trusting and believing in the writer. Britton has drawn attention to the importance of teacher as "trusted adult" for school children (67–68). No one can be good at private, reflective writing without some *confidence and trust in self*. A nurturing reader can give a writer a kind of permission to forget about other readers or to be one's own reader. I have benefited from this special kind of audience and have seen it prove useful to others. When I had a teacher who believed in me, who was interested in me and interested in what I had to say, I wrote well. When I had a teacher who thought I was naive, dumb, silly, and in need of being "straightened out," I wrote badly and sometimes couldn't write at all. Here is an interestingly paradoxical instance of the social-to-private principle from Vygotsky and Meade: we learn to listen better and more trustingly to *ourselves* through interaction with trusting *others*.

Look for a moment at lyric poets as paradigm writers (instead of seeing them as aberrant), and see how they heighten *both* the public and private dimensions of writing. Bakhtin says that lyric poetry implies "the absolute certainty of the listener's sympathy" (113). I think it's more helpful to say that lyric poets learn to create more than usual privacy in which to write *for themselves* — and then they turn around and let *others overhear*. Notice how poets tend to argue for the importance of no-audience writing, yet they are especially gifted at being public about what they produce in private. Poets are revealers — sometimes even grandstanders or showoffs. Poets illustrate the need for opposite or paradoxical or double audience skills: on the one hand, the ability to be private and solitary and tune out others — to write only for oneself and not give a damn about readers, yet on the other hand, the ability to be more than usually interested in audience and even to be a ham.

If writers really need these two audience skills, notice how bad most conventional schooling is on both counts. Schools offer virtually no privacy for writing: everything students write is collected and read by a teacher, a situation so ingrained students will tend to complain if you don't collect and read every word they write. Yet on the other hand, schools characteristically offer little or no social dimension for writing. It is *only* the teacher who reads, and students seldom feel that in giving their writing to a teacher they are actually communicating something they really want to say to a real person. Notice how often they are happy to turn in to teachers something perfunctory and fake that they would be embarrassed to show to classmates. Often they feel shocked and insulted if we want to distribute to classmates the assigned writing they hand in to us. (I think of Richard Wright's realization that the naked white prostitutes didn't bother to cover themselves when he brought them coffee as a black bellboy because they didn't really think of him as a man or even a person.) Thus the conventional school setting for writing tends to be the least private and the least public — when what students need, like all of us, is practice in writing that is the most private and also the most public.

Practical Guidelines about Audience

The theoretical relationships between discourse and audience are complex and paradoxical, but the practical morals are simple:

1. Seek ways to heighten both the *public* and *private* dimensions of writing. (For activities, see the previous section.)

2. When working on important audience-directed writing, we must try to emphasize audience awareness *sometimes*. A useful rule of thumb is to start by putting the readers in mind and carry on as long as things go well. If difficulties arise, try putting readers out of mind and write either to no audience, to self, or to an inviting audience. Finally, always *revise* with readers in mind. (Here's another occasion when orthodox advice about writing is wrong — but turns out right if applied to revising.)

3. Seek ways to heighten awareness of one's writing process (through process writing and discussion) to get better at taking control and deciding when to keep readers in mind and when to ignore them. Learn to discriminate factors like these:

   a. The writing task. Is this piece of writing *really* for an audience? More often than we realize, it is not. It is a draft that only we will see, though the final version will be for an audience; or exploratory writing for figuring something out; or some kind of personal private writing meant only for ourselves.

   b. Actual readers. When we put them in mind, are we helped or hindered?

   c. One's own temperament. Am I the sort of person who tends to think of what to say and how to say it when I keep readers in mind? Or someone (as I am) who needs long stretches of forgetting all about readers?

   d. Has some powerful "audience-in-the-head" tricked me into talking to it when I'm really trying to talk to someone else — distorting new business into old business? (I may be an inviting teacher-audience to my students, but they may not be able to pick up a pen without falling under the spell of a former, intimidating teacher.)

   e. Is *double audience* getting in my way? When I write a memo or report, I probably have to suit it not only to my "target audience" but also to some colleagues or supervisor. When I write something for publication, it must be right for readers, but it won't be published unless it is also right for the editors — and if it's a book it won't be much read unless it's right for reviewers. Children's stories won't be bought unless they are right for editors and reviewers *and* parents. We often tell students to write to a particular "real-life" audience — or to peers in the class — but of course they are also writing for us as graders. (This problem is more common as more teachers get interested in audience and suggest "second" audiences.)

   f. Is *teacher-audience* getting in the way of my students' writing? As teachers we must often read in an odd fashion: in stacks of 25 or 50 pieces all on the same topic; on topics we know better than the writer; not for pleasure or learning but to grade or find problems (see Elbow, *Writing with Power* 216–36).

To list all these audience pitfalls is to show again the need for thinking about audience needs — yet also the need for vacations from readers to think in peace.

Note

[1]There are many different entities called audience: (a) The actual readers to whom the text will be given; (b) the writer's conception of those readers — which may be mistaken (see Ong; Park; Ede and Lunsford); (c) the audience that the text implies — which may be different still (see Booth); (d) the discourse community or even genre addressed or implied by the text (see Walzer); (e) ghost or phantom "readers in the head" that the writer may unconsciously address or try to please (see Elbow, *Writing with Power* 186ff. Classically, this is a powerful former teacher. Often such an audience is so ghostly as not to show up as actually "implied" by the text). For the essay I am writing here, these differences don't much matter: I'm celebrating the ability to put aside the needs or demands of *any* or all of these audiences. I recognize, however, that we sometimes cannot fight our way free of unconscious or tacit audiences (as in b or e above) unless we bring them to greater conscious awareness.

Works Cited

Bakhtin, Mikhail. "Discourse in Life and Discourse in Poetry." Appendix. *Freudianism: A Marxist Critique.* By F. N. Volosinov. Trans. I. R. Titunik. Ed. Neal H. Bruss. New York: Academic, 1976. (Holquist's attribution of this work to Bakhtin is generally accepted.)

Berkenkotter, Carol, and Donald Murray. "Decisions and Revisions: The Planning Strategies of a Publishing Writer and the Response of Being a Rat — or Being Protocoled." *College Composition and Communication* 34 (1983): 156–72.

Blau, Sheridan. "Invisible Writing." *College Composition and Communication* 34 (1983): 297–312.

Booth, Wayne. *The Rhetoric of Fiction.* Chicago: U Chicago P, 1961.

Britton, James. *The Development of Writing Abilities, 11–18.* Urbana: NCTE, 1977.

Bruffee, Kenneth A. "Liberal Education and the Social Justification of Belief." *Liberal Education* 68 (1982): 95–114.

Bruner, Jerome. *Beyond the Information Given: Studies in the Psychology of Knowing.* Ed. Jeremy Anglin. New York: Norton, 1973.

_____. *On Knowing: Essays for the Left Hand.* Expanded ed. Cambridge: Harvard UP, 1979.

Chomsky, Noam. *Reflections on Language.* New York: Random, 1975.

Cicotello, David M. "The Art of Writing: An Interview with William Stafford." *College Composition and Communication* 34 (1983): 173–77.

Clarke, Jennifer, and Peter Elbow. "Desert Island Discourse: On the Benefits of Ignoring Audience." *The Journal Book.* Ed. Toby Fulwiler. Montclair: Boynton, 1987.

Cooper, Anthony Ashley, 3rd Earl of Shaftesbury. *Characteristics of Men, Manners, Opinions, Times, Etc.* Ed. John M. Robertson. 2 vols. Gloucester, MA: Smith, 1963.

Ede, Lisa, and Andrea Lunsford. "Audience Addressed/Audience Invoked: The Role of Audience in Composition Theory and Pedagogy." *College Composition and Communication* 35 (1984): 140–54.

Elbow, Peter. *Writing with Power.* New York: Oxford UP, 1981.

_____. *Writing without Teachers.* New York: Oxford UP, 1973.

Emerson, Caryl. "The Outer Word and Inner Speech: Bakhtin, Vygotsky, and the Internalization of Language." *Critical Inquiry* 10 (1983): 245–64.

Feldman, Carol Fleisher. "Two Functions of Language." *Harvard Education Review* 47 (1977): 282–93.

Flower, Linda. "Writer-Based Prose: A Cognitive Basis for Problems in Writing," *College English* 41 (1979): 19–37.

Goodman, Paul. *Speaking and Language: Defense of Poetry.* New York: Random, 1972.

Griffin, Susan. "The Internal Voices of Invention: Shaftesbury's Soliloquy." Unpublished. 1986.

Lawrence, D. H. *Studies in Classic American Literature.* Garden City: Doubleday, 1951.

Ong, Walter. "The Writer's Audience Is Always a Fiction." *PMLA* 90 (1975): 9–21.

Park, Douglas B. "The Meanings of 'Audience.' " *College English* 44 (1982): 247–57.

Perl, Sondra. "Guidelines for Composing." Appendix A. *Through Teachers' Eyes: Portraits of Writing Teachers at Work.* By Sondra Perl and Nancy Wilson. Portsmouth: Heinemann, 1986.

Progoff, Ira. *At a Journal Workshop.* New York: Dialogue, 1975.

Shaughnessy, Mina. *Errors and Expectations: A Guide for the Teacher of Basic Writing.* New York: Oxford UP, 1977.

Trimbur, John. Letter to the author. September 1985.

_____. "Beyond Cognition: Voices in Inner Speech." Forthcoming in *Rhetoric Review.*

Vygotsky, L. S. *Thought and Language.* Trans. and ed. E. Hanfmann and G. Vakar. 1934. Cambridge: MIT P, 1962.

Walzer, Arthur E. "Articles from the 'California Divorce Project': A Case Study of the Concept of Audience." *College Composition and Communication* 36 (1985): 150–59.

Wright, Richard. *Black Boy.* New York: Harper, 1945.

I benefited from much help from audiences in writing various drafts of this piece. I am grateful to Jennifer Clarke, with whom I wrote a collaborative piece containing a case study on this subject. I am also grateful for extensive feedback from Pat Belanoff, Paul Connolly, Sheryl Fontaine, John Trimbur, and members of the Martha's Vineyard Summer Writing Seminar.

Elbow's Insights as a Resource for Your Teaching

1. I'm sure you recognize the value of the "desert island mode" that Elbow discusses. Demonstrate to your students how valuable such private writing is to you by discussing how you have kept a journal or notebook and when you used it as a resource. Encourage your students to write a journal entry on any experience they had with writing entirely for themselves and without the distraction of a reader. A standard technique writing instructors use both to respect the "personal" in personal writing and to encourage private reflection is to require that students write daily but to give students the option of stapling together any entries that were not written with an outside reader in mind.

2. Try Elbow's recommendation to turn off the screen while writing with a computer and report to your class what happened to you when you ignored audience as you generated some writing. The authors of *The Bedford Guide for College Writers* recommend this exercise in "Strategies for Writing with a Computer" in Chapter 20 to help writers from becoming too self-conscious about tapping the resource of imagination and thus triggering a "writing block." Their concern there is clearly parallel to Elbow's concern about premature self-consciousness about audience.

Elbow's Insights as a Resource for the Writing Classroom

1. Elbow's "ghost reader" — a student's sense of an inflexible teacher-as-evaluator — surfaces frequently in early essays from first-year writers and most often in "diagnostic" essays written the first week. Photocopy a few samples of writing where the ghost reader clearly frightened the writer into dense or unclear or stuffy or inauthentic prose. Ask the class to decide where "thinking too much about the 'ghost teacher as reader' got in the way" and to suggest ways to exorcise the ghost reader.

2. Encourage the "desert island mode" by asking students to close their eyes and open their ears while you play something calming like Pachelbel's Canon in D Major or Albinoni's Adagio or some recent space or new age music. After five minutes, ask them to freewrite for twenty minutes. Repeat this technique several times during the semester; tell the writers that this sequence is for their private writing. Observe whether all writers are freewriting, but don't collect or read the writing. Will some students bluff you? Inevitably a few will waste the opportunity, but worry more about the writers who need some modeling of ways to move into self-discourse.

3. Ask students to supplement the discussion of "Setting Up Circumstances" in Chapter 16, "Strategies for Drafting," by describing, either in journal entries or a brainstorming session, ways they have set up their own circumstances for writing from imagination and for self-reflection.

PURPOSE

Easily the most frequent question posed to writers — by writers themselves, by peer readers, by a writing instructor, or by the instructor in another discipline who has requested student writing — is "Why are you doing this?" or "What are you after here?" Other synonyms abound — thesis, research question, controlling idea, focus — but readers and writers all assume that writing is generated from, informed by, and revised according to the *purpose* of the writing. The literature on purpose is extensive, both in textbooks and in scholarly books and journals of composition studies. The essay written by Linda Flower for *College English* presents an excellent introduction to current thought about and research into ways of talking about purpose.

THE CONSTRUCTION OF PURPOSE IN WRITING AND READING

Linda Flower

Linda Flower has puzzled over purpose in a new way. Most discussion of purpose in rhetoric and composition studies assumes that writers come to the writing process with a purpose, whether they generated it or were compelled to adopt it by writing assessments, class assignments, or directions for completing job and grant applications. Flower explores how writers — and then readers — construct purpose in the processes of writing and reading a text. She describes her purpose in this essay as the complementing of social/cultural and textual views of purpose with a "cognitive view of reading and writing as rhetorical acts" for a "more integrated theory."

Flower emphasizes that we can recognize in a text the purposeful process of a writer at work, but she demonstrates through the use of "protocol analysis" that a writer at work proceeds in a less orderly, linear, and controlled manner than the final text demonstrates. By looking at transcripts of writers "thinking out loud" about what they do as they generate and shape a draft, Flower concludes that writers construct "a web of purposes" and create a "multidimensional network of information — a web that radiates in all directions, anchored to points unknown."

The web of purposes cannot be fully recovered from a text; making assumptions about purpose from only the evidence of the text creates problems for readers, as contemporary literary criticism reminds us. A text can be generated from private intentions that the readers never know; those intentions can govern the text for both the writer and the reader.

Because a writer works with a web of purposes, a text may be affected by intentions the writer has not or may not be able to complete. Often, perceptive readers can see those intentions and assist the writer to better understand those intentions and to "realize" them. You'll find yourself describing to a writer in a conference what you infer as the "purpose" or as perhaps conflicting purposes of the draft you've read. Peer editors often advise writers about what, despite the formal statement of purpose they met, seems to be the "real purpose" or the writer's main interest in the text.

In her discussion of a web of purposes, Flower rejects sharp distinctions of intentional/ unintentional and of conscious/unconscious and uses metaphors that honor many ways of knowing. When a student complains, "Well, I know what I think but I don't know how to say it on paper," she would agree and would suggest a variety of strategies for reclaiming what that writer "knows."

Flower reports from research conducted with colleagues that a writer working with a web of purposes inevitably constructs purpose for a text through an ongoing process of planning, setting goals, and changing plans and goals as a text emerges. Flower emphasizes

that "expert writers" in these actions of constructing a purpose create "more richly elabo-
rated networks" and link "these plans and goals into a more fully integrated, coherent
structure." From this network the writer accepts, or discovers, or recovers, the rhetorical
purpose that informs the draft.

Flower's understanding of these planning processes prompted her to ask what readers
are doing as they construct in their minds some meaning from a text. The "reading protocols"
that Flower cites and analyzes demonstrate that experienced or "expert" readers use a
rhetorical reading strategy in their process of constructing meaning. They infer from the web
of purposes surrounding the text as well as from the text and individual parts of the whole text
and they shape an interpretation.

Flower emphasizes that use of a rhetorical reading strategy has great power for stu-
dents. She cites examples of readers who refused to give up the meaning they constructed
from their inferences about the author's purpose even when parts of the text directly contra-
dicted their constructed meaning. Often in literature courses or in class discussions prompted
by reading, you'll encounter students who are very confident about their interpretation of a
text. Leading them to review their interpretation in the light of a more complex rhetorical
reading and of "community response" to the text is much like the process of assisting a
student writer to revise more deeply. In both circumstances, the students are actively con-
structing meaning, even if their "texts" are not fully processed.

I infer from Flower's essay that such readers are "in process" and may become more
expert readers who use a rhetorical reading strategy not just to defend an early impression or
personal bias but also to resolve comprehension problems. She speculates that rhetorical
reading is both an "expert" strategy that first-year writers don't use and an important
strategy for constructing a meaningful interpretation. She suggests that rhetorical reading
may also help readers — and I would add writers-as-readers — to infer key, unstated claims
or informing assumptions of a text.

Flower calls for more research and reflection on reading as "a constructive cognitive
process and a rhetorical event in which readers use their knowledge of human purposes to
build a meaningful and coherent text." Such a discussion of reading should be particularly
useful for teaching peer evaluation strategies, and for working with Chapter 3, "Writing from
Reading," as well as "Generating Ideas" and "Planning, Drafting, and Developing" in
Chapter 27, "Writing from Library Research."

Purpose is problematic. Everyone agrees that it is an admirable thing: we encourage students to "have" one and we are justly impatient with texts that don't. However, our traditional ways of talking about purpose — as that singular, statable entity one should possess — seem painfully limited. We may question if a simple "authorial" purpose, as Michel Foucault defines it, even exists. We may conclude that the purposes behind any rhetorical or any human act are so multifold, so entangled and even contradictory that in the attempt to describe them, the notion of a willed, intentional act simply evaporates.

The current critical discussion has complicated our definition of purpose in healthy ways, trying to distribute much of the credit for human agency across a larger social and contextual reality. Reflecting its roots in literary criticism, this discussion has focused primarily on literary texts (broadly defined) and has tended to locate purpose either in the text itself or in the social context of the text. However, this analysis leaves us facing an uncomfortable fact: as writers ourselves, laboring over our journal articles, term papers, and love letters, we cannot escape the need to produce purposeful prose — nor do we wish to. As theorists we have not developed equally sensitive ways to describe how an individual writer creates a unique rhetorical purpose for each text he or she writes within the constraints of context. In the end we need a theoretical language that can recognize the shaping power of language and context and still respect and explain individual, human agency.

My interest in contributing to this conversation is motivated by two questions and an observation. The observation first. During the past ten years I have pored over the transcripts of people thinking aloud, watching them struggle not only to plan a paper and affect a reader but to fathom and form their own intentions and construct new meanings. These protocols are only data — a best effort to gather information on what we can't see directly — but they continually impress me with the constructive nature of writers' cognition and with the purposeful, goal-directed nature of such thinking. This raises the question of how such a dynamic situation operates: How do writers come by/find/create their sense of purpose? And are readers at all aware of or affected by this purposeful, sometimes elaborate rhetorical structure the writer labored to construct?

Although I can't answer those questions, I hope this paper is a step in that direction. What I would like to offer is a data-based discussion of the way purpose plays itself out in some of the readers and writers I have observed. My aim is theoretical. I want to use these observations not to test a hypothesis or make a statistically significant claim, but to show how looking closely at the cognition can help us track the *construction* of purpose and can give us a more precise view of one way purpose infuses the thinking process in individual writers and readers.

Talking about Purpose

Cleanth Brooks made it difficult for English professors in good standing to talk about authorial purpose by urging literary critics to beware the intentional fallacy. One should not impute intention to authors by assuming that they had intended the particular "meaning" one reads into a text. A healthy caution. On the other hand, classical and modern rhetorical theory is based on the notion of a rhetor as a purposeful agent in a rhetorical context who seeks through persuasion or identification to affect the minds of others. Likewise, good writing teachers are expected to infer the purpose(s) behind a student's text, to acknowledge even unrealized intentions, and to help develop the student's purpose rather than impose their own. Rhetoric and composition exist in a world of rhetorical purpose. Yet our theory says little about how individual writers fabricate the vigorous personal sense of purpose we value — our textbooks say less. The process of purpose-making in Aristotle is reduced to "stating the case" because the rhetor is presumed to come with a purpose firmly in mind. The intellectual work of invention is devoted to discovering proofs that secure argument. Similarly, Wayne Booth's rhetorical stance is taken on a pre-existing sense of purpose. But what would happen if we stepped behind the scenes and explored how purpose itself is constructed and represented in the mind of the rhetor?

Let me pose, as a case in point, a text I wish to return to later in this discussion. How shall we describe the rhetorical purpose of Stephen Jay Gould's typically multilayered, highly rhetorical introduction to *Ever Since Darwin*?

"One hundred years without Darwin are enough," grumbled the noted American geneticist H. J. Muller in 1959. The remark struck many listeners as a singularly inauspicious way to greet the centenary of the *Origin of Species,* but no one could deny the truth expressed in its frustration.

Why has Darwin been so hard to grasp? Within a decade, he convinced the thinking world that evolution had occurred, but his own theory of natural selection never achieved much popularity during his lifetime. . . . It is widely misunderstood, misquoted, and misapplied. The difficulty can not lie in complexity of logical structure, for the basis of natural selection is simplicity itself — two undeniable facts and an inescapable conclusion. . . . [a five-paragraph discussion of the theory follows]

Thus, Darwin's apparently simple theory is not without its subtle complexities and additional requirements. Nonetheless, I believe that the stumbling block to its acceptance does not lie in any scientific difficulty, but rather in the radical philosophical content of Darwin's message — in its challenge to a set of entrenched Western attitudes we are not yet ready to abandon. (11–12)

Dedicated readers of Stephen Jay Gould know the party line of his larger purpose: we need to understand Darwinian evolution thoroughly and come to terms with our place in a non-human-centered, biological system. But having stated the "purpose" of the text we have not distinguished it from the dozens of other Gould texts on the theme, nor have we achieved any insight into how Gould conceived and fulfilled the purposes he had for his Prologue to this book.

To discuss such purposes with accuracy is difficult because any speech act is highly overdetermined. It is not the result of any single purpose, but the confluence of many. College professors write papers in order to enter the academic community, to get tenure, to sway opinion and change practice, to state the importance of XYZ, and/or because they are compulsive meaning makers and can't help it. In the text itself, a given passage, a key word, or an image of a grumbling geneticist may well be reflecting multiple purposes driven by the demands of content, voice, claims in the making, or the conventions of the discourse — forces that may work in harmony or at complicating cross purposes to one another. In the face of this complexity, we often retreat. The very notion of authorial purpose has received a bad name because it is sometimes equated with simplistic single-liners of the sort, "Dickens wrote *Great Expectations* to show us that . . ." or with equally narrow statements about *the* "theme" or "meaning" of a poem, a symbol, or a powerful line.

However, even though some ways of talking about a writer's purpose are reductive and all ways are necessarily partial, we can't afford to avoid the subject. We need an interactive picture of writing as a purposeful act. Such a picture would include a broad cultural perspective in which purpose is inseparable from the social assumptions that help shape the text — assumptions that are often unexamined and may even seem unreachable. A cultural critic might point out an unexamined purpose of this sort in Gould's insistence that we understand the "great man," Darwin, correctly — a purpose, institutionalized by universities, that justifies academic scholarship. Or one might locate purpose in Gould's attempt to reduce this problem to a conflict within the Western belief system — a purpose that cultural critics have themselves valorized and institutionalized.

Our discussion of rhetorical purpose might also include a more text-based analysis such as Kenneth Burke's description of form as the "arousing and fulfillment of desires" (*Counter-Statement*). Some aspects of the form Burke describes, such as dramatic reversals or careful progressions toward an effect, show the marks of active intentionality and crafting. Other aspects of form, such as beginnings and endings, are so highly conventionalized that they may enter the rhetorical plan without a second thought on the part of the writer. In fact, forms and conventions can so quietly dictate local discourse moves that writers may not realize they have made a "choice." The text may end up being at "cross-purposes" to itself, and the "seams" or disjunctions in the text become a window into multiple but unintegrated rhetorical purposes at work. However, Burke notes that the role of forms and conventions is diminished when one turns from literature to writing in which information becomes more central, as in the texts studied here. As Burke puts it, "atrophy of form follows hypertrophy of information" (144).

Social/cultural and textual views of purpose each uncover distinctive dimensions of the rhetorical purpose embodied in texts. However, each gives us only a limited glimpse and speculative understanding of another part of the picture — the dynamic web of purpose that is constructed by the individual writer during composing. If we are to avoid reducing purpose to the tracks it leaves in text, we need a complementary cognitive view of reading and writing as rhetorical acts. We need a more integrated theory.

Consider the difference between some of the conventions that represent purpose in expository texts and the purposeful process one sees in writers at work. In texts, writers often signal one level of their purpose with a preface, an introductory paragraph, or a problem/purpose statement of the sort that heads this paper. And they may signal the linear plan that organizes the paper with previews, transitions, and indicators of key points and conclusions, as Gould did with "Thus Darwin's apparently simple theory . . ." and "Nonetheless, I believe . . ." When purpose is explicitly marked in a text, it gives the impression of orderly, linear, controlled intentionality and singularity of purpose.

However, when we look at a transcript of a writer thinking, even under the unusual condition of thinking out loud, it is as though we turned the nose of the kaleidoscope. The illusion of order and simplicity is replaced with an initial image of chaos and complexity. Writers at work do not decide on "their purpose" as the textbooks advise; they create a web of purposes. They set goals, toss up possibilities. They may respond to one of those ideas with a negative evaluation, which can lead to new criteria for what they have to do, if only they could figure out how to do it. They think through possible content and leap back into goal setting, generating provisional, tentative ideas of what they want to achieve, working hypotheses that they may soon ditch or even forget. They worry over questions ("Do I want to . . .?"), confusions, and conflicts as a workable plan or cherished goal seems at loggerheads with other goals or a piece of text they don't want to throw away. They create a multidimensional network of information — a web that radiates in all directions, anchored to points unknown.

We need to distinguish between this interconnected body of goals, plans, and criteria writers construct and the topical information they also generate, that is, that pool of ideas and pre-text about their topic that is destined for the page. Even though goals and content are naturally linked, a writer's network of purposes can not be simply equated with (or recovered from) the text. The web may contain many private intentions to which the reader is never privy, even though they quietly govern the text. Likewise writers may hold many intentions that they are unable to realize in text. A young writer trying to instantiate a grandiose plan with limited topic knowledge or only a seventh-grade vocabulary might feel the distinction between intention and text acutely. More important, because this web of purpose is an internal, cognitive construct, it embraces multiple ways of representing meaning. That is, meanings pulled into this web might be represented imagistically or in other nonverbal, structural ways or in episodic memories of experience. For instance, one of my goals is to convey the sense of interconnected goals and cumulative complexity that comes from reading a given protocol — to convey a form of "knowing" familiar to us as literary readers that is not easily expressed in direct statement. Writers' motives might also be mentally represented as parts of a schema or in code words that point to packages of information stored in memory. As John Hayes and I proposed with the "multiple representation hypothesis," this variety of representations with which writers work adds immeasurable richness to the act of planning ("Images, Plans, and Prose"). However, it is also a common source of frustration when it forces writers to translate from one highly personal or marginally verbal representation of meaning to a fully articulated, conventionally coded representation in standard written English.

Like other mental representations, this web of purpose may contain a great deal of nonlogical, unarticulated, associatively linked information. It likely contains tacit knowledge existing below our threshold of conscious awareness and generates thinking processes which have become so automated they require little attention. For instance, the schema for narratives, which most of us have begun to master by age three, specifies a set of highly conventional goals. Having acquired the schema, we can carry out the plan of telling a story almost automatically — there is little need for conscious attention or active planning. However, when our goals become complex (e.g., we want the story subtly to support a point), we may rise to awareness, reflect on our knowledge, and make our purpose and the goals of narrative the subject of active problem solving.

I should note that this view of cognition as a bubbling stew of various mental representations is at odds with some more dichotomous views of thought based on popular Freudianism and its sharp demarcation between conscious and unconscious knowing. Some readers of this paper, for instance, may have reserved the term "intentionality" (versus the more general term "purpose") for those purposes that are consciously held or even fully articulated. However, from a cognitive, process-oriented point of view, intentionality is a far more protean impulse and much harder to pigeonhole. For example, much of the thought that emerges, even in protocols, as goals, criteria, tentative notions, or possible plans is neither logical nor well articulated, even though it is clearly contributing to the web of purpose. Moreover, the threshold of awareness is a constantly moving boundary — knowledge and processes that were operating tacitly often become the subject of increased conscious attention when the situation demands. A cognitive view replaces the dichotomy of conscious/unconscious with metaphors that describe the changing and relative nature of awareness, using concepts such as "depth of processing," "focal and peripheral awareness," and shifting "levels of attention." A sharp distinction between conscious and unconscious seems useful only for talking about the extremes. The cognition this study aspires to understand, then, embraces many kinds of knowing, even though the tracks of that cognition are only that — tracks in the snow from which the event is interpreted.

It should also be clear that this cognitive image of the writer's purpose as a web of intertwined goals, plans, criteria takes issue with other views of purpose many of us have found problematic. The richness of the web argues against a reductive intentional fallacy (e.g., Shakespeare wanted to expose the way Oedipal conflicts can cause . . .), as well as the fallacy of paraphrasable content (e.g., Swift's response to the Irish problem was to propose that . . .), and against the tendency to reduce writers' intentions to single, statable purpose. Even the writer's own after-the-fact interpretations and/or functional "purpose" statements in the text are fragmentary indicators of the purposes that guided composing. However, this metaphor of a web alone does not let us answer the inevitable question: how does this seemingly chaotic process and its multiple networks of purpose ever contribute to an integrated plan and a coherent text? How do writers construct a guiding rhetorical purpose?

Constructing a Plan in Writing

One way to approach these questions is to look closely at the data of what writers do as they plan. Thinking-aloud protocols of writers in the act of composing contain a rich set of traces of cognition. Unlike a retrospective account, they offer an extended concurrent record of shifting content and focus of thought as writers concentrate on the task at hand. The protocol record is typically more detailed and explicit than one a writer could ever recall and is likely to capture conflict, contradictions and abandoned plans generated during the thought process. Protocols also have a number of limitations, as does any method, in that they are a record of that information that has entered the writer's conscious attention to at least the level of fleeting reference. This means that much of the writer's web of purpose (like his or her topic knowledge) remains invisible or can only be inferred. At the same time, when one's research is motivated by education, this limitation itself plays a useful role: it tends to focus observation on those thinking processes that are accessible to reflection and present in all writers, even those who are learning.

In a study of how expert and student writers plan, John R. Hayes, Karen Schriver, Linda Carey, Christina Haas, and I observed what we began to call a *constructive planning process* in which writers actively constructed and integrated a body of goals, plans for meeting those goals, criteria for success, and discoveries and new ideas (Flower et al., "Planning in Writing"). Some of the conclusions from the study are relevant here. In that analysis, the notion of a web was given more concrete form as we mapped out an explicit "working goal network" for each writer based on the data of the protocols. That is, each indication of a goal, plan, or criteria was treated as a node on a network the writer was constructing, a network in which new goals and plans formed multiple links to other nodes in the plan. Tracking the growth and structure of this network let us compare the way writers manage their planning process and describe certain features of the plans they give themselves. This goal network is, of course, a theoretical construct. It reduces complexity (and hence loses information that was actually present). But it throws a spotlight on the dominant, organizing goals and the structure of the plan, and it allows us to see patterns at this level of planning that will help us understand the larger process we can't observe. Three key features of the *constructive planning process* help explain how purpose is "constructed" over the course of writing and how it can lead both to coherent and to wildly fragmented writing plans.

1. Planning is a continuing, unpredictable, and often opportunistic process. Writers may aspire to one-shot planning, but plans often emerge by a stubborn timetable of their own. The process can seem to inch forward through a temporally connected, associative string of ideas. Yet, unlike some venerable libraries in which books are shelved according to the order of acquisition, the goals writers construct in working memory do not form a chain of ideas, organized by the order of appearance, by associations, or by the serendipity that generated an idea. Rather, this web of information has first the character of a network. That is, an individual idea can have multiple links to multiple other nodes or ideas. These links may be associative or causal ones or links of goal to subgoal and so on. We see this network of connections operating in reverse in texts when we notice that a single phrase is realizing multiple, disparate goals. Second, this network has the character of a hierarchy — that is, certain goals from the top-level structure of the network subsume and integrate other goals, plans, and criteria within their compass. As a result, the network that emerges over time is not a temporal log left by the process of invention, but is, to varying degrees, a purposeful, goal-directed structure of information.

The networks created by experienced and student writers in the study mentioned above had some striking differences. The expert networks were far more elaborated; the experienced writers gave themselves a richer rhetorical problem to solve. But elaboration carries a cost: as ideas, plans, and criteria mount so does the problem of organizing and integrating the whole. Experienced writers created networks that were also more integrated at their top levels, thanks in part to planning strategies such as creating subgoals or consolidating the current network into a new plan — a strategy rarely observed in our student writers.

2. The workaday significance of this network lies in its structure and power to guide composing. But the wonder of planning lies in its ability to change. The web of purpose one sees emerging in a protocol is a dynamic structure. It is built and developed, and sometimes radically restructured at even the top levels, as the writer imagines possibilities and responds to new ideas or to his or her own developing text.

3. Although this web of purpose (and the goal network we observe) may remain under construction throughout composing, it helps guide the construction of the text. This relationship between the structure of the plan and the structure of text is as problematic as it is important. An incoherent set of goals is likely to produce an incoherent text on some level. But since the network building process may extend over a series of visions and revisions, maintaining a meaningful hierarchy of one's own goals can be difficult. At other times, the structure of the network itself is not under revision, but different parts of it rise to attention and these foregrounded goals then govern composing, while other, perhaps conflicting, goals stand in the wings.

The following excerpts from the think-aloud transcript of a young graduate student illustrate a few of these features. She is writing notes and later text in response to an assignment that asked her to read various brief statements on the topic of revision, to interpret and synthesize that information, and write her own statement. In these excerpts we can see the interplay between her various readings of what the assignment "intended" and her own goals, interests, tendencies, and earlier plans. [The segmented comments are numbered to indicate location in the protocol. Brief pauses are indicated by dashes and written notes or text are underlined.]

52 Well maybe what I'll try and do is write down what I think of first.

53 Otherwise it will just be picking out the higher points from this paragraph.

54 And I don't know why I think that is wrong to do.

55 I guess I think that I'm supposed to do something original.

56 Ok. Revision—

57 Ok — There's a process — that experienced writers — use.

58 It is a process — that inexperienced — writers may use but not successfully

59 This is making me think of, of one of the things I read was that inexperienced writers jumped into their writing and experienced writers, um, would take a little longer time to plan.

60 I guess if I want to fall in the category of an experienced writer, I should make a little more of a plan myself.

61 Um — the plan that I have made so far is simply to write down either what I know or what I remember from reading this piece about revision.

62 And then I was going to go back and look at the paper and see how my ideas fit into that structure and maybe make an overall new structure myself.

63 I'm going to look at the assignment again. . . .

. . . .

69 I mean because I could just make a real general statement or I could make a more precise one.

70 I don't know — which one.

71 So I'm deciding right now what to do.

72 This is reminding me what the kids I'm teaching might do.

73 They might make more out of the assignment than they are asked to do.

74 [pause] I'm just thinking

75 I guess I'm supposed to say what I'm thinking.

76 I'm thinking about the kids I'm teaching

77 But I'm trying to get my mind back to — uh, the thing I'm trying to write.

. . . .

90 Hmm — I'm wondering if I could write this in a way that it could be used for my students.

91 That's one of the things I was thinking about when I read this was how could I adapt this to be helpful to them.

93 And one of the things that I do when I write is I have to get some overall goal or purpose to write.

94 Um, right now I'm doing it just to make it interesting to myself.

As even these brief excerpts show, this writer has multiple goals on the boil for not only her text but her own writing process. We might also think of these ideas functioning as multiple constraints, in the sense that the final text may have to satisfy a number of these needs simultaneously. Notice too how an association to her own students in Comment 72 (she was an instructor in the freshman course) grows into a reflection, which later emerges in Comment 91 as a possible goal for the paper. That goal, we can infer, might then embed within itself another rich and purposefully structured network of ideas, organized around what she wants her students to know.

The following comments show us another feature of planning. Even though I have stripped away the context for brevity, we can see how goals that had been momentarily pushed to the background as other goals governed composing may reassert themselves. These moments, when forgotten parts of the network rise to attention and demand their say, often lead writers to frustration or to yet another fresh start. But at times they also lead to acts of consolidation which restructure the goal network and let it do justice to the writer's larger web of purpose. [To make this debate among alternative goals easier to follow, I have added italics to key terms in the protocol.]

119

198 Well, I guess I'll just go with this this structure,
199 I don't know what else to do —
200 Umm — So I have my *three points* and I seem to have *three goals for revision.*

. . . .

276 My goal is [rereading the assignment] to make the statement about "the process of revision." — OK —
277 I'm not sure I have the structure right to answer about the *process of revision.*
278 Do I like my structure and talk about the *goals* of revision?
279 Looks like I'm beginning to include some *steps* for revision which I hadn't originally planned on.

. . . .

286 I'm just supposed to write about the *process* it says.
287 Humm — *good versus bad writers* [writes notes]
289 Humm — that's interesting.
290 Now I feel like what I originally started out to write.

. . . .

292 The *process of revision.*
293 I don't necessarily have to compare *good writers to bad writers.*

. . . .

416 No, I don't know how I want this organized —
417 Because if I talk about the three steps,
418 Then that seems to relate to what the good writers do.
419 But I want to talk about what the bad writers do too
420 Because that makes it more vivid what the good writers are doing.

This student writer is more aware, articulate, and given to internal debate than many writers. But she brings into focus some of the features we see in other writers: the tip of the iceberg complexity of some goals (such as "make it interesting to myself"), the way goals (such as adapt this for my students and make it vivid) can operate jointly — as well as the way such goals can come in conflict, and finally, the extended process by which writers construct and reconstruct a purposeful plan for the text. An open-ended task like this clearly calls for goal setting, yet one can observe some of the same features of construction and conflict operating on assigned papers and professional writing, where the constraints may make planning even more problematic.

Let me sum up the argument I have been making so far. Writing, as a rhetorical act, is carried out within a web of purpose. Some aspects of the purposes that guide writing exist in the culture and the conventions a writer uses, and many parts of this web will never rise to conscious attention or be subjected to reflective awareness. However, another part of the writer's purpose is in fact constructed in the act of planning each unique text. Writers build a network of working goals, plans, and criteria and, if planning becomes problematic, even those processes that often operate below awareness, such as making connections, drawing inferences, or responding to familiar cues in the situation will rise into the spotlight of conscious attention. Because this aspect of purpose making is the product of active cognition, it gives us insight into the writer's thinking process. In the act of building a sense of purpose, expert writers are doing at least two important things — they are creating more richly elaborated networks and at the same time they are linking these plans and goals into a more fully integrated, coherent structure. The part of this network that is accepted (or the part that is recalled) becomes the rhetorical plan that guides composing.

The performance of the writers I have observed, both expert and novice, is impressive — especially when one considers that building this plan is only part of what a successful writer must do. The problem of translating plan to prose, for instance, still looms (cf. Witte). However, this glimpse of the planning process raises an interesting question: what then is the *reader* doing, since readers too have to create a coherent text in their own minds? What becomes of this rich web of purpose and the rhetorical plan our writers have labored to construct?

Readers and Rhetorical Reading

Literary theorists have long explored the ways aesthetic goals influence (or should influence) interpretation. Recent psychological research on how purpose shapes comprehension offers additional insights. Readers bring a variety of goals to expository texts, including the goals of reading "to do" something, such as use one's new computer, versus reading "to learn" something, such as the theory of natural selection. We know that changing these goals can affect the reading strategies people use, the information they recall, and many features of prose processing in general. It can change the depth of processing (e.g., do you skim for key phrases or read and rehearse the argument to yourself?), the amount of mental elaboration done on the text, and the way information is clustered and recalled. (For a review of this work see Bransford; Frase.)

Designers of instructional texts naturally try to influence such reading purposes with priming questions, text cues, and suggested reading objectives (Anderson and Biddle). This makes sense since the agenda readers set for themselves often overcomes the effects of text structure. For instance, when two groups of adults were asked to read and recall a house description, their recall was significantly influenced by whether they were reading as potential house buyers or prospective burglars — one group remembered the color TV, the other a leak in the roof (Pichert and Anderson). It is perhaps not surprising that we structure information around our own purposes in reading and that we recall the "text" we ourselves construct. But what about the author's intentions — do readers perceive them? And if so, does this affect the reader's constructive process?

In an imaginative sequence of studies in the 1950s Solomon Asch showed that assumptions about the author's intention have a substantial effect on the meaning readers see. Two groups of people were asked to write down the meaning of a text which started, "I hold it that a little rebellion, now and then, is a good thing. . . ." When one group was told that this statement was by Lenin, and the other that it was by Jefferson, this attribution affected "*the cognitive content* of the statement" these readers perceived (422). Asch wanted to show that knowledge of the author contributes more than a subjective, or stereotypical, emotional response. He found that readers used their knowledge of the author and his historical context to interpret problematic terms such as "rebellion" (e.g., the Lenin readers systematically interpreted the term as "revolution," while the Jefferson readers saw "agitation.") These readers altered the actual propositional content of the message. In this and further studies with texts attributed to Adams, Marx, CIO leaders, and so on, Asch found that readers also altered the "direction" of the message (e.g., whether the text was speaking for or against its topic) even when both groups reported the same specific content. Readers also supplied differing versions of the reasons prompting the utterance and gave the text itself different significance (such as, this is a bit of breezy journalism, or a piece to be reckoned with).

The text, Asch argued from his evidence, is not an island of meaning; it is seen by readers as a part in a part/whole pattern. In more artificial conditions when the author/context was unknown (as it is in most experiments) Asch's readers did more leveling and reduced their responses to a more literal precis. But under more normal conditions of reading and interpreting, they actively used their assumptions about intentions to form the meaning of the message. Despite his strong results, it is interesting that half of his subjects appeared quite unaware of the impact of context and asserted that knowing who the author was would make no difference in their interpretation.

In many ways Asch's work complements observations of I. A. Richards and later work in literary and rhetorical theory and offers empirical support for at least some of the claims made by writers such as Louise Phelps, David Bartholomae, Patricia Bizzell, Stanley Fish, Wolfgang Iser, and Siegfried Schmidt, who argue for various constructive processes in reading. The meaning of a text is not an immutable feature residing in splendid isolation in the text itself. Instead it is a private construct created by a writer influenced by both text and the context in which he or she is reading. We might say that Asch's readers at some point aligned themselves with an interpretative community or a discourse community in which features in the text then became "cues" to the creation of a given reading.

Asch's work also suggests that the role of the perceived author should not be dismissed lightly even in our enthusiasm for the autonomy of the text or the constructive process of the reader. Because we prize the suggestive ambiguities and the multiple meanings literature strives for, we do need to be especially wary of reading based on an intentional *fallacy* in interpreting such texts. However, if we assume that a good reader will (or even could) ignore indications of an "author" in the name of a purer reading of the "text" we may misrepresent *how the reading process works as a psychological process,* at least for expository texts. Inferences about the writer's intentions appear to be an essential building block — one that readers actively use to construct a meaningful text. Because readers are participants in a rhetorical situation in which communications have a purpose, recognizing or attempting to infer those intentions is, indeed, a reasonable response.

Trying to unravel the place of authorial purpose in a reader's response only makes sense if we have a cognitively complex image of that purpose. So let me note some of my own premises. First, the authorial purposes which drive the creation of texts can not be reduced to after-the-fact authorial statements, historical inferences, or even in-the-text conventional statements of purpose. The web of purpose writers create is a cognitive construct: although it may well harbor information concerning the dominant "theme," or the "meaning" one reads about in blue book exams, it will also contain a cluster of goals for the effect a key paragraph should create and special criteria based on an imagined reader's response or based on a new possibility just seen in the text. It will contain plans for creating a sustained argument and anticipating points of misreading as well as profoundly complicated plans for creating a sustained voice and/or a personal stance toward one's own material and for a whole range of larger purposes for writing. Our critical tradition, and critical ingenuity, has made us expect complexity in texts, in language, and in authors as psycho/sexual/cultural entities. If we wish to talk equally well about the writer as agent and thinker and about the role individual purpose plays in composing, we need to expand our theoretical frameworks to include cognitive complexity as well. (We must also, I believe, accept the fact that we can infer only a small part of such cognition from finished text or writers' recollections and that other, richer sources, such as think-aloud protocols, are themselves still data that must be interpreted, with tests for reliability, within a theoretical framework.)

Secondly, if we adopt a cognitively sophisticated picture of purpose in the writer, we must ask: how is the author's purpose represented in the mind of the reader during the process of comprehension? Is the reader's mental representation going to reflect only a blue book exam vision of purpose? Or are readers, as complex rhetorical beings, likely to engage in a highly inferential interpretive process that picks up shimmers from the web? Purpose in the mind of the writer and the mind of the reader, I will suggest, are cognitive analogues — elaborate mental representations that we can only partially infer (cf. Flower, "Interpretive Acts"). However, an analogue is not a mirror image. If readers are in some way sensitive to the author's purpose, what sort of representations do they build as part of their own interpretive process?

122

Even though it is convenient to imagine this web of purpose as an object (a noun), we are in fact dealing with a verb, a psychological process of "purposing." This intellectual and emotional event unfolds in real time as writers construct a plan for rhetorical action and as readers infer something of that web to construct their own interpretive response. In the final section of this paper I would like to look at how a group of six readers responded to two descriptive/persuasive essays, one a cheerful, informal essay on "my job" and the other the Prologue by Stephen Jay Gould. I will draw my examples from the response to the Gould text, not to make any direct comparison to Gould's web of purpose, to which we have no access, but to talk about how the inferences these readers drew about the author's purpose played a role in their construction of a meaningful text. One purpose of this analysis is not to categorize or compare these *readers* — they were selected for diversity — but to build a data-based description of a *rhetorical reading strategy* they all employed. Rhetorical reading links reader and writer in a particularly direct way, since it is a strategy by which readers use their inferences about the author's plans, goals, and context to help construct a meaningful text. The strategy as it was defined in this study has a number of parallels with the "point-driven" or "information-driven" reading strategy Vipond and Hunt were at the same time describing in readers of literary texts. They observed that while some readers brought only a "story-driven" reading to short stories, others engaged in what they called a "point-driven" reading — a more complex act of interpretation concerned with seeing the "point" of plot, setting, dialogue, etc. — in which readers frequently imputed motives to the author of the literary text. Authorial purpose clearly figures in various kinds of reading; the question is how.

Let me place the observations which are to follow in a theoretical and procedural context. First, the theoretical one: because reading is a highly constructive cognitive process, the reader's own goals, assumptions, and context play an enormous role in meaning making. One can even see readers building more than one distinctive representation of "meaning" from the same text, in response to different sets of goals during reading (cf. Flower, "Interpretive Acts"). So we need to place the reader's perception of a writer's purpose in perspective; it is in no way equivalent to *the* meaning of the text. Rather it appears to be simply another piece of information (sometimes privileged, sometimes not) that readers use in constructing their own meaningful representations of a text.

Secondly, let me review the research context for this observation, which was designed to encourage reading for comprehension and to legitimize individual interpretation. The readers were adults who read frequently for their jobs, but had varying degrees of knowledge about the subject matter. They included a seventy-year-old businessman, a twenty-year-old research assistant, three English teachers and an educational psychologist. Since the processes I wanted to observe were the high-level ones that frequently demand conscious processing, I used thinking-aloud protocols in which readers were asked to think aloud as they read and/or paused to think. To encourage reading for comprehension, I told them they would be asked some questions at the end of the text.

For adults, much of the reading process is fluent; its strategies are automated. My subjects spent a good deal of their time simply mumbling along reading the text out loud. However, at certain points in reading, these automated processes are no longer adequate, and readers must rise to more conscious processing of the text. Reading protocols capture these moments. At such points people stop to draw inferences, to elaborate, or to use other problem-solving behaviors to understand and interpret the text (Waern).

However, we had discovered that reading protocols can miss much of even this conscious processing. In writing, the productive acts of planning and producing text soak up attention so fully that most of the information in focal attention is likely to be reported. But the time-consuming act of reading out loud gives people ample time to think silently — to actively make comparisons, pose questions, and draw inferences that they may not stop to report. Therefore, in addition to reading and thinking out loud, readers were also prompted to state their current understanding of the text at key boundary points, such as the end of a paragraph. The text had been typed on cards, and at these boundary points readers encountered the prompt card which asked them: "What is the gist of the passage so far?" "What do you expect will follow?" On the occasions readers fell silent and appeared perplexed, they were prompted orally with: "What are you thinking?" or "How do you interpret the text now?" Finally, at the end of the text they were asked to reconstruct what they recalled of their reading process and interpretation of the text, since this method had proved fruitful in other studies of inferences in reading (Collins, Brown and Larkin). Together, these three techniques — concurrent report of thinking, prompted statements on the current understanding of the text, and cued recall — gave converging evidence on readers' processes and on their developing image of the text.

Under these conditions, it is possible to engage in little or no high-level interpretation. One could simply read the text aloud with an occasional elaborative comment and, at the "gist" or "interpret" prompt, merely restate some portion of the content in a brief paraphrase (as the students we have observed often do). Although the research situation encourages verbalization, it is satisfied with a response based wholly on an automated reading process and a paraphrase of content. Readers rise to more conscious processing and inferential response at a cost and for a reason. The readers I observed were not content with paraphrase. In many cases they turned to active problem solving and unprompted interpretation near the end of key units, only to find the prompt on the next card which would elicit responses such as: "oh hell, what is the gist again. Well so far the gist is just what I said with some — a — additional information. [Details followed.]" At all these sites of more active interpretation, we should also note that readers engaged in a variety of comprehension strategies in addition to rhetorical reading. These included using their prior knowledge to interpret points or resolve difficulties, searching the text for information, and monitoring, testing, and elaborating their own understanding.

Within this context, then, the rhetorical reading strategy I observed was neither a predictable move nor one required by the method of observation; it was a choice among other choices to spend cognitive effort creating a context or a sense of purpose for the text by trying to infer the author's goals or rhetorical plan.

Inferences about the Writer's Purpose

If readers take time to draw inferences and construct their own mental representation of the writer's goals, what sorts of rhetorical information do they generate in their effort to interpret the text? We can divide the rhetorical reading responses of these readers into three categories: inferences about the rhetorical plan of the text, single inferences about specific authorial intentions, and complex rhetorical scenarios which involve a number of linked inferences.

The most straightforward group of inferences served to identify the *rhetorical structure* of the text. By "rhetorical" I mean not only the ordering of information, but the structure of this text as a speech act or social transaction between Gould and his readers. Drawing on cues in the text and their knowledge of genre and conventions, readers inferred a logic, behind the text's organizational plan, that was based on some larger sense of the writer's purpose. They wanted to understand the "why" that governed the "what next" sequence of information. The example below is even more interesting in that it came in response to the final comprehension question.

Okay — a — because this [the essay] was — a — what it was, celebrating the publishing of the *Origin of Species,* what he was trying to do was summarize the essence of the theory, . . . and then explain the difficulties that people had accepting it.

Although this reader has been asked to recall Gould's "main ideas," she begins by summing up the underlying logic of the entire essay, linking its organization to (what she saw as) its celebratory purpose. Note too how the reader is working with a gist statement of the content which, like her inference about the plan, allows her to see the text in larger, more meaningful chunks.

The following example shows a more local inference about the writer's plan. This reader has just encountered Gould's emphatic preview of what is coming: two facts and a conclusion. But his inferences are devoted to the implicit rhetorical plan, that is, to the intentions that erected this large signpost.

> The theory rests on [he reads] "two undeniable facts and an inescapable conclusion." So he's sort of forcing the reader, manipulating, almost berating. This is something that has to be perfectly clear according to what Gould is setting us up to. This [the theory] can not be difficult.

It is, of course, not surprising to find readers attributing a purpose to a text's structure and its conventional moves. As Burke would say, the purpose of structure is precisely to arouse such expectations. We know that readers in fact use their knowledge of standard text conventions to draw a steady stream of low-level inferences which we would not see, for which there is no need to rise to conscious processing.

More interesting are those inferences which go more directly to the human motives and larger purposes of the writer. They raise the kinds of questions you might expect a person to ask, such as, what is this speaker trying to do? And who is this I'm listening to anyway? And in certain cases, these inferences became part of an extended effort to forge a coherent reading of the text. That is, readers would sometimes elaborate their sense of an underlying intention into a dramatic portrait of an author who thinks, believes, and does things, who has a complex web of intentions, and who succeeds or fails at realizing those intentions in the text. These more elaborate portraits of purpose, these rhetorical scenarios, create an image of an agent who acts in some meaningful context. Their added complexity appears to give them special powers as they grow into vivid docudramas in which multiple speakers think and interact with each other in the mind of the reader.

At a time when we see the role of purpose excluded from so many theoretical discussions, it is important to look for the ways it surfaces in the process of writers and readers. In an earlier study of people struggling to read the federal regulations that govern small business loans, we found that readers coped with this impenetrable prose by turning abstract terms or definitions into scenarios. In the effort to interpret the text, terms such as "ineligible concern" were translated into: "Say that if a fellow has a bar and he's selling moonshine which is not taxed, and so on, then. . . ." Readers instantiated abstractions with a concrete example, that specified an agent (which was often lacking in the text), an action, and a context. For these difficult texts scenarios accounted for between 60 and 70 percent of the interpretative comments readers made (Flower, Hayes, and Swarts).

The beginning paragraph of the Darwin text seemed to require this sort of heightened interpretive effort. Every reader found it confusing, and this reader, who had very little prior knowledge about Darwin on which to draw, created an extended scenario in order to interpret the text. The essay begins:

> "One hundred years without Darwin are enough," grumbled the noted American geneticist H. J. Muller in 1959. The remark struck many listeners as a singularly inauspicious way to greet the centenary of the *Origin of Species*.

At this point the reader, who is clearly perplexed, comments:

> The *Origin of Species*. I'm not sure just what it — what it means, but apparently it was a book that was written in 1859, and this fellow, H. J. Muller thought that we had enough of Darwin and that we shouldn't be any — shouldn't be pursuing this particular — a — thoughts of Darwin any further.

125

The text goes on: "But no one could deny the truth expressed in its frustration." And the reader continues to puzzle out an interpretation:

> Apparently the *Origin of Species* — a — deals in a frustrated way, the teaching of Darwin and while he [Muller] didn't believe in them he was apparently frustrated that he didn't understand them or didn't believe in them or didn't have an answer to refute them. . . . This fellow Muller did not understand or believe them, but apparently has an open mind and is willing to — a — concede enough, enough to investigate it further.

This reader responds to his confusion by building an extended scenario which attributes a set of potential motives, attitudes, and personality traits to Muller, and by extension to the entire essay. One could draft an agent/action/context script from this protocol in which Muller, perceiving that we had had enough of Darwin, is himself vacillating between disbelief and multiple sources of confusion and frustration, but willing in the end to stand with an open mind.

A number of readers built scenarios at this apparently perplexing place in the text. The fact that these scenarios differed and that this reader is demonstrably wrong, shows us how clearly this is a constructed interpretation. As an attempt to create a coherent reading of the passage, this reading process looks beyond the textual elements of cohesion, unambiguous reference, and form, and attempts to find coherence in some sense of human purpose.

The reader in the next excerpt shows how scenarios can serve a more focused, local purpose. This interpretative effort appears to have been triggered when the reader encountered an assertion in the text that he could not integrate into his current interpretation. (It also suggests that the reader was keeping a running record of who was taking what position on the current topic.) The text reads, "Variation must be random. . . ."

> Who says? Maybe Darwin, or the nature of things, or something, or some abstract logic behind this. . . . Maybe according to Darwin. I mean, who said that it [variation] is preferential and comes prepackaged in a particular direction? I didn't say it, and he didn't say it, and I don't know that Darwin said it.

In these miniature docudramas, readers are trying out alternative hypotheses about the text by assigning intentions, roles, and statements not only to the writer, but to potential readers and to other people quoted in the text. Scenarios help readers understand the text in the way a single inference might not. Scenarios function as a simulation: "If I interpreted the text this way, what would happen? If Muller is critical of Darwin, then why is he writing this, and why is he frustrated? Maybe Gould is presenting Muller's quote because he is trying to . . ." and so on. Olson has argued that in writing, unlike speaking, one is obligated to produce what he calls an "autonomous text" — a text that can stand on its own. It needs to create its meaning without the aid of an immediate context — such as pointing or body language — and without the presumption of prior knowledge held by the reader. It is ironic to see that even if writers are laboring to create "autonomous texts," readers are hard at work trying to reconstruct that very context as a clue to interpretation.

Creating scenarios is a rather complex problem-solving strategy. It takes a good deal of effort and inferencing. Why would readers stop reading and bother to do this? Why not just read the text? One answer, I think, is that these scenarios let readers do a difficult thing: they allow people to represent to themselves a complex logical and rhetorical situation in which there are a number of forces and constraints at work. Moreover, these forces or variables interact with each other — one interpretation only makes sense if two other points are true, unless, of course, there is another explanation for the first fact, and so on. Tracing the effects of these interactions is a thinking task that humans, with their short-term memory limitations, find particularly exasperating. Yet reading and writing constantly call for decisions that are sensitive to multiple interpretations and interacting ideas — decisions which can at the same time yield a coherent text. It is interesting that these readers do not seem to opt for a more formal logical representation of the content, of the sort: If A is true then B, but not Q. Scenarios appear to offer a less cognitively demanding, yet apparently quite effective means of dealing with interactions among ideas. They locate textual coherence not merely in the logical coherence of propositions, but in the ordinary logic of human intentions.

The Function of Rhetorical Reading

Getting a vague "feel for" most writers' intentions requires no special effort. But why do more? Given the default response of reading aloud and paraphrasing content at the prompt that the reader could use and given the other comprehension strategies these readers could and did employ to arrive at a gist or a current understanding, one wants to know *why* readers choose to interrupt fluent reading and *why* they tried to express their current understanding by generating information about the writer's purpose. What function does rhetorical reading serve that makes it a noticeable part of their repertoire?

Some of the advantages already noted, such as letting one chunk and manage information, support the cognitive process of reading in ways the reader may not even be aware of. Other functions seem to be more directly under the reader's strategic control (even though a reader asked to introspect after the fact might not be particularly aware of the process). For these readers, rhetorical reading was used first of all to establish an initial framework for understanding the text. That is, five of the six writers I observed created a high-level statement of the framing purpose of this text very early in the reading. The reader who didn't struggle unhappily through five alternative theories about the point of the "my job" essay she was reading (e.g., "I think this writer doesn't know what she's doing and I am not sure what's going to follow but, I predict it isn't going to be very good") until she finally saw the light ("it is suddenly becoming clear to me . . .") and then made a detailed, confident prediction of the rhetorical plan for the rest of the essay.

The first reader quoted below (547) comes to a straightforward view of this framing purpose very early in the Darwin text (a frame which she elaborated in subsequent responses). The second reader exercises his critical distance and creates a more extended scenario of the author enlightening the masses — specifying the roles, relative IQ's, and an appropriate tone for everyone involved:

> I'm trying to figure out what he means by 100 years without Darwin are enough. Means he wants Darwin back? [Comment follows prompt at end of 1st paragraph] I guess . . . I guess it's going to sing the praises of Darwin and *Origin of Species*. Formula stuff again — misunderstanding Darwin. So our author here seems to be in the possession of the truth. I mean people for some centuries have been mistaken and Gould is going to let us know why they had so much trouble, being so dumb for 100 years. [Unprompted response within 2nd paragraph]

This initial sense of purpose creates a framework for interpreting the text which stands in contrast to a naive, information-driven focus on content. Among these readers it also appeared to be a stable framework in the sense that nearly every subsequent inference about purpose was either directly related to it, consistent with it, or simply a local inference. The power this initial representation wields also suggests one problem with rhetorical reading. It is a powerful tool, and when readers misread the purpose, they create a mental "set" that may guide the rest of their reading. This is, of course, true of any inference readers make or any interpretive schema they bring to reading. One might speculate that poor readers may make premature decisions about the purpose of a text and not display the same willingness some of these experienced readers showed to debate with contradictory information and test their hypotheses about purpose and meaning.

Rhetorical reading supported sophisticated reading in a second way by allowing readers to maintain a critical distance from the text. For example, in a series of comments one reader distinguishes the factual level of a statement from the inference the author wants us to draw from it; she then notes that underlining indicates the author's emphasis and sense of what is important; she remarks that the text sets up two ideas as separate, but she thinks they overlap, and she distinguishes between Darwin's meaning of materialism and other potential meanings. This reader appears to be drawing inferences about the author's perspective in order to keep sensible distinctions between her interpretation, the author's interpretation, and the information presented or referred to in the text.

This critical reading is obviously a desirable stance. (Although, as Asch showed, readers may overestimate their critical awareness and underestimate the effect of their own assumptions.) Sometimes readers actually seem ready to agree with the author, but to be maintaining their critical distance as a matter of good reading form (e.g., "A nice little if/then thing here, though I'm questioning the 'if.' ").

Finally, and I think most importantly, rhetorical reading appears linked to trouble spots and problems of interpretation. Reading a moderately complex text seems to produce a constant stream of problems the reader must resolve in order to build a coherent, meaningful interpretation. The reader doesn't understand a term; she can't see the connection among ideas in the text or between the text and her prior knowledge. Or what she reads may conflict with her prior knowledge or current predictions about the text. Until this occurs, adult reading is a relatively automatic process, but a problem or an occasion to elaborate can shift the process into conscious attention and shift the reader into active problem solving. Reading aloud protocols are particularly good at capturing this level of the interpretive process. In the example below, the reader creates a detailed scenario in order to deal with a conflict between her assumptions about Darwin and Gould's claims about the meaning of Darwin's work. One can read the thought going on in this reader's mind as a dialogue among different voices. We hear Gould, speaking out of the context of a scholarly debate, claim that Darwin has violated Western beliefs, to which the reader responds, in a more tentative voice, that she had a different impression. Then Darwin's voice, as this reader imagines it, emerges out of the context of his personal life as the reader begins a catalogue of inferences and remembered facts.

Okay, I'm going to read on. *Darwin was not a moral dolt; he just didn't care to fob off upon nature all the deep prejudices of Western thought . . . didn't care to fob off on nature all the deep prejudices of Western thought* [reads text]. I'm not sure that — a — a — That doesn't — I'm not sure that my impression of Darwin would not be that he — a — that he took sort of an active philosophical stance to all this, but that he was just describing what he saw, and so in a sense was simply trying to give an, a moral interpretation. I don't think he was sort of actively rejecting — a — Western beliefs [as the text claims]. Now what I know about Darwin now that I look back is that he was really shy, and that he didn't want to publish this, and that he was really afraid of getting a lot of criticism. And this statement makes it sound like he was a radical going out to change the world, which I know he wasn't from what I've heard of him.

The schematic diagram below shows how this scenario allowed Gould, Darwin, and the reader to interact. It presents a paraphrase of the protocol (except for the notes on "context" which I supplied) in order to foreground how the three players in this dialogue (lined up in the left column) create an extended scenario in which voices can be seen as agents and ideas as actions occurring in a rhetorical context. Scenarios of this sort appear to help readers deal with their interpretive difficulties by constructing a rhetorical event.

Agent	Action	Context
Gould	claims that Darwin's theory violates Western beliefs	[a scholarly debate in the history of ideas]
Reader	has different impression	
Darwin	took no philosophical stance was just describing tried to give a moral interpretation	[Darwin's personal and professional life]
Reader	doesn't agree with claim [see quote]	
Darwin	was shy didn't want to publish was afraid of criticism	
Gould	implies a contradictory view	
Darwin	was a radical wanted to change the world	
Reader	knows that Darwin wasn't a radical	

Scenario used to construct an interpretation: This reader is clearly perplexed by Gould's claim that Darwin (with his notion that evolution has no other purpose than adaptation) violated Western beliefs. Why is she perplexed? Because Gould's assertion violates two of her own assumptions about Darwin's *intentions,* namely: (1) Darwin was trying to be observational, not philosophical and (2) Darwin's personality — as she constructed it — was a shy and retiring sort, so that in order to avoid criticisms, he would have not wanted to challenge our beliefs. In effect, this reader is rewriting evolution by natural selection into a tamer theory in order to make it congruent with her inferences about Darwin's personality and private intentions.

Analysis of the protocols showed that all of these experienced readers turned at times to a rhetorical reading strategy, using inferences about the web of purposes surrounding the text to construct coherent meaning. But, one might ask, "so what?" How much stability and power do these inferences about the author's purpose have? There were two pieces of evidence to suggest that they may have had a good deal of power. One is the fact that when readers' inferences were incompatible with seemingly bald statements in the text, the text did not always win. Some readers simply refused to give up their image of what the text *should mean* (based on their inferences about the author's intentions), in the face of conflicting information in the text itself. Other readers gaily read through statements that directly contradicted their interpretation and seemed not to notice.

A second kind of evidence for the significance of rhetorical reading comes from the frequency with which readers used this strategy to resolve difficulties. As the following table shows, if we examine the protocols of these six writers for any indication of problem spots or conflicts in the reading process, we find a total of 52 points at which readers were momentarily confused, uncertain, or in difficulty. We can then see if these problems were resolved (10 were not) and, if so, what strategies writers used. As this analysis makes clear, rhetorical reading is just one of the strategies these readers used to deal with problems. Sometimes readers returned to the text to reread or search for information they may have missed (7 times). At other times they resolved the problem by referring to their own prior topic knowledge (a total of 6 times). However, 31 of the conflicts to which these readers attended were followed by inferences about the author's purpose. This means readers turned to some form of rhetorical reading to solve nearly 60 percent of the interpretive problems they encountered. (One instance was double coded as both a topic and scenario.) The table lets us see how these responses are distributed and distinguishes between readers' brief inferences about goals or the rhetorical plan and the more extended scenarios. Although the scenarios often contained multiple comments, they were counted as a single response.

The role of rhetorical reading in resolving conflicts: Although these numbers are too small to discuss statistically, this is a surprising observation. For these experienced readers, at least, rhetorical reading appears to play a meaningful role in resolving comprehension problems. On the basis of these suggestive results, Christina Haas and I designed a controlled study of experienced and inexperienced readers on a more difficult text. In that study it appears that rhetorical reading is not only an "expert" strategy the freshmen are not using, but an important tool for building a meaningful interpretive context. It may even play a role we didn't predict in helping readers infer key, unstated claims in a text.

Reader	Problems or Conflicts	Rhetorical Reading		Topic Info.	Text Info.	Not Resolved
		Goals	Scenarios			
#1	14	4	8	1	1	0
#2	3	3	0	0	0	0
#3	14	3	5	3	3	2
#4	6	0	2	0	0	4
#5	8	1	1	2	1	3
#6	7	4	—	—	2	1
Total	52	15	16	6	7	10
		31				

This view of purpose, as a complex web of meaning which writers build and which readers in their own, independently constructive way infer, leaves us with some provocative questions to answer. On one level it asks us to refine our theoretical understanding of how individual purposes interact with context and convention in the creation of a text. And it asks for a broader vision of reading as both a constructive, cognitive process and a rhetorical event in which readers use their knowledge of human purposes to build a meaningful and coherent text. On another level it invites us to close and careful observation of both of these processes. We need to trace, for instance, the connections between the active, constructive cognition of readers and writers and the coherence and structure of texts. And we need to discover new ways to make the strategic knowledge we see in experienced writers and readers more accessible to our students. For me at least, the expert/novice differences I have seen in the research on planning and rhetorical reading bring me back to my own primary aims as a teacher, which are to help students take control of their own reading and writing processes, in the service of their own rhetorical purposes. A more robust view of literate purposes may help us do this.

Note

One of the most valuable forms of collaboration comes from people who are willing to think through problems with you, trying to build a conceptualization that is one step closer to doing justice to the experience of writer and readers. Although the questions raised here are far from resolved in my mind or theirs, this paper has received the invaluable help of Mike Rose, Patricia Sullivan, Stephen Witte, Andrea Lunsford, Richard Enos, and Russell Hunt.

Works Cited

Anderson, R. C., and W. B. Biddle. "On Asking People Questions about What They Are Reading." *Psychology of Learning and Motivation*. Vol. 9. Ed. G. Bower. New York: Academic, 1975. 90–132.

Asch, Solomon. *Social Psychology*. New York: Prentice, 1952.

Bartholomae, David. "Inventing the University." *When a Writer Can't Write: Studies in Writer's Block and Other Composing-Process Problems*. New York: Guilford, 1985. 134–65.

Bizzell, Patricia. "College Composition: Initiation into the Academic Discourse Community." *Curriculum Inquiry* 12.2 (1982): 191–207.

Bransford, J. D. *Human Cognition: Learning, Understanding, and Remembering*. Belmont, CA: Wadsworth, 1979.

Burke, Kenneth. *Counter-Statement*. Berkeley: U of California P, 1986.

Burtis, P. J., C. Bereiter, M. Scardamalia, and J. Tetroe. "The Development of Planning and Writing." *Exploration of Children's Development in Writing*. Ed. C. G. Wells and B. Kroll. England: J Wiley, 1983. 135–74.

Collins, Alan, John Seely Brown, and Kathy M. Larkin. "Inference in Text Understanding." *Theoretical Issues in Reading Comprehension*. Ed. R. Spiro, B. Bruce, and W. Brewer. Hillsdale: Erlbaum, 1980. 385–410.

Fish, Stanley. *Is There a Text in This Class?* Cambridge: Harvard UP, 1980.

Flower, Linda. "Interpretive Acts: Cognition and the Construction of Discourse." *Poetics* 16 (1987): 109–30.

_____, and John R. Hayes. "Images, Plans, and Prose: The Representation of Meaning in Writing." *Written Communication* 1 (1984): 120–60.

_____, John R. Hayes, and Heidi Swarts. "Revised Functional Documents: The Scenario Principle." *New Essays in Technical Writing and Communication*. Ed. P. Anderson, J. Brockmann, and C. Miller. Farmingdale: Baywood, 1983. 41–58.

_____, Karen Schriver, Linda Carey, Christina Haas, and John R. Hayes. "Planning in Writing: A Theory of the Cognitive Process." Technical Report. Berkeley: Center for the Study of Writing, University of California at Berkeley and Carnegie Mellon, 1988.

Foucault, Michel. "What Is an Author?" *Language, Counter-Memory, Practice*. Ed. Donald Bouchard. Ithaca: Cornell UP, 1977. 113–38.

Frase, Lawrence T. "Prose Processing." *Psychology of Learning and Motivation*. Vol. 9. Ed. G. Bower. New York: Academic, 1975. 1–47.

Gould, Stephen Jay. *Ever Since Darwin*. New York: Norton, 1977.

Haas, Christina, and Linda Flower. "Rhetorical Reading Strategies and the Construction of Meaning." *College Composition and Communication* 39 (1988): 167–83.

Iser, Wolfgang. *The Act of Reading*. Baltimore: Johns Hopkins, 1978.

Olson, David. "From Utterance to Text: The Bias of Language in Speech and Writing." *Harvard Educational Review* 47 (1977): 257–81.

Pichert, J. W., and R. C. Anderson. "Taking Different Perspectives on a Story." *Journal of Educational Psychology* 69 (1977): 209–315.

Phelps, Louise. "Dialectics of Coherence: Toward an Integrative Theory." *College English* 47 (1985): 12–29.

Richards, I. A. *Practical Criticism*. New York: Harcourt, 1929.

Schmidt, Siegfried. *Foundations for the Empirical Study of Literature*. Trans. Robert de Beaugrande. Hamburg: Buske, 1982.

Waern, Y. "Thinking Aloud during Reading: A Descriptive Model and Its Application." *Scandinavian Journal of Psychology* 21 (1980): 123–32.

Witte, Stephen. "Composing and Pre-Text." *College Composition and Communication* 38 (1987): 297–425.

Flower's Insights as a Resource for Your Teaching

1. We often teach as much about strategies for critical reading as we teach about strategies for writing. Because, as the author's of *The Bedford Guide* so frequently demonstrate, reading is a major resource for writing, you'll want to know a great deal about both the reading and the writing processes of each writer you assist. Ask students, in journal entries and in short "response" writings, to discuss and reflect on their reading experiences.

2. During individual conferences, invite each student to read his paper out loud, commenting to you either on his writing or on his reading of his writing. Don't be surprised if the

student suddenly shifts from talking about his process of writing to an evaluation of how it reads and then to a question to you as a reader about whether a particular revision would improve the passage. This recursiveness and shifting from a writer's to a reader's perspective is a behavior you want to encourage in apprentice writers.

Flower's Insights as a Resource for the Writing Classroom

1. Early in the semester and again when you work with Chapter 3, "Writing from Reading," focus classroom attention on critical reading by using the techniques Flower used for her research. Introduce an essay that class members have not been previously assigned and have the group read it aloud together. Select one of the essays from *The Bedford Guide* described as college level in the "Guide to the Readings" in *Teaching with* The Bedford Guide for College Writers: *Practical Suggestions*.

Ask for reports of current understanding of the text at key points in the essay. If the class seems puzzled by your questions, ask several class members to describe their perplexity and what that makes them think or how it affects their interpretation of the reading so far. Once the reading aloud ends, ask all students to write about what they recall of their own reading processes and individual interpretations of the text.

This process should seem familiar to you and your students; it's a technique used to teach reading in grammar school as well as in study skills courses. The only difference may be the complexity of the reading that you select and the importance that college students gain additional control over their reading processes. Using the technique in a college-level class lets the novice readers who don't understand how their peers "read between the lines" practice a reading heuristic as well as observe the conventions of academic reading. College students need to learn both to write and to read in the several discourse communities that they enter.

In addition, this class experience with a reading protocol encourages peer readers/editors to reflect on their process of constructing purpose and meaning from a text. They can see how to report their reading experiences back to the writer as comments that both validate the success of the text and report any difficulty the reader has constructing meaning.

2. Ask for a self-assessment writing to accompany a submitted draft. Encourage the writers to describe both the rhetorical purpose of the final draft and the choices they made during drafting and revision that were influenced by their understanding of purpose in their essay. Ask the writers to assess how successfully they have accomplished their main purpose in the paper. In your commentary on the papers, evaluate both the success in which the writers met their "rhetorical purpose" and any elements of the "web of purpose" that affects their drafts.

THINKING CRITICALLY

Many colleges and universities define the ability to think critically as a primary outcome of a baccalaureate degree. At the same time, many faculty members are uncertain about how or whether they can teach students to think critically. From Janet Emig forward, contemporary writing teachers assume that writing is a mode of thinking and is often the major way that novices to the academic community come to a critical consciousness about their world. The catchphrase "academic writing" appears in textbook titles and conference programs, embedding an assumption that we improve our abilities to think critically by reflecting on and writing about course content. Some of the impetus of the writing across the curriculum movement comes from a concern that writing prompts and demonstrates critical thinking and should be a mode of inquiry available to learners in all disciplines.

Some institutions offer courses in "critical thinking" and teach problem solving and analysis as generic skills. Most frequently, courses in "critical thinking" include a focus on argumentation, both spoken and written.

Part Two of *The Bedford Guide for College Writers*, "Thinking Critically," constantly encourages student writers to realize that they already think critically in their everyday lives but need to use those cognitive strategies for increasingly complex problem solving in new knowledge communities. The chapters elicit practice of kinds of analysis, argumentation, and evaluation. Throughout the text the authors encourage a heightened awareness about the writers' thinking out loud on paper through analysis and self-assessment prompted by discovery and revision checklists and through peer analysis and evaluation. Consequently, "metacognition" or thinking on thinking and dialogue about thinking, two conditions that developmentalists consider requisite to cognitive growth, are prompted in first-year writers. The following essays offer some practical strategies for helping writers to discover and recover their critical thinking ability.

EXTRAORDINARILY RE-EXPERIENCING THE ORDINARY: THEORY OF CRITICAL THINKING

Ira Shor

The authors of The Bedford Guide for College Writers *continuously emphasize the power of writing for self-discovery and for thinking critically. Many readings in this ancillary discuss the challenges for novice writers both to learn and to practice the thinking and discourse conventions of university communities; Bartholomae and Flower make this most explicit. Increasingly, cognitive theorists emphasize the essentially social nature and process of adult cognitive development. Educational theorist Ira Shor focuses on adult learners, inside and outside classrooms, in* Critical Teaching and Everyday Life. *In this excerpt, Shor describes a pedagogy that fosters critical thinking when it shapes a social environment in which learners engage in dialogue and in dialectic.*

Although Shor discusses this theory of critical teaching for a large audience of teachers, the "dialogic method" is particularly compatible with — and often the source of — strategies for teaching writing as process. It certainly congrues with the discussion of a "community of writers," "writing for a reader," "collaborative evaluation and learning," and "writing conferences" that you find in The Bedford Guide for College Writers.

Shor focuses here on the role of the instructor in prompting and nurturing critical thought and expression. He shares with Paulo Freire (author of The Pedagogy of the Oppressed*) the assumption that the "dialogue of learners and master-learners" can effect a transition from a passive and naive consciousness to an active and critical consciousness. I think that this active learning and critical consciousness — what Peter Elbow might call "writing with power" — is exactly the outcome we desire both for writing instruction and for college education.*

Freire and Shor — and an increasing number of writing instructors — believe that when a class examines familiar situations in the unfamiliar ways of analysis, synthesis, and inquiry they learn to reperceive and to rename their world. In what Shor calls a "liberatory classroom," writers reflect on the familiar and often personal themes of student experience and use those real contexts for posing problems and generating responses, evaluations, and even solutions. This dialogic method emphasizes co-investigation and collaboration of instructor and writers within a community of writers. Such a pedagogy impels students to become active, critical, and independent learners and writing instructors to assume a major responsibility for empowering writers as critical thinkers. You'll want to think about Shor's descriptions of the multiple and complex roles of an instructor who uses a "pedagogy of liberation" as you reflect on your own experiences as a student writer, as an experienced writer, and as a writing instructor.

Counter-Structures: Doing, Un-Doing, Re-Doing

The dialogic method asserts counter-structures against behavioral models. It dis-orders reality with modes for self-ordering. An example of this is the methodology of literacy teaching used by Freire.[1] He and his associates employed flexible agendas for each session and a variety of pedagogical materials. Before using phonetic cards to teach the alphabet, the Freirian teams showed slides to the class, to provoke a long discussion on the culture-making powers of humans. In addition to phonetic cards and pictorial representations, there is also systematic teacher-training. The design of transcendent counter-structure is an art which demands a high level of consciousness in the teacher who initiates the process. Freire found that

> A major problem in setting up the program is instructing the teams of coordinators. Teaching the purely technical aspect of the procedure is not difficult; the difficulty lies rather in the creation of a new attitude — that of dialogue, so absent in our own upbringing and education. The coordinators must be converted to dialogue in order to carry out education rather than domestication.[2]

Throughout his writing, Freire remarks on the need for teacher reconstruction, which will facilitate the reconciliation of teachers and students. This theme receives its greatest prominence in *Pedagogy in Process,* the report of his work with the revolutionary government in Guinea-Bissau.[3] His insistent use of the term "class suicide" is not a melodramatic approach to the problem of teacherly manner. Instead of self-flagellation or guilt-tripping, Freire rather realistically assesses how indispensable the teacher is to the liberatory learning process. It is a difficult task to use dialogue as the means to systematically and problematically *re-present* to students what they have unsystematically and uncritically taught the teacher. The teacher is the architect of this un-doing and re-doing. The extraordinary re-experience of the ordinary cannot begin or proceed without the teacher's counter-structures. This is an inspiring and awesome situation for teachers, who so often feel trapped in the slough of despond. So much can be gained or lost in the project of liberatory teaching.

Conversions: The Object-Subject Switch

The teacher who changes to liberatory modes accepts responsibility for a process which converts students from manipulated objects into active, critical subjects. This empowering conversion is the result of re-perceiving reality. The teacher can prepare for this eventuality by studying the students in advance of teaching, and by grasping the overall process as *self and social inquiry designed for consciousness-raising skill development.* This formulation asserts the integral development of the liberatory process in each student. For each class, the teacher qualitatively assesses the initial levels of cognitive skills and political awareness, while listening to the thematic and linguistic profile of student reality. Cognitive and affective growth, informational resources and political awareness, emerge concurrently through the critical study of life by critical lives in study. The structure of values underlying these conceptions remains the same: social practice is studied in the name of freedom, for critical consciousness; democracy and awareness develop through the form of dialogue; dialogue externalizes false consciousness, changing students from re-active objects into society-making subjects; the object-subject switch is a social psychology for empowerment; power through study creates the conditions for reconstructing social practice.

The conversion of popular consciousness from mass to liberatory culture mobilizes students into a struggle for "ownership of self."[4] The dramatic distinction between owning yourself or being owned involves a democratic or a massified form for society, a humanized or dehumanized model of social relations. The humanization of reality starts with humanization of students into subjects, who insert themselves into history. Reflecting on subject-making dialogics, Joel Spring writes "To be human is to be an actor who makes choices and seeks to guide one's own destiny. To be free, to be an actor, means knowing who one is and how one has been shaped by the surrounding social world."[5] Liberatory teaching thus leads a symbolic exodus from oppression.

The Withering Away of the Teacher:
Separation, Transformation, Re-Integration

One goal of liberatory learning is for the teacher to become expendable. At the start and along the way, the teacher is indispensable as a change agent. Yet, the need to create students into self-regulating subjects requires that the teacher as organizer fade as the students emerge. It is useful to examine how the teacher's profile changes, how the evolution of the liberatory process demands and then rejects direction.

The critical learning initiated by the teacher effects a symbolic expulsion of students from daily life so that they may re-enter with critical consciousness. The separation, transformation and re-integration of students can be looked at from a number of perspectives. First, from an epistemological point of view, there is the method of abstraction which dissociates routine thought, behavior, language and situations. Single features of everyday life are isolated as themes for study. This is the method which uproots the ordinary pieces of experience for extra-ordinary reflection. A critical dialogue around an abstracted part of life permits students to gain detachment from the structure of social relations inside and outside their minds. Abstraction serves to evict mass culture from thought. A reflective detachment on daily life is a means to push yourself away from the ordinary by pushing the ordinary away from you. This is the starting point of separation, which allows a transformative process to begin. A second aspect of dissociating from routine consciousness is less metaphysical. It involves the classroom being a physical reality separate in time and space from the other dimensions of living. The temporary separation permitted to the classroom, as a formal study space apart from the routines of earning money, commuting, raising children or arranging leisure-time, allows it room to experiment with reflection on all aspects of social life. A third way of understanding the symbolic separation achieved by the liberatory class is to see the sessions as an experiential matrix distinct from the emotional, political, social and intellectual values familiar to the rest of life. The experience of separation can only occur if these dimensions are arranged to trip the onrushing flow of experience. The liberatory classroom is a break from routines which offers a study of routines so that the familiar shape of life is appreciated with criticism rather than acceptance. As a separate zone for consciousness change, the liberatory classroom can break with the flow of events, the students' routine immersion in mass culture. The object-subject switch relates to this process of separation. Students are separated from the culture which has made them into manipulable objects, and with critical consciousness replacing false thought, they leave the class as subjects, that is, as people mentally armed against domination. If the liberatory process takes hold, then expulsion/ reconstruction/re-entry represents a model for humanization through learning. In a society devoted to humane social relations, philosophical and physical separation will not be crucial to liberatory growth. All institutions and situations would promote critical awareness. In mass culture, separation is fundamental to transcendent change.

The person responsible for provoking separation and critical re-entry is the teacher. By identifying, abstracting and problematizing the most important themes of student experience, the teacher detaches students from their reality and then re-presents the material for their systematic scrutiny. As the process evolves, one measurement of student development is how much direction the teacher needs to offer. If separation-reconstruction and the object-subject conversion are progressing, then the teacher will have to offer less direction and more support in other ways. This internal, organic test of development — assessing how much direction the teacher is responsible for — is a means for determining the progress of humanization. When the liberatory process is working well, the learners themselves assume more responsibility for the class. The students' emergence as subjects involves their growing self-regulation, which suggests that the teacher will simply regulate the class less. A successful class begins preparing students with the critical skills they need to pursue learning. They become their own systematizers, organizers, and cultural analysts.

This ideal eventuality — the full subjective emergence of the students and the withering away of the teacher — means that the initiating/organizing function has become generalized in class, distributed to the group rather than an expertise possessed by one person. The class can then set for itself more advanced problems, which may require calling in specialists at the discretion of the group or doing special investigations of a body of knowledge. In my own teaching practice, several of these moments have occurred. It was refreshing and startling to feel the process lifted from me into the class as a whole. Most often, this kind of development was only partial. This progress towards subjective emergence and self-regulation is a very difficult one: it is not a direct march forward, but is rather full of advances and regressions, inconsistencies, surprises and reversals. The classes which did become self-organizing did not order me out of the room. In fact, the more autonomous the students, the more they wanted my presence. Perhaps they enjoyed the sense of power in disciplining me into my role in the process. Perhaps they wanted me around for reassurance, in case something went wrong. Perhaps they simply enjoyed my participation in the reconstructive process. In any event, as my teacher/initiator role receded in the most advanced classes, I found myself assuming a number of other functions. The first new role was that of *peer-discussant,* a member of the dialogue on equal terms with all the others in class. As long as the process moved ahead, I could be peer-discussant and other things too; but when it broke down in ways the class itself could not repair, I needed to separate myself out from the group to become problematizer/ coordinator again. Instances of regression are the acid-tests of dialogic education; the temptation for the teacher to lecture is great. Re-focusing the class on its thematic problem tests the teacher's own evolving skill as a cultural organizer.

Given this conception of liberatory education, the teacher's function is in constant motion in class. The teacher accepts a variety of roles, at oscillating distances from the action. The teacher is the person whose intellectual skills make her or him responsible for provoking conceptual literacy in the critical study of a subject area. However, as the process takes, the teacher is not always the leading factor in class. After catalyzing discussion, at moments of the greatest success, the teacher experiences a dissolution, blending into the group deliberation. At moments of partial or full breakdown, the teacher experiences her or his role reconstituted, separated out for the restoration of the process.

Listening: Ready for Anything

A liberatory learning process is very demanding on the teacher. Changing roles and operating at varying distances from the activity requires that the teacher pay careful attention to what's going on. At every moment, the teacher must be a sensitive listener, to assess the forward, lateral or regressive motion of the session. There will be ideal moments for intervention, withdrawal and re-entry. A process which unsettles the routines of life is itself unsettling and non-routine.

The teacher needs to come to class with an agenda, but must be ready for anything, committed to letting go when the discussion is searching for an organic form. The teacher's initiating agenda and pedagogical materials start a process which keeps redesigning itself in-progress. By offering problem-statements, the teacher begins as provocateur of conceptual inquiry, but eventually the class can set its own agenda by reflecting on its previous session, thus making each phase of its own development grounded in a recognition of its growth so far. As the responsibility of self-reflection generalizes in class, the spectrum of roles performed by the teacher become much broader than those of initiator/coordinator and peer-discussant. At times, the teacher may simply be a *convenor* of the class hours. In other circumstances, the teacher may be called upon to be a *facilitator* of a special study or project needed by the class. Still other functions are *advocate* for a perspective missing in the discus-

136

sion or *adversary* to a line of thought or to a kind of oppressive behavior appearing in the discussion. The class may call upon the teacher to be a *lecturer* on a body of information or a problem about literacy or about conceptual habits of mind, which will propel the class across an impasse. On occasion, the teacher may serve as *recorder* of the sessions, whose minutes enable the class to examine its own learning process. Sometimes the teacher will need to be a *mediator* for divisive tendencies in the class, and at other times the teacher will be a *clearinghouse* or *librarian* through which resource materials pass. A process which mobilizes the critical consciousness of the students places the teacher into a mobile complex of roles. Down from the pedestal and out from behind the lectern, the teacher leaves behind the simplicity of lectures and term papers for something much more rigorous and compelling.

Working in a matrix of roles and functions, the teacher finds that her or his responsibilities increase and decrease at the same time. There are moments when the teacher plays a high profile role, in the initiation of the dialogue and in restoring the process along the way. The teacher is the class member with the greatest command of critical literacy and academic discipline, so the passing on of these skills begins with the initiative of the instructor. Yet, as the class develops, it adjusts the teacher's profile. An unorthodox and self-shaping process brings with it many surprises and rewards. When initiative begins to pass to the class, a great weight is taken from the teacher, whose experience of reconciliation with the class is inspiring. Quite simply, as the students' sense of responsibility emerges, the responsibilities of the teacher ease. One of the larger rewards in this development is the unconventional pace of growth. Students learn so quickly once they emerge as subjects of the learning process. In the object-subject switch, self-regulation decreases alienation, and alienation is the largest learning problem of students. The quick pace of learning in the non-alienated classroom raises a fundamental challenge to the behavioral/mechanical modes of education — one lesson plan for each class hour, four class lessons each week, fifteen class weeks each term, two terms a year, etc. These arbitrary and regimented time frames for learning become strikingly inappropriate, once the liberatory process takes hold. People then learn in remarkably brief and unpredictable spans and moments, reflecting their organic needs. This organic time span in liberatory learning concretely humanizes education. Education is not ruled or timed by an alienating institution but sets its own chronology. What this means in practice is that single sessions may be longer or shorter than the time allotted for them by the schedule grid; single courses may actually finish before semester's end, or may need one and a half, two or three terms to mature. Time itself is one of the controlling routines of life challenged by an extraordinary process. When a class acknowledges that its learning has ended before the term is officially over, or that its work is not complete by end-term, it has an experience of being in command of its own education. The authenticity of this moment is exciting, after so many years of being ruled by artificial, clocked regimens. The teacher has a place in this authentic community of learners, no longer responsible for furiously filling the air with words, in those painfully slow weeks dragging on to final exams.

This ideal development of teacher and students, where both mutually evolve the class, permits the students to grow into an intellectual character which is not mere mimicry of the professorial style. Through a prolonged process, the transfer of initiative opens up unfamiliar personality development. A venerable architecture of power, like the temple of the Philistines, falls unexpectedly around us. People pass beyond the ordinary models of life.

Using Daily Life: Hamburgers and the Ordinariversity

The irony of liberatory learning is that profound changes can occur through a critical study of ordinary life. Transcendence lies in the reversal of everyday conditioning. University training has left teachers with little experience in mass culture or in problem-posing dialogics. The turn in pedagogy towards daily life can open vast resources of subject matter. For every class and discipline, themes lie around us.

Further, the adaptation of study to the situations of mass life will make intellectual work of tangible relevance to students. This will be a novelty to them. Prior years of mass schooling have been ridiculously remote from their needs, so school itself has helped invalidate mental work. As it now stands, the power of the mainstream runs separately from the power of structural thought. Bringing the two together is a simple idea. It will also be catalytic.

For this project, some conceptual shapes or objectives are useful to bear in mind. One of the first operational shapes for liberatory teaching could be called *contextual skill-development*. This suggests that cognitive skills — reading, writing, comprehension, laboratory techniques, etc. — will be developed through a problematic examination of a real context, drawn from student life. As a basic method, contextual skill-development points to teaching introductory techniques through materials or activities which express a critical view of daily life. Traditionally, an academic discipline tends to teach its special body of knowledge abstractly, conservatively or narcissistically. The examples drawn in texts or lectures relate to no one's experience, or promote the experience of an elite, or else are simply couched within the discipline's own terminology. This prevents the study of any discipline from being a critical encounter with social life. The results are so absurd that the orthodox disciplines become their own worst enemies, repelling the masses of students from taking their methods seriously. Students leave such history, psychology and chemistry classes little wiser about the concrete problems they live with. The liquidation of their interests from academics serves to liquidate academic life from their interests. The idea of contextual cognition asserts the need to integrate concrete reality into formal study, so that the shape of official knowledge is transformed.

If skills are not learned in a problematic context drawn from experience, then the teaching will serve to domesticate the students to the methods of the discipline. The course will involve the submission and adjustment of the learners to the transmitted expertise of the teacher. This kind of passive structure for education will preclude the students separating from and then re-entering their experience. The memorizing form of study has been called by Freire the "banking system" of education, in which professors make deposits of knowledge in the empty accounts of their students' minds:

> The role of the educator is not to "fill" the educatee with "knowledge," technical or otherwise. It is rather to attempt to move towards a new way of thinking in both educator and educatee, through the dialogical relationships between both. The flow is in both directions. The best student in physics or mathematics, at school or university, is not one who memorizes formulae but one who is aware of the reason for them. . . . In the process of problematization, any step made by a subject to penetrate the problem-situation continually opens up new roads. . . . This is why educators continue to learn.[6]

The teacher's conviction that she or he can learn important things from the students is a keystone of this process. Without that belief, the educator will be rejecting student reality as a rich resource for thematic problems. Also, the teacher who does not seek to learn from the class will not listen carefully to what students offer, and hence will condition students into non-speaking. With a feeling for student resources, the liberatory teacher can embark on the experimental design of problem-models for each discipline. These models can animate an authentic encounter between student consciousness, reality and intellectual methods. Skills developed through consideration of an experiential problem will make education an ongoing process of life — a state of being rather than a course in an institution. Critical learning enters life because learning has absorbed life as its source for problematic themes. Without this dialectic between an academic discipline and reality, the transcendent conversion of students from objects into subjects is not possible.

The concrete contents for problem-posing education need to be relevant to each class situation. . . . In a number of my classes, we studied hamburgers or made video plays from our experience or investigated family life through the writing of marriage contracts. Each class began with a very familiar feature of experience — what Freire would call the "codification," or representation of an ordinary piece of reality, abstracted from its habitual place in society, as a theme for class study. We studied each object or situation structurally, using writing, reading, speaking and analysis to unveil the meaning of this event in our lives and in the totality of social life. In the case of the hamburger we recreated the largely invisible commodity relations which deliver a fried piece of dead beef to our palates. I brought hamburgers to class so that the familiar object would be as close at hand as possible, for the launching of unfamiliar analysis. The separation and re-entry from this exercise was rewarding, as the dialogue moved to consider "junk food" versus "health food," and the need to cooperatize the school cafeteria. In another class, one which studied dramatic writing, both literacy skills and awareness grew through the students' self-design of scripts based on their lives. The study of literary form was also a study of their lives. In our sessions, we discussed the meaning of their reality as well as the means for their aesthetic re-presentation of real life. The final teaching example involves a class which examined sexist dimensions of family life through the writing of marriage contracts. The contracts were literate documents which exercised numerous skills — writing, reading, organizing, editing, group and individual composing, etc. This project facilitated critical awareness because the emerging goal became the writing of a contract for an egalitarian marriage. There were long and interesting debates on how to shape equality in male-female bonding.

In each of these exercises, the classes had a chance to develop literacy skills through a real context. They also were called upon to use conceptual habits of mind. *Conceptual exercise* is as important as the development of literacy. The structural perception of social life depends on the command of analytic methods. To this end, techniques for rigorous scrutiny need to be integrated into the problem-contexts posed to the class. My teaching has left me optimistic that conceptual habits can emerge in the course of a few months. Some conceptual paradigms for teaching structural thought will be offered in the next section. There are analytic capabilities in each student, which are rarely exercised. Through rational analysis, the class not only reverses mysticism in its mind, but it simultaneously exposes the shape of social life and the unused powers of thought in every brain. By using their conceptual skills, students reverse their own disempowering consciousness. They gain an immediate sense of power which accompanies their emerging awareness of reality. Together, the sense of power and the clarity about self and society serve to restore the self-confidence eroded through years of depressant schooling. The restorative implications of analytic thought need recognition, especially when its context involves revealing the structure of social relations which have disempowered the students.

Creation and Re-Creation: Shaping the Re-Shaping

Contextual and conceptual studies are pedagogical foundations for expelling false consciousness. Along with democratic dialogue, they are the basic vehicles for conscientization. Each vehicle has a distinctly egalitarian character. A class of equals critically examining everyday life is the kind of setting to mobilize people as subjects of their own learning process. This interest in democracy and daily life is by itself a means to delegitimize the absence of democracy in our day to day experience. At the same time that social life is demystified, the students inside the process are validated, for powers they possess but have not been taught to use. Such development is provoked by a teacher whose success can be measured by the gradual dissolution and replacement of her or his teaching function.

The teacher is an exorcist confronting a panoply of dybbuks. Having expelled anti-dialogue from her or his own teaching style, the person who provokes liberatory learning must then investigate the students' world, gain some working measure of the level of literacy and politics extant, and then design the thematic problems which will develop skills and awareness. Building on the foundations of dialogue, contextual and conceptual study, there are more advanced modes for facilitating transcendent education. One of these pedagogical techniques could be called *self-creation of media and texts.*

The liberatory class can gain a lot from writing its own texts and designing its own forms of communications. These activities could complement the critical study of printed works and mass media which habitually fill school and daily life. The preparation of its own expressions is an active way for the class to criticize the debased communications and art which surround it. As part of the process, students can create printed, plastic and visual media to give presence to their own idiom. These expressions would magnify their own voices against the sensory saturation of mass culture. Each self-creation could serve as an object of reflection as well as a process of development. By examining the product, the class can gain some detached evaluation on its own progress.

The act of separation from routine reality can be aided through creating your own media and art. This activity pushes away the enveloping world. It changes people from being passive consumers of expression to being creators of meaning. In these efforts, it is reasonable to expect amateurism as well as mimicry of the forms found in everyday life. The class projects need to be evaluated from the bottom up and from inside the process, rather than in comparison to commercial culture or high art. Each class expression registers a certain moment of development. The value can be assessed in terms of where the class began and where it has come to. My own classes have done slide-shows, newspapers, and small texts, as well as video plays. The pride each class has taken in its self-designed media has propelled their emerging presence as critics of culture. There have been lessons even in the projects which went awry.

Diving into the Wreck

Besides action-projects like self-created media or the writing of marriage contracts, there are reconstructive techniques which relate to the *work-style* of the class. One purpose of a liberatory form for class interaction is the restoration of community. Mass culture interferes with the self-organizing capacities people can use for designing common purpose. The liberatory class can address this problem through collective work styles, self and mutual instruction, and peer/group evaluation. These activities are *integrative study formats* which speak to the alienation and atomization of students through mass culture. Isolated from each other, and alienated from their own powers, students need collective vehicles for two key developmental processes: *ego-restoration* and *character-structure awareness.* For the object-subject switch to succeed, the liberatory class must challenge the ego-damaged characters of the students. Years of processing through the institutions of mass society have left students divided, frustrated, and defensive about their own skills. Integrative study formats offer peer-group validation. That is, the students need to appreciate each other as competent, effective and worthy human beings. They don't enter class feeling this way. Their conditioned self-images interfere with their taking command of the learning process. Each student through group interaction has to shed her or his disempowered character. This can be achieved through modes of study which depend on critical peer transactions. The object-subject switch revolves around a turn away from authority-dependence, towards self-regulation. The kind of self-validation here is not simply a person-centered turn-to-yourself. Because disempowerment is social, empowerment has to be social. In the liberatory matrix, reconstruction involves people-in-a-process and a process-in-people. This dialectic permits an encounter between self and the cultural conditions which interfere with critical growth.

Collective work is a bonding experience for people who live with a low level of solidarity. A developmental rule-of-thumb is that people generally rise or sink to the amount of responsibility placed in them. A cooperative style of work in the liberatory class locates decision-making among students who have reacted to orders all their lives. Thus, an exercise in collective work and group deliberation is therapeutically restoring. A class project which cannot get done without student cooperation structures a high level of mutual responsibility into the pedagogy. The idea, once again, involves the withering away of the teacher, which is another way of formulating the withering away of authority-dependence, through the delegation of responsibility into a community of learners. One technique which eases the generalizing of power from the teacher to a group of equals is the *component method*. This simple idea calls for breaking down a large theme — like "work" — into smaller units or sub-themes. The activity of breaking a theme into component parts is itself a conceptual analysis helpful in developing structural perception. Each sub-theme is a problem which a grouping of students can develop for class presentation. After each group has discussed its single dimension, the class as a whole reconvenes for a dialogue which reconstitutes a focus on the larger theme.

The component method not only offers the students an exercise in the conceptual deconstruction of a theme, but it also deconstructs the teacher-centered learning process. Through component analysis, in their sub-groups, the students will have to look to each other more and to the teacher less. The single teacher in the room cannot be continually present in each group. Less supervised in their own work-teams, the students will need to supervise themselves, or else the study will not get done. Such a process structures the retreat of the teacher from direction and opens space for the advance of self-regulation. Within each sub-group, peer-instruction will replace teacher instruction, given that the teacher is only intermittently available. When the class as a whole re-convenes to receive each team's deliberation, students will again be addressing each other. The gradual emergence of a dialogue among peers, mediated by a commonly acknowledged problem, is another in-process test of development. The more students talk to each other about their deliberations on the problem-theme, the more they are emerging as subjects. This is not the same thing as scheduling a mechanical debate between students on an issue, or having students raise hands to ask the teacher's permission to speak. Peer-dialogue through component analysis involves students addressing each other without mediation by the teacher, but only mediated by a commitment to the inquiry. This simple idea amounts to an extraordinary change in the classroom gestalt. Teachers and students have become so conditioned to having all talk pass through the teacher's authority, that no one in class will have experience in self-regulating dialogue. As a skill, democratic discussion becomes easier the more you practice it. Some ways to ease into it include having a rotating chairperson for the sessions, and exchanging hand-raising with self-discipline, that is, people who want to talk can defer to each other, the first rights to the floor going to whoever has not yet spoken.

The democratization of social relations in the classroom will not be automatic. Regression to authority will be continual. In the sub-groups, students may set up a replica of their old schooling. The most advanced student in the team can dominate the others, become the new teacher-authority, and sabotage the collective process through anti-dialogue. To deal with the students' re-assertion of hierarchy, it helps to ask each member of the team to take part in issuing a verbal report, when the class as a whole reconvenes to hear the group deliberations. The most aggressive students and the most passive will each play out their own forms of alienated behavior, so the teacher has to study the reconciliation of the students with each other as well as the teacher's reconciliation with the class. Another problem can emerge when each team reports. The groups may start talking to the whole class, but as they go on, their words become directed more and more towards the teacher. When I notice this happening I try to do a few things. First, I refuse to make eye-contact with the people who have begun addressing their remarks only for my appreciation. This dissolves my presence as a focal point and encourages the talking student to generalize her or his discourse to the whole class. If I sense that I am the only one to whom a question or issue is addressed, I next rephrase the committee report as a question for class discussion, and resist responding myself. This helps wither my presence and decondition the students' authority-focus. Still another way to subjectivize student focus is to take the issue addressed to me and not simply raise it as a question for discussion, but either throw it to another of the teams for comment, or to ask each person in class to draw on their own experience or opinions for an answer. For example, in dialogue around the theme of work, at moments where the discussion-reports are giving me too high a profile as primary respondent, I can ask each person in class to list and talk about the worst jobs he or she has ever had and the best jobs she or he can imagine having. This not only generalizes the dialogue away from the teacher but it also offers a way to practice the structural perception of ordinary experience. The discussion then stays centered on the students' critical discovery.

Collective work process and peer education can address the problems of social fragmentation and self-doubting egos. They build confidence and community. In addition, the activity of testing for development should be supportive and organic. So far, internal and egalitarian measurements of the process have shaped up around the withering away of the teacher and the advance of student self-regulation. Concretely, these developments can be evaluated by determining how much direction the teacher needs to offer and how much peer-dialogue is emerging in the class. These are appropriate vehicles for assessing an interactive and democratic process. A standardized testing instrument brought in from the outside, or designed by the teacher separate from the class, would only contradict the emergence of students as subjects. Similarly, the liberatory class resists levels of learning; it is not easy to standardize it as a stepping-stone to higher level courses. An authentic learning process rejects mechanical agendas or limits on its growth. This does not mean that cognitive as well as affective and political growth cannot be determined. By comparing the class's early, middle and late expressions, projects, dialogues, writings, interactions and component team-work, it is apparent what progress is being made in literacy and conceptual thought. This kind of in-progress and in-process evaluation is an extraordinary challenge to the ordinary shape of power. Institutional testing through the agency of an empowered teacher is a way of keeping students paralyzed as objects. The liberatory class rejects alienation through its own means of organic self-measurement.

The ideal is for evaluation to be a learning activity consistent with the process. A class session can begin with group reflection on the work done so far, and it can end with mutual feedback on the day's interaction. Students can offer verbal and written evaluations of themselves, each other and their sub-groups. Each person can reflect on how much or how little distance has been traveled since the sessions began. The teacher can offer group and individual assessments, and should receive both collective and personal evaluations of his or her role from the students. The two most concrete problems with implementing this approach is that students need to be socialized into self-evaluation and that the institutions we work for will insist on behavioral testing and grading. Both the students below the liberatory teacher and the authorities above will attempt to impose mechanical models on teachers who attempt liberatory experiments. From the students' point of view, democratic discipline will be unfamiliar, disturbing, demanding and appealing. It's common for a period of classroom anarchy to accompany the transition from orthodox to liberatory structure. The teacher can only create the conditions for the practice of freedom, and cannot command anyone to be free, so the consciousness in each class will determine the limits of egalitarian reconstruction. From the institutional point of view, some experiments may be tolerated, some encouraged for window-dressing or as contained ghettoes for trouble-making teachers and students, and many will be discouraged by administrative fiat. In each school or college, teachers need to assess what level of liberatory learning they can assert, given student consciousness and institutional politics. Mass alienation and bureaucratic repression set limits on all phases of a critical pedagogy. Caught in the middle, the teacher needs to remember that liberatory learning is not a professorial conspiracy, but is rather a mutual effort of teacher and students. This suggests that it can only work if the students cooperate, and that the students are a mass of potential allies. They are, in fact, the ones who have the most to gain by the success of democratic learning. This is a support teachers can turn to.

Notes

[1]Paulo Freire, *Education for Critical Consciousness* (Seabury, NY, 1973) 63–84. Freire reproduces some of the slides-representations he used in Brazil to animate critical thinking prior to the start of literacy teaching.

[2]Freire 52.

[3]Paulo Freire, *Pedagogy in Process* (Seabury, NY, 1978).

[4]Joel Spring, *A Primer of Libertarian Education* (Free Life, NY, 1975). See chapter 2 on "Ownership of Self."

[5]Spring 63.

[6]Freire, *Education for Critical Consciousness* 125, 153.

Shor's Insights as a Resource for Your Teaching

1. Shor demonstrates that "critical teaching" demands flexibility; an instructor shifts roles as class members become more active learners. If you keep a journal about your teaching experiences, you can, several times during the course, review and evaluate your own teaching strategies. Use Shor's list of "a multiple complex of roles" for the instructor and analyze your instruction. Should you find that lecture dominates your instruction, you can design additional classroom activities to provoke students into taking responsibility for shaping the learning.

2. Shor states that "the gradual emergence of a dialogue among peers, mediated by a commonly acknowledged problem, is another in-process test of development." That dialogue is as critical for instructors who are learning how to teach writing as it is for the students with whom they work. Initiate or propose a forum in which teaching colleagues can identify, abstract, and set as "problems" the most important themes of their experiences as writing teachers. Some of that dialogue might find its way to "brown bag" sessions with peer instructors or to publication in campus writing across the curriculum newsletters. Or, it might end up in the "Staffroom Exchanges" of *College Composition and Communication*.

Shor's Insights as a Resource for the Writing Classroom

1. Take advantage of the multiple discussions of writing in groups that you find in *The Bedford Guide for College Writers*. In particular, Chapter 19, "Strategies for Working with Other Writers: Collaborative Learning," sets a mood for dialogue. Assign the chapter and follow up with several of the writing activities; each of the other chapters also recommends at least one collaborative activity.

2. Ask class members to take responsibility for a class-to-class dialogue by writing and running off "minutes" of class meetings. At each class meeting, a student takes notes and then writes up the minutes. The next class begins with a collective reading and discussion of the minutes. Anticipate a wide range of written minutes, from the highly formal to the unpredictably imaginative.

3. Peer evaluation is central to assisting reader/writers to analyze and evaluate writing and to develop self-assessing skills. The revision checklists and peer editing checklists that accompany each writing assignment in the textbook can be used for small-group discussion of intermediate and final drafts.

4. Shor recommends that a class write its own texts and asserts that such activity "can change people from being passive consumers of expression to being creators of meaning." Prompt student publication of class writing. You'll find recommendations for initiating this activity in *Teaching with* The Bedford Guide for College Writers: *Practical Suggestions*.

INVESTIGATING

Investigating and writing from investigation are two expectations of an academic community. Many first-year writers come to a university prepared to write a "term paper"; some are puzzled when they confront new definitions of research. *A Writer's Research Manual*, in *The Bedford Guide for College Writers*, focuses on "new" definitions of research: critical reading and evaluation of library research, thoughtful design and evaluation of field research, analysis and synthesis of research materials, and reflective drafting and redrafting of a sustained essay informed by independent judgment. Novice researchers and writers need guidance when they experience research writing as a recursive process. *The Bedford Guide* and the article that follows offer practical, student-centered guidance.

RESEARCH AS A SOCIAL ACT

Patricia Bizzell and Bruce Herzberg

When they discuss student "investigating," Bizzell and Herzberg reject a definition of research as discovery of new knowledge by a solitary researcher. They also reject a definition of research as recovery of information previously discovered by others. Research-as-recovery leads only to report; students do not actively learn or come to "own" research-as-recovery. On the other hand, research-as-discovery requires a shared body of knowledge as a prerequisite to constructing a purpose for research and writing. Students do not yet have access to or grasp of that prerequisite knowledge. How then can investigating be a mode of learning and writing across the curriculum?

Bizzell and Herzberg offer an alternative definition of research: "a social, collaborative act that draws on and contributes to the work of a community that cares about a given body of knowledge." They demonstrate that no researcher is solitary in a process of investigating. A sense of what can be researched and should be researched develops from the "knowledge community" to which the researcher belongs. They explain that every researcher communicates with other researchers in a knowledge community and converses with them about preliminary results and directions of future research and writing. The "original" research produced extends the body of knowledge and also creates new channels for new knowing.

With this definition of research as a social act, the authors also provide a new definition of research-as-recovery. They report that this researcher "is interpreting and reinterpreting the community's knowledge in light of new needs and perspectives, and in so doing creating and disseminating new knowledge." You can see in this discussion that Bizzell and Herzberg share many assumptions with Bartholomae (14).

After defining research as a social and collaborative act, Bizzell and Herzberg suggest that we think about a writing classroom as one neighborhood in the larger academic community. The apprentice researchers in this small neighborhood are participating in the same processes of investigation as are the "experts" in the larger academic community.

With these definitions, the writers demystify research as an experience beyond the grasp of novice readers and writers. Notice how the discussion in A Writer's Research Manual *also shows student researchers interpreting and reinterpreting community knowledge and disseminating new knowledge.*

"Research" can be defined in several ways. First, it may mean discovery, as in the discovery of new information about the world by a researcher. We often call this work "original" research and think of the researcher as a solitary genius, alone in a study or, more likely, a laboratory. Second, "research" may mean the recovery from secondary sources of the information discovered by others. This is often the way we think of student research: students go to the library to extract information from books for a research paper. These two definitions call for some examination.

The first kind of research — discovery — seems more valuable than the second kind — recovery. Discovery adds to the world's knowledge, while recovery adds only to an individual's knowledge (some might add, "if we're lucky"). No matter how we protest that both kinds of research are valuable, there is a distinctly secondary quality to recovery. After all, recovery is dependent entirely upon discovery, original research, for its materials. Discovery actually creates new knowledge, while recovery merely reports on the results of the work of those solitary geniuses.

Common sense tells us that students, with rare exceptions, do not do original research until graduate school, if then. Students and teachers quite naturally share the feeling that research in school is, thus, mere recovery. Consequently, students and teachers often conclude that students are not likely to produce anything very good when they do this kind of research. Indeed, one cannot be doing anything very good while piling up the required number of facts discovered by others. Research-as-recovery seems to justify writing a paper by copying others' accounts of what they have discovered.

If we try, however, to remedy the defects of the research-as-recovery paper by calling for actual discovery, we run into more problems. Those who hope to do original research must know, before anything else, where gaps exist in current knowledge. And, of course, knowing where the holes are requires knowing where they are not. For most (perhaps all) students, this takes us back to research-as-recovery, that plodding effort to find out some of what others have already figured out.

Even research that evaluates sources of information, relates the accounts of information to one another, frames an argument that ties them together, and either reveals something important about the sources themselves or develops into a new contribution on the same topic requires, like discovery, a grasp of a field of knowledge that students cannot be expected to have.

The problem with both kinds of research, then, hinges on knowledge itself. The popular image of the solitary researcher in the lab or the library does not hint at the problem of knowledge — that these people are workers in knowledge who need knowledge as a prerequisite to their work. According to the popular image, they simply find facts. If that were all, presumably anyone could find them. But we know that is hardly the case.

What successful researchers possess that our students typically do not is knowledge, the shared body of knowledge that helps scholars define research projects and employ methods to pursue them. Invariably, researchers use the work of others in their field to develop such projects and consult others in the field to determine what projects will be of value. In short, all real research takes place and can only take place within a community of scholars. Research is a social act. Research is always collaborative, even if only one name appears on the final report.

This, then, is the third definition of research: a social, collaborative act that draws on and contributes to the work of a community that cares about a given body of knowledge. This definition is also a critique of the popular images that we have been examining. For, by the social definition of research, the solitary researcher is not at all solitary: the sense of what can and should be done is derived from the knowledge community. The researcher must be in constant, close communication with other researchers and will likely share preliminary results with colleagues and use their suggestions in further work. Her or his contributions will be extensions of work already done and will create new gaps that other researchers will try to close. Finally, his/her work of discovery is impossible without continuous recovery of the work of others in the community.

The social definition also allows us to revise the notion of research-as-recovery, for the recoverer in a community of knowledge is not merely rehashing old knowledge or informing himself/herself about a randomly chosen topic — he/she is interpreting and reinterpreting the community's knowledge in light of new needs and perspectives, and in so doing creating and disseminating new knowledge. The activity of interpretation reveals what the community values and where the gaps in knowledge reside. "Study knows that which yet it doth not know," as Shakespeare recognized long ago.

In many fields, the activities of synthesis and interpretation are primary forms of research. Think, for example, of the fields of history, philosophy, art and literary criticism, even sociology, economics, and psychology. But the important point is that no field of knowledge can do without such work. Clearly, the lab-science image of research is inaccurate, unrepresentative, and unhelpful. Research as a social act makes far more sense.

This new definition of research changes what it means for students to do research in school. In what ways do students participate in knowledge communities? One well-known and successful research assignment — the family history — suggests that in this very real community, student researchers find material to be interpreted, contradictions to be resolved, assertions to be supported, and gaps to be filled. They share the information and interpretations with the rest of the community, the family, who do not possess such a synthesis and are grateful to get it. But how do students fit into academic knowledge communities that are so much larger and colder than the family?

First, we must recognize that secondary and middle level students are novices, slowly learning the matter and method of school subjects. But they need not master the knowledge of the experts in order to participate in the sub-community of novices. They will need to know what other students know and do not know about a subject that they are all relatively uninformed about. In other words, they need to have a sense of what constitutes the shared body of knowledge of their community and a sense of the possible ways to increase that knowledge by useful increments. Imagine the classroom as a neighborhood in the larger academic community. Students contributing to the knowledge of the class are engaged in research in much the same way that expert researchers contribute to the larger community. They find out what is known — the first step in research — and identify what is unknown by sharing their knowledge amongst themselves. Then, by filling in the gaps and sharing what they find, they educate the whole community.

There are several practical implications for reimagining research in this way:

1. The whole class must work in the same area of inquiry — not the same topic, but different aspects of the same central issue. A well-defined historical period might do: by investigating work, play, social structure, literature, politics, clothing styles, food, and so on, students would become local experts contributing to a larger picture of the period. We will look at other examples later.

2. Students will need some common knowledge, a shared text or set of materials and, most of all, the opportunity to share with each other what they may already know about the subject. By collaborating on a questionnaire or interviewing each other, students learn valuable ways of doing primary research.

3. They will need to ask questions, critically examine the shared knowledge, and perhaps do some preliminary investigation to determine what the most tantalizing unknowns may be. Here again, some free exchange among class members will be helpful.

4. The exchange of ideas must continue through the process of discovery. Like expert researchers, students need to present working papers or colloquia to the research community, distribute drafts and respond to feedback, and contribute to the work of others when they are able. Finally, their work must be disseminated, published in some way, and made available to

the group. The early framework of the research community ought not to be reduced to a way to introduce the regular old term paper.

A perfectly good way to choose the general area of research for a class is simply to choose it yourself. Teachers represent the larger community and can be expected to know something about the topic at hand and provide guidance, so if the topic interests the teacher, all the better. Of course, the teacher can lean toward topics that may interest the class. Students may be asked to choose from among several possibilities suggested by the teacher, but it is likely to be needlessly daunting to the students to leave the whole selection process to them. Among the possibilities for class topics: utopia, Shakespeare's England, Franklin's America, the jazz age, the death of the dinosaurs, the year you were born, images of childhood, the idea of school, work and play, wealth and poverty, country and city, quests and heroes, creativity — it's easy to go on and on.

Central texts can be books, photocopied selections, a film, or videotapes. More's *Utopia* might work for some classes, but a utopian science fiction book might be better for others, and the description of the Garden of Eden, a well-known utopia, is only three pages long. Shakespeare plays are easy to come by, as is Franklin's *Autobiography* or selections from it. Not every topic will require such materials, of course. For some topics, the students' interviews or other initial responses might be compiled into the central text.

The shared knowledge of the group might be elicited through alternate writing and discussion sessions, the students answering questions like "what do you know about *x*?" or "what would you like to know about *x*?" Interviews and questionnaires also work, as noted. All of this preliminary reading, writing, and discussion will help to create a sense of community and give students a jump-start on writing for the group, rather than for the teacher. Needless to say, the teacher ought not to grade and need not even read such preliminary work, beyond requiring that it be done.

Identifying a gap in the group's knowledge and choosing a topic for individual research may still be difficult, and it helps to be armed with suggestions if the students run out of ideas or need to be focused. Have a list of questions about utopias, a list of attempted utopian communities, the names of prominent figures in the period under discussion, some key ideas or events or issues to pursue, and so on. Students may not see, in the central text, problems like class differences in opportunities for schooling, or assumptions about the place of women, or attitudes linked to local or historical circumstances. If discussion and preliminary research do not turn them up, the teacher can reasonably help out. We need not pretend that we are inventing a new field of inquiry, but we must beware of the temptation to fall back on assigned topics.

Having students share drafts and give interim reports takes time, but it is usually time well spent. Students can learn to provide useful feedback to other students on drafts of papers — teachers should not read every draft. Students acting as draft-readers can respond to set questions (what did you find most interesting? what do you want to learn more about?) or work as temporary collaborators in attacking problem areas or listen to drafts read aloud and give oral responses. Other kinds of sharing may be worthwhile. Annotated bibliographies might be compiled and posted so that resources can be shared. Groups might lead panel discussions to take the edge off formal oral presentations. Reading aloud and oral reporting are good ways, too, of setting milestones for writing, and public presentation is important for maintaining the sense of community. Oral reports, by the way, tend to be better as drafts than as final presentations — the feedback is useful then, and anxiety about the performance is muted. Publishing the final results is the last step — copies of the papers might be compiled with a table of contents in a ring binder and put on reserve in the school library, for example.

These activities do not eliminate problems of footnote form and plagiarism, but in the setting of a research community, the issues of footnoting and plagiarism can be seen in a fresh light. Students should be able to articulate for themselves the reasons why members of a

147

community would want to enforce among themselves (and their novices) a common and consistent method of citation. When knowledge exists to be exchanged, footnotes facilitate exchange. So too with plagiarism: members of the community would love to see themselves quoted and footnoted, but not robbed.

An excellent way to teach citation and reinforce community cohesion is to ask students to cite each other. How do you cite another student's paper, especially in draft form? How do you cite an oral report? How do you thank someone for putting you onto an idea? These citation forms may be used rarely, but they are good ways to stir up interest in the need for and uses of footnotes.

If the students are discovering the process of drafting, peer-review, and interim reports for the first time, the problems of discussing work-in-progress may come up in that context. Many students have learned that it is "wrong" to look at someone else's paper and will just be learning about the way professionals share and help each other with their work. A good place to see how collaboration works is to look at the pages of acknowledgments in books. Students will find, in all of their textbooks, long lists of people who are acknowledged for help in the process of writing. Writing their own acknowledgments will allow students to talk about how their ideas were shaped by others, especially by those who cannot reasonably be footnoted.

If the social act of research is successful, students have the opportunity to learn that knowledge is not just found, but created out of existing knowledge. And if people create knowledge, it is reasonable to expect knowledge to change. What people regard as true may be something other than absolute fact. Indeed, it may be only a temporary formulation in the search for better understanding. We can hope that our students will develop ways to evaluate knowledge as a social phenomenon and progress toward a critical consciousness of all claims to knowledge.

Bizzell and Herzberg's Insights as a Resource for Your Teaching

1. If you decide to conduct research in your writing classroom — whether it is an ethnographic study like Robert Brooke's (188) or protocol analysis like Linda Flower's (112) — keep in mind that your colleagues can assist you in defining a research question, in interpreting preliminary research, in determining the next steps to take in your research, and in preparing your essay for a scholarly journal or for presentation at a conference focused on composition studies. Notice how many of the writing theorists in this ancillary acknowledge collaboration in their research and writing.

Bizzell and Herzberg's Insights as a Resource for the Writing Classroom

1. Bizzell and Herzberg offer some very practical advice about designing research units or building a syllabus for a research writing course (a frequent second-semester requirement in American universities). If you are including a research unit in a writing course, invite the class members to brainstorm "central issues" that either the entire group or smaller research groups can use for inquiry. If you as the "expert" in the knowledge community decide on a central issue or theme, be prepared to assist students to generate topics from that central issue.

2. Particularly in the sciences and social sciences, students are required to work collaboratively and to conduct research that leads to a group essay. I have seen no discussion of this process as excellent as "For Group Learning" in Chapter 27, "Writing from Library Research." The authors of *The Bedford Guide* also suggest that students team up to write field research papers, because of the size of such projects (Chapter 29, "Writing from Research in the Field"). Be ready to facilitate the group process of research writing groups; most first-year

writers are unaccustomed to group research and group writing and will appreciate your guidance when they meet snags.

3. Bizzell and Herzberg emphasize that the instructor should not read every draft but should organize peer reading sessions. If you encourage students to use word processing for research writing, ask each writer to print several hard copies and distribute them for fellow writers to carry away and read and respond to.

4. Oral reports on research in process, as the authors suggest, provide additional opportunities for peer evaluation. In addition, you can hold conferences with writers about drafting a sustained essay from the research because your "preparation time" is freed up by students preparing for and presenting oral reports and/or syntheses.

5. Publication of completed researched essays is critical to defining a knowledge community. You'll find advice about publishing student writing in *Teaching with* The Bedford Guide for College Writers: *Practical Suggestions.*

PART THREE

OPTIONS

Notice the abundance of options in the third edition of *The Bedford Guide for College Writers*. You'll find more suggestions for assignments, group learning activities, reading activities, and writing with computers than you could use in one semester. The text could easily work for an entire year's sequence — a curriculum pattern at many colleges and universities — yet it encourages you to choose among options to design each writing course.

But for the semester when you can make use of more options, I've included this series of readings. The annotated bibliography that concludes this volume suggests even more options for you to read and think about as you shape your teaching self. I hope you'll enjoy the "plenty" here.

COLLABORATIVE LEARNING

The Bedford Guide for College Writers features a serious and systematic focus on collaborative learning in the writing classroom. Each chapter of the text includes a box recommending activity for writing in a group; Chapter 19, "Strategies for Working with Other Writers: Collaborative Learning," advises students about forming a writing community and acquiring peer editing expertise. Because of the "take what pleases and helps you" attitude of the authors, you aren't constrained to foster collaborative learning in your writing classroom. However, I think that your students will be intrigued by the inventiveness of each box of suggestions about writing in groups, and they may well establish informal learning communities outside the formal classroom if they don't encounter them in the classroom.

I suspect that the following readings will persuade you that collaborative learning should be a major objective for your course. Bruffee explains the benefits of collaborative learning and reminds us that collaboration is a natural process for professional writers — and for other professionals who write. Wiener provides some measures to use when you want to evaluate both how effectively students use collaborative learning and how skillfully you encourage and prompt it.

THE ART OF COLLABORATIVE LEARNING:
MAKING THE MOST OF KNOWLEDGEABLE PEERS

Kenneth A. Bruffee

Kenneth Bruffee argues that collaborative learning empowers students to work more successfully in and beyond college. He concludes that "it teaches effective interdependence in an increasingly collaborative world that today requires greater flexibility and adaptability to change than ever before." His argument appeared in Change, *the bimonthly publication of the American Association for Higher Education, and speaks to all college-level teachers.*

The theme that knowledge is a social construct recurs in all of Bruffee's discussions of collaboration. (See Bruffee, "Social Construction, Language, and the Authority of Knowledge: A Bibliographical Essay," College English *48 [Dec. 1986]: 773–90.) This theme provides a unique insight for instructors who organize their classroom as a "writing commu-*

*nity"; by assuming that learning occurs among persons, they can help writers understand the
reader-writer "dialogue" and relationships.*

*Like many of the writing specialists whose work appears in this ancillary, Bruffee uses
personal narrative to introduce and clarify a concept that may be new to some of his readers.
His citations would be excellent titles to add to your "when I have time to do extra reading"
list.*

Late last spring, a colleague of mine at a university out West — I'll call him Jim —
wrote and asked if I would read a manuscript of his. He felt he was finally ready for someone
to take a close look at it.

Jim's an old friend. I dashed off a note saying of course I'd read it, with pleasure. At the
beginning of June, which luckily for both of us was right at the end of exams, I got a weighty
package in the mail — 279 pages plus notes. I read it, scribbled clouds of barely decipherable
marginal notes, and drafted a six-page letter to Jim congratulating him on first rate work,
suggesting a few changes and mentioning one or two issues he might think through a bit
further.

He phoned to thank me when he got the letter and asked some questions. We then spent
an hour or so discussing these questions and supporting AT&T in the manner to which it has
become accustomed.

Before the snow blows, I expect I shall see some of Jim's manuscript again. I doubt that
he needs another reading, but I'm happy to do it if he wants me to. I learned a lot reading his
book. We both learned something talking out the few stickier points in it. Anyway, I owe him
one. He did the same for me five years ago, when I was thrashing about in the terminal throes
of the book I was finishing. His name appeared prominently on my acknowledgments page; I
suppose mine will appear prominently on his.

The experience I have just described is familiar to most readers of *Change*. To enjoy
such an experience, you don't have to write a book. All you have to do is work with an
intelligent, compatible committee on an interesting grant proposal or a new development plan
for your college. You know how it can go. Joe gets an idea and sketches it out in a couple of
pages. Mary says, hey, wait a minute — that makes me think of. . . . Then Fred says, but
look, if we change this or add that. . . . In the end everyone, with a little help from his and her
friends, exceeds what anyone could possibly have learned or accomplished alone.

If I'm right that this kind of experience is familiar, then no one reading this article is a
stranger to collaborative learning, however strange the term may be. Jim and I are peers.
When Jim asked me to read his work and I agreed, we became an autonomous collaborative
learning group of two with the task of revising and developing the written product of one of
its members.

The term "collaborative learning" has become increasingly familiar today because it is
applied not only to voluntary associations such as my work with Jim, but also to teaching that
tries to imitate that experience in college and university classrooms. Teachers of writing at
institutions throughout the country are discovering that teaching students in a variety of ways
to work productively on their writing demonstrably improves students' work.

And it is not just writing teachers who are interested. Clark Bouton and Russell Y.
Clark's useful book, *Learning in Groups,* reports on the way collaborative learning is being
applied in subjects from business management to medicine to math. And there is at least one
physics lab manual in the country (at Montana State University) that presents an extended
rationale of collaborative learning on its front cover.

Perhaps more to the point for some of us, at least one trenchant article exists that
explains collaborative learning for the benefit of faculty and administrators who find them-

selves evaluating teachers. Harvey S. Wiener's "Collaborative Learning in the Classroom: A Guide to Evaluation" [the next selection in this ancillary] suggests ways to tell when teachers are using collaborative learning most effectively. It is also, therefore, a useful guide to effective use of collaborative learning for teachers.

Admittedly, there is not much research to date on the effects of collaborative learning in college and university education. But recent work on its effect in primary and secondary schools is relevant. Surveys of research by David Johnson (*Psychological Bulletin* 89) and by Shlomo Sharon (*Review of Educational Research* 50) tend to support the experience of college and university instructors who have used collaborative learning. Students learn better through non-competitive collaborative group work than in classrooms that are highly individualized and competitive. Robert E. Slavin's *Cooperative Learning* reports similar results.

Interest in collaborative learning in colleges and schools is motivated in part by these results. It is motivated also by the observation that the rest of the world now works collaboratively almost as a universal principle. Japanese "Theory-Z" quality circles on the factory floor aside, there is hardly a bank, legal firm, or industrial management team that strives — much less dares — to proceed in the old-fashioned individualistic manner. Physicians are increasingly collaborative, too, although they prefer to call it "consultation." At Harvard Medical School, 25 percent of each entering class currently studies in collaborative groups, bypassing systematic lecture courses almost entirely.

Interest in collaborative learning is motivated also by recent challenges to our understanding of what knowledge is. This challenge is being felt throughout the academic disciplines. That is, collaborative learning is related to the social constructionist views promulgated by, among others, the philosopher Richard Rorty (*Philosophy and the Mirror of Nature*) and the anthropologist Clifford Geertz. These writers say (as Geertz puts it in his recent book, *Local Knowledge*) that "the way we think now" differs in essential ways from the way we thought in the past. Social constructionists tend to assume that knowledge is a social construct and that, as the historian of science Thomas Kuhn has put it, all knowledge, including scientific knowledge, "is intrinsically the common property of a group or else nothing at all." (See Bruffee, "Social Construction, Language, and the Authority of Knowledge: A Bibliographical Essay," *College English* 48 [Dec. 1986]: 773–90.)

Collaborative learning is related to these conceptual changes by virtue of the fact that it assumes learning occurs among persons rather than between a person and things. It even turns out that some teachers who are using collaborative learning have found that social constructionist assumptions enhance their understanding of what they are trying to do and give them a better chance of doing it well.

So, although the term "collaborative learning" may be unfamiliar for some, collaborative learning itself is not new. Our understanding of its importance to higher education began in the late 1950s with Theodore Newcomb's work on peer group influence among college students (*College Peer Groups, The American College,* ed. Nevitt Sanford) and with M. L. J. Abercrombie's research on educating medical students at University Hospital, University of London. Newcomb demonstrated that peer group influence is a powerful but wasted resource in higher education. Abercrombie's book, *The Anatomy of Judgement,* showed medical students learning the key element in successful medical practice, diagnosis — that is, medical judgment — more quickly and accurately when they worked collaboratively in small groups than when they worked individually.

Abercrombie began her important study by observing the scene that most of us think is typical of medical education: the group of medical students with a teaching physician gathered around a ward bed to diagnose a patient. Then she made a slight but crucial change in the way that such a scene is usually played out. Instead of asking each individual medical student in the group to diagnose the patient on his or her own, Abercrombie asked the whole group to examine the patient together, discuss the case as a group, and arrive at a consensus — a single diagnosis agreed to by all.

When she did this, what she found was that students who learned diagnosis collaboratively in this way acquired better medical judgment faster than individual students working alone.

With the exception of small, recently instituted experimental programs at the medical schools of the University of New Mexico and Harvard University, Abercrombie's conclusion has had little impact as yet on medical school faculties anywhere, in Britain or America. But when I read the book in 1972, a dozen years or so after it was published, her conclusion had an immediate and, I believe, positive impact on my thinking about university instruction and, eventually, on the role I see myself in as a classroom instructor.

The aspect of Abercrombie's book that I found most illuminating was her evidence that learning diagnostic judgment is not an individual process but a social one. Learning judgment, she saw, patently occurs on an axis drawn not between individuals and things, but among people. But in making this observation, she had to acknowledge that there is something wrong with our normal cognitive assumptions about the nature of knowledge. Cognitive assumptions, she says, disregard "the biological fact that [the human being] . . . is a social animal." "How [do] human relationships," that is, relations among persons, she asked, "influence the receipt of information about apparently non-personal events?"

In trying to answer this question, Abercrombie makes the brilliant observation that, in general, people learn judgment best in groups; she infers from this observation that we learn judgment well in groups because we tend to talk each other out of our unshared biases and presuppositions. And in passing, she drops an invaluable hint: The social process of learning judgment that she has observed seems to have something to do with language and with "interpretation."

These three principles underlie the practice of collaborative learning. One thing that college and university instructors most hope to do through collaborative learning is increase their students' ability to exercise judgment within the teacher's field of expertise, whatever that field is.

But there is today another thing that instructors hope to do through collaborative learning. They hope to raise their students' level of social maturity as exercised in their intellectual lives. In doing so, instructors are trying to prepare their students for the "real world." They are preparing them to enter law, medicine, architecture, banking, engineering, research science — any field, in fact, that depends on effective interdependence and consultation for excellence.

This discovery that excellent undergraduate education also depends on effective interdependence and consultation awaited the work of William Perry. Perry's book, *Forms of Intellectual and Ethical Development in the College Years,* has made an indelible impression on the thinking of many college and university instructors, but not in every instance for the right reason. Like Abercrombie, Perry makes cognitive assumptions about the nature of knowledge, and most readers to date have found his developmental "scheme" of greatest interest.

Yet Perry himself is not entirely comfortable with the cognitive assumptions underlying his scheme. He has read Thomas Kuhn's *The Structure of Scientific Revolutions,* and he acknowledges that our current view that "knowledge is contextual and relative" is only the most recent phase in a tendency toward the assimilation of cultural diversity that needs for its fulfillment "a new social mind."

As a result, again like Abercrombie, Perry implies that the central educational issues today hinge on social relations, not on cognitive ones: relations among persons, not relations between persons and things. Learning as we must understand it today, he concludes, does not involve people's assimilation of knowledge, it involves people's assimilation into communities of knowledgeable peers. Liberal education today must be regarded as a process of leaving one community of knowledgeable peers and joining another.

Perry's discomfort with this conclusion when it comes to educational practice, however, suggests that he himself may never have quite recognized the full implications of his study. He denies that the creating of communities of knowledgeable peers among students is a legitimate part of rationally and consciously organized university education. He prefers to rely on "spontaneity" to organize knowledge communities among students. He politely dismisses as unprofessional attempts to foster communities among students by using "particular procedures or rituals." Students must independently manage their "identification with the college community" as they go about "divorcing themselves" from the communities they have left behind.

Fortunately, Perry quotes liberally from his raw material — statements made by a sizeable number of informants among the Harvard College undergraduate body. And these undergraduates are not at all as ambivalent as Perry seems to be about regarding learning as a social process. Many of them see their undergraduate education quite explicitly as a difficult, perhaps even treacherous passage from one homogeneous community — the one they came from — to another homogeneous community — the college community of their student peers.

This "marrying into" the new community of students at college is clearly, as the students describe it, an informal, autonomous variety of collaborative learning that challenges students to define their individuality not as starkly and lonesomely independent, but as *inter*dependent members of their new undergraduate community.

The more formal varieties of collaborative learning organized by instructors in classrooms imitate this informal type. And they imitate the "real world" interdependence and consultation that goes on in much business and professional work, including the work my friend Jim and I did together on his book and mine. In classroom collaborative learning, typically, students organized by the teacher into small groups discuss a topic proposed by the teacher with the purpose of arriving at consensus, much as Abercrombie's medical students practiced diagnosis on patients chosen by the teaching physician. Or students may edit each other's writing, or tutor each other, or develop and carry through assigned (or group-designed and teacher-approved) projects together.

But this classroom work, however collaborative, differs in striking ways from autonomous, "real world" interdependence. Classroom collaborative learning is inevitably no more than *semi*-autonomous, because students don't usually organize their own groups or choose their own tasks, as Jim and I did. In most cases, teachers design and structure students' work for maximum learning as part of a course of study. And teachers evaluate the work when it is completed, comparing it with professional standards and the work other students have done, both currently and in the past.

Now, to be accurate to a fault, of course, Jim and I were not an absolutely autonomous group either, any more than any interdependent consultative professional work is. Like most independently organized groups — such as political clubs, golf foursomes, and sand-lot baseball teams — he and I organized our working group on our own initiative for our own purposes, but we played the game, so to speak, by a set of rules we held in common with many other such groups.

The mores, conventions, values, and goals of our professional organization (in our case, the Modern Language Association), of that motley class of human beings called "university faculty," of promotion and tenure committees whose values are probably similar at Jim's college and mine, and so on — these large institutional communities determine to some extent what Jim and I did and said, how we did it and said it, and in point of fact, that we were doing it and saying it at all. Institutional motives and constraints always apply when people prepare themselves to take a hand in what is going on in the prevailing economic, legal, and educational world.

Formed within the immediate confines of a college's institutional structure, however, working groups in a collaborative learning classroom are clearly *semi*-autonomous. Like the New York Yankees, a Boy Scout troup, or the United States Supreme Court, their collaboration is organized by a larger institutional community and with its sanction. Group members abide by the conventions, mores, values, and goals of that institution. The autonomy of classroom groups derives from the fact that once the tasks are set and the groups organized, instructors step back, leaving peers to work in groups or pairs to organize, govern, and pace their work by themselves and to negotiate its outcome.

That this partial autonomy is the key to the impact of collaborative learning is evident when we compare semi-autonomous work with work that is entirely *non*-autonomous. The work of non-autonomous groups cannot reasonably be called collaborative learning at all. Like life in a Trappist monastery or an army platoon, in which activity is rigorously controlled, classroom group work is non-autonomous whenever instructors do not step back from the groups of working students, but rather "sit in" on them or "hover," predetermining the outcome of the work and maintaining the students' direct dependency on the teacher's presence, resources, and expertise.

Degree of autonomy is the key to collaborative learning because the issue that collaborative learning addresses is the way authority is distributed and experienced in college and university classrooms. It would be disingenuous to evade the fact that collaborative learning challenges our traditional view of the instructor's authority in a classroom and the way that authority is exercised.

This issue is much too complex to go into here. But perhaps we can get a provocative glimpse of the possible rewards that might accrue from pursuing it further if we take a brief look at the nature and source of the authority of knowledge in any autonomous working group. Return for a moment to may friend Jim and me at work together on his manuscript. What was the source of the authority exercised in that work? Where was it placed and how did it get there? Not to put too fine a point on it, where did I get the authority to comment on his writing?

The answer, of course, is that Jim and I together generated the authority in our group of two. And to occur at all in this way, that generation of authority required certain conditions. For starters, we like each other. We have read each other's stuff. We respect each other's intelligence. We have similar interests. We have worked together professionally in other circumstances. In short, we were *willing* to collaborate.

It was under these conditions that *Jim granted me* authority over his work by asking me to read it. The authority of my knowledge with regard to his manuscript originated primarily with him. I mean "primarily" here in the strongest possible sense. My authority began with his request, and the principal claim to the validity of my authority resulted from that request.

Furthermore, and equally important, when I responded positively, *I agreed to take on and assert* authority relative to him and his work. In that sense the authority of my knowledge with regard to his manuscript originated primarily not only with his granting me the authority, but also with my accepting it, both, of course, in a context of friendliness and good grace.

Willingness to grant authority, willingness to take on and exercise authority, and a context of friendliness and good grace are the three ingredients essential to successful autonomous collaboration. If any of these three is missing or flags, collaboration fails. These three ingredients are essential also to successful semi-autonomous collaboration, such as classroom collaborative learning.

But when instructors use semi-autonomous groups in classes, the stark reality is that willingness to grant authority, willingness to take it on and exercise it, and a context of friendliness and good grace are severely compromised. Classroom authority does not necessarily begin — as Jim's and mine began — with the participants' (that is, the students') willing consent to grant authority and exercise it. In a classroom, authority still begins in most cases with the representative or agent of the institution, the instructor. Furthermore, except in highly unusual classrooms, most students start the semester as relative strangers. They do not begin, as Jim and I did, as friends. It is not surprising that, as a result, in many classrooms students may at first be wary and not overly eager to collaborate.

That is, collaborative learning has to begin in most cases with an attempt to *re-acculturate* students. Given most students' almost exclusively traditional experience of classroom authority, they have to learn, sometimes against considerable resistance, to grant authority to a peer ("What right has he got to . . . ?"), instead of the teacher. And students have to learn to take on the authority granted by a peer ("What right have I got to . . . ?"), and to exercise that authority responsibly and helpfully in the interest of a peer.

Skillfully organized, collaborative learning can itself re-acculturate students in this way. Once the task is set and the groups organized, collaborative learning places students working in groups on their own to interpret the task and invent or adapt a language and means to get the work done. When the instructor is absent, the chain of hierarchical institutional authority is for the moment broken. Students are free to revert to the collaborative peership that they are quite used to exercising in other kinds of extracurricular activities from which faculty are usually absent.

Of course, students do not always exercise effective collaborative peership in classrooms, especially at first, because they have all so thoroughly internalized our long-prevailing academic prohibitions against it. And it need hardly be added that non-autonomous groups, in which the instructor insists on remaining in direct authority even after the task is set and the groups organized, cannot re-acculturate students in these ways, because the chain of hierarchical institutional authority is never broken.

Because we usually identify the authority of knowledge in a classroom with the instructor's authority, the brief hiatus in the hierarchical chain of authority in the classroom that is at the heart of collaborative learning in the long run also challenges, willy-nilly, our traditional view of the nature and source of the knowledge itself. Collaborative learning tends, that is, to take its toll on the cognitive understanding of knowledge that most of us assume unquestioningly. Teachers and students alike may find themselves asking the sorts of questions Abercrombie asked. How can knowledge gained through a social process have a source that is not itself also social?

This is another aspect of collaborative learning too complex to go into here. But raising it momentarily gives us a hint about why collaborative learning may empower students to work more successfully beyond the confines of college or university classrooms. Collaborative learning calls on levels of ingenuity and inventiveness that many students never knew they had. And it teaches effective interdependence in an increasingly collaborative world that today requires greater flexibility and adaptability to change than ever before.

Bruffee's Insights as a Resource for Your Teaching

1. Bruffee offers writing teachers an alternative to the role of "gatekeeper" that Elbow cited and that has become characteristic of a "writing as process" pedagogy. Rather than predetermining the outcome of all student discussion and work, and rather than keeping students dependent on the teacher as the chief resource, expert, and authority, collaborative learning exercises allow students to tap skills they already use in extracurricular activities and

to discover peers as resources. This frees you from shouldering all the responsibility for the class and gives you opportunities for "hearing" what and how writers are learning.

2. Using collaborative learning, as Bruffee reports, enhances your own understanding of what you are trying to do as you teach writing. In your teaching portfolio, you can log the tasks you set and the way you organized groups along with the results of the group work. As you analyze and review these materials, you may discover ways of clarifying tasks for groups that will help you improve the writing prompts you design. As you think about group dynamics and facilitating successful discussion and problem solving for a group of three or four, you may learn techniques to use for large-group discussion. Because you won't be as confined by having to examine what you did "right or wrong" as the central worker in a class, you can observe more carefully how group members interact and figure out ways of prompting and reinforcing the three kinds of "willingness" in the larger class discussions and activities.

Bruffee's Insights as a Resource for the Writing Classroom

1. To help students become semi-autonomous (and, in the long range, autonomous) learners, you will need to "re-acculturate" many students who come from a background where students competed against each other and where writing was perceived as a solitary task. Peer editing is a major activity in which students learn to trust their right to make and resources for making judgments about a writing and to trust the responses of fellow writers who, because they struggle with the same assignment, might have more sense of the difficulty of the task and the achievement of the writer. Before introducing peer evaluation, prompt a discussion of the role of a peer editor; some class members will be able to cite previous experiences and the benefits and drawbacks of their experiences. Use that discussion to "negotiate" procedures and a checklist for peer editing the assignment in process.

2. Although it is not unique, *The Bedford Guide for College Writers* is one of a handful of composition texts that offer imaginative and carefully organized activities to promote collaborative learning. Sample them freely.

COLLABORATIVE LEARNING IN THE CLASSROOM: A GUIDE TO EVALUATION

Harvey S. Wiener

The Bedford Guide for College Writers *repeatedly emphasizes the value of collaborative learning in a writing classroom. The authors have devoted an entire chapter to collaborative learning and peer evaluation; in addition, each chapter in Parts One, Two, and Three features boxed assignments for writing in groups.* Teaching with The Bedford Guide for College Writers: Practical Suggestions *consistently recommends using small-group discussion sessions for active reading and learning, collaborative prewriting activities, and peer evaluation. In this essay, Harvey Wiener defines what constitutes collaborative learning and describes student and instructor behaviors that demonstrate that a classroom is collaborative.*

Like Kenneth Bruffee, who has written cogently and frequently about collaborative learning as the "conversation" of a "knowledge community," Wiener emphasizes "negotiation" and working to a consensus — to agree or not to agree —which are hallmarks of collaborative learning. He defines collaborative learning as "generating knowledge as a social construct." He explains that we learn collaboratively when we discuss and come to agreement with our peers about what constitutes "knowledge" and the "authority of knowledge" within our community.

157

The teacher in a writing community assists students to engage in active learning by working together, tolerating diversity of opinion and style, and thinking critically as they make decisions. The teacher also assists the class to move into a larger community of knowledgeable peers. The writing teacher assists writers to learn from each other and shape their learning about writing from conversation about all the writing — by students, the instructor, professionals — that happens or appears in the classroom. The writing teacher assists students to discover and analyze some of the writing they meet and may be challenged to produce in knowledge communities across the curriculum.

For the philosophical underpinnings of such a pedagogy, I recommend the essays by Bruffee listed in the annotated bibliography at the end of this book. From his stance both as an instructor who values and prompts collaborative learning and as a master teacher who observes and assesses classroom instruction, Wiener provides practical advice about determining whether collaborative learning occurs in a writing classroom. You can use the list of "indicators" he provides to think about the responsibilities and tasks for both students and instructor in a writing classroom.

Over the last decade collaborative learning has become an important method for college English teachers, who now realize that their own education rarely taught them how colleagues work together to learn and to make meaning in a discipline, and who have rejected philosophically the kinds of approaches to teaching that isolate learners instead of drawing them together. In addition, the problems for education in the seventies and eighties — the changes in student populations, the growth in the number of nontraditional learners in the collegiate body, the alienating nature of learning in large classrooms with too many students, the acknowledged decline of freshmen entry-level skills in reading, writing, speaking, listening, and thinking — these and other challenges to an earlier educational paradigm have shaken our faith in conventional teaching strategies and have called to question our obsession with the major metaphor for learning over the last three hundred years, "the human mind as the Mirror of Nature."

As Ken Bruffee has put it, this old metaphor insists that teachers give students as much information as they can "to insure that their mental mirrors reflect reality as completely as possible" and also insists that we help our students "through the exercise of intellect or development of sensibility, to sharpen and sensitize their inner eyesight" ("Liberal Education" 98). In this ground-breaking essay, Bruffee, drawing upon the works of Thomas Kuhn, L. S. Vygotsky, Jean Piaget, M. L. J. Abercrombie, and Richard Rorty, advances an alternate concept of knowledge as *socially justified belief*. According to this concept, knowledge depends on social relations, not on reflections of reality. Knowledge is "a collaborative artifact" (103) that results from "intellectual negotiations" (107). Bruffee explores the curricular implications of knowledge collaboratively generated, always with one eye on the classroom and the other on the philosophical underpinnings of the new paradigm.

But Bruffee's model, built on the delicate and necessary tension between theory and practice, may not, I suspect, have guided much of what teachers are calling collaborative learning today. I mention this suspicion out of my recent investigations into the issue of assessment generally as a force in postsecondary education and also out of my recent frustration as formal observer of classroom teaching performances in a university-mandated system of evaluation for promotion, retention, and tenure. I realized as I watched these attempts at instruction through collaboration that to apply to the new paradigm the standards we had in place for the old was inappropriate. Our elaborate student evaluation forms and classroom observation checklists had little relation to the classroom activities I observed. What was worse, I realized that we had not established either as an institution or as a profession any standards for judging our attempts to implement the evolving concept of teaching and learning as a social act. Hence the question I intend to address in this essay: How do we assess the effectiveness of collaborative teaching models in the classroom?

Asking this question on evaluation now, as collaborative learning grows more and more popular, is to seize an advantage we have missed many times before. Formal assessment has always been the stepchild of the profession. In the past we have given up important evaluation activities for certifying the success of our students as learners and of ourselves as teachers. Professional testing agencies, for example, not classroom teachers, develop, and oversee college entrance tests for graduates and undergraduates. Despite the obligatory committees of teachers and researchers who are invited to establish standards in general terms and to high-light areas of learning, professional test writers are the ones who produce specifications on most commercially prepared large-scale examinations. Worse still, legislatures, seeing a void, have leaped in to define competencies we have not. In many states, legislatures, not teachers, have mandated and overseen the development of tests for college writers. The Florida Depart-ment of Education, for example, has created the College Level Academic Skills Test (an essay and an objective test) for all students in the state, and has prescribed the number of pages to be written each week in writing classes. Georgia has a similar test in progress. Even current measures for judging a teacher's classroom effectiveness have been influenced insufficiently by the teachers themselves who are being judged. Administrative committees, education school faculty, and evaluation specialists often develop the standards for classroom observations and create atomistic, overly-generalized checklists for use in assessing teaching. Or, institutions develop no standards whatsoever, and classroom observation is an exercise in a senior professor's effort to characterize someone else's teaching by means of some vague, unarticulated, and as yet socially unjustified vision of perfection. Even useful efforts by the profession are often too late to do as much good as they might have done had they flowered earlier. The evaluation instruments developed by the Conference on College Composition and Communication's Committee on the Evaluation of the Teaching of Writing, for example, reached English teachers ten years after the City University of New York's faculty negotiating unit, the Professional Staff Congress, wrote an evaluation system into the University's faculty contract, long after precedent set most of the institutional evaluation procedures in cement.

By advancing collaborative learning as a productive instructional mode for teaching literature and writing, however, English teachers have a rare opportunity to evolve a set of standards by which to judge classroom performance in the new paradigm. Our first obligation is to define for ourselves what we see as efficient classroom models for collaborative learn-ing. Our next obligation is to pass on to beginners the standards by which we measure our own performances so that new teachers seeking membership in this intellectual community have a clear paradigm to study. And, finally, we are obliged to lay out for classroom observ-ers what to look for as hallmarks of collaboration so that any judgments evaluators make about teaching performance are judgments our community has justified through thoughtful, disciplined discussion.

In an effort to move forward this evolution of standards for appropriate collaborative teaching models and to provide a temporary set of guidelines for the classroom observer of collaborative learning, I will look at the teacher's role in a collaborative session sequentially. I will confine my remarks to one of the most common kinds of collaborative learning, collaborative group work. Here, students perform some common task in small study and discussion groups. The class is divided into clusters of three to seven students each. Each group chooses a recorder to take notes on the conversation and, when the discussion ends, to report the group's deliberations to the whole class. The time required for a collaborative effort depends on the task, but fifteen or twenty minutes is a bare minimum. The teacher helps the class compare results, resolve differences, and understand features of the task that students did not work out on their own.

The Teacher as a Task Setter

The success of the collaborative model depends primarily upon the quality of the initial task students must perform in groups. Hence, the instructor's role as task setter is one that any observer must view with great attention. "What is essential," Bruffee writes, "is that the task lead to an answer or solution that can represent as nearly as possible the collective judgment and labor of the group as a whole" (*Short Course* 45).

The group's effort to reach consensus by their own authority is the major factor that distinguishes collaborative learning from mere work in groups. What is consensus? Unfortunately the word is widely misunderstood as a dimension of collaborative learning. It is not an activity that stifles differences or intends to make conformists out of divergent thinkers. John Trimbur asserts that those new to collaborative learning often miss

> the process of intellectual negotiation that underwrites the consensus. The demand for consensus that's made by the task promotes a kind of social pressure. Sometimes, to be sure, this pressure causes the process of negotiation to short circuit when students rush to an answer. When it works, however, the pressure leads students to take their ideas seriously, to fight for them, and to modify or revise them in light of others' ideas. It can also cause students to agree to disagree — to recognize and tolerate differences and at best to see the value systems, set of beliefs, etc. that underlie these differences.

Consensus, he points out, "is intellectual negotiation which leads to an outcome (consensus) through a process of taking responsibility and investing collective judgment with authority."

Certainly methodology in education for many years has depended upon group work, but it is generally not an activity that demands collective judgment. In elementary and secondary schools, for example, teachers of reading, spelling, and mathematics divide students into groups for skills instruction, each group at a different level. Such groupings permit those with like abilities to investigate topics at the same rate and with the same intensity as their peers. But this kind of group work is by no means collaborative learning. It merely subdivides the traditional hierarchical classroom into several smaller versions of the same model. Despite the groups, the teacher remains the central authority figure in the students' attempts to acquire knowledge. Other popular yet perhaps more imaginative types of group activity — clusters of students working on a common project or experiment, say — also rarely build upon the idea of a learning community that leads to joint decisions. Much group work on projects and experiments of this sort is only the sum of its parts, each student contributing his or her piece without the vital "intellectual negotiation" that "places the authority of knowledge in the assent of a community of knowledgeable peers" (Bruffee, "Liberal Education" 107). Students put into groups are only students grouped and are not collaborators, unless a task that demands consensual learning unifies the group activity.

To assure that the teacher in a collaborative learning classroom is guiding students to collective judgments in groups, evaluators are right to insist that the task be written down. A written task provides the language that helps to shape students' conversations. An observer asked to judge a class session in collaborative learning must first scrutinize the task and then comment on it in the evaluation report in the same way he or she would comment on the teacher's preparation for any lesson. To look only at the outward manifestations of the collaborative classroom — the fact that students group together and talk within their groups — is to look at the activity with one eye closed.

Peter Hawkes points out important differences between collaboration and group work and these differences inhere in the nature of the task:

> Sometimes in mere group work the teacher sets a task or poses a question that has an answer that the teacher has already decided on. Groups take on the role of the smart kid in class who guesses what's on the teacher's mind. The evaluator should examine the task assigned and the way the teacher responds to the student reports in the plenary session to see whether the authority of knowledge has been shifted temporarily in the classroom. In CL, the teacher should ask questions that have more than one answer or set problems that are capable of more than one solution. In other

words, sincere questions rather than pedagogical ones. The CL teacher is interested in the way the students come up with their consensual answer, the rationale for that answer, the opportunities for debate among groups, the suggestion of how knowledge in a discipline is arrived at rather than in leading students toward an already acknowledged "right answer." CL changes the student-teacher relationship; mere group work appears to but does not.

A good written statement of task will probably have a number of components: general instructions about how to collaborate in this particular activity; a copy of the text, if a single text is the focus of the collaboration; and questions appropriately limited in number and scope and offered in sequence from easier to more complex, questions requiring the kind of critical thinking that leads to sustained responses from students at work in their groups. Since collaborative group work normally should move toward consensus, instructions almost always should require a member of a group to record this consensus in writing. But although one member writes the report, the group as a whole shapes it. Some experienced collaborative learning teachers insist that the recorder do something more like a performance after the work in the group ends — a formal presentation to the class, participation in a debate with recorders from other groups, or some other responsible social activity that may be subjected to group judgment. When recorders must perform, these teachers argue, the recorders keep the groups functioning smoothly and efficiently.

The teacher's role as task-setter often must go beyond simply writing the assignment down and distributing it. This is especially true when students consider varied texts collaboratively (their own papers, for example). The instructor may have to guide the manner in which students attack the task by reviewing some of the principles that need attention if activity is to move forward before the group work begins. For example, in a typical collaborative session, dividing students into small groups to read and provide commentary on the coherence of a practice essay, an instructor might explain to the class at the beginning of the hour some of the principles of coherence in expository writing. Or, if students are to comment on drafts of each other's essays, the teacher could begin by asking student groups to generate a *Reader Response Guide.* Asking the class "Which two or three vital questions do you wish to have answered about your draft so that you can take it to the next stage" and then collecting the questions for everyone to see is effective because it reviews whatever was taught in an earlier class or in advance of the assignment; it highlights for the whole class the major issues to be addressed in this writing task; it calls attention immediately to the students' own most pressing concerns; and it gives the class an opportunity to buy into the collaborative process as shapers of their own learning.

For evaluators the key issue here once again is that the task and the teacher's role in setting it must stimulate active learning that leads to an important outcome: consensus (either agreement or agreement to disagree) on the issue at hand. Many collaborative settings I've witnessed do not pay much attention to consensus. Students divided into groups to examine drafts and to "discuss" their papers, but who lack specific guidelines, will flounder. I saw one class session like this where students told to discuss their drafts discussed only their errors in spelling and sentence structure, probably the least valuable things to talk about in the early stages of composing. Perhaps even more troublesome than activities inappropriate to the task is no collaboration at all. The risk is great that, without clear guidelines, students will just pat each other on the back, attack each other counterproductively, or fall silent.

An observer in a collaborative setting, then, must consider the task set by the teacher as the first essential element in any evaluation. The task must figure very prominently in judgments about the class. Questions an observer might ask about the task are: is it clearly worded and unambiguous? does it split the exercise into workable segments? do students know what to do and how to do it? is the task pertinent to the students' needs, goals, and abilities? does the exercise move toward consensus? do the questions students deal with stimulate critical thinking? and, perhaps most important of all, does it call on what students can be expected to know in a way that will lead them together beyond what they already know — is the task difficult enough to challenge but not too difficult to stonewall conversations?

The Teacher as Classroom Manager

The second aspect of collaborative learning for evaluators to consider is the teacher as classroom manager. With the task laid out, how does the teacher implement the actual act of collaboration? How does the teacher organize the social relations in which learning will occur? Have students learned to form groups easily and with relative speed? Are chairs organized in well-spaced clusters so that group conversations do not drown each other out? Do group members demonstrate an ability to work together, one person talking at a time, others listening? Are time limits clear and generally adhered to, and yet flexible? Does the teacher check on how much more time the groups may need as the prescribed end point draws near, and perhaps urge the groups to move on to complete their tasks? If a recorder or reporter is required — the member of each group who acts as synthesizer of the discussion — are his or her functions clear? Does the recorder or reporter take down statements carefully and check with group members for accuracy?

The Teacher's Role during Group Work

The third aspect of collaborative learning that evaluators should examine carefully is the teacher's behavior while the groups are working. Most teachers I have observed travel from group to group answering questions from students, participating in discussions, probing with further questions, guiding responses, and focusing students' attention on the task. Although some of these steps may be necessary from time to time, the teacher's presence as a group member challenges one of the basic tenets of collaboration in the classroom. "The purpose of collaborative learning . . . ," Bruffee points out, "is to help students gain authority over their knowledge and gain independence in using it" (*Short Course* 49). In the classroom "teachers create social structures in which students can learn to take over the authority for learning as they gain the ability and confidence to do so" (49). A teacher joining a group can easily undermine the development of that authority and that confidence. All attention will turn to the teacher as the central figure in the learning process. Usually, collaboration advances best when groups are left pretty much to the students themselves. At this point in the process, in most cases the best teacher is usually the seemingly most idle teacher, busy with other tasks or even going out of the room from time to time as the groups conduct their business. Evaluators, then, should not judge harshly a practitioner of collaborative learning who reads papers or who leaves the class during small group discussions.

An observer can learn a great deal about prior instruction by watching how students engage in the group task. The noise level in the room, the arrangement of furniture, the ease with which the groups are formed, the tone of conversation among students, the nature of reports emerging from groups all indicate how much the class has practiced efficient collaborative schemes in the past. Evaluators, therefore, should note very carefully how students behave in their groups as a signal of the teacher's advance preparation. Group management is the teacher's responsibility and the collaborative learning teacher pays careful attention to dynamics and composition. Are there too many monopolizers in one group? too many withdrawn students? too many unprepared students? If a group is not working at the task or if a group delivers a weak report, how does the teacher respond? Evaluators should pay particularly close attention to the reporter's role after group activity ends. If selected students make thoughtful, responsible, well-planned presentations to the whole class, the evaluator knows that the teacher has built collaboration theory into the structure of the course prior to the evaluation session. Student behavior in groups and at the reporting stage is an important signal for the teacher's skill in the uses of collaborative learning.

The Teacher as Synthesizer

The fourth aspect of collaborative learning that the classroom observer must consider is how the teacher performs in the role of synthesizer after the activity in groups is complete. Once the groups finish their work, it is important for each recorder to share the group's consensus with the rest of the class. With this done, the teacher must help the class as a whole to make sense and order out of the sometimes conflicting and contradictory reports. Writing the points raised by each group on the chalkboard or on a transparency for the overhead projector (or asking recorders themselves to do this) allows everyone to discuss and evaluate the conclusion arrived at by the groups. Even when a consensus report does not follow inevitably from the task, when, for example, students read their drafts aloud to each other for revision, report on the process itself or on what people think they learned from it may be useful. Questions from the teacher like "What were the general recommendations made to members of the group?" or "What did readers of your paper suggest that you do to take it to the next stage?" help to reinforce what has been learned as well as to establish the value of learning communities and of peer review in any intellectual process.

How the teacher conducts this plenary discussion is very important to the success of collaborative learning. First, the teacher helps students synthesize each group's results with the results produced by other groups. The teacher should lead the class to consider the similarities and contradictions in the recorded points of view and should unite them all, if possible, into a larger vision. The instructor must help students see their differences and to reconcile them. Here "the teacher acts as a referee, directing the energies of the groups on two sides of a divided issue to debate the matter until the parties either arrive at a position that satisfies the whole class or until they agree to disagree" (Bruffee, "Liberal Education" 52).

With agreement, then, the teacher's role once again changes. The teacher now must help the class move further toward joining another community of knowledgeable peers, the community outside the classroom, the scholars who do research in the discipline, who establish the conventions of thinking and writing in those disciplines, who write books and articles and read papers on the problem at hand. "What happens when we learn something," Bruffee writes, "is that we leave a community that justifies certain beliefs in a certain way and join another community that justifies other beliefs in other ways. We leave one community of knowledgeable peers and join another" ("Liberal Education" 105). By synthesizing results of the individual groups, and comparing that synthesis with the consensus of the larger community of knowledgeable peers — the teacher's own community — the teacher helps complete the movement into this larger community.

An observer considering these last two features of the teacher's role — as synthesizer and as representative of the academic community — must be prepared to evaluate the teacher's knowledge of content as well as the teacher's ability to bring the class to perceive differences and similarities in the conclusions of the groups. The teacher must guide students to classify the ideas presented by the various groups without judging one idea right and the other wrong, but by helping the class to investigate the reasoning used to develop and shape the ideas. The teacher also must lead the class to consider how their consensus differs from the consensus of the larger community, and must lead the class to speculate about how that larger community might have arrived at its decision. The skill with which the teacher manages the stages of collaboration is directly related to the teacher's knowledge of and commitment to the philosophical principles upon which collaborative learning is based (see Bruffee, "Collaborative Learning"). An instructor who understands and believes in knowledge as a social construct will see group reporting as an important means of advancing knowledge in the classroom. On the other hand, an instructor willing to experiment with group work but clinging to the Mirror-of-Nature metaphor will find it hard to avoid using the group setting as anything other than a microcosm of the lecture hall. Many teachers who attempt collaborative learning but abandon it are frequently trying to achieve the same ends in groups that they tried to achieve in the more familiar lecture-recitation session or Socratic dialogue. Thus, an appropriate evaluation should consider the teacher's understanding of collaboration as a means to generate knowledge as a social construct and not simply as the use of a new configuration of students in the classroom.

Yet a one-hour class does not always easily reveal a teacher's knowledge of the rationale for collaboration. Evaluators, therefore, may find it useful to consult with teachers either before or after the class in order to uncover the roots of the particular program of learning for the session. Furthermore, the evaluator's interests must extend to the whole course of study and should not be confined exclusively to a single hour's instruction. Too often collaborative activities are a chain of exercises, unrelated to each other. Thus, in a conference with the teacher an evaluator should aim to discover the goals for the course as a whole and the relation of those goals to the collaborative task observed.

Summary

I am not unaware of the problems that inhere in the kind of evaluation that this essay is advocating. Collaborative learning is messier in practice than in theory; no one can "live" the theory as clearly as the model suggests. As Harvey Kail points out:

> One doesn't simply eradicate the "mirror-of-nature metaphor" from one's life as if one were changing from Crest to Colgate. Sometimes I find myself back in the old world, the one where knowledge is "out there" and my job is to find it and my students' job is to model my search. Other times, more frequently now, I see conversation, its give and take, as the central manufacturing process of knowledge and appropriate ways of talking (and writing) as the goal. At the same time, I also believe that the lecture is a perfectly legitimate mode of teaching, even within the boundaries established by CL theory. So . . . I contradict myself . . . very well. . . .

Certainly, a commitment to collaborative learning is based on a desire to confront the traditional view of knowledge in our own lives. Like all confrontations, this too is anything but smooth and simple.

Yet my purpose here is to move the practitioner of collaborative learning to an ideal model that will help students achieve knowledge in the classroom. Toward that end, I wish to summarize the features of the collaborative session that an outside evaluator should consider:

1. the nature and quality of the task statement
2. the social setting of the collaborative activity and the behavior of students during the execution of the task
3. the teacher's behavior during the execution of the task
4. the teacher's role in group composition and management
5. the nature and quality of the reports made by each group
6. the teacher's performance as synthesizer and as representative of the academic learning community
7. the relation of the collaborative activity to the design of the course
8. the teacher's knowledge of and commitment to the rationale of collaborative learning

The critical underlying principle for evaluators is that in the collaborative learning classroom the instructor is in no sense a passive figure. Collaborative learning is not unstructured learning; it replaces one structure, the traditional one, with another, a collaborative structure. The roles I have attempted to outline here define some of the elements to consider in evaluating a teacher's effectiveness as a leader of collaborative learning within this new structure.

Expecting students to engage in productive conversation simply by reshuffling chairs, by telling them to work together in groups, or by requiring, without further guidance, that they read each other's papers, can easily stymie collaboration and not stimulate it. I have seen reflected in the attitude of teachers inexperienced with collaboration and inattentive to its complexities as a mode of learning an often unfulfilled plea to students: "Don't just sit there — collaborate!" Neither inactive nor nondirective, the teacher in the collaborative classroom must plan and organize the session so that students know that the end is not simply to work in groups but to work in groups in an effort to reach consensus for an important task. The effective collaborative learning teacher is one who understands the basis and structure of collaborative learning and who knows how to lead students to work productively within it.[1]

Note

[1]I have based my comments in this essay upon many years' experience in observing college English teachers as part of a required program of classroom observation as well as upon my work in supervising teachers across the curriculum in LaGuardia's ongoing faculty development effort, the Integrated Skills Reinforcement Project. But I have shared this paper with a number of colleagues who have long been at the forefront of collaborative learning — including my mentor in all this, Kenneth Bruffee (Brooklyn College), and Marian Arkin (LaGuardia Community College), John Bean (Montana State University), Peter Hawkes (Dutchess Community College), Harvey Kail (University of Maine at Orono), Carol Stanger (John Jay College), and John Trimbur (Boston University). Of course, I assume all responsibility for the points made here, but I acknowledge with gratitude the thoughtful comments and suggestions of my colleagues as this paper evolved from draft to draft.

Works Cited

Bruffee, Kenneth A. "Collaborative Learning and the 'Conversation of Mankind.' " *College English* 46 (1984): 635–52.

_____. "Liberal Education and the Social Justification of Belief." *Liberal Education* 68 (1982): 95–114.

_____. *A Short Course in Writing.* 3rd ed. Boston: Little, 1985.

Hawkes, Peter. Letter to the author. n.d.

Kail, Harvey. Letter to the author. 25 Feb. 1985.

Trimbur, John. Letter to the author. 10 Feb. 1985.

Wiener's Insights as a Resource for Your Teaching

1. Use Wiener's list of features of collaborative learning to observe and assess situations in which collaboration is expected: committee meetings, small-group discussion in your classroom or in graduate or postgraduate seminars you attend, and so on. If you find an absence of collaboration, list problems or obstructions to collaboration. Then generate possible solutions for some of those problems. Use that analysis to think about "what's happening" the next time you organize group learning in your classroom.

2. Invite your colleagues to join you in a study group meeting once or twice a month to discuss collaborative assignments used for writing across the curriculum. Ask one member of the group to be responsible each time for describing a classroom situation in which he or she promoted collaboration. Such a study group is a collegial and social opportunity to swap teaching strategies, explore philosophies about teaching and learning, and enhance the writing-as-learning environment on your campus.

Wiener's Insights as a Resource for the Writing Classroom

1. Wiener emphasizes the need for a plenary session in which small groups report their findings or "consensus" to the larger group. When you use small-group discussion for a reading such as Quammen's "A Republic of Cockroaches," set a task that makes each group decide on the author's purpose. Then ask each group to report its conclusions and direct the larger community to evaluate each interpretation and to decide, through some voting process, on the interpretation that is "most literal as paraphrase," "most insightful," "most effective" and the interpretation that most requires a reader to connect the author's thinking to a larger issue, in Quammen's case the danger of being specialized and unable to adapt.

2. Reinforce the value of collaborative activities by frequently assigning journal entries that ask writers to reflect on and describe how their reading and writing has been influenced by the conversation of peers.

3. Follow up peer evaluation sessions with some self-assessment writing prompts that ask the individual writers to describe their choices about using peer advice.

4. Invite the class to collaborate by inventing and editing prompts for use in in-class writing or for simulations of essay exams.

ESL STUDENTS AND WRITING COURSES

"ESL students" is itself a misleading phrase. Used generically to describe students who are nonnative speakers of English, it includes learners who are immigrants or refugees planning to live in a country where the English language dominates, international students who must use the language skillfully enough to pursue a degree in an "English-speaking" institution, and citizens whose first language is not English and who may not be sufficiently fluent in the second language to communicate ideas as effectively as they desire and need. ESL students are as diverse as the institutions they attend, the reasons they are attending, their undergraduate or graduate status, the variety of first languages they speak, the expertise they have in writing in English, and their level of language proficiency.

However, they share the arduous task of becoming fluent enough and proficient enough to think and write in a second language with its unique rhetorical expectations and cultural perspectives. Many of their writing instructors confess that they feel less than competent in and confident about their abilities to assist these writers as effectively as they can assist native speakers. When ESL students are "mainstreamed" in writing classrooms, how can writing instructors more ably assist them as writers?

This is an area of teaching and writing where the "practitioners' lore" and research do not yet meet the needs of instructors. I've coupled two readings to suggest ways of getting started. Ann Raimes's essay provides a clear survey of changes in writing instruction over the last twenty-five years and the implications for ESL teachers and researchers as they focus on writing. Muriel Harris's essay discusses the influences of a writer's culture and language on the task of writing in English as a second language. Both writers resist thinking about the first language (L1) as an impediment and something that "interferes" in the tasks of communicating in a second language (L2). Both encourage us to reperceive the first language as an important resource for ESL students as they grapple with thinking in a foreign language.

OUT OF THE WOODS: EMERGING TRADITIONS IN THE TEACHING OF WRITING

Ann Raimes

Ann Raimes has taught English as a second language with its four interconnected skills of listening, speaking, reading, and writing in a nonnative language, for twenty-five years. Her primary audience in this essay is other ESL teachers and researchers, but her emphasis on writing instruction as it helps or hinders nonnative speakers makes her ideas a valuable resource. You'll notice the citations of several writing theorists whom you have encountered in your reading about composition theory and pedagogy: Emig, Bruffee, Hairston, and Elbow. You'll also gain a good idea of "whom to read" to learn about what the "specialists" — ESL teachers of writing — can tell you about working with student writers.

The emerging traditions Raimes identifies have influenced the authors of The Bedford Guide for College Writers; *I suspect they will also influence you positively. Raimes cites shifts in assumptions about how to teach writing and how to teach English as a second language that seem to be "new traditions." Writing teachers today, however they might disagree about approaches, designs, and procedures for teaching writing, seem to recognize the complexity of composing, the diversity of students as learners, the necessity that language and writing teachers know about the process of language acquisition as well as the writing process, the fact that pedagogic decisions are political, and the value of classroom practice and classroom teaching to learn how better to assist ESL students as they write.*

Most good fairy tales, at least the ones that delight us and make us or our children beg for more, begin with looking back to "once upon a time." Since the TESOL [Teachers of English to Speakers of Other Languages] organization has now reached its 25th anniversary, this seems a good way to begin looking at the story of how the teaching of writing to adult (secondary and higher education) nonnative speakers of English has developed since 1966; we can follow it up with an account of the thickets and thorny problems we face as we journey into the woods. Despite false trails, we might still, true to the best endings of fairy tales, be able to find a way out of the woods and live happily ever after. But that last is only speculation. Let's begin by looking back at the trails we've followed up to now, keeping in mind that we might not all have met the same witches, wizards, wolves, or good fairies along the way. Readers should be aware that the author of this article has been teaching ESL for more than 25 years, and so her telling of the story is inevitably influenced by the paths she chose to follow.

Once Upon a Time: Writing Instruction and Research 1966–1991

This brief historical survey delineates four approaches to L2 [second language] writing instruction that have been evident in the last 25 years. Each approach, at least as it emerges in the literature, has a distinctive focus, highlighting in one case the rhetorical and linguistic *form* of the text itself; in another, the *writer* and the cognitive processes used in the act of writing; in another, the *content* for writing; and in the last, the demands made by the *reader*. The dates given mark the approximate time when each focus first appeared consistently in our literature; no final dates are given, since all the approaches are still, in varying degrees, subscribed to in theory and certainly in practice.

Focus on Form, 1966–

Once upon a time, when the TESOL organization first was founded in 1966, the audiolingual method was the dominant mode of instruction. The view that speech was pri-

167

mary meant that writing served a subservient role: to reinforce oral patterns of the language. So in language instruction, writing took the form of sentence drills — fill-ins, substitutions, transformations, and completions. The content was supplied. The writing reinforced or tested the accurate application of grammatical rules. In the 1970s, the use of sentence combining (O'Hare, 1973; Pack & Henrichsen, 1980), while still focusing on the manipulation of given sentences and thus, according to Zamel (1980), ignoring "the enormous complexity of writing" (p. 89), provided students with the opportunity to explore available syntactic options.

In the early 1970s, too, passages of connected discourse began to be used more often as classroom materials in the teaching of writing. Controlled composition tasks, still widely used today, provide the text and ask the student to manipulate linguistic forms within that text (see, for example, Byrd & Gallingane, 1990; Kunz, 1972; Paulston & Dykstra, 1973). However, the fact that students are using passages of connected discourse does not necessarily guarantee that the students view them as authentic. If the students are concentrating on a grammatical transformation, such as changing verbs from present to past, they "need pay no attention whatever to what the sentences mean or the manner in which they relate to each other" (Widdowson, 1978, p. 116).

It was not only grammatical form that was emphasized in the 1960s and early 1970s. Concern for rhetorical form was the impetus for Kaplan's influential 1966 article that introduced the concept of contrastive rhetoric. His "doodles article," as he calls it (Kaplan, 1987, p. 9), represents the "thought pattern" of English as "dominantly linear in its development" (Kaplan, 1966, p. 4) in contrast to the paragraph patterns of other languages and cultures. It has led to compensatory exercises that offer training in recognizing and using topic sentences, examples, and illustrations. These exercises often stress imitation of paragraph or essay form, using writing from an outline, paragraph completion, identification of topic and support, and scrambled paragraphs to reorder (see, for example, Kaplan & Shaw, 1983; Reid & Lindstrom, 1985).

Formal considerations are also the basis for a great deal of current L2 writing research. Textual features, such as the number of passives or the number of pronouns, are counted and compared for users of different cultures (Reid, 1990). Researchers examine the structure of such features as introductory paragraphs (Scarcella, 1984), the form of essays in various languages (Eggington, 1987; Hinds, 1987; Tsao, 1983), cohesion and coherence (Connor, 1984; Johns, 1984), and topical structure (Lautamatti, 1987). A large-scale study of written composition across 14 countries established to codify tasks and describe the state of writing instruction has provided a rich data base for cross-cultural discourse analyses (Purves, 1988). (For a summary of text-based research, see Connor, 1990.) A form-dominated approach has the largest body of research to inform and support it; it has been with us for a long time, and lends itself to empirical research design.

Focus on the Writer 1976–

The 1970s saw the development of more than sentence combining and controlled composition. Influenced by L1 [first language] writing research on composing processes (Emig, 1971; Zamel, 1976), teachers and researchers reacted against a form-dominated approach by developing an interest in what L2 writers actually do as they write. New concerns replaced the old. In place of "accuracy" and "patterns" came "process," "making meaning," "invention," and "multiple drafts." The attention to the writer as language learner and creator of text has led to a "process approach," with a new range of classroom tasks characterized by the use of journals (Peyton, 1990; Spack & Sadow, 1983), invention (Spack, 1984), peer collaboration (Bruffee, 1984; Long & Porter, 1985), revision (Hall, 1990), and attention to content before form (Raimes, 1983a; Zamel, 1976, 1982, 1983). Zamel (1983) has recommended that teachers not present instruction in the use of thesis sentences and outlines before the students have begun to explore ideas. In response to theory and research on writers' processes, teachers have begun to allow their students time and opportunity for selecting topics, generating ideas, writing drafts and revisions, and providing feedback. Where linguistic accuracy was formerly emphasized from the start, it is now often downplayed, at least at the beginning of the process, delayed until writers have grappled with ideas and organization. Some practitioners even entirely omit attention to grammar, as in ESL writing textbooks that contain no grammar reference or instructional component (e.g., Benesch & Rorschach, 1989; Cramer, 1985).

Research publications on L2 writing processes grew rapidly in the 1980s to inform and support the new trends in instruction (e.g., Cumming, 1989; Friedlander, 1990; Hall, 1990; Jones, 1982, 1985; Jones & Tetroe, 1987; Raimes, 1985, 1987; Zamel, 1982, 1983; for a summary, see Krapels, 1990). However, although we are beginning to discover much about the writing process, the small number of subjects in case study research limits generalizations, and we are rightly warned that the "lack of comparability across studies impedes the growth of knowledge in the field" (Krapels, 1990, p. 51).

Despite the rapid growth in research and classroom applications in this area, and despite the enthusiastic acceptance of a shift in our discipline to a view of language as communication and to an understanding of the process of learning, teachers did not all strike out along this new path. The radical changes that were called for in instructional approach seemed to provoke a swift reaction, a return to the safety of the well-worn trail where texts and teachers have priority.

Focus on Content 1986–

Some teachers and theorists, alienated by the enthusiasm with which a process approach was often adopted and promulgated (Horowitz, 1986a), interpreted the focus on the writer's making of personal meaning as an "almost total obsession" (Horowitz, 1986c, p. 788) with "the cognitive relationship between the writer and the writer's internal world" (Swales, 1987, p. 63). Those who perceived the new approach as an obsession inappropriate for academic demands and for the expectations of academic readers shifted their focus from the processes of the writer to content and to the demands of the academy. By 1986, a process approach was being included among "traditional" (Shih, 1986, p. 624) approaches and in its place was proposed what Mohan had already proposed in 1979 — a content-based approach. In content-based instruction, an ESL course might be attached to a content course in the adjunct model (Brinton, Snow, & Wesche, 1989; Snow & Brinton, 1988) or language courses might be grouped with courses in other disciplines (Benesch, 1988). With a content focus, learners are said to get help with "the language of the thinking processes and the structure or shape of content" (Mohan, 1986, p. 18). It is interesting to note here that the content specific to English courses — language, culture, and literature — is largely rejected (see Horowitz, 1990) in favor of the subject matter of the other fields the ESL students are studying.

The research studies that inform this approach include analysis of the rhetorical organization of technical writing (Selinker, Todd-Trimble, & Trimble, 1978; Weissberg, 1984), studies of student writing in content areas (Jenkins & Hinds, 1987; Selzer, 1983), and surveys of the content and tasks L2 students can expect to encounter in their academic careers (Bridgeman & Carlson, 1983; Canseco & Byrd, 1989; Horowitz, 1986b). While classroom methodology might take on some of the features of a writer-focused approach, such as prewriting tasks and the opportunity for revision, the main emphasis is on the instructor's determination of what academic content is most appropriate, in order to build whole courses or modules of reading and writing tasks around that content.

This content-based approach has more repercussions on the shape of the curriculum than the two approaches previously described, for here the autonomous ESL class is often replaced by team teaching, linked courses, "topic-centered modules or mini-courses," sheltered (i.e., "field specific") instruction, and "composition or multiskill English for academic purposes

(EAP) courses/tutorials as adjuncts to designated university content courses" (Shih, 1986, p. 632–33). With an autonomous ESL class, a teacher can — and indeed often does — move back and forth among approaches. With ESL attached in the curriculum to a content course, such flexibility is less likely. There is always the danger that institutional changes in course structure will lock us into an approach that we want to modify or abandon.

Focus on the Reader 1986–

Simultaneously with content-based approaches came another academically oriented approach, English for academic purposes, which focuses on the expectations of academic readers (Horowitz, 1986a, 1986b, 1986c; Reid, 1987, 1989). This approach, in which the ESL teacher runs a theme-based class, not necessarily linked to a content course, is also characterized by its strong opposition to a position within a writer-dominated process approach that favors personal writing. A reader-dominated approach perceives language teaching "as socialization into the academic community — not as humanistic therapy" (Horowitz, 1986c, p. 789).

The audience-dominated approach, focusing on the expectations of readers outside the language classroom, is characterized by the use of terms like *academic demands* and *academic discourse community*. Attention to audience was, in fact, first brought to the fore as a feature of the process approach, but the focus was on known readers inside the language classroom, as peers and teachers responded to the ideas in a text. An English for academic purposes approach focuses on the reader, too — not as a specific individual but as the representative of a discourse community, for example, a specific discipline or academia in general. The reader is an initiated expert who represents a faculty audience. This reader, "particularly omniscient" and "all-powerful" (Johns, 1990a, p. 31), is likely to be an abstract representation, a generalized construct, one reified from an examination of academic assignments and texts.

Once the concept of a powerful outside reader is established, it is a short step to generalizing about the forms of writing that a reader will expect, and then an even shorter step to teaching those forms as prescriptive patterns. Recommendations such as the following: "Teachers must gather assignments from across the curriculum, assess the purposes and audience expectations in the assignments, and present them to the class" (Reid, 1987, p. 34) indicate a return to a form-dominated approach, the difference being that now rhetorical forms, rather than grammatical forms, are presented as paradigms.

A reader-dominated approach, like the other approaches, has generated its own body of research: mostly surveys of the expectations and reactions of faculty members (Johns, 1981; Santos, 1988), studies of the expectations of academic readers with regard to genres (Swales, 1990), and identifications of the basic skills of writing transferable across various disciplines (Johns, 1988).

These four approaches are all widely used and by no means discrete and sequential. Certainly the last three appear to operate more on a principle of critical reaction to a previous approach than on cumulative development. In all, our path through the woods of writing instruction is less clearly defined now in 1991 than it was in 1966. Then there was one approach, form-dominated, clearly defined, and relatively easy to follow in the classroom. Now teachers have to consider a variety of approaches, their underlying assumptions, and the practices that each philosophy generates. Thus, leaving the security of what Clarke and Silberstein call the "explicitly mandated reality" (1988, p. 692) of one clear approach, we have gone in search of a new theoretical approach or approaches to L2 writing instruction.

170

Into the Woods: Thickets and Thorny Issues

Once we have left the relative safety of a traditional form-dominated approach and set off into the woods in search of new theories, our process is hampered by many thickets and thorny issues. These we have to confront and negotiate before we can continue our journey. Particularly thorny are five classroom-oriented issues that arise in our literature and in teachers' discussions frequently enough to trouble L2 writing instructors, issues that in my more than 25 years of teaching have provided cause for reflection and uncertainty: the topics for writing; the issue of "real" writing; the nature of the academic discourse community; the role of contrastive rhetoric in the writing classroom; and ways of responding to writing. These areas, difficult to negotiate, will be described as discrete items, each posing its own set of problems. A word of caution is in order, though: Readers should not expect to find here miracle solutions or magic charms to lead the way past these thickets and out of the woods.

The Topics for Writing

One of the major problems teachers face is what students should write about. Topics for writing are an integral part of any writing course, and the four approaches outlined above lead to what can be a bewildering array of topics for teachers. In a form-dominated approach, topics are assigned by the teacher; since the interest is in how sentences and paragraphs are written rather than in what ideas are expressed, each piece of writing serves as a vehicle for practicing and displaying grammatical, syntactic, and rhetorical forms. For this purpose, almost any topic will serve. In a writer-dominated approach (usually called a process approach), the students themselves frequently choose the topics, using personal experience to write about what concerns them, or responding to a shared classroom experience, often a piece of expository writing or a work of literature (Spack, 1985). In a content-dominated approach, topics will be drawn from the subject matter of either a particular discipline or a particular course, supplied either by the content teacher when content and writing course are linked in the adjunct model (Snow & Brinton, 1988) or by the language teacher in theme-based EAP courses. And in a reader-dominated approach, the model is one of the writing-across-the-curriculum movement, with language teachers examining what other disciplines assign and training students how to respond to those assignments by "deconstructing" (Johns, 1986a, p. 253) the essay prompt and by following a model of the appropriate form of academic writing.

The problem of whether to teach personal or academic writing has surfaced frequently in recent years (Mlynarczyk, in press) and has no easy solution. Approaches that focus on rhetorical form and on the reader's expectations look to the larger community for guidance. ESL instruction is seen as a service "to prepare students to handle writing assignments in academic courses" (Shih, 1986, p. 617). For EFL students and for international students in the U.S., who will probably only write in English as part of their educational requirement and not at all thereafter, this might be suitable. However, the purposes are different for the many ESL immigrant and refugee nonnative speakers in secondary and college classrooms. This last group, a rapidly growing one, Leki (1990) equates with native speakers of English, who, she says, are "more likely to write for many different contexts in the course of their professional lives" (p. 14). For native speakers — and, by extension, certain large groups of ESL students — Hairston (1991) rejects the idea that writing courses should be "service courses" taught for the benefit of academic disciplines, since "writing courses taught by properly trained teachers do have important content: learning how to use language to express ideas effectively" (p. B1)

"Real" Writing

A great deal of the recent controversy about the teaching of writing has centered not only around the topics students write about but also around the dichotomy of process and product.

Horowitz initiated lengthy debate (see Braine, 1988; Hamp-Lyons, 1986; Horowitz, 1986a, 1986b, 1986c; Liebman-Kleine, 1986; Lyons, 1986; Reid, 1984; Spack, 1988; Zamel, 1983) by questioning the effectiveness of the process approach with its focus on the writer. In particular, Horowitz (1986) criticized what he termed the "cavalier view" (p. 141) of a process proponent (this author) who said at the 1985 TESOL Convention that examination writing was not "real" (p. 141) writing. Horowitz is not alone in his complaint. Cited as a major flaw in a process approach is the fact that "the Process Approach fails to give students an accurate picture of university writing" (Johns, 1990b). The issue of what university writing is and what kind of writing ESL students should be doing is a thorny one, and the use of the term *real* relates to this issue in practice as well as in theory.

In practice, I and many of my colleagues teach two types of writing in our classes: writing for learning (with prewriting, drafts, revisions, and editing) and writing for display (i.e., examination writing). Our students are aware of the different purposes and different strategies. They recognize that these are distinct. The use of the term *real* in this context was initiated by Searle (1969), who makes a clear distinction between real questions and exam questions. In real questions, the speaker wants to know the answer; in exam questions, the speaker wants to know if the hearer knows. Similar distinctions can be made with writing. In a writing class, students need to be taught both how to use the process to their advantage as language leaners and writers, and also how to produce an acceptable product upon demand. A shortcoming of the debate around these issues is that process and product have been seen as *either/or* rather than *both/and* entities. However, while students certainly need to learn how to pass exams, they also need to perceive writing as a tool for learning, a tool that can be useful to them throughout their professional and personal lives.

As evidence of the difficulty of defining authentic writing, it is interesting to note that even Horowitz (1986b) has used the designation *real* to describe writing. He suggests ways to simulate "the essential characteristics of *real* university writing assignments" (p. 449) and discusses the context of "a *real* academic task" [italics added] (p. 459). Here, too, the use of the term *real* could be questioned. However, we should not assume that the implication is necessarily that the topics and tasks that come from ESL teachers' own repertoire are somehow unreal; it is, rather, that Horowitz and others find them less appropriate in certain settings. In any case, the L2 debate provides a great deal of evidence for what Harris (1989) has observed in L1 writing: "One seems asked to defend either the power of the discourse community or the imagination of the individual writer" (p. 2). Obviously, the whole area of the types of writing students are expected to do and the types of writing we should teach is one surrounded by controversy.

The Nature of the Academic Discourse Community

Frequently cited as important in determining the nature of "real" writing and the topics we should assign are the demands of the "academic discourse community." These demands provide a set of standards that readers of academic prose, teachers in academic settings, expect. So some L2 writing teachers look to other disciplines to determine their course content, their readings, their models, and their instruction of rhetorical form. One thorny issue here is whether we should put our trust in this community, or whether we shouldn't rather be attempting to influence and change the academic community for the benefit of our students, while teaching our students how to interpret the community values and transform them (for discussion of similar issues, see Auerbach, 1986, 1990; Peirce, 1989).

According to Johns (1990a), teachers who emphasize the conventions of the discourse community will begin with "the *rules* [italics added] of discourse in the community" (p. 32), since academic faculty "insist that students learn to 'talk like engineers,' for example, *surrendering their own language and mode of thought* [italics added] to the requirements of the target community (p. 33). The language used here — "rules" and "surrender" — reveals perceptions regarding who exercises power in the community and the value of that power. In contrast Patricia Bizzell (cited in Enos, 1987) sees the academic community as synonymous with "dominant social classes" and has recommended that we not direct our students towards assimilation but rather find ways to give them "critical distance" on academic cultural literacy, so that eventually "elements from students' native discourse communities can be granted legitimacy in the academic community" (p. vi).

Another thorny problem is whether we view the academic discourse community as benign, open, and beneficial to our students or whether we see discourse communities as powerful and controlling, and, as Giroux (cited in Faigley, 1986) puts it, "often more concerned with ways of excluding new members than with ways of admitting them" (p. 537). These opposing views point to the validity of Berlin's (1988) statement that every pedagogy implies "a set of tacit assumptions about what is real, what is good, what is possible, and how power ought to be distributed" (p. 492). Teaching writing is inherently political, and how we perceive the purposes of writing vis-à-vis the academic community will reflect our political stance.

Reflecting our stance, too, is how we interpret the information that comes to us from members of the academic community. In a survey of 200 faculty members' opinions in response to the question, "Which is more important for success in your classes, a general knowledge of English or a knowledge of English specific to the discipline? (Johns, 1981, p. 57), most faculty members ranked general English above specific purposes English. This result was interpreted in the following way:

> There could be a number of reasons for the general English preferences, the most compelling of which is that most faculty do not understand the nature and breadth of ESL. They tend to think of it as an aspect of the discipline that has to do with vocabulary alone. (p. 54)

The mix of signals perhaps reflects a more generalized ambivalence of TESOL practitioners: Subject-area faculty are viewed as a valuable resource; however, when they do not support what ESL teachers and researchers expect, it is tempting to discount their perceptions.

A focus on the academic discourse community also raises issues as to whether academic writing is good writing, whether academic discourse "often masks a lack of genuine understanding" (Elbow, 1991, p. 137) of how a principle works, and indeed whether there is a fixed and stable construct of academic writing even in one discipline. Elbow goes so far as to say that we can't teach academic discourse "because there's no such thing to teach" (p. 138). This issue of the nature, requirements, even the existence of, an academic discourse community is a thicket in which we could be entangled for a long time.

Contrastive Rhetoric

Although it has been 25 years since contrastive rhetoric research was introduced (Kaplan, 1966; Leki, 1991) and the concept is frequently mentioned in discussions of theory and research, its applications to classroom instruction have not developed correspondingly. Published research informs teachers about the different ways in which the written products of other languages are structured (e.g., Eggington, 1987; Hinds, 1987; Tsao, 1983), but the nature of transfer in L2 writing remains under debate (see Mohan & Lo, 1985) and transfer has been found not to be significant in certain types of task, such as paraphrase (Connor & McCagg, 1983). The declared intention of contrastive rhetoric research is, however, "not to provide pedagogic method" but rather to provide teachers and students with knowledge about how the links between culture and writing are reflected in written products (Grabe & Kaplan, 1989, p. 271).

Rather than abstracting a principle of the "linear" development of English prose (Kaplan, 1966) as a pedagogic principle, contrastive rhetoric is more useful as a consciousness-raising device for students; teachers can discuss what they have observed about texts in different cultures and have students discover whether research findings hold true in their experience of their L1 texts.

The thicket that contrastive rhetoric presents for teachers as they wander into the woods of theory is the question of the value of prescribing one form of text — English form — not just as an alternative, but as the one privileged form of text, presented as the most logical and desirable, with which other learned systems interfere. Land and Whitley (1989), in discussing how readers read and judge ESL students' essays, found that nonnative speaker readers could "accommodate to more kinds of rhetorical patterns" (p. 287) than could native-speaker readers. If we are to move away from courses that are "as retributive as they are instructive" and away from "composition as colonization," we need, they say, to "recognize, value, and foster and alternative rhetorics that the ESL student brings to our language" (p. 286), not treat them only as features that interfere with language learning. Land and Whitley fear that "in teaching Standard Written English rhetorical conventions, we are teaching students to reproduce in a mechanical fashion our preferred vehicle of understanding" (p. 285).

In the same way that multiple "literacies" (Street, 1984) are posed against the idea of one dominant cultural literacy (Hirsch, 1987), so a broad use of contrastive rhetoric as a classroom consciousness-raising tool can point to linguistic variety and rhetorical choices; a narrow use would emphasize only prescriptions aimed at counteracting L1 interference. An extensive research study (Cumming, 1989) of the factors of writing expertise and second-language proficiency of L2 writers revealed in the qualities of their texts and their writing behaviors warns against such a narrow use of contrastive rhetoric: "Pedagogical prescriptions about the interference of learners' mother tongue in second-language performance — espoused in audiolingual methodologies and theories of linguistic transfer or contrastive rhetoric — appear misdirected" (pp. 127–128) since students' L1 is shown to be an important resource rather than a hindrance in decision making in writing.

Responding to Writing

With a number of approaches to teaching writing to choose from, teachers are faced with a similar variety of ways to respond to students' writing. Since a response on a student's paper is potentially one of the most influential texts in a writing class (Raimes, 1988), teachers are always concerned about the best approach. Some of the options follow, illustrating the variety at our disposal. We can correct errors; code errors; locate errors; indicate the number of errors (see Robb, Ross, & Shortreed, 1986, for a discussion of these); comment on form; make generalized comments about content, e.g., "good description" or "add details" (Fathman & Whalley, 1990, p. 182); make text-specific comments, e.g., "I'm wondering here what Carver tells the readers about the children"; ask questions; make suggestions; emote with comments like "Nice!" or "I'm bored" (Lees, 1979, p. 264); praise; ask students to comment on the source of the error (Raimes, 1990); or ask L1 peers to reformulate the students' texts (Cohen, 1983). Given the range of choices, it's hardly surprising that responding is a thorny issue. It is, in fact, so problematic that much of our written response to students' texts is inconsistent, arbitrary, and often contradictory (Zamel, 1985).

In an effort to understand more about teachers' responses, researchers are looking at students' responses to feedback (Cohen, 1987; Cohen & Cavalcanti, 1990; Radecki & Swales, 1988), finding mainly that students simply "make a mental note" of a teacher's response. The fact that little of the research examines activities that occur after the act of responding seems to get at the heart of the problem. If teachers see their response as the end of the interaction, then students will stop there. If, however, the response includes specific directions on what to do next, an "assignment" (Lees, 1979, p. 265), there is a chance for application of principles.

False Trails

The five thorny issues just discussed are ones that trouble teachers and concern theorists and researchers. There are many others, too, rendering our journey into the woods exciting, even hazardous. As teachers read the theories and research and try to figure out what approach to adopt in a writing classroom, they will sometimes confront a false trail that seems to promise a quick way out of the woods, an easy solution. We have seen evidence of false trails in the rise and demise of various methods (Clark, 1982, 1984; Richards, 1984). Similarly, prescriptions of one approach for our whole profession and all our students can be seen as false trails, too, since they actually lead back to another "explicitly mandated reality" (Clarke & Silberstein, 1988) to replace the mandate of form-focused instruction. Such a prescription in the teaching of writing appears in proposals for the widespread adoption of content-based language teaching as "the dominant approach to teaching ESL at all levels" (Celce-Murcia, 1989, p. 14).

I regard proposals like this as false trails because they perpetuate one of the errors that has been at the heart of many of our thorny problems about writing. That problem, alluded to earlier, is that we tend to discuss ESL/EFL students as if they are one or at the most two groups. Most of the dissension and controversy that has surfaced at conferences and in our literature would, I submit, simply cease to exist if we defined our terms. Our field is too diverse for us to recommend ways of teaching ESL in general. There is no such thing as a generalized ESL student. Before making pedagogical recommendations, we need to determine the following: the type of institution (high school, two-year college, four-year college, research university?) and the ESL student (undergraduate or graduate? freshman or junior? international student [returning to country of origin] or immigrant/refugee? with writing expertise in L1 or not? with what level of language proficiency?) If we are to prescribe content, we need to ask, Whose content? For the nonnative-speaking first-year students in my university, to offer modules of marketing, accounting, and nursing is to depart from the very tradition of a liberal arts education. On the other hand, for very specialized international graduate students, a content approach might be the most appropriate. When Johns and Connor (1989, reported in Leki, 1990) maintain that no such thing as general English exists, they are referring to international students, but immigrant students need general English; that is, they need more than ways to adapt to course requirements for a few years. They need to be able to write in English for the rest of their working and earning lives. They need to learn not only what academia expects but how to forge their place in it, and how to change it. Indeed, on many campuses now, a diverse student body is urging the replacement of the male Eurocentric curriculum model with one emphasizing gender representation and cultural diversity. Adopting a content-based approach for all ESL students would be succumbing to what I have called "the butler's stance" (Raimes, in press), one that overvalues service to other disciplines and prescribes content at the expense of writer, reader, and form.

Being lost in the woods might be uncomfortable, but we have to beware of taking an easy path that might, in fact, lead us back to where we started, to a reliance on form and prescription.

Out of the Woods: Emerging Traditions in the Teaching of Writing

What is the story now after a 25-year journey, beset by thickets, thorns, and false trails? Are new traditions emerging?

I am reminded of an article I wrote for this journal 8 years ago (Raimes, 1983b), in which I argued that in spite of the thrust towards communicative competence, there had been no real revolution in our field. While there were then signs of some shifts in the assumptions about what we do, we were still enmeshed in tradition but were beginning to raise important questions. At that time Kuhn's (1970) description of a paradigm shift seemed apt for the field of ESL/EFL in general: "the proliferation of competing articulations, the willingness to try anything, the expression of explicit discontent, the recourse to philosophy and to debate over fundamentals" (p. 91). That description seems still to be apt for the teaching of writing, where there is certainly evidence of competition, discontent, and debate, and where now, given the plurality of approaches, designs, and procedures, it seems more appropriate to talk of *traditions* rather than of one *tradition*.

If any clear traditions are emerging, they have more to do with recognition of where we are now rather than delineation of exactly where we are going. I see five such emerging traditions of recognition: recognition of the complexity of composing, of student diversity, of learners' processes, of the politics of pedagogy, and of the value of practice as well as theory. I end with a brief discussion of each.

Recognition of the Complexity of Composing

Despite all of the false trails and some theorists' desire to offer one approach as the answer to our problems, what seems to be emerging is a recognition that the complexity of the writing process and the writing context means that when we teach writing we have to balance the four elements of form, the writer, content, and the reader. These are not discrete entities. Rather,

> writers are readers as they read their own texts. Readers are writers as they make responses on a written text. Content and subject matter do not exist without language. The form of a text is determined by the interaction of writer, reader, and content. Language inevitably reflects subject matter, the writer, and the writer's view of the reader's background knowledge and expectations. (Raimes, in press)

This complexity may mean that no one single theory of writing can be developed (Johns, 1990a) or it may mean that a variety of theories need to be developed to support and inform diverse approaches (Silva, 1990). In either case, recognition of complexity is a necessary basis for principled model building.

Recognition of Student Diversity

While there is still a tendency to discuss our field as if it were the easily definable entity it was 25 years ago, there are signs that we are beginning to recognize the diversity of our students and our mission, and to realize that not all approaches and procedures might apply to all ESL/EFL students. Reid (1984) notes this when she reminds Zamel of the differences between advanced students and novice writers, particularly with regard to cognitive development; Horowitz (1990) notes this when he lists the questions that we need to ask about our students before we decide to use literature or any other content. For heterogeneous classes, a "balanced" stance is recommended (Booth, 1963; Raimes, in press), one that presents a governing philosophy but pays attention within that philosophy to all four elements involved in writing: form, writer, content, and reader. The combination of complexity and diversity makes it imperative for us not to seek universal prescriptions, but instead to "strive to validate other, local forms of knowledge about language and teaching" (Pennycook, 1989, p. 613).

Recognition of Learners' Processes

Amidst all the winding and intersecting paths and false trails, one trail seems to be consistently well marked and well traveled. While there is controversy about what a process approach to teaching writing actually comprises and to what extent it can take academic demands into account, there is widespread acceptance of the notion that language teachers need to know about and to take into account the process of how learners learn a language and how writers produce a written product. Such a notion of process underlies a great deal of current communicative, task-based, and collaborative instruction and curriculum development (Nunan, 1989a, 1989b). Even writing theorists who are identified with content-based and reader-based approaches frequently acknowledge the important role that the writer's processes play in the writing class (Johns, 1986b; Shih, 1986; Swales, 1987). The process approach more than any other seems to be providing unifying theoretical and methodological principles.

Recognition of the Politics of Pedagogy

Along with the recognition of the complexity of composing and the diversity of our students and their processes has come a more explicitly political understanding: The approach we take to the academic discourse community and the culturally diverse students in our classrooms will inevitably reflect "interested knowledge," which is likely to be "a positivist, progressivist, and patriarchal" view presented as "a method" (Pennycook, 1989, p. 589). All approaches should, therefore, be examined with a set of questions in mind: Who learns to do what? Why? Who benefits? (See Auerbach, 1986, 1990.) Recognizing the power of literacy, we need to ask "what kind of literacy we want to support: literacy to serve which purposes and on behalf of whose interests" (Lunsford, Moglen, & Slevin, 1990, p. 2) and to keep in mind that "to propose a pedagogy is to propose a political vision" (Simon, 1987, p. 371).

Recognition of the Value of Practice

Both in L1 and in L2 instruction, the power that theory, or method, has held over instruction is being challenged by what Shulman (1987) calls "the wisdom of practice" (p. 11). North (1987) argues that in L1 writing instruction we need to give credit to "practitioners' lore" as well as to research; teachers need to use their knowledge "to argue for the value of what they know and how they come to know it" (p. 55). Before we heed our theorists and adopt their views, it will help us if we first discover how often they teach writing to ESL students, where they teach it, how they teach it, and who their students are. We need to establish a context. We need to know the environment in which they have developed what Prabhu (1990, p. 172) calls "a teacher's sense of plausibility about teaching," which is the development of a "concept (or theory, or in a more dormant state, pedagogic intuition), of how learning takes place and how teaching causes and supports it." But better than putting the research into a teaching context is for teachers to become researchers themselves. Classroom-based research and action research is increasingly recommended to decrease teachers' reliance on theorists and researchers (Richards & Nunan, 1990). Teachers can keep sight of the forest as well as the trees.

These recognitions characterize our position at the end of our 25-year journey from "once upon a time," journeying into the woods, facing the tangle of thickets and thorny problems to trying to recognize — and avoid — false trails. Our own telling of the story might also include having taken some false trails or having met and vanquished a few big bad wolves in our travels. The fact that we are beginning to emerge from the woods with new recognitions but not a single new approach is perhaps the happiest 1991 ending that we can expect, given the diversity and complexity of our students and of learning and teaching writing. But by the turn of the century, we could well be reading (and writing) a different story.

References

Auerbach, E. R. (1986). Competency-based ESL: One step forward or two steps back? *TESOL Quarterly, 20*(3), 411–429.

Auerbach, E. R. (1990). Review of *Alien winds: The reeducation of America's Indochinese refugees*. *TESOL Quarterly, 24*(1), 85–91.

Benesch, S. (Ed.). (1988). *Ending remediation: ESL and content in higher education*. Washington, D.C.: TESOL.

Benesch, S., & Rorschach, B. (1989). *Academic writing workshop II*. Belmont, CA: Wadsworth.

Berlin, J. A. (1988). Rhetoric and ideology in the writing class. *College English, 50*(5), 477–494.

Booth, W. C. (1963). The rhetorical stance. *College Composition and Communication, 14*(2), 139–145.

Braine, G. (1988). Comments on Ruth Spack's "Initiating ESL students into the academic discourse community: How far should we go?" *TESOL Quarterly, 22*(4), 700–702.

Bridgeman, B., & Carlson, S. B. (1983). *Survey of academic writing tasks required of graduate and undergraduate foreign students* (TOEFL Research Rep. No. 15). Princeton, NJ: Educational Testing Service.

Brinton, D., Snow, M. A., & Wesche, M. (1989). *Content-based second language instruction*. New York: Newbury House.

Bruffee, K. (1984). Collaborative learning and the "conversation of mankind." *College English, 46*(7), 635–652.

Byrd, D. R. H., & Gallingane, G. (1990). *Write away 2*. New York: Newbury House.

Canseco, G., & Byrd, P. (1989). Writing required in graduate courses in business administration. *TESOL Quarterly, 23*(2), 305–316.

Celce-Murcia, M. (1989). Models for content-based curricula for ESL. *CATESOL Journal, 2*(2), 5–16.

Clarke, M. A. (1982). On bandwagons, tyranny, and common sense. *TESOL Quarterly, 16*(4), 437–448.

Clarke, M. A. (1984). On the nature of technique: What do we owe the gurus? *TESOL Quarterly, 18*(4), 577–594.

Clarke, M. A., & Silberstein, S. (1988). Problems, prescriptions and paradoxes in second language teaching. *TESOL Quarterly, 22*(4), 685–700.

Cohen, A. D. (1983, December). Reformulating compositions. *TESOL Newsletter*, p. 1, 4–5.

Cohen, A. D. (1987). Student processing of feedback on their compositions. In A. Wenden & J. Rubin (Eds.), *Learner strategies in language learning* (pp. 57–68). Englewood Cliffs, NJ: Prentice Hall.

Cohen, A. D., & Cavalcanti, M. C. (1990). Feedback on compositions: Teacher and student verbal reports. In B. Kroll (Ed.), *Second language writing: Research insights for the classroom* (pp. 155–177). New York: Cambridge University Press.

Connor, U. (1984). A study of cohesion and coherence in English as a second language students' writing. *Papers in Linguistics: International Journal of Human Communication, 17*, 301–316.

Connor, U. M. (1990). Discourse analysis and writing/reading instruction. *Annual Review of Applied Linguistics, 11*, 164–180.

Connor, U., & McCagg, P. (1983). Cross-cultural differences and perceived quality in written paraphrases of English expository prose. *Applied Linguistics, 4*, 259–268.

Cramer, N. A. (1985). *The writing process: 20 projects for group work*. Rowley, MA: Newbury House.

Cumming, A. (1989). Writing expertise and second language proficiency. *Language Learning, 39*(1), 81–141.

Eggington, W. G. (1987). Written academic discourse in Korean: Implications for effective communication. In U. Connor & R. B. Kaplan (Eds.), *Writing across languages: Analysis of L2 text* (pp. 153–168). Reading, MA: Addison-Wesley.

Elbow, P. (1991). Reflections on academic discourse: How it relates to freshmen and colleagues. *College English, 53*(2), 135–155.

Emig, J. (1971). *The composing processes of twelfth graders*. Urbana, IL: National Council of Teachers of English.

Enos, T. (1987). *A sourcebook for basic writing teachers*. New York: Random House.

Faigley, L. (1986). Competing theories of process: A critique and a proposal. *College English, 48*(6), 527–542.

Fathman, A. K., & Whalley, E. (1990). Teacher response to student writing: Focus on form versus content. In B. Kroll (Ed.), *Second language writing: Research insights for the classroom* (pp. 178–190). New York: Cambridge University Press.

Friedlander, A. (1990). Composing in English: Effects of a first language on writing in English as a second language. In B. Kross (Ed.), *Second language writing: Research insights for the classroom* (pp. 109–125). New York: Cambridge University Press.

Grabe, W., & Kaplan, R. B. (1989). Writing in a second language: Contrastive rhetoric. In D. M. Johnson & D. H. Roen (Eds.), *Richness in writing: Empowering ESL students* (pp. 263–283). New York: Longman.

Hairston, M. (1991, January 23). Required writing courses should not focus on politically charged social issues. *Chronicle of Higher Education,* pp. B1–B3.

Hall, C. (1990). Managing the complexity of revising across languages. *TESOL Quarterly, 24*(1), 43–60.

Hamp-Lyons, L. (1986). No new lamps for old yet, please. *TESOL Quarterly, 20*(4), 790–796.

Harris, J. (1989). The idea of community in the study of writing. *College Composition and Communication, 40*(1), 11–22.

Hinds, J. (1987). Reader versus writer responsibility: A new typology. In U. Connor & R. B. Kaplan (Eds.), *Writing across languages: Analysis of L2 text* (pp. 141–152). Reading, MA: Addison-Wesley.

Hirsch, E. D., Jr. (1987). *Cultural literacy: What every American needs to know.* Boston: Houghton Mifflin.

Horowitz, D. M. (1986a). Process, not product: Less than meets the eye. *TESOL Quarterly 20,* (1), 141–144.

Horowitz, D. M. (1986b). What professors actually require: Academic tasks for the ESL classroom. *TESOL Quarterly, 20*(3), 445–462.

Horowitz, D. M. (1986c). The author responds to Liebman-Kleine. *TESOL Quarterly, 20*(4), 788–790.

Horowitz, D. M. (1990). Fiction and nonfiction in the ESL/EFL classroom: Does the difference make a difference? *English for Specific Purposes, 9,* 161–168.

Jenkins, S., & Hinds, J. (1987). Business letter writing: English, French, and Japanese. *TESOL Quarterly, 21*(2), 327–349.

Johns, A. M. (1981). Necessary English: A faculty survey. *TESOL Quarterly, 15*(1), 51–57.

Johns, A. M. (1984). Textual cohesion and the Chinese speaker of English. *Language Learning and Communication, 3,* 69–74.

Johns, A. M. (1986a). Coherence and academic writing: Some definitions and suggestions for teaching. *TESOL Quarterly, 20*(2), 247–265.

Johns, A. M. (1986b). The ESL student and the revision process: Some insights from schema theory. *Journal of Basic Writing, 5*(2), 70–80.

Johns, A. M. (1988). The discourse communities dilemma: Identifying transferable skills for the academic milieu. *English for Specific Purposes, 7,* 55–60.

Johns, A. M. (1990a). L1 composition theories: Implications for developing theories of L2 composition. In B. Kroll (Ed.), *Second language writing: Research insights for the classroom* (pp. 24–36). New York: Cambridge University Press.

Johns, A. M. (1990b, March). *Process, literature, and academic realities: Dan Horowitz and beyond.* Handout for paper presented at the 24th Annual TESOL Convention, San Francisco, CA.

Jones, C. S. (1982). Attention to rhetorical form while composing in a second language. In C. Campbell, V. Flashner, T. Hudson, & J. Lubin (Eds.), *Proceedings of the Los Angeles Second Language Research Forum* (Vol. 2, pp. 130–143). Los Angeles: University of California, Los Angeles.

Jones, C. S. (1985). Problems with monitor use in second language composing. In M. Rose (Ed.), *Studies in writer's block and other composing process problems* (pp. 96–118). New York: Guilford Press.

Jones, C. S., & Tetroe, J. (1987). Composing in a second language. In A. Matsuhashi (Ed.), *Writing in real time: Modeling production processes* (pp. 34–57). Norwood, NJ: Ablex.

Kaplan, R. B. (1966). Cultural thought patterns in intercultural education. *Language Learning, 16*(1), 1–20.

Kaplan, R. B. (1987). Cultural thought patterns revisited. In U. Connor & R. B. Kaplan (Eds.), *Writing across languages: Analysis of L2 text* (pp. 9–20). Reading, MA: Addison-Wesley.

Kaplan, R. B., & Shaw, P. A. (1983). *Exploring academic discourse.* Rowley, MA: Newbury House.

Krapels, A. (1990). An overview of second language writing process research. In B. Kross (Ed.), *Second language writing: Research insights for the classroom* (pp. 37–56). New York: Cambridge University Press.

Kuhn, T. S. (1970). *The structure of scientific revolutions* (2nd ed.). Chicago: University of Chicago Press.

Kunz, L. (1972). *26 steps: A course in controlled composition for intermediate and advanced ESL students.* New York: Language Innovations.

Land, R. E., & Whitley, C. (1989). Evaluating second language essays in regular composition classes: Toward a pluralistic U.S. rhetoric. In D. M. Johnson & D. H. Roen (Eds.), *Richness in writing: Empowering ESL students* (pp. 284–293). New York: Longman.

Lautamatti, L. (1987). Observations in the development of the topic in simplified discourse. In U. Connor & R. B. Kaplan (Eds.), *Writing across languages: Analysis of L2 text* (pp. 87–114). Reading, MA: Addison-Wesley.

179

Lees, E. O. (1979). Evaluating student writing. *College Composition and Communication, 30*(40), 370–374.

Leki, I. (1990). Potential problems with peer responding in ESL writing classes. *CATESOL Journal, 3*(1), 5–19.

Leki, I. (1991). Twenty-five years of contrastive rhetoric: Text analysis and writing pedagogies. *TESOL Quarterly, 25*(1), 123–143.

Liebman-Kleine, J. (1986). In defense of teaching process in ESL composition. *TESOL Quarterly, 20*(4), 783–788.

Long, M. H., & Porter, P. A. (1985). Group work, interlanguage talk, and second language acquisition. *TESOL Quarterly, 19*(2), 207–228.

Lunsford, A., Moglen, H., & Slevin, J. (Eds.). (1990). *The right to literacy.* New York: Modern Language Association.

Mlynarczyk, R. (in press). Personal and academic writing: A false dichotomy? *TESOL Journal.*

Mohan, B. A. (1979). Relating language teaching and content teaching. *TESOL Quarterly, 13*(2), 171–182.

Mohan, B. A. (1986). *Language and content.* Reading, MA: Addison-Wesley.

Mohan, B. A., & Lo, W. A. (1985). Academic writing and Chinese students: Transfer and developmental factors. *TESOL Quarterly, 19*(3), 515–534.

North, S. M. (1987). *The making of knowledge in composition: Portrait of an emerging field.* Portsmouth, NH: Boynton/Cook, Heinemann.

Nunan, D. (1989a). *Designing tasks for the communicative classroom.* Cambridge: Cambridge University Press.

Nunan, D. (1989b). Toward a collaborative approach to curriculum development: A case study. *TESOL Quarterly, 23*(1), 9–25.

O'Hare, F. (1973). *Sentence combining: Improving student writing without formal grammar instruction.* Urbana, IL: National Council of Teachers of English.

Pack, A. C., & Henrichsen, L. E. (1980). *Sentence combination.* Rowley, MA: Newbury House.

Paulston, C. B., & Dykstra, G. (1973). *Controlled composition in English as a second language.* New York: Regents.

Peirce, B. N. (1989). Toward a pedagogy of possibility in the teaching of English internationally: People's English in South Africa. *TESOL Quarterly, 23*(3), 401–420.

Pennycook, A. (1989). The concept of method, interested knowledge, and the politics of language teaching. *TESOL Quarterly, 23*(4), 589–618.

Peyton, J. K. (Ed.). (1990). *Students and teachers writing together: Perspectives on journal writing.* Alexandria, VA: TESOL.

Prabhu, N. S. (1990). There is no best method—Why? *TESOL Quarterly, 24*(2), 161–176.

Purves, A. C. (Ed.). (1988). *Writing across languages and cultures.* Newbury Park, CA: Sage.

Radecki, P. M., & Swales, J. M. (1988). ESL student reaction to written comments on their written work. *System, 16,* 355–365.

Raimes, A. (1983a). Anguish as a second language? Remedies for composition teachers. In A. Freedman, I. Pringle, & J. Yalden (Eds.), *Learning to write: First language/second language* (pp. 258–272. Harlow, England: Longman.

Raimes, A. (1983b). Tradition and revolution in ESL teaching. *TESOL Quarterly, 17*(4), 535–552.

Raimes, A. (1985). What unskilled ESL students do as they write: A classroom study of composing. *TESOL Quarterly, 19*(2), 229–258.

Raimes, A. (1987). Language proficiency, writing ability, and composing strategies: A study of ESL college student writers. *Language Learning, 37*(3), 439–468.

Raimes, A. (1988). The texts for teaching writing. In B. K. Das (Ed.), *Materials for language learning and teaching* (pp. 41–58). Singapore: SEAMEO Regional Language Centre.

Raimes, A. (1990). *How English works: A grammar handbook with readings.* (Instructor's Manual). New York: St. Martin's Press.

Raimes, A. (in press). Instructional balance: From theories to practices in teaching writing. *Georgetown University Round Table on Languages and Linguistics 1991.*

Reid, J. (1984). Comments on Vivian Zamel's "The composing processes of advanced ESL students: Six case studies." *TESOL Quarterly, 18*(1), 149–159.

Reid, J. (1987, April). ESL composition: The expectations of the academic audience. *TESOL Newsletter,* p. 34.

Reid, J. (1989). English as a second language composition in higher education: The expectations of the academic audience. In D. M. Johnson & D. H. Roen (Eds.), *Richness in writing: Empowering ESL students* (pp. 220–234). New York: Longman.

Reid, J. (1990). Responding to different topic types: A quantitative analysis from a contrastive rhetoric perspective. In B. Kross (Ed.), *Second language writing: Research insights for the classroom* (pp. 191–210). New York: Cambridge University Press.

Reid, J., & Lindstrom, M. (1985). *The process of paragraph writing*. Englewood Cliffs, NJ: Prentice Hall.

Richards, J. C. (1984). The secret life of methods. *TESOL Quarterly, 18*(1), 7–23.

Richards, J. C., & Nunan, D. (Eds.). 1990. *Second language teacher education*. Cambridge: Cambridge University Press.

Robb, T., Ross, S., & Shortreed, I. (1986). Salience of feedback on error and its effect on EFL writing quality. *TESOL Quarterly, 20*(1), 83–93.

Santos, T. (1988). Professors' reactions to the academic writing of nonnative-speaking students. *TESOL Quarterly, 22*(1), 69–90.

Scarcella, R. C. (1984). How writers orient their readers in expository essays: A comparative study of native and nonnative English writers. *TESOL Quarterly, 18*(4), 671–688.

Searle, J. R. (1969). *Speech acts: An essay in the philosophy of language*. Cambridge: Cambridge University Press.

Selinker, L., Todd-Trimble, M., & Trimble, L. (1978). Rhetorical function shifts in EST discourse. *TESOL Quarterly, 12*(3), 311–320.

Selzer, J. (1983). The composing processes of an engineer. *College Composition and Communication, 34*(2), 178–187.

Shih, M. (1986). Content-based approaches to teaching academic writing. *TESOL Quarterly, 20*(4), 617–648.

Shulman, L. S. (1987). Knowledge and teaching: Foundations of the new reform. *Harvard Educational Review, 57*(1), 1–22

Silva, T. (1990). Second language composition instruction: Developments, issues, and directions in ESL. In B. Kroll (Ed.), *Second language writing: Research insights for the classroom* (pp. 11–23). New York: Cambridge University Press.

Simon, R. (1987). Empowerment as a pedagogy of possibility. *Language Arts, 64*(4), 370–382.

Snow, M. A., & Brinton, D. M. (1988). The adjunct model of language instruction: An ideal EAP framework. In S. Benesch (Ed.), *Ending remediation: ESL and content in higher education* (pp. 33–52). Washington, DC: TESOL.

Spack, R. (1984). Invention strategies and the ESL college composition student. *TESOL Quarterly, 18*(4), 649–670.

Spack, R. (1985). Literature, reading, writing, and ESL: Bridging the gaps. *TESOL Quarterly, 19*(4), 703–725.

Spack, R. (1988). Initiating ESL students into the academic discourse community: How far should we go? *TESOL Quarterly, 22*(1), 29–51.

Spack, R., & Sadow, C. (1983). Student-teacher working journals in ESL freshman composition. *TESOL Quarterly, 17*(4), 575–593.

Street, B. V. (1984). *Literacy in theory and practice*. Cambridge: Cambridge University Press.

Swales, J. (1987). Utilizing the literatures in teaching the research paper. *TESOL Quarterly, 21*(1), 41–68.

Swales, J. M. (1990). *Genre analysis: English in academic and research settings*. Cambridge: Cambridge University Press.

In the *TESOL Quarterly*, from which this selection is reprinted, the references end here.

Raimes's Insights as a Resource for Your Teaching

1. You could be one of the authors of the "different story" that Raimes speculates writing teachers "could well be reading" (and writing) by the end of the century. For your teaching portfolio, log the process you used to work with each nonnative speaker/writer. Depending on the population of ESL students in your course, keep these notes over several semesters or until you observe a pattern of student writing behavior. Conduct some classroom research — perhaps structured interviews with your students — about what "worked" and why. Then invite a peer instructor to help you research and analyze teaching practice that "worked" to discover other "applications" for that practice.

2. Select one or two historical events or new traditions that Raimes cites and read her sources. Invite peer instructors to a "brown bag" session where you summarize what you've learned about that event or tradition and ask your colleagues about their questions and reactions to what you've described.

Raimes's Insights as a Resource for the Writing Classroom

1. Raimes explains that "a broad use of contrastive rhetoric as a classroom consciousness-raising tool can point to linguistic variety and rhetorical choices." Ask students to write in their journals in response to either of these questions: "What contrasts have you noticed between the way you talk and use words and the way that a student from another geographic location or another culture would discuss the same content?" "What differences have you noticed between the way you send nonverbal messages and the way used by a student from another geographic location or another culture?" Ask students to use that prewriting for a classroom discussion on linguistic choices and variety.

2. Native speakers who peer edit might make hasty assumptions about "errors" in the drafts of ESL students and give advice that is proscriptive. Nonnative speakers might be hesitant to evaluate the language and rhetorical patterns of a native speaker. Ask peer editors to select a short passage or a pattern of language use that created problems for them and a passage or a pattern of language use that pleased them. Ask the peer editors to explain their reactions.

Then ask the writers to reflect on what the peer editors said and to explain, as part of a self-assessment, whether and how they revised in response to the peer editors' descriptive comments. Keep a tally of instances where "alternative rhetorics" enhanced the writing and share those examples with students in your next course.

CULTURAL DIFFERENCES WHICH INFLUENCE WRITING

Muriel Harris

Muriel Harris synthesized her reading in linguistics and anthropology with her experience working with writers and directing a writing center in this excerpt from a larger text, Teaching One to One: The Writing Conference. *Harris's primary audience is tutors and consultants in a writing center, but her advice is useful for all composition instructors. Rhetorical traditions of a student's culture influence the ways he or she writes in English. Writing instructors need to become aware of cultural differences that affect the written communication of students.*

Harris recaps some of the cultural thought patterns that affect the content, development, and style of writing. She reminds us, for example, that assumptions about the writer's relationship to the audience in written English may be at odds with the assumptions about the world embedded in, say, the Japanese or the Chinese language. She cautions tutors to realize that second-language writers need assistance in "trying to learn — and to accept — cultural perspectives that may overturn or upset many of their unconscious assumptions about the world."

Harris reminds us that, when we teach "students from other cultures about the rhetorical expectations and standards of English discourse," we must remember that their writing will improve slowly because of the difficulty of "adjusting to the mental frameworks that go with such new standards." She cites the conference as a particularly helpful teaching strategy.

Notice that Harris refers to "students [who] are not members of the dominant American culture," not just students whose first language is other than English. She doesn't define "dominant American culture" but describes one of its features as having "the rhetorical expectations and standards of English discourse."

Cultural Differences

When our students are not members of the dominant American culture, there is yet another area of differentiation important for diagnostic work, that of culture. Students brought up in other cultures acquire habits, behavior patterns, perspectives, ways of delivering information, and other cultural filters that can affect writing in ways we often do not sufficiently attend to — and indeed are in danger of ignoring. For example, if another person's culture displays a strong preference for conveying information indirectly, merely criticizing paragraphs written in English by that person as too diffuse, wordy, or unclear is not likely to produce improvement. Instead, we must first recognize that we are dealing with a cultural difference and then discuss with that person the appropriate rhetorical patterns for prose in English.

That such differences abound is clear, for, as Robert Kaplan has noted, "Each language and each culture has a paragraph order unique to itself, and . . . part of the learning of a particular language is the mastering of its logical system."[1] In a later article Kaplan looks back at his earlier statements about the rhetorical structures of different languages and concludes that those earlier statements may have been too strongly worded.[2] But he still maintains that while all forms are possible in different languages, they don't occur with equal frequency. Such a statement reminds us not to form stereotypes about such cultural differences but, at the same time, to be aware of them as teachers, evaluators, and diagnosticians of writing. These students are not committing errors but employing a rhetoric and sequence of thought which are appropriate for them but which violate the expectations of a native English-speaking reader.

Kaplan's work on cultural thought patterns has defined for us the rhetorical structures of paragraphs and whole pieces of discourse — that is, how the text is organized and developed — for several languages. As Kaplan explains ("Cultural Thought Patterns" 4–9), English thought patterns are predominantly linear in development, allowing for little or no digression, while paragraph development in Semitic language is based on a complex series of parallel constructions. Thus, maturity of style in English is often gauged by the degree of subordination rather than the coordination required in the extensive parallelism of a Semitic speaker's prose. In Karyn Thompson-Panos and Maria Thomas-Ruzic's analysis of Arabic, they note that coordinating conjunctions frequently appear at the beginning of Arabic sentences because of an Arabic predilection for emphasizing sequence of events and balance of thought, forms that favor coordination.[3] We might, therefore, see Arabic students' attempts to write English paragraphs as riddled with excessive *ands* and *buts,* as evident in the following excerpt from an Arab student's paper developed by coordination and parallelism:

> At that time of the year I was not studying enough to pass my courses in school. *And* all the time I was asking my cousin to let me ride the bicycle, *but* he wouldn't let me. *But* after two weeks, noticing that I was so much interested in the bicycle, he promised me that if I pass my courses in school for that year he would give it to me as a present. *So* I began to study hard. *And* I studying eight hours a day instead of two.
>
> My cousin seeing me studying that much he was sure that I was going to succeed in school. *So* he decided to give me some lessons in riding the bicycle. After four or five weeks of teaching me and ten or twelve times hurting myself as I used to go out of balance, I finally knew how to ride it. *And* the finals in school came *and* I was very good prepared for them *so* I passed them. My cousin kept his promise *and* gave me the bicycle as a present. *And* till now I keep the bicycle in a safe place, *and* everytime I see it, it reminds me how it helped to pass my courses for that year. (From Kaplan, "Cultural Thought Patterns" 9)

Since students from a Semitic culture will value this form of development, they need to learn not just how to subordinate in English but also why they should adopt patterns of expression they will not initially value as good writing.

Another difference in Arabic thought, noted by Edward Hall, is that history is used by Arabs as the basis for almost any modern action.[4] The chances are that an Arab won't start a talk or a speech or analyze a problem without first developing the historical aspect of his or her subject. Here again, we can imagine the response of a composition teacher, unaware of such a propensity, to a paper whose topic would not seem (to a native speaker of English) to require a historical perspective in the introduction. We can also imagine the Arab student's response when told that such an introduction is unnecessary or not to the point. Such a student might also be told that his or her writing is wordy and repetitious and perhaps too prone to overstatement because of stylistic differences which also mark Arabic prose. Thompson-Panos and Thomas-Ruzic (619) note that as part of the Arabic linguistic tradition main points are overasserted and exaggerated, thus calling for increased use of superlatives. Frequent rewording and restatement are also devices used for clarity of communication. Measured against the preferences of readers whose cultural conditioning leads them to favor moderation, understatement, and/or conciseness, typical Arabic structure and style may seem inadequate.

The prose of Oriental students, when evaluated in terms of rhetorical traditions taught in American schools, can appear deficient in other ways. After having taught in China, Carolyn Matalene warns us that some advice dispensed by Western teachers of writing is not easily understood by Chinese students learning English.[5] As Matalene explains, students trained in Chinese traditions absorb a cultural heritage that emphasizes memorization of phrases from classical sources and that values working within given traditions, not departing from them. To such students our recommendations that they avoid clichés and seek to use original phrases are counseling them "to write like uneducated barbarians" (792). In Kaplan's analysis ("Cultural Thought Patterns" 10), Oriental paragraphs are marked by indirection. The Oriental writer will circle around a subject, showing it from a variety of tangential views, but not looking at it directly. Development can be in terms of what things are not rather than what they are. For example, consider the following paragraphs written by a Korean student:

Definition of College Education

College is an institution of an higher learning that gives degrees. All of us needed culture and education in life, if no education to us, we should go to living hell.
One of the greatest causes that while other animals have remained as they first man along has made such rapid progress is has learned about civilization.
The improvement of the highest civilization is in order to education up-to-date.
So college education is very important thing which we don't need mention about it. (From Kaplan, "Cultural Thought Patterns" 10)

It is not uncommon in writing labs for Oriental students who have written such paragraphs to appear with notes from teachers asking for help in learning how to get to the point and to use more concrete details and examples. But merely giving these students such advice is not likely to effect much change if they continue to see the direct approach as rude. As one Oriental student admitted to me, "I would rather not offend my readers." Similarly, the Japanese preference, noted by Edward Hall, for going around and around a point can be frustrating to an American while the American preference for getting to the point so quickly is just as frustrating to the Japanese, who do not understand why Americans have to be so "logical" all the time.[6]

While Kaplan's analysis of cultural thought patterns concentrates heavily on Semitic and Oriental methods of development, he also notes that writers in French and Spanish exhibit much greater freedom to digress from their subjects than do writers in English. Kaplan offers

English   Semitic   Oriental   Romance   Russian

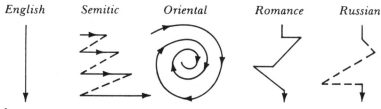

Figure 1

the graphic representation in Figure 1 of the movements of paragraphs from five different cultures.[7]

Although Kaplan reminds us that "much more detailed and more accurate descriptions are required before any meaningful contrastive systems can be elaborated" ("Cultural Thought Patterns" 15), his work can serve as an important reminder in our evaluation and diagnostic work that we cannot merely label as errors or problems those characteristics in the discourse of nonnative speakers of English which they bring with them from the rhetorical traditions of their own languages. Instead, we must realize the difficulty these students will have in trying to learn — and to accept as appropriate — cultural perspectives that may overturn or upset many of their unconscious assumptions about the world.

The depth to which cultural differences influence the content and development of written communication can also be seen in another factor, the degree of reader/writer involvement assumed by writers in different cultures. As explained by John Hinds, the concept of reader versus writer responsibility considers the degree of involvement the reader will have, a degree which will depend on the language being used.[8] In some languages, such as English, the writer (or speaker) is the person primarily responsible for effective communication, for making clear, well-organized statements. In other languages, however, such as Japanese, the reader (or listener) is the person primarily responsible, meaning that if a breakdown in communication occurs, it is the reader who assumes the burden of responsibility because he or she hasn't exerted enough effort. Muneo Yoshikawa's explanation for the Japanese view of reader responsibility is that because the Japanese mistrust verbal language what is not verbalized counts more than what is verbalized.[9] The Japanese reader/listener, who is supposed to know by "intuition" what is not said aloud, is therefore aware that what is expressed and what is actually intended are two different things. Similarly, Carolyn Matalene's study of Chinese rhetoric leads her to conclude that to be indirect, to expect the audience to infer meanings rather than to have them spelled out, is a defining characteristic of Chinese rhetoric.

A related perspective on the same cultural distinction is offered by Edward Hall, who differentiates between high-context and low-context cultures. It is typical of people in a high-context culture, Hall notes, to communicate less directly than do those in a low-context culture because they assume that much of what they think and mean can go without saying. This is possible in a high-context culture because of an extensive information network among family, friends, coworkers, and clients, who keep each other informed and reduce the need for context (or background information). Hall lists as examples of high-context cultures the French, Spanish, Italian, peoples of the Middle East, and Japanese. Examples of low-context cultures, notes Hall, are Americans and northern Europeans such as the Germans, Swiss, and Scandinavians. Thus, in intercultural communication, explains Hall, a German would seek detailed, explicit information, while a Japanese would be likely to feel uneasy if he or she were being too direct.[10] Because international business can suffer unless adjustments are made for different cultures, businesspeople are training themselves to become more aware of such differences. Similarly, as we read written communication from writers of other cultures, we too must be aware of such differences as we offer instruction and evaluate and diagnose papers. It is best, of course, to start by presenting these writers with the rhetorical information they need to write English prose, explaining not just the syntax and grammar of the language but its rhetorical standards and its readers' expectations as well. And we must be patient and realize that learning the intricacies of English verb tenses is still far easier than learning the role of the English-speaking reader.

The differences in reader/writer responsibility will also affect writing skills other than development and amount of information, since the distinction also impinges upon the unity of a text. English-speaking readers will, as Hinds explains, expect transition statements to be provided by the writer so that they can piece together the threads of the writer's logic. In Japanese discourse such landmarks may be absent or attenuated because it is the reader's responsibility to determine relationships between any one part of an essay and the essay as a whole. Transition statements do exist in Japanese, but Hinds characterizes them as more subtle and requiring a more active role on the reader's part, since it remains the reader's responsibility to create bridges. Edward Hall finds the same cultural perspective evident in the Japanese use of space, which illustrates what Hall describes as the Japanese "habit of leading the individual to a spot where he can discover something for himself." Hall also notes that in Arabic thinking, the conveyor of information is not responsible for building bridges because one is expected to connect widely separated points on his or her own, and very quickly too.[11]

Yet another writing skill, revision, can be affected by differences in reader/writer responsibility, for the inference drawn by Hinds from reader-responsible languages is that there is greater tolerance for ambiguity and imprecision of statement. While English-speaking writers go through draft after draft in order to produce a clear final product, Japanese authors frequently compose exactly one draft, which becomes the finished product. While this can hardly be equated with all reluctance to revise, Hinds's inference does serve to remind us that more generalized attitudes toward the world around us in different cultures can impinge upon writing processes. For example, Edward Hall notes that American Indians, who have a different sense of time, exhibit an indifference to finishing tasks all at once that is translated by whites as indolence. This is particularly true when the perceiver is a member of what Hall calls a monochronic culture, characterized by schedules, punctuality, and a sense that time forms a purposeful straight line. Typical monochronic people, says Hall, are Germans, Swiss, some other European cultures, and Americans. Rather than doggedly pursuing one task, as a person from a monochronic culture is likely to do, people in polychronic cultures, such as Hispanics, are comfortable with multiple tasks going on simultaneously and do not feel as constrained by deadlines and schedules.[12]

Only a few cultural distinctions that should concern us as writing teachers have been mentioned here, but it is clear that we need to be aware of such differences in our teaching and in our responses to students from other cultures. Yet much is still unknown about such differences. Hall estimates that the cultural systems that have never been made explicit probably outnumber explicit systems by a factor of one thousand or more.[13] The best we can do, then, is to be aware of how much we need to teach students from other cultures about the rhetorical expectations and standards of English discourse. And when their writing does not immediately seem to improve, we also have to realize the difficulty involved in adjusting to the mental frameworks that go with such new standards. It is not likely that these students can even verbalize for us the standards they have been using, for each system consists largely of what Hall calls "out-of-awareness" characteristics, the unconscious level of cultural norms. Every culture has a system, but the people who live by the system can tell others very little about its laws. As Hall points out, they can only tell you whether you are using the system correctly or not (*Beyond Culture* 165–66). When someone is not using the system in English discourse, we can see from this discussion how that person's writing might be labeled as wordy, lacking in coherence, unfocused, unclear, or any of a number of other terms denoting writing problems at the rhetorical level. It is a challenge to our instructional skills to help these writers learn "the system" in English. The conference is a helpful place to do so, since we can keep probing and asking as we go to see how much each student understands of what we are explaining. The conference is also an excellent place to invite such students to discuss their feelings of bewilderment, confusion, and even embarrassment, as they try to conform to standards that are even more foreign than English vocabulary or the bewildering system of prepositions in English syntax.

Notes

[1]Robert B. Kaplan, "Cultural Thought Patterns in Inter-Cultural Education," *Language Learning* 16 (1966): 14.
[2]Robert B. Kaplan, "Cultural Thought Patterns Revisited," *Analyzing Writing: Models and Methods,* ed. Ulla Connor and Robert B. Kaplan (Reading: Addison, forthcoming).
[3]Karyn Thompson-Panos and Maria Thomas-Ruzic, "The Least You Should Know About Arabic: Implications for the ESL Writing Instructor," *TESOL Quarterly* 17 (1983): 620.
[4]Edward T. Hall, *The Silent Language* (New York: Doubleday, 1959) 172.
[5]Carolyn Matalene, "Contrastive Rhetoric: An American Writing Teacher in China," *College English* 47 (1985): 792.
[6]Edward T. Hall, *The Hidden Dimension* (Garden City: Anchor-Doubleday, 1969) 151.
[7]Kaplan, "Cultural Thought Patterns" 15.
[8]John Hinds, "Reader versus Writer Responsibility: A New Typology," *Analyzing Writing.*
[9]Summarized in Hinds.
[10]Quoted in Gary Blonston, "The Translator," *Science 85* 6.6 (1985): 84.
[11]Hall, *Hidden Dimension* 154.
[12]Quoted in Blonston 82–84.
[13]Edward T. Hall, *Beyond Culture* (Garden City: Anchor-Doubleday, 1977) 165–66.

Harris's Insights as a Resource for Your Teaching

1. Although writing instructors can usually tell whether someone is using the system of rhetorical expectations and standards of English discourse "correctly," they frequently can't explain the laws of the system, for reasons explained by the linguist Edward Hall. It may happen that, as you work one on one with a writer who has difficulty with English discourse, you will discover some interconnections among cultural perspectives, behavior patterns, habits of discourse, and rhetorical expectations that will make you understand English discourse better. Be careful to write down those insights, both to share with ESL instructors and other students and to research for yourself.

2. Linguists, foreign language faculty, and cultural anthropologists are good campus resources for educating yourself about the verbal and nonverbal behaviors of students who are not completely comfortable with English discourse. When a Japanese student nods and smiles and moves his head in agreement during a conference about his writing, you may think that he understands your explanation or question. He may be demonstrating with behavior appropriate to his culture how a student should respond toward a professor or how a reader or listener should actively participate in the communication.

3. Although many ESL writers fear the campus writing center because they must confront their fears about writing, many ESL students seek out that service. Investigate the resources of your campus writing center and inquire how you, the tutor, and the student might collaborate.

Harris's Insights as a Resource for the Writing Classroom

1. Many students find examples of cultural differences interesting. Ask students to discuss in their journals any observations they have made about how students "not from the dominant American culture" use English discourse, written or spoken. Ask for journal entries in which they discuss their own experiences in trying to learn a second language. In a class

discussion on cultural differences that you might prompt by a mini-lecture, ask students to share material from their journals.

2. Harris explains that differences in cultural perceptions of reader/writer responsibility will affect transition statements and attitudes toward revision. Peer editing and other collaborative work may also be affected. To assist students to participate most effectively, devise an attitude or learning inventory for students to describe their expectations for peer editors and group members. Use those descriptions in a class discussion where class members "negotiate" a list of responsibilities of writers and of readers. Use the list to generate a peer editing checklist.

3. ESL writers often complain that they don't receive enough help from peer editors fluent in English. In return, peer editors comfortable with English are sometimes intimidated by the range or nature of "problems" they encounter in writings of ESL students. Use the information you gain from conferences with individual ESL students to individualize a peer editing checklist. Ask each student to decide on three or four specific questions for the peer editor who reads his or her paper. Build in opportunities for the writer and reader to talk over the written peer editing comments.

READING AND WRITING CONNECTIONS

Like the authors of *The Bedford Guide,* many contemporary theorists and writing instructors assume that reading is an important resource for the writer and that writing, whether personal or critical, and rewriting prompt growth in readers. You will discover in composition studies a lively controversy over what, where, when, who, and why reading should be part of any writing course. Teachers puzzle over how best to incorporate reading in their composition syllabus, and teachers-as-researchers carefully observe the interconnections of writing and reading within the processes of composing. The following two essays provide some useful responses to some of these questions.

MODELING A WRITER'S IDENTITY: READING AND IMITATION IN THE WRITING CLASSROOM

Robert Brooke

Robert Brooke offers a sanguine defense of "imitation" and reading in the composition classroom. Historically, the current-traditional paradigm for understanding and teaching composition led instructors to focus on imitation of models of great writing. They assumed that reading and analyzing literary models would lead writers into the production of good writing. When the writing-as-process paradigm came to dominate composition theory and pedagogy, some instructors and theorists renounced both imitation and reading as useful pedagogic strategies. More recently, composition theorists have argued for reading — particularly the reading of literature — in the writing classroom because it models both forms and processes for writers to imitate. Brooke agrees that reading should be an important part of the writing classroom but disagrees that writers should imitate forms and processes. He argues that writers learn to write and improve as writers by imitating a person — a writer — and not a text or process.

Brooke asserts that the forms, processes, and texts are less important as models than are the writers who use the forms, engage in the processes, and construct the texts. When he discusses the implications of his research, he concludes that "being a writer involves taking a stance towards experience, towards reading, towards writing" and "involves taking on a particular identity, a way of being a certain person in a social world."

Brooke studied the way writing students negotiate the identities offered by a classroom context and the identities they brought to the classroom. He observed the process of learning writing by imitating writers' identities in a course that used literature as a major prompt. However, Brooke explains that the "reading" used can vary dramatically from writing course to writing course. What's most important for writing teachers to understand, argues Brooke, is that we effectively model identities of writers such that our students "come to see that being a writer in their own way is a valid and exciting way of acting in the world."

In The Bedford Guide for College Writers, *the authors enable student writers to observe a wide variety of writers at work. Students find multiple examples of how specific student writers have responded to a writing assignment and descriptions of how other student writers shaped the essays provided as models. In* A Writer's Research Manual *students learn from other writers by reading narratives about how one student wrote from library research and a second wrote from research in the field. Add to all this your presentation of yourself as a writer and you have offered to your students a heady mix of writers' identities that they can try on and imitate in part as they develop identities for themselves as language users.*

Reading (especially the reading of literature) has often been justified in the writing classroom because reading gives students something to imitate (see, for example, Miller's "Composition and Decomposition" and Comley and Scholes's "Literature, Composition, and the Structure of English"). The text, it is argued, provides a "model" of effective writing which students can copy, and the process of reading critically, practiced on literature, can become a "model" of how writers should behave in reading their own work. Reading is thus seen as useful because it models both forms and processes for writers to imitate.

But is this kind of imitation how writers really learn to write? Or does imitation in learning actually work some other way? In this article, I'll suggest an alternative understanding of imitation and reading in the writing classroom, and I'll exemplify this alternative using material from a semester-long participant-observation study of a freshman "Composition and Reading" course.

The alternative runs as follows: when a student (or any writer) successfully learns something about writing by imitation, it is by imitating another *person,* and not a text or a process. Writers learn to write by imitating other writers, by trying to act like writers they respect. The forms, the processes, the texts are in themselves less important as models to be imitated than the personalities, or identities, of the writers who produce them. Imitation, so the saying goes, is a form of flattery: we imitate because we respect the people we imitate, and because we want to be like them.

Imitation as a learning/teaching strategy, thus, is more concerned with the *identity* of the writer than the form of the text. When imitation works, it is because the student writer admires the teacher (or professional writer) enough to want to act like her. When it doesn't, it is because there is no respect, and the exercise in imitation becomes an empty exercise in reduplicating sterile form.

This, in simple form anyway, is the alternative I propose. The purpose of the rest of this article will be to explore the complexities of this alternative, to show just what it entails in the actual give-and-take of the classroom. I'll proceed with this exploration in the following way. First, I'll explain a bit of the theoretical work that supports seeing imitation this way. Then, I'll describe in some detail how these ideas operated in a particular course. Lastly, I'll address some implications of this stance towards learning, reading, and writing in the college curriculum.

Imitation, Reading, and Identity

Underlying the connection between reading, writing, and imitation is a more fundamental connection between imitation and identity. People often learn to be certain sorts of people by imitating those they admire, by trying to take on the "identity" of those they'd "like to be like." In some cultures, such learning by imitation is even the primary way of instructing the young. Shirley Brice Heath's studies of Asian-American families ("Ethnography and Education"), for example, show that Asian-American parents train their children in their familial and social duties not by listing expected behaviors (as a typical Anglo-American parent would) but by acting as a model to be imitated. In training for professional life, Asian-Americans learn through a sort of "apprentice" system — they watch and imitate the master craftsman rather than receiving explicit "textbook" instruction. A young Asian-American, thus, becomes an adult by respect and imitation. The adults she respects, she watches and imitates; her own adult identity is formed through the imitation of adults she respects.

By imitating those one respects, one forms aspects of one's "identity," one's public and acknowledged "sense of self." The term "identity" as used here needs some explanation. I do not have in mind "identity" as the sort of cosmic singleness of spirit or enduring mystical aura at the core of the self — "identity" in the sense of personal essence, spirit, or soul. Instead, I have in mind a fairly widespread psychosocial definition of the term: your identity is the sense of self attributed to you by yourself and other participants in your social situation. Such a definition is interactional in nature, and derives primarily from the work of Goffman, Erikson, and Laing, although versions of this view are widely held. An individual's identity, in other words, is a consequence of the way that person acts around others. On the basis of their actions (occupation, hobbies, mannerisms, quickness or slowness to anger, likes and dislikes, etc.), individuals come to be recognized and come to recognize themselves as certain sorts of people. This mutual recognition of self by self and others becomes one's identity. In interacting with others, then, one negotiates and is assigned a kind of consistent stance towards the world, based on the pattern of one's past and present interactions. This assigned consistent stance is, as far as anyone in the situation can tell, one's identity.

In this sense of the term, "identities" can be imitated, because they are a product of the ways individuals interact with those around them. One can try to react to experience in ways that are similar to those one respects, so that one will be assigned an identity also similar to them. Taking on certain occupations, certain hobbies, certain mannerisms, and the like all will help form the identity one is assigned; if you take these things on because someone else you admire does them, then imitation is at work.

I expect that a good deal of the identities we develop as we mature is a consequence of such imitation. Furthermore, I expect that a great deal of college teaching, especially in the humanities, works on this principle: teachers try to offer themselves or the writers they are teaching as valid "identities" for students to model. This is a fairly common strategy, and has a rich history. The teacher as model to be imitated, after all, was in classical Greece the educational stance of rhetoricians like Gorgias (according to Kennedy's *Classical Rhetoric*), and Aristotle's *Rhetoric* suggests that "ethos" or character is close to the most important ingredient in persuasion. Furthermore, literature classrooms, as Applebee points out in his history of English studies, have often been charged with teaching "culture," and for many teachers this charge has been realized by offering themselves as models of a cultured person. Further, most of us who have been influenced to become English teachers ourselves can remember some great teacher (or teachers) who really "turned us on" to reading, writing, and literature — teachers we self-consciously imitated in our attempts to be literate. For me, this person was my junior-year high school teacher. I can date my first attempts to write self-sponsored fiction and criticism to my experience in Ms. Johnson's classroom, and my desire to be the sort of person she respected. The identity of the teacher, it seems, can be a strong positive influence on learning.

But, as most of us English teachers also know, such identity-modeling doesn't always work. We can remember classmates in those "great" classes who hated our Ms. Johnsons, and hoped never to be like them. We also can remember, usually with regret, some of our own students who wanted no part of who we were, and consequently battled us, misunderstood assignments, and complained about grades all semester long. Identities, as Goffman, Erikson, and Laing all point out, are *negotiated* in interaction between people. Just because an identity is offered as a model doesn't mean it will be imitated. In fact, it was the problems in the process of identity negotiation that first led Erikson (*Childhood and Society*) to think about identity in this way, and to develop his oft-repeated theory of the "identity crisis" in adolescence. Laing's work as a psychotherapist (*The Divided Self; Self and Others*) similarly shows that people whose interpretations of themselves don't match the interpretations others have of them are consistently labeled "mentally ill." The processes of identity modeling and negotiations are anything but smooth.

The identity developed from a modeled identity, then, is a product of interpretation. You interpret your own actions and the actions of the model, and so do others; you interpret their responses, and so do they. From this web of mutually dependent interpretations arises the identity that gets assigned to you. But, as critics like Norman Holland have shown, the web of interpretation doesn't simply cause identity — in the process of interpretation, identity is already at play. Each person's identity is certainly a product of the interpretations that form it, but each person interprets experience according to the ways in which his or her identity has already been shaped. Writing of the process of reading literature, for example, Holland claims:

> *Interpretation is a function of identity,* specifically, identity conceived as variations upon an identity theme. . . . Identity re-creates itself, or, to put it another way, style — in the sense of personal style — creates itself. That is, all of us, as we read, use the literary work to symbolize and finally to replicate ourselves. We work out through the text our own characteristic patterns of desire and adaptation. We interact with the work, making it part of our psychic economy and making ourselves part of the literary work — as we interpret it. ("UNITY IDENTITY" 123–24, his italics)

What Holland shows, in other words, is that new experience (in his case, new literary experience) is interpreted in relation to one's identity as developed to that point. Students don't come into classrooms as blank slates. They come with a wealth of past experience and, by the time they reach college, a fairly well-defined sense of the kinds of persons they are. Their interaction with any attempt to model an identity for them, then, must take into account the identities they have already developed for themselves. The actual experience of any classroom that involves identity modeling, then, can be seen as a negotiation between the identities offered by the classroom context and the identities of the students as already fairly well formed individuals. It is within this negotiation that learning-by-imitation occurs.

One way of looking at what goes on in classrooms, then, would focus on the identities modeled for the students by the classroom interaction and materials and on the resulting identities negotiated for themselves by students. In the rest of this article, I will describe how such negotiations operated in one introductory English class, a "Composition and Reading" course taught in Spring 1986 by a teacher I'll call Janet Rich.[1] As a writing course, this class was highly successful: according to formal course evaluations at the end of the semester, students rated it easily the best writing course they had ever taken. The reason the course worked, I think, was because of the possibilities for learning by imitation the course provided.

In this course, a particular way of being a writer was modeled, and students were allowed to imitate this model if they chose to. The modeling was a product of two things. In part, the course focused on Margaret Laurence, author of *A Bird in the House,* as the model of writer to be imitated. But this model only existed because of the way the teacher, Janet Rich, connected Laurence's work to the students' own writing through her behavior as reader and writer. Janet thus served as the bridge between the published, professional writer Margaret Laurence and

191

the students as beginning writers — students grew to consider themselves potentially like Laurence because they could understand and imitate the ways Janet read and wrote in response to Laurence.

In what follows, I will describe the writer's identity that Janet's course modeled and some of the ways in which she established this model. Then I will present some student responses characteristic of the range of response in this classroom. Lastly, I will suggest some implications of this way of teaching for the learning of writing and the theory of writing instruction.

The Writer as Explorer

Writer Identity: One of the tensions in Margaret Laurence's *A Bird in the House* is the tension between the fanciful, escapist stories people would like to tell themselves and the real, difficult stories that people live. The book, in fact, chronicles the development of the young Vanessa through a childhood in which she writes escapist plots about pirates and explorers to a realization of the intense honesty required to write from real life. In the final chapter of the novel, she describes such a moment, a moment in which she abandons a plot she's just started because she recognizes the falseness of it:

> [D]isenchantment began to set in. Marie [her escapist heroine] would not get out of the gray stone inn. She would stay there all her life. The only thing that would ever happen to her was that she would get older. . . . I felt I could not bear it. I no longer wanted to finish the story. What was the use, if she couldn't get out except by ruses which clearly wouldn't happen in real life? (153)

Although it isn't explicitly stated in this novel, this same Vanessa grows in time to write *A Bird in the House,* a book which scrupulously details events from this character's childhood. Writing, for Vanessa, comes to be a tool for honest exploration of one's own life, instead of a tool for escape. The difficulty of real life and the difficulty of understanding it, thus, become central aspects of the novel, and writing for Vanessa becomes one way to explore these difficulties. The problems of what to tell, how to understand it to tell it, and the courage required to be honest enough to tell it all come together as central ingredients in the process of writing.

The identity of the writer in Margaret Laurence's novel, thus, is of a person who uses writing to explore, present, and hopefully understand the complexity of life around her. This identity, furthermore, is presented as a difficult identity because of the intense honesty it requires of the self, and the recognition of the tendency to escape from this honesty into self-protecting fantasy. The writer, in short, is a kind of intrepid explorer of the self, requiring as much stamina and bravery as would explorers of any other unknown regions.

It was exactly this sense of writer as explorer that Janet's course modeled. Janet used Margaret Laurence's book and the class to model a certain stance towards experience, a certain way of writing and thinking in response to experience. Instead of focusing the students on the text as a model for imitation or as a place to practice literary reading, she turned reading and writing into an exploration of situations in their own lives. As the course progressed, she began to point explicitly to Margaret Laurence (and inexplicitly to herself) as models of the sort of person who typically approaches the world this way, and suggested that writing allows and depends on exactly such an approach. Her final goal was to improve the students' writing and reading by encouraging them to see themselves as language users like Margaret Laurence, using writing to explore the complexity of experience and to communicate what they find. The goals of her class, thus, were much in keeping with the writer's identity presented in *A Bird in the House.* The way Janet structured the course and the way she handled class discussion contributed to the presentation of this identity as a valid model of how to be a writer.

Class Structure: Janet's class was planned as a sequence of six units, each dealing with a particular paper topic and a major revision. Each unit prompted students to consider writing as a tool for self-exploration and communication.

At the beginning of each unit, Janet provided a hand-out describing the project and conducted an in-class guided memory invention exercise to help students find their own ideas within the general topic. Students usually had a week to write the paper after it had been assigned. In the meantime, Janet would have students read and discuss *A Bird in the House,* material from *The Bedford Reader,* and suggestions on rhetoric from Young, Becker, and Pike's classic text, *Rhetoric: Discovery and Change.* Although she didn't always hold to this schedule, Mondays were usually spent discussing student writing in small groups, Wednesdays were spent discussing their reading, and Fridays were spent doing activities from the rhetoric.

Each of the six units involved writing an original paper, reading it to a small group of other students and submitting it to Janet, and rewriting it (or writing a completely new paper) to shift focus, purpose, or emphasis from the first draft. Students thus turned in a total of twelve papers, two in each unit.

Two representative units proceeded as follows:

Papers 3 and 4: Students wrote about an experience they'd had from which they learned something, the purpose being to help the reader share both the experience and what it taught them. For the second paper, students were asked to think about how they went about changing some important idea they'd held about the world, focusing this time on describing the process of change that led to their present understanding of the situation.

Papers 5 and 6: Students wrote about a "phase" someone they knew had gone through, again describing for their readers what had happened and how they understood it. For their revision, students were encouraged to expand their descriptions by conducting interviews with the subject or others who knew the person, considering other perspectives on the phase, and considering the long term changes in which the phase played a part. These revisions were suggested under the general rubric of "making the paper more appropriate for a wider audience."

Each of Janet's assignments asked students to explore some aspect of their experience and thought, and to share what they found with their readers. Each assignment, in short, prompted students to explore aspects of the writer's identity her course modeled.

Furthermore, during each unit, *A Bird in the House* featured prominently. When students wrote about an experience from which they learned, they read about the birth of Vanessa's brother and Grandmother MacLeod's demand that he be named after the dead Rodrick. As they wrote about a phase, they read about Grandmother Connor's death and the "mask" that Grandfather put on. And so on — the events in *A Bird in the House* and the treatment of those events paralleled Janet's assignments.

Kinds of Discussion: Janet used discussions of *A Bird in the House* to focus more clearly the *behaviors* she thought were important in dealing with writing, reading, and experience. On the days when *A Bird in the House* was discussed, Janet did not focus on technique, symbolism, theme, or any other "English teacher" sort of talk. Instead, she began by posing a question about the events of the sort "how do we understand X?" and then let students develop their own lists of answers. For the first chapter, for example, Janet divided the class into small groups and provided each group with cards for each of the characters in the story. She then asked each group to arrange the cards so that characters who were like one another were together. Each group's arrangement was then put on the board, and the groups took turns explaining, attacking, and defending their arrangements. As the class ended, Janet encouraged the students to think about two things: (1) whether in their own families people "took after" other people, and (2) how Margaret Laurence's description of the house at the beginning of the story might clue us in to the relationships between the characters.

This kind of class exercise didn't focus on reading the story as the traditional English class might. Instead, it provided students an opportunity to reflect on personalities and how those personalities were formed, using the characters in the book as examples. And Janet suggested that students extend this kind of thinking beyond the book to their own families. The focus on writing/reading itself was not as strong as the focus on understanding and thinking about interactions between people.

Late in the course, when students were explicitly writing to "an audience" about issues and problems which concerned them, Janet brought Margaret Laurence explicitly into the picture. While discussing the last two chapters, she began to ask if ideas or patterns from these chapters connected with earlier chapters, and what Laurence might have been up to in writing this book. At the same time, she asked students to come to grips in their writing with real problems they faced and real readers who might think differently than they. On other days during this time, Janet brought in drafts of her own letters on such topics as her anger at sensationalist TV newscasts and discussed how she had to work through her anger before she could write a persuasive letter; Janet took students to the student art gallery and had one of the student artists come in and talk about why he painted what he painted. And she said things in class like "Is this story Margaret Laurence's essay #9?"

In other words, as the course progressed Janet led students from only considering ways of thinking about families, pasts, and events to considering why someone might write about such events. She moved from using writing/reading/thinking to explore surrounding social life to explicit questions about using writing/thinking/reading as a public forum in which to communicate ideas about what students explored. In both of these activities, Laurence's *A Bird in the House* served as a cornerstone. It was never really "analyzed" for theme, plot, and symbols as in traditional English classes. Instead, it came to offer two kinds of opportunities for students: an opportunity to think about lives in the way Janet had them think about the book, and an opportunity to act as writers like Margaret Laurence, using writing to explore the complexity of their own lives and to communicate this complexity to other readers. The identities of writer, of reader, of thinker were modeled through Margaret Laurence's novel.

Student Responses

To describe the identity modeled by Janet's course is only half the description; the more important part is how the students responded to the modeled identity. Janet's course, as I have shown, created a situation in which a certain kind of writer's identity, a certain stance toward reading and writing, was modeled for students. In looking at student response, we begin to see how this kind of presentation affects people — how they negotiate an identity for themselves in the face of pressure from the class environment to become a certain sort of person and in the face of the person they already feel themselves to be. At issue, in short, are three complex processes: (1) how the individual students interpreted the model of writer being offered; (2) how they negotiated an identity in response to this interpretation; and (3) how their past identity influenced their interpretation and negotiation.

As the course progressed, I followed eight students closely, conducting out-of-class interviews with them at three points during the semester. These students' responses suggest three general patterns of dealing with the modeled identity: acceptance, transformation, and rejection. Of the eight students, two left the course excited about being writers and defended their excitement with explanations of writing and reading which were similar to those Janet had offered. Five other students felt good about the course and about their writing, but felt tense, confused, or uncertain about aspects of what Janet expected of them. These students all provided a rationale which justified their mixed reactions and posited a different sort of writer's identity from the one Janet offered. The final student claimed to like Janet as a person, but rejected the course as a waste of time because it didn't help her with what she thought "writing" was. In this section, I will briefly describe four of these students' responses, using excerpts from my interviews to illuminate these general patterns.

Pattern One: Acceptance

One of the students, Amy, exemplified most clearly acceptance of the modeled writer's identity. In interviews, she articulated a connection between her writing and Margaret Laurence's, and claimed this connection contributed to writing in general. Furthermore, she connected these ideas to her sense of herself as a person outside the classroom.

According to Amy, the way she responded to *A Bird in the House* and to the course in general was a function of the person she was. She described herself as someone who had always liked English courses, particularly courses with literature. For her, what was important about reading literature was what it allowed you to see about yourself. This stance informed Amy's positive evaluation of *A Bird in the House:*

> I'm a people person I suppose that's why I like it. It's interesting to read about somebody else . . . you can tie your family to things that happened in their family, you know, there's always somebody in your family that's either like Grandfather or Vanessa.

For Amy, the book was not really different from other books she'd read in English class — the connection between reading and understanding one's own family was one she had already made.

When she turned to writing, however, Amy made much greater claims for this particular course. Although she had been presented before with the idea of reading as a way of exploring one's own experience, she claimed she never had experienced writing in this way. In her words, her past writing courses had forced her to copy forms, but this course allowed her to use writing to explore and communicate:

> I think I've learned more in sixteen weeks here, how to write, than I have in like my three years of writing in high school. Here you had to write about what, your experience, what you wanted to write about and they told you what, you know, an audience to put it towards. I mean in, in high school you were just writing because they wanted you to write something — you had to, you were, you practiced more on writing the, you know, correct form instead of how you felt about what you were writing and who your, your audience was for.

In Amy's mind, then, the course allowed her to connect reading and writing as activities in a new way. Following Janet's lead, she could now see writing as a way to explore experience, just as reading had been for her in the past. Her own writing, she could see, didn't have to be overwhelmingly worried about "form" as it had been in the past. Instead, it could be just like Margaret Laurence's writing — an exploration of experience.

For Amy, then, the exciting part of the course was the idea that writing could be used to explore and understand experience. She already saw herself as a person who was interested in understanding experience and who used reading for this purpose; writing thus became an added tool. Her acceptance of the identity of a writer as "one who explores experience," thus, seems primarily an embellishment of a stance towards the world she already held. Through Janet's course, she was able to connect the idea of writing to the sense of herself as a person she had already developed.

Pattern Two: Transformation

While Amy both articulated the connections between writing, reading, and experience that Janet modeled and felt good about seeing herself in this way, the most common responses from a second group of students were to enjoy the experience and feel uncomfortable about it. Where Amy felt confirmed in the sort of person she was, several students felt both excited and threatened. In responding to the course, these students had to find a way of justifying their responses to themselves, of transforming their understanding of Janet's course so that they could keep what excited them and avoid what was threatening. I will describe the responses of two such students, Clark and Melody.

Clark's response to the course was twofold. On the one hand, he enjoyed the course and the opportunities for writing it allowed. On the other, he disliked Margaret Laurence's book:

> Nothing ever, I mean nothing good ever happens in that book, it's always drab and morbid, I mean people are dying, people are running away, people are going crazy. . . . The only good thing that happens is Aunt Edna gets married. The rest of it, I mean something good will start to happen and it turns bad. . . . I don't understand, she must (pause) had a bad life, she wrote, she wrote it from her own experience, 'cause, I mean, I've never known anybody that had that bad a life. . . . I mean, I hope my life never turns out like that.

As a reader and writer, Clark seemed unable to handle the kind of thinking about experience Laurence's book provided. This fit in many ways with his general personality in the course. He had his life planned out — after college, he would enter the Air Force and become a fighter pilot, maybe get married, and have a successful career. He wrote papers about the steps he would go through to become a fighter pilot, about funny events from his childhood, and, when given an "open" assignment, a fantasy story about a Dungeons and Dragons warrior. He claimed to read only sword and sorcery novels for fun. He complained loudly throughout the course that assignments were too hard or that the readings were a waste of time. Overall, then, Clark's response to *A Bird in the House* seems to connect with other aspects of his personality. He almost seemed to want to appear as the stereotypic "military male," and to play down any other of his responses.

But, at the same time, Clark really liked Janet as a teacher, and admitted in interviews that even though he complained he thought he had learned something. In particular, he singled out "audience" as a concept that was helpful. Although he had resisted revising his papers to comply with an audience's needs during the course, he felt it would help him in the future when he needed to speak to groups of people. Also, he really enjoyed writing his "sword and sorcery" paper, and admitted it was always something he wanted to do but hadn't until Janet allowed them to write "whatever they wanted."

Clark, in short, responded to the class by segmenting his experience of it into discrete parts. When I asked him explicitly if he saw connections between the reading and writing in the course, he said he couldn't see any. When I asked him to summarize what he might think in the future he'd learned from the course, he responded with a list of disconnected things — he'd learned how important audience was, he'd learned how to analyze stuff (although he doubted authors really put all that stuff in books), and he expected he'd keep his last paper because he liked it. Instead of perceiving the activities of the class as a whole, Clark separated them and, in separating them, obscured the identity Janet was modeling. This separation allowed him to justify his differing responses to the parts of the course — he could remain puzzled and scornful of Laurence's book, but he could also hold on to his positive sense of his own writing, his positive sense of Janet, and the idea of the importance of audience for writing and speaking.

What emerges from Clark, then, is a division of Janet's model of writer into two parts which can be responded to separately. On one side is Laurence's book and the whole way of exploring experience which it represents. On the other is the idea of writing as fun and purposeful, writing as something people do because they like to and because they want to affect other people. Clark keeps the two separate, and consequently can see the first as worthless or unintelligible ("do authors really put all that stuff in there?"), the second as useful. Such a division, it could further be argued, allows Clark to protect his sense of self while still admitting he liked the course — it keeps the elements of the course that prove useful to his "planned" life, and eliminates the elements that challenge it. In this sense, Clark's transformation of the identity offered seems quite possibly a defense against having to think aspects of his position through — his most telling statement about Laurence's book becomes "I hope my life never turns out like that." His transformation of the modeled identity becomes a way of preserving his current identity while still allowing parts of the course to filter through.

Unlike Clark, Melody entered the course seeing herself as a writer. As a theater arts major, Melody described herself as associated with creative writers and actors and really interested in writing. During the semester, she confirmed this sense of herself by joining an experimental theater group, and writing for and acting in four improvisational one-act plays. Nevertheless, Melody responded much the same way to the course as Clark did. She transformed the model of writer being offered by the course into a model much more in keeping with her current identity, and consequently understood her experience with Laurence's book as an unimportant part of the course.

A passage from my final interview with Melody illuminates these transformations:

Interviewer: In these last two weeks, we haven't done much actual writing, instead we've finished *A Bird in the House* and gone to the [student] art gallery. Why do you think we're doing it?

Melody: I don't know, I think it still has to do with writing though, 'cause when we went over to the gallery we were writing about what we were looking at. It makes you look more as to not just what you're writing but why you're writing it and what, what makes you write it. Um 'cause every week we get deeper into it, deeper into why we're writing, you know, than what we're writing. Instead of just the basic rules of writing . . .

Interviewer: Do you think [*A Bird in the House*] connects with the writing?

Melody: Uh. Yes, some of it does. But, as many people have said the book is so morbid in itself that you really don't think about what it's teaching you or what you're learning from it, you just think how morbid it is. . . . I figured we read it because she's a good writer, a good way of writing . . . I just figured she wrote it because she wanted to write it, it was semiautobiographical and you know, why else would you write, you know. I don't really see a purpose for writing all this.

Melody shows on the one hand an insightful awareness that Janet's course has slowly been moving towards the question "why do we write?" — a question Melody finds exciting. She has a sense of an answer: we write, she seems to say, to communicate and explore thoughts. She sees the exploration of "what makes us write" as exciting, and sees many aspects of the course converging at this point. Like Amy, she sees the focus on "why we write" as an exciting contrast with her earlier classes, which focused on the "rules of writing." The image of writer Melody seems to be developing is an image of someone driven to write, perhaps by parts of her personal history, and of someone who writes to communicate with others. Much of the identity Janet modeled is encapsulated in such an image.

But Melody finally doesn't connect this answer with *A Bird in the House* because she finds the book so morbid that she distances herself from it. She claims that the book probably does connect, but that she finds it so morbid that she has stopped thinking about it. For her, the particular stance Laurence provides in the book is not important to her sense of writers as people who explore and communicate — she can accept being a writer without accepting the depressing events of Laurence's book. As she explained, she doesn't like to think about morbid things. This rationale seems connected to her sense of herself as a theater person.

Melody came from a wealthy Omaha family, and was excited about her future as an actress and playwright, but frightened that she wouldn't succeed. The thought of life not turning out positively, but closing in like it did for the families in Laurence's book, may have been more than she could accept at this point in her life. In this way, Melody is very much like Clark — both transform their experience in Janet's class to eliminate those aspects of the modeled identity that threaten parts of their own, while allowing them to keep those aspects that support who they feel themselves to be. Melody's model of the writer, however, is closer to Janet's than Clark's: she keeps the idea of self-exploration as well as the idea of communication with readers, leaving out only the possibility that the self to be explored is a self in a depressing environment.

Pattern Three: Rejection

Not everyone saw connections between the course and their own writing, however. One of the most interesting responses to the book (and to English classes in general) was given by Clare, an "A" student in Janet's course who had been an "A" student since junior high school. In talking with Clare, it became apparent that her identity as "A" student in many ways interfered with her considering the identity of writer being offered by the course. When asked to draw connections between parts of the course, Clare focused on the mechanics of course procedure rather than on the ideas underlying the procedures.

> I never really think, I mean, is it supposed to tie together, I mean, I thought it was just part of the (laughs) English course. I mean you write papers you read books, and now we're ending them up and getting it all finished, you know, it's the end of the semester.

Clare was baffled by the questions — the course, to her, was just an English course. You read books, you wrote papers, and that was it. When I asked her later if she saw a connection between her work and Laurence's, she denied it — even though Janet had written in response to one of her papers "do you realize how much like *A Bird in the House* this is?":

> Maybe if I looked at it and she explained what she meant then I'd go "Oh." You know (laughs) but I don't from — what she wrote on my paper it said "did you notice how much this correlated with *A Bird in the House?*" And I wrote about my childhood and um, how my old place where I used to live, um, in my mind subconsciously I think of it as a happy place because that's where my family was a whole, then we moved from there my sister (pause) went insane and my (pause) parents got divorced and (laughs) you know. And that's the only thing I wrote about and then she said that it correlates with *Bird in the House,* I don't, I don't know. (laughs) It's nothing like what happened in there.

Clare, much like Clark and Melody, can't see the connection between herself and Margaret Laurence. We can see a connection though — her work sounds very similar. It describes family changes by focusing on a place, it reflects on events that are hard to understand in family life. But because the plots aren't similar, Clare won't see the connection even when it's pointed out. Later in her interview, she provides some reasons why she can't see the connection. Basically, she says she's only read literature for "symbolism" in the past, and is highly aware that she didn't use symbolism and real writers do (thus, she can't be like Laurence). Secondly, she says writing classes should teach form — the forms for different types of essays will help students succeed in other classes. She says Janet helped with content but not form, and she can't see how writing personal stuff in this class will help her in her future history and business classes. The identity of writer that Clare posits, thus, is an identity that is wholly connected to the school environment. Form and technique — that is what writers are concerned with, not with "personal" aspects of life. Clare already has a strong image of a writer as someone who succeeds in English classes, writing formal papers and explicating the symbolism of literary works. She thus experiences Janet's course as an enjoyable break from such real work, but a break that is finally not worth her time.

In general, then, Clare never considers that writing could go on outside the school setting, or that writing could be used to "explore and communicate" one's own life. Unlike Amy and Melody who are excited to find Janet's course focusing on purpose rather than form, Clare is worried by it. It doesn't fit with her experience in other classrooms, and therefore will not help her. For Clare, it appears, the identity of writer or reader is an identity that belongs only to the classroom. She can't imagine being a writer in any other context. In her refusal to consider such other possibilities lies her inability to see connections — and, of course, in her own mind she may be right. Janet's course very well may not help in future courses, if all one writes for is to satisfy course demands.

Implications

Janet's course, and the students' responses to it, provide us with examples of identity-modeling in action. They allow us to see how this teaching strategy operates in the classroom, and how the imitation of identity influences student learning. In particular, this description of Janet's class suggests three significant implications for the teaching of writing. First, the course suggests that the imitation of identity is a more powerful means of learning, at least in the experience of students, than the imitation of forms and processes. Second, the course suggests that students will interpret a modeled identity (and negotiate their own) in a wide variety of ways — as a learning process, identity-modeling is only slightly in the teacher's control. Finally, the course suggests that composition instruction can work profitably when it presents a stance towards experience, when its goal is to model a consistent way of viewing the self as language-user. These three implications help clarify the role of the writing teacher in the writing classroom.

1. *Imitation: Form or Identity?* For most of the students in this course, following Janet and focusing on purpose, exploration, and communication through writing was much more exciting and beneficial than copying accepted forms in their papers or imitating literary reading processes. To be exploring why people write and to be trying to act as writers themselves was more worthwhile than imitating forms. Both Amy and Melody, in the excerpts given above, described their experience in the course in terms of this difference — their past courses had been "not as useful" because they were forced to copy "forms" or "rules," but this course was very useful because they explored purposes for writing.

It would seem, then, that the experiences of these students confirm the alternative model of imitation proposed at the beginning of this article: students feel they learn more by imitating identities rather than imitating forms or processes. Imitating an identity gives students a reason for the behavior — they perceive a model of someone they'd "like to be like," and try to copy it. Imitating a form or process is only a forced exercise, divorced from the identity and life of the student. When students perceived "a writer" as something they were or would like to be, they strove to act appropriately. Amy, Melody, and Clark all show this process at work — they defined a version of "writer" they wanted to be through their experience in this course, and strove to be it (although their versions transformed in significant ways the one Janet was modeling). All three students found they could understand themselves, as a consequence of the class, as certain kinds of language-users, and this understanding led to their learning. Given the overwhelmingly positive response of the students as a whole to the class (21 of 23 students gave both the teacher and class "excellent" marks on formal course evaluations), it would seem that this method of teaching connected with most students as it had connected with Amy, Clark, and Melody. Connecting the behaviors of writing and reading to themselves was important to these students once they could imagine the sort of person they would become by doing so. Janet's course allowed them to develop an image of this potential person by interaction with her, Margaret Laurence, and each other.

2. *Modeled Identity and Student Identities:* While Janet's course did model a particular way of being a writer, the students in her course found their own ways of interpreting and

199

understanding what a writer is. Amy, Clark, and Melody, for example, all ended up under-standing the identity of writer in different ways. The teacher's model influenced them by providing an opportunity to explore the writer's identity, but it did not control the particular identity students developed. The process of modeling a consistent stance towards reading, writing, and experience may thus be more crucial for learning by imitation than the particular content of the identity model.

Such an implication, I believe, is significant for meeting the charges of "sophistry" or "indoctrination" so often raised against an identity-modeling approach to teaching. If Kennedy is right in suggesting the ancient Sophists taught primarily by offering themselves as models to be imitated, then we must recognize that identity-modeling as a teaching strategy has been attacked as immoral since the beginning of rhetoric. Plato's Socrates, after all, attacked such teaching in the "Gorgias" because for it to work the teacher must be truly good. For Plato, the ethical problem of who the identity-model is constitutes a significant problem, for he worked under the assumption that the pupil would turn out like the model. His argument, conse-quently, was to reduce the Sophist's claims of "good teaching" to rubble because they occa-sionally turned out students who were immoral and evil. If the students are just imitating their teachers, then their teachers must themselves be immoral (or, worse, ignorant of what they're about).

The responses of students in Janet's class, however, show how unfounded these fears are. The teacher, no matter how exciting a model she presents, just isn't in control of the identity the students will develop. Students are not as tractable as that — the identities they negotiate in any class are the result, to a large extent, of the identities they already have. The transformations of the writer's identity by Clark and Melody in Janet's classroom should make this point clear. The process of identity-formation is not as simple as Plato apparently imagined in his dialogue. It involves a complex interrelationship of model, past experience, and interpretation, much of which cannot take place at a conscious level.

3. *Composition as a Stance towards Experience:* The final implication is, I believe, the most powerful. Being a writer involves taking a stance towards experience, towards reading, towards writing. It involves taking on a particular identity, a way of being a certain person in the social world. Janet's course suggests that modeling a writer's identity, modeling a particu-lar stance towards written language and experience, is a powerful method of bringing students to understand themselves as writers. It seems a way of instilling in them the motivation to write, to see themselves as writers and readers, to act as writers in their world. A writer's identity, I would argue, is what composition courses should be fostering, for it is in a writer's *stance* towards experience that written language, both writing and reading, moves from being just a "skill" to being a way of acting in the world.

Furthermore, it strikes me that such a focus on developing a writer's identity is exactly what many of the very best pedagogical changes in the last ten years have brought about, even though they haven't explicitly recognized it. The entire "process, not product" revolution can be seen as a change of focus from results to behaviors, from texts to people — in its best forms, the goal is to teach people to be writers, not to produce good texts in the course of a semester. "The growth of students as writers," claim Knoblauch and Brannon, "is not the same as the improvement of texts" (*Rhetorical Traditions* 151). Behind the development of abilities stands the development of identities, of the sense of self as a writer, reader, and responder to experience.

Such a view is implicit (though not developed) in the pedagogical systems of Knoblauch and Brannon, Peter Elbow, and Ann Berthoff, to cite three currently-fashionable examples. Knoblauch and Brannon's "community of writers," in which teachers and students dialogue with one another on important academic questions, would seem to model a kind of writer's identity just as powerful as the one Janet modeled. In such classrooms, students experience themselves as writers in important, ongoing debates to which they have something to contribute. Elbow's "teacherless" classrooms similarly provide a model of writers motivated to find their own meanings through self-searching and sharing — a stance towards language-use and experience very similar to the one Janet modeled. Ann Berthoff's notion of composing as forming, as an activity students do every day in a whole variety of ways, is yet another way of offering a model of who a writer is. In each of these classrooms, what's important is that students are presented with valid, exciting models of writers as people who take consistent stances towards language and experience, and work with it to create their own meanings.

Seeing these classrooms as places where identity is modeled provides a clear way of meeting the common criticism of such classrooms as inappropriate for academic study. Recently, James Reither and Mike Rose have argued that writing classes which focus on "personal experience" harm students more than help them. The experience of entering students, it is claimed, is too divorced from the real world of college education for their experience to lead to significant academic writing. Their objection, in short, is somewhat like Clare's objections to Janet's course, only more sophisticated. The objection falls flat, I believe, once we recognize (as Clare could not) that identity is at issue in the writing classroom. A teacher like Berthoff, Elbow, or Janet is modeling a way of being, an identity, a stance towards written language use; the actual shape of the student's finished product is less important than the stance towards writing the student develops. Identity-modeling, it could be said, works on the motivation of students. Students leave such courses (as Amy, Clark, and Melody did) excited about themselves as writers, more aware of how they might develop a piece of writing, and more eager to attempt writing in the future.

Reither and Rose's objections, consequently, miss the point of so-called "personal experience" teaching. By focusing on the appropriateness of student texts for the academy, they obscure the development of the student's identity as writer. The data from Janet's class suggest that developing a sense of oneself as a writer is perceived by students as "more useful" than developing better command of forms appropriate for academic inquiry. Developing a writer's identity is what classes like Janet's are all about. It may not finally matter what version of writer's identity is modeled or in what context (academic or otherwise) the identity is cast, because what emerges for students is a stronger sense of themselves as writers. Students, thus, feel better able to write in other settings because they know more about themselves as writers, and trust themselves more.

Modeling how written language fits into a consistent stance towards experience, a consistent, productive way of seeing human action in the world, would thus appear to be one of the primary insights of modern composition practice. Seeing this insight in terms of identity is what this study allows. Composition teaching works, in the modern sense, when it effectively models an identity for students which the students can in some way accept. It works when part of their identity becomes a writer's identity, when they come to see that being a writer in their own way is a valid and exciting way of acting in the world. The modeled identities may differ — clearly Janet's "writer" differs from Berthoff's, and Berthoff's from Knoblauch and Brannon's — but the process of modeling identity is what composition teaching is all about. Behind the processes of reading and writing lie stances towards the world, and behind our teaching of these processes lie the identities of ourselves and our students as language users. The processes of identity-formation are the processes we are in, and the processes we teach.

Note

[1]I studied this course using a version of the participant-observation method described by researchers like Graves and Calkins for elementary schools and Kantor for high schools. I participated as a member of the class for the entire semester, writing papers, interacting with students, and working in small groups, as well as recording observations daily in a sort of anthropologist's field notebook. Three times during the semester, I conducted individual thirty-minute taped interviews with eight selected students. The instructor and I met weekly to discuss what was happening in the classroom. As Kantor et

al. ("Research in Context") and Heath ("Ethnography in Education") have argued, these ways of gathering data uncover qualitative information about classroom interaction and language use that traditional research designs omit. In this course in particular, this research method made available the experience of the students in revealing ways, since on paper the course appeared to be much the same as many a traditional "reading and writing" course. The participant-observation method allowed me to see how this course differed from traditional courses, at least in the experience of students.

Works Cited

Applebee, Arthur. *Tradition and Reform in the Teaching of English*. Urbana: NCTE, 1974.

Aristotle, *Rhetoric*. Trans. W. R. Roberts. New York: Modern Library, 1954.

Berthoff, Ann. *Forming/Thinking/Writing*. Rochelle Park, NJ: Hayden, 1978.

Calkins, Lucy. *Lessons from a Child*. Portsmouth, NH: Heinemann, 1983.

Comley, Nancy, and Robert Scholes. "Literature, Composition, and the Structure of English." Horner 96–109.

Elbow, Peter. *Writing without Teachers*. New York: Oxford UP, 1973.

Erikson, Erik. *Childhood and Society*. New York: Norton, 1950.

_____. *Identity, Youth and Crisis*. New York: Norton, 1968.

Goffman, Erving. *Asylums*. New York: Anchor, 1961.

_____. *Stigma: Notes on the Management of Spoil Identity*. Englewood Cliffs: Prentice, 1963.

Graves, Donald. *A Researcher Learns to Write*. Portsmouth, NH: Heinemann, 1984.

Heath, Shirley Brice. "Ethnography in Education: Toward Defining the Essentials." *Ethnography and Education: Children in and out of School*. Ed. P. Gilmore and A. Glatthorn. Washington: Center for Applied Linguistics, 1982. 33–55.

_____. "Ethnography and Education." Seminar given at the University of Nebraska–Lincoln, March 1986.

_____. *Ways with Words*. New York: Cambridge UP, 1983.

Holland, Norman. *5 Readers Reading*. New Haven: Yale UP, 1975.

_____. *The I*. New Haven: Yale UP, 1985.

_____. "UNITY IDENTITY TEXT SELF." *PMLA* 90 (1975): 813–22. Rpt. in *Reader-Response Criticism*. Ed. Jane Tompkins. Baltimore: John Hopkins, 1980. 118–33.

Horner, Winifred, ed. *Composition and Literature: Bridging the Gap*. Chicago: Chicago UP, 1983.

Kantor, Ken. "Classroom Contexts and the Development of Writing Intentions." *New Directions in Composition Research*. Ed. Richard Beach and Lillian Bridwell. New York: Guilford, 1984. 72–94.

Kantor, Ken, Dan Kirby, and Judith Goetz. "Research in Context: Ethnographic Studies in English Education." *Research in the Teaching of English* 15 (1981): 293–309.

Kennedy, George. *Classical Rhetoric and Its Christian and Secular Tradition from Ancient to Modern Times*. Chapel Hill: North Carolina UP, 1980.

Knoblauch, C. H., and Lil Brannon. *Rhetorical Traditions and the Teaching of Writing*. Upper Montclair: Boynton/Cook, 1984.

Laing, R. D. *The Divided Self*. London: Tavistock, 1960.

_____. *Self and Others*. 2nd ed. New York: Penguin, 1969.

_____. *The Voice of Experience*. New York: Pantheon, 1982.

Laurence, Margaret. *A Bird in the House*. Toronto: Seal, 1978.

Miller, J. Hillis. "Composition and Decomposition: Deconstruction and the Teaching of Writing." Horner 38–56.

Plato. "Gorgias." Trans. W. D. Woodhead. *The Collected Dialogues of Plato*. Ed. Edith Hamilton and Huntington Cairns. Princeton: Bollington, 1961. 229–307.

Reither, James. "Writing and Knowing: Toward Redefining the Writing Process." *College English* 47 (1985): 620–28.

Rose, Mike. "The Language of Exclusion." *College English* 47 (1985): 341–59.

Young, Richard, Alton Becker, and Kenneth Pike. *Rhetoric: Discovery and Change*. New York: Harcourt, 1970.

Brooke's Insights as a Resource for Your Teaching

1. It's no accident that Brooke, who works with the Nebraska Writing Project, would recommend that we provide models of ourselves in our writers' identities to our students. This "modeling" is one of the first principles of the National Writing Project, which was originally funded by the National Endowment for the Humanities and which has dramatically assisted writing instructors from kindergarten through college. Check out your state and regional writing projects and apply for admission to a summer or year-long workshop. You will then be able to co-investigate with teachers from every discipline, from every educational level, and with varying teaching and writing backgrounds the common issues and insights of composition theory and pedagogy.

2. Talk with your students about your own writing. Show them drafts and describe how you are constructing a purpose and attending to or ignoring audience. Ask for evaluative comments and show them revisions that followed their commentary. Demonstrate to them that even "expert" writers are continuously engaged in the processes of learning to write.

Brooke's Insights as a Resource for the Writing Classroom

1. Invite your students to research a writer and to develop a sequence of readings in which class members can see and reflect on that writer in action. Ask each small research group to "teach" the class by organizing a discussion both of the readings and of the reasons why the writer uses written language in a "consistent stance towards experience."

If you set this project up as an end-of-term project, groups may have opportunities to interview the writer whom they select or to correspond with him or her. Many of the professional writers included in *The Bedford Guide for College Writers* have written about or been interviewed about issues of "a writer's identity." In particular, such interviews about or reflections on a writer's identity by Alice Walker, Russell Baker, Stephen Jay Gould, William Least Heat Moon, Annie Dillard, Richard Rodriguez, Toni Morrison, and Michael Dorris can be fairly easily researched in libraries.

2. Encourage students to write to you early in the course about whether and how they define themselves as writers. Ask them to invent some metaphors that describe specific aspects of their identities as writers. Ask for a letter during the last class meeting about their current definitions of themselves as writers. Reinforce the modeling of the readings by having class members compare themselves with one or more of the writers in the guide.

FROM STORY TO ESSAY: READING AND WRITING

Anthony R. Petrosky

Petrosky argues that despite a historical separation among reading, response to literature, and composition, they are "similar processes sharing both the dependence on peoples' models of reality (or, schemata) and the essential 'putting together' as the act of constructing meaning from words, text, prior knowledge, and feelings." Petrosky traces the shifts in research and theory for each of the fields that led him to conclude that all "represent reading as a process arising from the interactions of texts, readers, and contexts."

He argues that reading "comprehension, like composition, means making public what is private — a process dependent on explication, illustration, and critical examination of perceptions and ideas." After explicating these themes, Petrosky demonstrates a technique he has used successfully in graduate literature courses for engaging students in inquiry.

203

Most of the work in reading, response to literature, and composition has gone on independently. Few people have crossed the boundaries of their disciplines to examine the relationships between these aspects of human understanding. Consequently, both research and pedagogy are hard pressed to describe and apply integrated notions of these three aspects of language.

As a result of separate instruction and assessment of progress in reading, literature, and composition, curricula in language are fragmented to the point where literature is often kept out of reading, and composition instruction seldom includes reading or study of literary works, except as models of writing. We even train teachers to be one kind of teacher, say a reading specialist, and not the other. Our obsessions with specialization pose unnecessary and artificial problems that have serious consequences for students. How can they learn to play the spectrum of discourse, as James Moffett says, when the spectrum is broken into wholly independent components, and otherwise intelligent people go around claiming that we can not ask students to write about their reading because the writing confounds reading, especially the assessment of reading ability.[1]

Although I do not intend to discuss assessment, the implications will, I hope, be clear. I do intend to focus on the relationships between reading, response to literature, and composition from theoretical and pedagogical perspectives. In order to do this, I need to first draw attention to research and theory in reading, and then show how recent reading research is telling us the same things about understanding that we know from literary and composition research. Essentially, my argument is that our comprehension of texts, whether they are literary or not, is more an act of composition — for understanding is composing — than of information retrieval, and that the best possible representation of our understandings of texts begins with certain kinds of compositions, not multiple-choice tests or written free responses.

I also want to claim that this process of writing in response to reading is heavily subjective, and, as such, depends on the reader's models of reality, the text, and the context in which it occurs. We set our expectations and goals for understanding, in other words, according to our personal frames of reference, according to the particular kind of text we face, and according to the group of people we are interacting with. We need, therefore, to share, read, and comment on each other's written responses if we are to understand ourselves as readers and writers and, equally important, if we are to understand the myriad aspects of texts.

Along the way to making these claims, I first review the radical change in thinking about reading that has come about over the past decade — change that goes from seeing reading as straight information retrieval to seeing it as a process dependent on and subject to readers' models of reality (in the technical jargon of reading, "schema"), which are mental configurations or maps built from prior knowledge, feelings, personality, and culture which readers then apply to, or impose on, new experiences. I then tie these notions of reading into the work of Louise Rosenblatt, Norman Holland, and David Bleich in literary study to demonstrate that these three theorists are, basically, making the same claims about readings as the reading people. After making these connections, my attention turns to demonstrating how comprehension of texts — the putting together of understanding — is the same kind of putting together, or composing, that David Bartholomae discusses when he talks about writers, especially basic writers, as people caught within their own worlds to the point where it is difficult for them to see how they must change their private discourse to meet the demands of public discourse. I will argue, like Bartholomae, that there is a way out of these worlds and that comprehension, like composition, means making public what is private — a process dependent on explication, illustration, and critical examination of perceptions and ideas.

Finally, I come full circle and make a very simple claim that in order to help students understand the texts they read and their response, we need to ask them to write about the texts they read. I demonstrate the differences between written free response to texts and a response heuristic taken from the work of David Bleich; and, consequently, I argue that Bleich's response heuristic is a good beginning point for teaching students how to represent their comprehension in writing.

We must begin, I think, by reseeing our language use as a whole, not as discrete pieces. Reading, responding, and composing are aspects of understanding, and theories that attempt to account for them outside of their interactions with each other run the serious risk of building reductive models of human understanding. Yet we continually focus our attention on them as if they exist in isolation from one another. Consequently, we end up with theories of comprehension, for example, that discount any reliance on composition or extended response. In the same vein, reading researchers are careful not to contaminate assessments of comprehension by asking readers for extended written or oral response to texts. Generally, this kind of research looks to memory as if it were an exact and orderly storehouse, identical for everyone, that can account for comprehension. But by eliminating extended written or oral discourse as a representation of comprehension, we box ourselves into the position of equating comprehension with definitions of recall that ignore the constructive roles of affect and interpretation in remembering. Comprehension can not be simple literal recall for recall is, as F. C. Bartlett pointed out in 1932,[2] never simple and hardly literal. Readers recall, either accurately or inaccurately, for reasons, and those reasons are driven by affect, cognitive frameworks (or, in Bartlett's language, "schemata"), and the context in which the reading and recalling are taking place. To put it another way, the process of recollecting usurps the reality that is recollected.

Putting these arguments aside for a moment, there is another problem with representing comprehension through recall rather than through some kind of structured response that leads to a dialectic which represents the interaction of readers with a text. When we tell students that their job is to remember information or details from texts they read, we limit their senses of reading to one narrow slice of the whole domain of reading and, in effect, we tell them that reading is the kind of activity we do when we have to pass tests based on information in textbooks. And whereas this certainly goes on in schools, it is not the kind of reading that teaches how to think — it teaches, instead, how to memorize and regurgitate. The reading that teaches us how to think lets us read without the pressures of recall and then, when we are finished, it begs us to speak our minds about what we have read and, in the process, it asks us to substantiate our interpretations and opinions — our readings — with evidence from our lives and the texts. When we only ask students to recall or engage in quick, easy-answer type discussions about their reading, we do not give them a chance to form interpretations and opinions with documentation from themselves and texts. One of the best ways to begin giving them this chance is, I will argue, to ask them to write about readings, using Bleich's response heuristic.

To pick up the main threads of my argument, let me say that I think there is compelling evidence to support the claim that comprehension is heavily subjective and is a function of the reader's prior knowledge, the text, and the context. I also think we can argue that we compose as we comprehend, and that our composition arises from these same factors: the text, our affective and cognitive frameworks (or prior knowledge), and the context for reading. When we put together our comprehension — however consciously or unconsciously — the "putting together" is more an act of composition than of information retrieval. And if, as I argue, comprehension is heavily dependent on these three factors, then a convincing representation of it must focus on how they enter into our responses as public statements derived from private experience. To see how we do this, we can and should turn to extended written response to texts. If we take this stance toward comprehension, then it is not enough for readers to demonstrate their comprehension by saying what they perceive in texts (as multiple-choice tests and quick, easy-answer type discussions lead them to do);[3] they have to explain why they see what they do by explicating the forces that drive their discussions, because they often see things differently for legitimate reasons. The authority for their explanations comes, then, from the personal associations (that is, from their prior knowledge) —

205

the thoughts and feelings they generate in response to what they read — that flesh out their connections to the texts and from textual evidence. And just as the believability or credibility of a text comes from these associations, comprehension arises from an immersion in the particulars of texts, readers' knowledge, and contexts.

These response compositions are best judged, I want to argue, by the standards usually applied to academic essays: adequacy of elaboration, coherence, clarity, and aptness of illustration. This kind of academic discourse derives its validity from examples and illustrations that anchor the explanations and generalizations in readers' knowledge. The knowledge bases, in the case of reading, are readers' prior experiences, the texts, and the contexts for reading. The personal narratives — which are, in fact, illustrations and examples of personal knowledge — that reveal readers' approaches to comprehending link readers to texts in the same way that examples and illustrations link writers to essays by connecting statements, generalizations, explanations, and conclusions to the knowledge or evidence that informs them.

When we see reading, then, as composing, we see also the need for readers to have ways to express and explain the connections between their prior knowledge and the texts they read. Clearly, this kind of meaning-making requires something more than multiple-choice questions or quick, easy-answer type discussions. If we are looking for compositions that begin to represent comprehension, then there are two elements, I would argue, that must be present in the composition. There must be, of course, reference to and reconstruction of the text to some degree; but there must be, also, reference to and reconstruction of the reader's associations — the reader's schema — so we, the reader's public, can see how he or she is putting it all together.

Recent research in reading by people like Robert Anderson,[4] David Rumelhart,[5] and Robert Schank and Robert Abelson[6] focuses on readers as meaning-makers in reading and gives us a theoretical base for making connections between reading, response to literature, and composing as similar processes sharing both the dependence on peoples' models of reality (or, schemata) and the essential "putting together" as the act of constructing meaning from words, text, prior knowledge, and feelings. Basically, and although their research differs in large and small ways, they represent reading as a process arising from the interactions of texts, readers, and contexts. As Marilyn Jager Adams and Allan Collins put it, "A fundamental assumption of schema-theoretic approaches to language comprehension is that spoken or written text does not in itself carry meaning. Rather, a text only provides direction for the listener or reader as to how he should retrieve or construct the intended meaning from his own, previously acquired knowledge."[7] Schemata — frequently referred to as "plans" (Schank and Abelson), "frames" (Minsky), and "scripts" (Schank and Abelson) — are knowledge structures that provide a framework from which we view the world, including texts. What we know and can know, then, is dependent on what we already know and believe. Current thinking along these lines[8] suggests that schemata consist of categories that control our perceptions of both format and content in our reading. In other words, as our models of reality develop in breadth and depth through our experience, we develop categories for our knowledge that help us organize what we know, believe, and feel. This organized knowledge, then, influences both the shape and content of our comprehension, and by extension, of our response and writing.

Prior to this work in schema-theoretic approaches to comprehension, researchers tended to see reading as the act of retrieving information from a text with little or no consideration for the reader as a meaning-maker in a relative and interpretive process. In contrast, the schema-theoretic approach says, simply, that readers put together their comprehension from not just the text, but from the interactions of their personal knowledge, feelings, and experiences with the text under the constraints of the context for reading. This is quite a radical change from seeing reading as the straightforward retrieval of information.

Somewhat the same kind of turnabout in our understanding of reading has taken place in literature. When scholars like I. A. Richards[9] first started to wonder publicly why their students made so many unique interpretations of works of literature, they set in motion the thinking that eventually yielded the notion that readers transact with texts using their personal models of reality to construct meaning and interpretations. Currently, variations on this position are championed by Louise Rosenblatt,[10] who maintains that reading is a transaction between readers and texts; Norman Holland,[11] who asserts that this transaction is dependent on the reader's personality; and David Bleich,[12] who contends that reading is essentially and necessarily subjective.

Rosenblatt, unlike Holland or Bleich, makes an important distinction between readers' purposes for reading. She argues for two basic stances towards texts, efferent and aesthetic (actually she sees them as ends of a continuum). When readers approach a text efferently, they look only for information, not an aesthetic experience. When they approach a text aesthetically, their primary concern "is with what happens *during* the actual reading event. . . . In aesthetic reading, the reader's attention is centered directly on what he is living through during this relationship with a particular text."[13] And while she argues for close attention to texts by readers as the way of letting them confirm the accuracy of their comprehension, she also argues for equally close attention to "what that particular juxtaposition of words stirs up within each reader."[14] Like schema-theoretic approaches to comprehension, Rosenblatt's transactive model — built on the work of John Dewey and Arthur F. Bentley[15] — emphasizes the role of the knower's prior knowledge in knowing. Her distinction between efferent and aesthetic stances, like the current emphasis on context for reading, gives us a way of discussing the problems of students who read everything like textbooks. And while it is certainly true that readers can take these stances towards anything they read, the process of reading is in all cases transactive. Although Rosenblatt does not herself assert the point, writing about reading is one of the best ways to get students to unravel their transactions so that we can see how they understand and, in the process, help them learn to elaborate, clarify, and illustrate their responses by reference to the associations and prior knowledge that inform them.

Norman Holland also views reading as a transaction. Although he does not discuss efferent and aesthetic reading, nor the contexts for reading, he sees the process as a transaction where comprehension is completely dependent on the reader's fixed, invariant identity — the unchanging core of personality formed, according to Holland, in the early months of life. David Bleich, on the other hand, working from a subjective paradigm of knowledge, a paradigm that assumes knowledge is always relative and unique to the knower, argues that the constraints of the text are trivial because they can be changed by individual, idiosyncratic action. Unlike Rosenblatt and Holland, he is unwilling to admit the constraints of the texts because, as he claims, "they function as any real object functions, since they can be changed by subjective action."[16] Bleich's views are radical, and he is, I think, too easily seduced by what he refers to as "subjective action" — the possibilities of people seeing things differently because of their unique models of reality. Even though we can, as he says, change things, including texts, by subjective action, we in fact do not always do this. And, furthermore, we share an enormous set of beliefs and expectations that make it possible for us to understand each other. Bleich argues persuasively, though, for the power of the individual's unique experience to control interpretation and for the power of the community that must then evolve when readers come together to determine reality. He takes the position that texts are symbolizations resymbolized, understood, and interpreted within the context of a community. The community channels and defines reality through the dialectic that ensues when readers get together in various contexts to understand texts and each other. For Bleich, the only way to demonstrate comprehension is through extended discourse where readers become writers who articulate their understandings of and connections to the text in their responses. Response is, then, an expression and explanation of comprehension; and comprehension means using writing to explicate the connections between our models of reality — our prior knowledge — and the texts we recreate in light of them.

207

Unlike retrieval models of reading, this approach gives readers a way to discuss their thoughts, feelings, and references while making meaning for themselves by writing expressive and explanatory prose in response to their readings. Essentially, *they are asked to write, first, what they perceive in the text, and then how they feel about what they see, and finally what associations— thoughts and feelings — inform and follow from their perceptions.* This "response" heuristic yields an essay that represents comprehension much more accurately than multiple-choice questions, quick-and-easy-answer type discussions, or free responses. This approach to writing about reading is derived from a powerful heuristic — explanation conducted by description and association — that is used widely in philosophical, psychoanalytic, and psychological inquiry. It can tease out structured response and, therefore, encourage respondents to discover their orientations to just about anything. Like all frequently repeated experiences, its effect is paradigmatic, altering the way we "see" and respond, "affecting by analogy much beyond the immediately seen. . . ."[17] When used as a writing prompt, it yields a first draft of what can, with revision based on comments from a teacher or a group of students, become a sophisticated essay.

Within the past ten years, the field of composition has begun to concern itself with the same heuristic. David Bartholomae, working towards a pedagogy for basic writers,[18] has found that writing produced by basic writers relies heavily on the writers' unarticulated knowledge, with little or no exposition of that knowledge through examples, illustrations, and details. He maintains that a characteristic of a sophisticated essay, on the other hand, is the writer's critical examination, through examples and illustrations, of the assumptions, beliefs, and knowledge that inform the writing. In other words, Bartholomae contends that the roots of public academic discourse rest in the writer's subjectivity — that is, in the power of the writer's unique experience and prior knowledge, which control perceptions and interpretations. One of the important distinctions between good and bad public academic discourse is, then, that good public discourse articulates this prior knowledge or individual point of view so that it is accessible to others who need the information in order to understand the writer and his or her contexts. Once a student writer has made this information accessible, he or she can then, with help from the teacher and other students, go back to his or her other essay and begin a critical examination of both the essay and the assumptions underlying it.

Bartholomae's approach to composition asks writers to do what Bleich's heuristic for writing responses asks readers to do: use examples and illustrations as the basis for explanations, generalizations, and critical examinations. The examples and illustrations in a response come from the reader's associations, beliefs, assumptions, knowledge, and perceptions of the text. Writing about reading in this way gives readers a way to make meaning for themselves through a process of discovery rooted in inferential thinking.

Roland Barthes,[19] discussing writing in a more global sense, extends the metaphor of a writer's "schemata" to help us see the role of personal background and cultural conventions in writing. He expands the notion of personal influences on writing to include not only the "familiar personal past" of the writer but also influences beyond the immediate control of the writer, such as the pressures of history and tradition that limit and define writing and its conventions. So in a narrow sense writers, like readers, are influenced in responding by the exigencies of their familiar personal past, but they are also influenced in responding and writing by pressures beyond their immediate awareness, such as the broad cultural expectations and influences of history and tradition — frames and schemes of much more inclusive proportions.

In summary, one of the most interesting results of connecting reading, literary, and composition theory and pedagogy is that they yield similar explanations of human understanding as a process rooted in the individual's knowledge and feelings and characterized by the fundamental act of making meaning, whether it be through reading, responding, or writing. When we read, we comprehend by putting together impressions of the text with our personal, cultural, and contextual models of reality. When we write, we compose by making meaning from available information, our personal knowledge, and the cultural and contextual frames we happen to find ourselves in. Our theoretical understandings of these processes are converging, as I pointed out, around the central role of human understanding — be it of texts or the world — as a process of composing.

The pedagogical implications of making these theoretical connections are actually quite simple: readers and writers need help in the form of heuristics and dialogue to articulate their understandings of texts, themselves, and the world. Bleich's response heuristic works to this end by giving students a way to flesh out the models of reality that inform their understandings of texts. Once this happens and students have explained their readings, they can enter into critical discussions with teachers and other students that lead them to examine their readings *and* the assumptions that inform them.[20]

Let me now turn to an example. Here is a response that a student, Dan, wrote in a free response style with no direction except to write a statement that would represent his understanding of William Faulkner's "A Rose for Emily." Prior to this response, he had written in a free response style after reading Donald Barthelme's "The Balloon," and Shakespeare's sonnet 138. It is characteristic of the eight free responses he wrote in a graduate seminar on reading and psychology that I taught at the University of Pittsburgh in 1981. His free responses, like almost everyone else's in the seminar, tended to be sketchy and unfocused.

Upon Reading "A Rose for Emily"

How beautiful:
How otherwise?
The thing's as we expect and
Wouldn't, couldn't change.

No blemish Emily
But hybrid
Of the stubborn rose
That yields diverse perversity.

That yields perverse integrity
And loyalty and spoils
All notion garden walks
Are through once briar and thicket catch to tear.

Maybe that would be enough if I had any confidence in my poetry. The temptation is to say it again, now in prose, but the thing is so fleeting . . . I guess that's why poetry seemed like the right way to express it. I wonder if I can capture how "A Rose for Emily" affects me in any other way? It's almost a violation of something strong and basic in me to pull this wonderful mess of emotion out, so fishnet tangled up, and give it a shape it shouldn't have.

I love William Faulkner for doing this to me. And he took me so by surprise. I rushed to get the story in the first few pages and suffered reader's doldrums in the next few and was cynical when toward the end I wondered if Estella might appear chasing after a story to hide in. And then, the man himself lay in the bed, and sweetly, no, I can't understand it either, I don't know why it's with such a rush of pleasure that I see it, Emily had joined him there. I thought so many things that were the same thing when Faulkner finished writing. I thought, Yes, that's right, of course she'd done this thing. It's not so hard to understand or even wish it as a romantic and symbolic act. It's those crazy people who are always giving us the symbols. They must be the only ones with any vision.

Links with the text are missing from this response, and it is difficult to see why Dan says the things he does. It is particularly difficult to see why this story moves him as much as he claims it does. And even though I like the poetic sense of his response, I have to admit, finally, that I need more from Dan if I am to understand his understanding of the story.

Before going on to look at Dan's use of the heuristic in his response to *The Great Gatsby,* I think another glimpse at one of his free responses will help me complete the picture of free response that I am trying to paint. For this example, I turn to Dan's response to Robert Frost's poem "Once by the Pacific." The poem begins with someone looking out at the ocean and seeing waves shatter on the rocks, "forming a misty din." It builds to an awesome foreboding of the sea's destructive power and, finally, in the last stanza God enters to put out the light.

Although Dan wrote this as a free response, it is one of the last such responses and came at a time in the semester when he was growing frustrated with the sketchy, unfocused nature of the free responses. Here he deliberately moves his attention to a central idea and tries to focus his response on the poem — more so than he did on the story in his response to "A Rose for Emily." But, again, it does not work; he begins well enough with a statement defining his attempt to find a central idea, but he finally ends up digressing in what he claims Frost makes him see and, finally, a private association he has with Niagara Falls.

Response to "Once by the Pacific"

What to say. How to begin. What central idea to express and tie in with "Once by the Pacific." I don't know. I see dusk at all the ocean spots I've stood in — as a boy with jellyfish in the Atlantic, as an adolescent with the black sand and the hucksters in the Mediterranean, as a young man with my insecurities in an inlet, on a penninsula, on the edge of a continent in any water anywhere stretching my imagination out and out.

Great water, I conclude, had life. Frost hasn't surprised that reaction in me. So what has he done? He has made me answer, Yes, that's right — if tales come carried from the tale giver they will reach shore on wing if they are good and on wave if they are ominous and bad. He has made me answer, Yes, the word will be too loud to hear, too spendrift to be held for long before, once shattered into bits of night, new words, greater than before, succeed those old. And he has made me answer, Yes, the earth absorbs initial shocks to fall back upon upright earth, but it is *someone* who had best put affairs in order, for what continent will make a man secure?

He makes me see a privileged man alone, exposed, host-like by the door he is standing, privy to a drama played out. And he is not surprised and he does not seem to be afraid. Another, look, another hurries on below, over washing slabs of stone, wraps up his eyes under his coat, about his business, off to supper, and privy to nothing. No eyes, no ears for hearing any noise save the muttering he gives way to — the gust that swallows it.

The caves of Niagara. Creep along the narrow caves, edge along the walls of the caves of Niagara and hear what you can see at the mouths of the caves. Hear the thunder unabated as the water walls explode forever hour upon hour. Come closer to the cruelty, let it last at you. See death in the mouths of the caves of Niagara and ask what sort of man can be here and think his own thoughts, not hear the roar and change.

He makes me remember. He makes me know what I know.

While the first two paragraphs seem, to me, to be the barest beginnings of a response that other readers can understand, he never quite puts the response together with his private associations that drive it so we could see the links he might be making in his mind. We end up with the barest structure of a response that lacks support in the form of explicit connections between what Dan sees in the poem and why he sees what he does. As a reader, my reaction is puzzlement. I am left with a handful of important unanswered questions. Why, for instance, is he so heavy-handed in the second paragraph? Why is there a second man in the third stanza? What does this person represent? And, finally, how is this association to Niagara Falls connected to his reading of the poem? What is it that Dan knows from Niagara that this poem makes him remember?

All in all, Dan's attempt at a more focused response with the free response format is only a little better, a little clearer than his response to "A Rose for Emily," and, as we will see, is nowhere near as clear and explicit as his response to *The Great Gatsby,* where he uses the response heuristic. There is, though, an aspect of Dan's response to the Frost poem that deserves some attention because it highlights the relative uselessness of personal associations in a response unless they are connected in some explicit way to the reader's impressions or interpretations of the text. Dan's first and last paragraphs of this response are free associations very much in the manner of what the response heuristic is meant to produce; but unlike the associations encouraged by the response heuristic they are not connected to statements of perception or interpretation, so they appear to come from and go nowhere.

When Dan began to use Bleich's response heuristic — writing first what he perceived in the text, then how he felt about what he saw, and finally what associations followed from his perceptions — his responses blossomed into three- and four-page single-spaced essays that flip back and forth between sections of the texts and specific personal references. The following selection from his response to *The Great Gatsby* is typical of the way he interrelates the text with his memories and associations. He tells us, in short, how he relates to the text he writes about. This is part of his first response from the heuristic.

> Nick's house. The first thing I remember, having just finished Gatsby, is Nick's house. It sits hidden (mostly by grass) and because it is hidden, it provides Nick with a good private spot for making observations and for making judgements. I like the house. I think its walls are probably white and rough and the rooms crowded with furniture. It is always warm, and it is always a smarter place to be than is Gatsby's. Houses are important to me. I always think of my childhood *in* some house. My favorite house was in Butler, Pa. I spent a romantic adolescence there, writing awful short stories on Sunday mornings while my parents were in church, smoking my father's Camel cigarettes on the sly, feeling very grown up and melancholy. It was in this house that I spent a year convalescing after an operation that straightened my spine from a radical curve into a soft curve. I was encased in plaster from my head to my knees — helpless. Every Sunday morning, after he came back from church, my father, a practical, even rough business man, ministered to my needs. And though my mother spent her time during the week doing the same things and doing them with more finesse and doing them gently, it is with greater fondness that I remember the way my father roughed me up with towels and brushes and soapy water. My room was on the second floor and looked out over a small reservoir completely surrounded by old trees. I watched the seasons change and start to change again before I was on my feet again. And if it hadn't happened. I wouldn't know the depth of my father's love for me.

Nick's house reminds him of his favorite childhood house where he grew close to his father. Clearly, he has strong feelings about the whole scene that the house brings to mind and, in a direct way, these feelings shape his stance towards the text. Dan's use of his family as a sounding board for characters and events in the text is one of the recurring characteristics of his affective and cognitive framework. In his response to *Gatsby,* he develops every textual reference into a statement about some member of his family. He discusses Fitzgerald's humor, and then begins discussing his father by beginning with his sense of humor. Later on in the same response, he discusses the scene in the hotel room where Tom Buchanan confronts Gatsby with his fabricated story of his life, and then he slips into a monologue on his relationship with his brother by referring to Gatsby's relationship with Tom. The response heuristic teases out these kinds of references and Dan was one of the two people in the seminar who continually returned to their families in their responses.

When Dan wrote using Bleich's response heuristic in response to *Gatsby,* he developed his statements around characters and events that related to recollections of his family, but he also wrote, for the first time during the semester, statements that began with specific retellings of the text, then moved to explanations of his connections to the text *vis à vis* his feelings and associations; finally, he concluded by generalizing from his discussion.

Not everyone in the seminar wrote from family recollections, and not everyone had Dan's initial success with the response heuristic. One student, Bob — a clinical psychologist — managed to double the length of his responses using Bleich's heuristic, but still his responses were not explicit enough to be accessible to others in the class. He relentlessly saw everything in the stories and poems from a clinical perspective. He would not discuss a character or event unless he could frame the discussion as an illustration of a clinical phenomenon. He saw Faulkner's Emily, for instance, as a person who never understood her options in life; and, therefore, she needed therapy to help her see these options. He saw *Gatsby* as a book that "carried some good descriptions of character behavior disorders." He continually placed himself in the role of a therapist and he took great pleasure from treating characters as patients. His responses prompted lengthy seminar discussions — most of which were devoted to fleshing out what he was saying — and he literally recreated every story and poem in light of his clinical experiences.

Millie, another student in the seminar, had a difficult time writing responses that articulated the prior experiences underlying her perceptions and judgments. Here are the first two paragraphs of her response to *Gatsby*. They are typical of her two-page response to this book. Notice how they never quite get off the ground, although the barest bones of the heuristic are evident — perceptions of the text, feelings, and spare associations. She stops short of the depth of explanation that Dan achieves in his response to *Gatsby,* and she did not at all try to interpret texts as we will see Dan doing later in his response to Penelope Mortimer's *The Pumpkin Eater*. Notice, too, how Millie introduces pertinent information about her associations with Nick's sense of powerlessness when Tom and Gatsby begin to fight, but she does not develop that discussion into any kind of elaborated description or explanation that might allow us to get a concrete sense of her perception of the powerlessness that she attributes to Nick.

> Whenever I think over what I remember from the novel, sensory impressions come to mind first. One of the most vivid impressions is dust. The grayness in the valley of ashes between the City and the Eggs depresses me. I can see the bareness and sterility of the landscape and Myrtle's body lying in the dusty road. I can also visualize the grayness of Wilson's face. The valley of ashes reminds me of a depressing strip of highway leading into New Kensington which is littered with shacks, coal tipples, junked cars, and greasy diners. This strip puts the rider in the right frame of mind for entering New Kensington, "a good place to work, trade, and live."

> Another memorable sensory impression is the heat. I can feel the enervating heat the afternoon Nick first visits Daisy and Tom. I am oppressed by the boiling tense environment the afternoon the couples go to the city. It's no surprise to me that violent activity explodes because the oppressive air keeps swelling along with the palpable tension between Tom and Gatsby. I know how the heat enervates me and makes me short tempered. I love summer storms that finally give some relief from oppressive heat. I know how Nick must have felt as the tension built between Gatsby and Tom. I've been in unpleasant situations like the one that afternoon and I was powerless to stop the inevitable progression that led to a violent outburst.

While Millie does *tell* us that she understands the tension and powerlessness that Nick must have felt, she does not give us the description and explanation that would allow us to see or understand her experience with powerlessness so we might know what it means to her. Her narrative is thin compared to Dan's, and as such it is less compelling than Dan's. In short, Millie begins to use the heuristic, but unlike Dan, she stops short and does not make the commitment to description and explanation through association with prior personal knowledge that Dan does. Consequently, I have only a vague sense of the prior knowledge driving her response; in order to have a more concrete sense of her associations with the text, I need more explanation. My response was to ask her to say more — to specifically tell the story of that afternoon she felt powerless and then to tell how her sense of powerlessness is related to Nick's. And although I kept asking her for more explanation and critical examination, she never did write anything nearly as sophisticated as Dan.

Dan's response to Penelope Mortimer's *The Pumpkin Eater* is another good example of how the response heuristic helps him discuss his associations with the story, so that unlike Millie's response to *Gatsby,* his response gives us a good sense of the mental map that is guiding his reactions. But this response also differs in an important way from his earlier *Gatsby* response in that it takes a more critical, speculative stance towards the text. The second paragraph — presented below — goes beyond the description of houses in his *Gatsby* response by exploring "desperation" and commenting on what Mrs. Armitage might have felt in her desperate state. Notice, too, how this paragraph follows a pattern. First, he describes Mrs. Armitage, confused and desperate, awaking in Giles' bedroom (a perception of the text); then Dan recalls the desperation of his brother and he explains that experience as a comment on desperation (a statement of his feelings couched in the associations); finally, he concludes by generalizing from his discussion. Dan cues to this scene because he has strong associations with desperation. He tells us what those associations are so that we can see why this scene is important enough for him to want to discuss it, and then he takes his experience with desperation and turns it into critical speculation on desperation and Mrs. Armitage's situation.

> A awakes. Eleven hours unconscious in Giles' bedroom. Night? Late day? I can't say, but were I to film the scene the lights would burn without shades from the sockets and the room would be sick with their paleness. Giles tells A the truth about Jake's calls and she is desperate to go. She is confused with so much sleep, disoriented and not certain about time. She goes, and what is left behind is the room — rumpled, stale, yellow with some bright spots that turn out to be bare lights. And I am reminded that what surrounds me when I awake and just before I sleep and as I work has a profound effect upon whether I stay all sane. And I remember how one evening my brother David and I sat arguing in our room, our parents insulated downstairs with their papers from our racket and thumping around. I held my head in my hands and wailed that he had to clean up the room, for he'd made a mess. He became frightened and set to work without delay. I was calm again before long. But I also had a new kind of memory and one that had come too early in the life of a boy — I had done something and felt some way without reason and without control and had scared myself and David. Face to face with an altered consciousness that would test me again in dreams and in wakefulness whenever it was time to be a little crazy. Desperate. David slipped over the edge before any of the rest of us, though, and did it without witness. I could have helped had I known he was nuts because I had seen the other side though I hadn't embraced it. I could have helped, and I remember how it isn't good to be desperate all alone.

Dan's last paragraph in the same response is another good example of the same pattern. First, he describes Jake's father in the context of a haunting statement he left behind when he died; then he recalls a boy from his youth and relates a moving story about his death; and, finally, he concludes the response by generalizing about death and memory. Notice, too, how explicit his links are to the text in this response compared with those in his responses to "A Rose for Emily" and "Once by the Pacific." His connections are much more visible and concrete in his responses, like this one, that follow from the heuristic than they are in his responses, like the one to "A Rose for Emily," that are essentially free response. Here too, he goes beyond his earlier *Gatsby* response by making a critical judgment in guessing "that Mortimer is claiming Jake's father purposely held back important things for the reasons A suspects." Once Dan makes the interpretive judgment, he goes on to explore it and its implications by commenting on private and public feelings. We get a good sense of the mental map that directs his explorations because he recreates the experience that bears directly — or, at least, associatively — on his sense of public and private feelings.

> I felt close to the strange character of Jake's father. We don't know a lot about him, but he left behind a haunting statement in which the nature of God is examined. A calls it his only great statement and accuses him of leaving his life still uninvolved because the statement came after his

213

death. I guess that Mortimer is claiming Jake's father purposely held back important things for the reasons A suspects. Good. We peer into people's lives and make them ordinary by it. Holding portions away from public view seems a small, dignified price to pay, whatever the results. One's children don't know the depths of your feelings toward God. Small price for owning something private, that. I can feel a reaction against the process that we are all currently undergoing rising up in me. We are peering into one another's lives, and worse, we assist one another. Billy Fennick. A boy from my youth named Billy taught me how to set trees on fire and to smoke. He was bad for me. He went to the Navy and never came home because he drowned. His submarine went under and didn't come up. He was as close to me, to my hands, as this typewriter once and then he was under the sea drowning. My friend Billy. And do you know what I wondered when I heard? I wondered if he saw my face and heard me laugh when he talked dirty. Because Billy left nothing. The submarine was lost. Billy never came home, even dead. But, in my little age, I was convinced if he had thought of me, he left me behind. I was his statement and the sign of his involvement with the world. That sort of mystic link with the dead is important to me. It is not ordinary, first of all, and I think the dead deserve being remembered unusually. And second of all, those kinds of memories give the living a chance to make amends for the shortcomings of living so close beside the people we love that the only thing that makes them important to us is their death.

Dan's responses are particularly moving, but then so were almost everyone's in the seminar once we began using Bleich's response format. But the responses were not only moving, they had explanatory power because they used examples and illustrations derived from associations as a way of revealing the readers' mental maps that were guiding their responses. There was very little explaining or illustrating in the free responses and in the responses, like Millie's, that only flirted with the heuristic. Generally, readers free responded in terms of what they liked, and then they drew conclusions or generalizations about the work, about some aspect of it, or about reality. And while it was interesting to see these varied and individual perceptions, they were not compelling as acts of comprehension in the ways essays are compelling when they illustrate with examples to flesh out the knowledge — personal, factual, or textual — that shapes one's comprehension.

Throughout the seminar we duplicated and shared our responses so that at the end of the semester we had complete sets of responses from everyone in the group. We used these as the basis for our theoretical and literary discussions. The final project for the seminar was a self-study paper. The group members were asked to write case studies on their reading. They examined all of their responses in light of the readings and discussions. From this, they wrote case reports of themselves as readers. The papers were interesting for a number of reasons. First, everyone looked for and found consistent patterns in their readings that indicated how they were using their personal knowledge to create both the format and content of their responses. Second, the readers took varied theoretical stances to explain their readings, but regardless of their bent, they were able to explain them. And third, they recognized that they wrote considerably more sophisticated papers when they used the response heuristic. By having a way to flesh out the personal knowledge that informed their comprehension, they were better able to explain themselves to each other. And while I would be hard pressed to argue that elaboration like this will always lead to more sophisticated response — for I can certainly imagine elaborated but empty responses — I do think that this kind of elaboration and explanation is a necessary beginning to more critical examinations of texts and the assumptions underlying readers' readings of them.

Teaching reading this way means teaching composition as the most compelling and persuasive representation of comprehension. If we are willing to consider that comprehension is more than limited recall and retelling (although it certainly contains these), and if we are willing to see reading as a kind of transaction between readers and texts in specific contexts, then we need to ask readers to represent their comprehension through composition by asking them to follow a sequence of assignments that begins with Bleich's response heuristic and then moves to more critical examination of responses and the assumptions underlying them.

When readers in my seminar used Bleich's response heuristic, their responses began with references to the text and then moved into personal narratives that told the story of their associations with the text. The personal narratives served a function similar to that served by examples and illustrations in essays — they fleshed out assumptions, feelings, and prior knowledge to give authority to what the author had to say. When these examples and illustrations are missing from essays, the writing becomes a set of empty assertions with little or no evidence to give them authority. And like essays that follow conventions but say nothing, they turn into a kind of "themewriting."[21] The same is true of the responses the readers in my seminar wrote when they followed the free response format. Like Dan in his response to "A Rose for Emily," they wrote vague statements that were difficult to understand and were like essays without compelling examples and illustrations — responses that lacked evidence and failed to show the essential connections of knower to known.

Statements of comprehension are most compelling, on the other hand, when they make connections between knower and known, text and reader, reading and context. And, equally important, when we ask readers to write about their readings using Bleich's response heuristic, we are asking them to engage in one of the most fundamental intellectual processes. We ask them to use a basic heuristic of inquiry. The process is similar to making interpretations and documenting them; as such, it is fundamental to the beginnings of any dialogue or dialectic that must ensue when people come together to understand reality. Writing plays a crucial role in this heuristic because it can commit and compel the reader to discover meaning by articulating one's responses in extended discourse that is meant to be public within the community of the classroom.

Once readers have used Bleich's heuristic to generate a response, the class can move to a discussion of everyone's responses, and then, using comments from the group and from the teacher, the readers can begin treating their responses as both critical statements whose assumptions and stances need to be examined, questioned, and discussed, and as pieces of writing that can be revised and edited. By following a procedure like this, students can accumulate experience in reading, writing about their reading, discussing each other's reading, commenting on responses as pieces of writing, and revising and editing. Teachers, on the other hand, need to learn how to read responses with an eye to helping students flesh out the personal knowledge and critical judgments that inform them. In order to do this, I read and wrote along with my students. I am convinced that doing this is necessary if the teacher is to become a member in the community of readers; but, perhaps more importantly, I am convinced that doing it is necessary because it teaches me how to talk about responses in the context of trying to help students do what I am trying to do for myself. The entire process is, I think, one of the most meaningful ways to integrate reading and writing in composition, reading, and literature classes.[22]

Notes

[1]This argument that we should not ask students to write about their reading because the writing confounds our assessment of their reading is a familiar one in assessment circles. I first encountered it in its most entrenched form when I held a contract to develop test specifications and items for the third national assessment of reading and literature. It resides, I believe, in the notion that reading and writing are discrete mental processes — a notion that I hope this paper begins to dispel.

[2]F. C. Bartlett, *Remembering* (Cambridge: Cambridge UP, 1932). The term "schemata" is used by Bartlett to include both affective and cognitive frameworks, but it is often the case that people quoting him use it only to mean cognitive frameworks. The varied use of the term has lead me to prefer "models of reality" or "frames" in lieu of "schemata."

[3]For decades multiple-choice tests have dominated reading comprehension assessment and instruction. College skills programs have students read short paragraphs and answer multiple-choice questions as comprehension instruction, and classrooms at all levels of education are dominated by quick, easy-answer type discussions of texts. Finally, from the third national assessment of reading and literature, we

have empirical evidence indicating that students at ages 9, 13, an 17 do much better on multiple-choice questions than on essays that require them to explain answers to multiple-choice questions. About 70% of all 17-year-olds can do the multiple-choice questions while only 20 to 30% can adequately explain and substantiate their answers. To me, this is a clear indication of the kinds of instruction students are getting in reading and literature classes — a situation that must change if we are going to move beyond superficial reading and literature instruction.

[4]Robert Anderson, "The Notion of Schemata and the Educational Enterprise," *Schooling and the Acquisition of Knowledge*, ed. R. Anderson, R. Spiro, and W. Montague (Hillsdale: Erlbaum, 1977).

[5]David Rumelhart, "Schemata: The Building Blocks of Cognition," *Theoretical Issues in Reading and Comprehension*, ed. R. Spiro, B. Bruce, and W. Brewer (Hillsdale: Erlbaum, 1980).

[6]Robert Schank and Robert Abelson, *Scripts, Plans, Goals, and Understanding* (Hillsdale: Erlbaum, 1977).

[7]Marylin Jager Adams and Allan Collins, *A Schema-Theoretic View of Reading* (Urbana: Center for the Study of Reading, 1977). It is interesting, I think, to see both the idea of retrieval and construction applied to reading in this quotation. Although the gist of the statement is clearly along the lines of readers constructing meaning, there is still a tension in the author's reluctance to completely give up the retrieval notion of reading. This is, I think, typical of the tensions in the field of reading.

[8]Robert De Beaugrande, "Design Criteria for Process Models of Reading," *Reading Research Quarterly*, 16 (Feb. 1981): 261–315.

[9]I. A. Richards, *Practical Criticism: A Study of Literary Judgment* (New York: Harcourt, 1929).

[10]Louise Rosenblatt, *The Reader, the Text, the Poem: The Transactional Theory of the Literary Work* (Carbondale: Southern Illinois UP, 1978).

[11]Norman N. Holland, *5 Readers Reading* (New Haven: Yale UP, 1975).

[12]David Bleich, *Subjective Criticism* (Baltimore: Johns Hopkins UP, 1978). Although I have taken the response heuristic from this book, there is much more here for the reader who wants to go beyond the heuristic to critical examinations of responses and texts.

[13]Rosenblatt 24–25.

[14]Rosenblatt 137.

[15]John Dewey and Arthur F. Bentley, *Knowing and the Known* (Boston: Beacon, 1949).

[16]Bleich 112.

[17]John Fowles, *Daniel Martin* (Boston: Little, 1977). Fowles talks about reading and writing throughout this marvelous book. His comments are as insightful as the best reading and writing research.

[18]David Bartholomae, "Teaching Basic Writing: An Alternative to Basic Skills," *Journal of Basic Writing* (Spring/Summer 1979): 85–109.

[19]Roland Barthes, *Writing Degree Zero and Elements of Semiology* (Boston: Beacon, 1970). This is one of the most helpful books for understanding writing in the contexts of history and tradition, governed by cultural codes and conventions. Even though Barthes changed this position on writing well before his death, his work here seems relevant to reading and writing.

[20]See David Bartholomae and Anthony Petrosky, "Facts, Artifacts, and Counterfacts: A Basic Reading and Writing Course for the College Curriculum," *Building the Bridges Between Reading and Writing*, ed. Marilyn Sternglass and Douglas Butturff. (Akron: L&S Books, 1981) for a more detailed discussion of a basic reading and writing pedagogy emanating from these notions of comprehension as composition.

[21]William E. Coles, Jr., *The Plural I: The Teaching of Writing* (New York: Holt, 1978). Coles characterizes writing that says nothing but says it well as "themewriting." He claims, and my experience supports his claim, that students learn how to do this kind of writing in schools where teachers spend little or no time commenting on the meaning and content of papers, but, rather, spend time teaching composition forms and formats.

[22]A version of this paper was originally presented at the New York University Language and Reading Conference, New York City, May 1981. I am grateful to my friends and colleagues Arthur Applebee, David Bartholomae, Charles Cooper, and Susan Wall for their careful readings of earlier drafts.

Petrosky's Insights as a Resource for Your Teaching

1. Petrosky explains that he reads and writes along with his students, a recommendation from day one of the National Writing Project. He explains that responding to a writing prompt himself teaches him how to talk about students' responses to the same prompt. This practice can also help you discover the effectiveness of writing assignments you design; practice writing in response to those assignments before you give them out, both as a means of evaluation and revision and as a way to anticipate and explain to more hesitant writers what kinds of heuristics they might use to succeed.

2. Keep a two-sided or dialectical reading journal for yourself. On the left side, write your response to a reading from *The Bedford Guide* or to some literature you assign as class reading, borrowing Bleich's heuristic. On the right side, write further about your own process of comprehending the material. Keeping in mind that you are an expert reader, use the insights from your journal to decide what prompting questions to use in conferences or class discussions of writing about reading.

Petrosky's Insights as a Resource for the Writing Classroom

1. Imitate Petrosky and Bleich and use the three-part heuristic for an assignment to write about literature. Petrosky offers useful advice about responding to and using the student responses to build "an interpretive community."

2. Students like Millie may not use a heuristic to respond as fully as Dan because of previous experiences with critical reading and writing, because of previous socialization in academic writing, or because of fear or reluctance to tap personal feelings and associations. Journal use and one-minute letters — "How did this aspect of the setting make you feel?" or "Can you cite, in one sentence, an event from your life that triggered a feeling similar to how you felt about this work?" — are good warmup exercises.

3. Petrosky recommends having students work through the entire heuristic before "they . . . enter into critical discussion with teachers and other students that lead them to examine their readings *and* the assumptions that inform them." In fact, one step of the heuristic could be used on each of successive days for class discussion. On the first day of discussion, ask students to write down what meaning they made of a work and on a subsequent day to write down what meaning they make after having participated in a discussion of it. This helps them to think about their thinking and to look at their process of making meaning. These writings can help them appreciate peers as a resource for constructing knowledge and provide prewriting for the self-study essay Petrosky describes.

LITERACY, DIVERSITY, AND MULTICULTURALISM

Recognition of and respect for the individual engaged in learning permeates the shifting of paradigms from writing as product to writing as process. At the same time, this skill of recognition and this attitude of respect are the results of working with paradigms of writing as recursive process, of language acquisition as recursive process, and of reading as recursive process. This insightful recognition of and respect for the individual informs the research into, discussion of, and practice in teaching basic, novice, and mature writers. It also informs the research into, discussion of, and practice in open admissions policies, teaching English as a second language, collaborative learning, whole-language learning, and multicultural perspectives on and approaches to writing, reading, and gaining of wisdom.

In writing classrooms, we define the group of learners as a community of writers. We ask students to assess and reflect on what is unique to each person and what is shared with others in the community. We simultaneously individualize instruction and "acculturate" students to discourse communities. We attempt to balance recognition of and tolerance for diversity with recognition of and tolerance for common ground and "universal" beliefs and values.

Terms like "literacy," "diversity," and "multiculturalism" seem descriptive. However, competing definitions are offered daily. We hear national, state, local, and institutional mandates for increasing and enhancing literacy, for acknowledging and respecting diversity, and for broadening our awareness of and inquiry into the multiple cultures (ethnic, regional, social, political, gender-linked, religious, and so on) that make up the mosaic of "America" and of the world community. Equally often, we hear critical voices stipulate alternative definitions for literacy (lowering standards, weakening education), for diversity (exclusivity and prejudice), and for multiculturalism (attempts by the "other" to break down the coherent tradition and value system of the "majority"). We teach and work with a community of writers comprising individuals who have been traditionally included in knowledge communities and individuals who have been excluded in times when vigorous debate ensues about how education can or should serve all those learners. The task is daunting and exciting. Many of the readings in this ancillary demonstrate that recognition of and respect for diversity. The annotated bibliography cites other readings to guide you in your teaching of literacy — linguistic and cultural — and the power of writing.

CROSSING BOUNDARIES

Mike Rose

This excerpt from Lives on the Boundary: The Struggles and Achievements of America's Underprepared *by Mike Rose strikes me and many teachers as eloquent, precise, and inspiriting. In the concluding chapter, "Crossing Boundaries," Rose calls for a "revised store of images of educational excellence, ones closer to egalitarian ideas — ones that embody the reward and turmoil of education in a democracy, that celebrate the plural, messy human reality of it." We couldn't reprint the entire book, but I suspect that after reading and reflecting on this chapter you'll decide to go and read it yourself.*

Through all of my experiences with people struggling to learn, the one thing that strikes me most is the ease with which we misperceive failed performance and the degree to which this misperception both reflects and reinforces the social order. Class and culture erect boundaries that hinder our vision — blind us to the logic of error and the everpresent stirring of language — and encourage the designation of otherness, difference, deficiency. And the longer I stay in education, the clearer it becomes to me that some of our basic orientations toward the teaching and testing of literacy contribute to our inability to see. To truly educate in America, then, to reach the full sweep of our citizenry, we need to question received perception, shift continually from the standard lens. . . .

> The humanities presume particular methods of expression and inquiry — language, dialogue, reflection, imagination, and metaphor. . . . [and] remain dedicated to the disciplined development of verbal, perceptual, and imaginative skills needed to understand experience.
> *The Humanities in American Life,* Report of the
> Rockefeller Commission on the Humanities[1]

Two young men have walked in late and are standing around the back of the classroom, halfheartedly looking for seats. One wears a faded letterman's jacket, the other is bundled up in a bright red sweater and a long overcoat. A third student has plopped his books by the door and is hunkering down against the wall. This is Developmental English in a state college in

Ohio. It is December, and the radiators are turned up high. Occasional clanks are emitted by some distant valve. The room is stuffy with dry heat. The teacher directs the latecomers to some seats in the front, and he begins the lesson. The class is working on pronoun agreement. They have worked on it for a week and will continue to work on it for another. The windows are frosted at the edges. In the distance, a tall smokestack releases a curling black stream diagonally across the sky.

Students designated "developmental" at this school must take a year's worth of very basic English before they can move into standard Freshman Comp. Their year is broken into two semesters. During the first semester they inch through a thick workbook. During the first semester they inch through a thick workbook filled with grammar exercises: "Circle the correct pronoun in this sentence: That was her/she in the lecture hall" or "Supply the correct pronoun for the following sentence: The recruits were upset by _____ scores on the fitness tests." Some of this they do at home. Most of it they do in class. That way, the teacher can be sure they are doing it. They hand in their workbooks regularly to have the teacher check their answers.

The course involves very little writing, except for words and phrases the students must scribble in the blanks on the pages. Some class discussion is generated when the teacher has the students read their answers. Periodically he will explain a rule or illustrate its use on the blackboard. Young men along the back wall fill in a blank now and then; the rest of the time, they're eyeballing the teacher and talking softly. A girl is filing her nails. Students in the middle of the room are bent over their workbooks, penciling in answers, erasing them, looking up and out the frosted windows. A skinny boy in the front is going down the page as mechanically as Melville's pallid scrivener.

There are sentences being written in this class, but not by mandate of the dean of instruction. Two girls close to the door have been passing notes all hour; they are producing the class's most extended discourse. Students are not asked to write here because it is assumed — as it is assumed in many such basic courses — that they must first get all their workbook pronouns to agree with their workbook antecedents. When they reach the second semester, they will, for fifteen weeks, do some small amount of writing, but that writing will be limited to single sentences. At this school, and many others, the English Department and the program that coordinates remedial courses are philosophically and administratively separated. Different schools have different histories, but often — as was the case here — the separation was strongly influenced by the English department's desire to be freed from basic instruction. The two departments at this school, though, have an unusually stringent agreement: Anything longer than the sentence (even two or three sentences strung together) is considered *writing,* and the teaching of writing shall be the province of the English Department. Anything at the sentence level or smaller (like filling words and phrases into a workbook) is to be considered grammar review, and that falls within the domain of the remedial program. For one academic year, then, students who desperately need to improve their writing will not be writing anything longer than the sentence. This particular slicing of the pedagogical pie is extreme in its execution, but the assumptions about error, remediation, and the linguistic capabilities of poorly prepared students that undergird it remain widespread in America — and they influence everything from lesson plans to the sectioning of academic territory. Given the pervasiveness of these assumptions, it would be valuable to consider, for a moment, their origins.[2]

A good place to begin is with the encounter of educational psychology and schooling. Turn-of-the-century English education was built on a Latin and Greek-influenced grammar, primarily a set of prescriptions for conducting socially acceptable discourse. So when psychologists began investigating the teaching of writing, they found a pedagogy of memory and drill, one concentrating on the often arcane dos and don'ts of usage. They also found reports like those issuing from the Harvard faculty in the 1890s that called attention to the presence of errors in handwriting, spelling, and grammar in the writing of that university's entering

219

freshmen. The twentieth-century writing curriculum, then, was focused on the particulars of usage, grammar, and mechanics. Correctness became, in James Berlin's words, the era's "most significant measure of accomplished prose."[3]

Such a focus suited educational researchers' approach to language: a mechanistic orientation that studied language by reducing it to discrete behaviors and that defined growth as the accretion of these particulars. Quantification and measurement were central to the researchers' method, so the focus on error — which seemed eminently measurable — found justification in a model of mind that was ascending in American academic psychology. This approach was further supported and advanced by what Raymond Callahan has called "the cult of efficiency," a strong push to apply to education the principles of industrial scientific management.[4] Educational gains were defined as products, and the output of products could be measured. Pedagogical effectiveness — which meant cost-effectiveness — could be determined with "scientific" accuracy. What emerges, finally, is a combination of positivism, efficiency, and a focus on grammar that would have a profound influence on pedagogy and research.

Textbooks as well as workbooks reflected this orientation. One textbook for teachers presented an entire unit on the colon. A text for students devoted seven pages to the use of a capital letter to indicate a proper noun. Research, too, focused on the details of language, especially on listing and tabulating error. You rarely find consideration of the social context of error, or of its significance in the growth of the writer. Instead you find studies like those of W. S. Guiler's tally of the percentages of 350 students who, in misspelling *mortgage,* erred by omitting the *t* versus those who dropped the first *g*.[5]

Despite the fact that the assumptions about language and learning informing these approaches to teaching and research began to be challenged by the late 1930s, the procedures of the earlier era have remained with us. This trend has the staying power it does for a number of reasons: It gives a method — a putatively objective one — to the strong desire of our society to maintain correct language use. It is very American in its seeming efficiency. And it offers a simple, understandable view of complex linguistic problems. The trend reemerges most forcefully in times of crisis: when budgets crunch and accountability looms or, particularly, when "nontraditional" students flood our institutions. A reduction of complexity has great appeal in institutional decision making, especially in difficult times: a scientific-atomistic approach to language, with its attendant tallies and charts, nicely fits an economic decision-making model. When in doubt or when scared or when pressed, count.

This orientation to language complements the way we conceive of remediation.

The designation *remedial* has powerful implications in education — to be remedial is to be substandard, inadequate — and, because of the origins of the term, the inadequacy is metaphorically connected to disease and mental defectiveness. The etymology of the word *remedial* places its origins in law and medicine, and by the late nineteenth century the term generally fell into the medical domain. It was then applied to education, to children who were thought to have neurological problems. But *remedial* quickly generalized beyond the description of such students to those with broader, though special, educational problems and then to those learners who were from backgrounds that did not provide optimal environmental and educational opportunities.

As increasing access to education brought more and more children into the schools, the medical vocabulary — with its implied medical model — remained dominant. People tried to *diagnose* various *disabilities, defects, deficits, deficiencies,* and *handicaps,* then tried to *remedy* them. So you start to see all sorts of reading and writing problems clustered together and addressed with this language. For example, William S. Gray's important monograph, *Remedial Cases in Reading: Their Diagnosis and Treatment,* listed as "specific causes of failure in reading" inferior learning capacity, congenital word blindness, poor auditory memory, defective vision, a narrow span of recognition, ineffective eye movements, inadequate training in phonetics, inadequate attention to the content, an inadequate speaking vocabulary, a small meaning vocabulary, speech defects, lack of interest, and timidity.[6] The remedial paradigm was beginning to include those who had troubles as varied as bad eyes, second language interference, and shyness. The semantic net of *remedial* was expanding and expanding.

It is likely that the appeal of medical-remedial language had much to do with its associations with scientific objectivity and accuracy — powerful currency in the efficiency-minded 1920s and 1930s. Consider, as illustration, this passage from Albert Lang's 1930 textbook, *Modern Methods in Written Examinations*. The medical model is explicit:

> Teaching bears a resemblance to the practice of medicine. Like a successful physician, the good teacher must be something of a diagnostician. The physician by means of a general examination singles out the individual whose physical defects require a more thorough testing. He critically scrutinizes the special cases until he recognizes the specific troubles. After a careful diagnosis he is able to prescribe intelligently the best remedial or corrective measures.[7]

The theoretical and pedagogical model that was available for "corrective teaching" led educators to view literacy problems from a medical-remedial perspective. Thus they set out to diagnose as precisely as possible the errors (defects) in a student's paper — which they saw as symptomatic of equally isolable defects in the student's linguistic capacity — and devise drills and exercises to remedy them. (One of the 1930s nicknames for remedial sections was "sick sections." During the next decade they would be tagged "hospital sections.") Such corrective teaching was, in the words of one educator, "the most logical as well as the most scientific method."

Though we have, over the last fifty years, developed a richer understanding of reading and writing difficulties, the reductive view of error and the language of medicine is still with us. A recent letter from the senate of a local liberal arts college is sitting on my desk. It discusses a "program in remedial writing for . . . [those] entering freshmen suffering from severe writing handicaps." We seem entrapped by this language, this view of students and learning. We still talk of writers as suffering from specifiable, locatable defects, deficits, and handicaps that can be localized, circumscribed, and remedied. Such talk carries with it the etymological wisps and traces of disease and serves to exclude from the academic community those who are so labeled. They sit in scholastic quarantine until their disease can be diagnosed and remedied.

This atomistic, medical model of language is simply not supported by more recent research in language and cognition. But because the teaching of writing — particularly teaching designated remedial — has been conceptually and, as with the Ohio program, administratively segmented from the rich theoretical investigation that characterizes other humanistic study, these assumptions have rarely been subjected to rigorous and comprehensive scrutiny. *The Humanities in American Life,* the important position paper from which the epigraph to this section is drawn, argues passionately for the wide relevance of the humanities and urges the serious engagement of humanists in teacher training, industry, and adult basic education — areas they, for the most part, have abandoned. But until the traditional orientations to error and remediation are examined to their core, until the teaching of writing and reading to underprepared students is fundamentally reconceived, then the spirited plea of the Rockefeller Commission will be, for many in America, just another empty homiletic. Consider, after all, what those students in Developmental English are really learning.

The curriculum in Developmental English breeds a deep social and intellectual isolation from print; it fosters attitudes and beliefs about written language that, more than anything, *keep* students from becoming fully, richly literate. The curriculum teaches students that when it comes to written language use, they are children: they can only perform the most constrained and ordered of tasks, and they must do so under the regimented guidance of a teacher. It teaches them that the most important thing about writing — the very essence of writing —

is grammatical correctness, not the communication of something meaningful, or the generative struggle with ideas . . . not even word play. It's a curriculum that rarely raises students' heads from the workbook page to consider the many uses of written language that surround them in their schools, jobs, and neighborhoods. Finally, by its tedium, the curriculum teaches them that writing is a crushing bore. These students traverse course after remedial course, becoming increasingly turned off to writing, increasingly convinced that they are hopelessly inadequate. "Writing," one of the students tells me. "Man, I've never been any good at writing." "English," says another, "is not my thing." . . .

We seem to have a need as a society to explain poor performance by reaching deep into the basic stuff of those designated as other: into their souls, or into the deep recesses of their minds, or into the very ligature of their language. It seems harder for us to keep focus on the politics and sociology of intellectual failure, to keep before our eyes the negative power of the unfamiliar, the way information poverty constrains performance, the effect of despair on cognition.

"I was so busy looking for 'psychopathology,' . . ." says Robert Coles of his early investigations of childhood morality, "that I brushed aside the most startling incidents, the most instructive examples of ethical alertness in the young people I was getting to know."[8] How much we don't see when we look only for deficiency, when we tally up all that people can't do. Many of the students in this book display the gradual or abrupt emergence of an intellectual acuity or literate capacity that just wasn't thought to be there. This is not to deny that awful limits still exist: so much knowledge and so many procedures never learned; such a long, cumbersome history of relative failure. But this must not obscure the equally important fact that if you set up the right conditions, try as best you can to cross class and cultural boundaries, figure out what's needed to encourage performance, that if you watch and listen, again and again there will emerge evidence of ability that escapes those who dwell on differences.

Ironically, it's often the reports themselves of our educational inadequacies — the position papers and media alarms on illiteracy in America — that help blind us to cognitive and linguistic possibility. Their rhetorical thrust and their metaphor conjure up disease or decay or economic and military defeat: A malignancy has run wild, an evil power is consuming us from within. (And here reemerges that nineteenth-century moral terror.) It takes such declamation to turn the moneyed wheels of government, to catch public attention and entice the givers of grants, but there's a dark side to this political reality. The character of the alarms and, too often, the character of the responses spark in us the urge to punish, to extirpate, to return to a precancerous golden age rather than build on the rich capacity that already exists. The report urge responses that reduce literate possibility and constrain growth, that focus on pathology rather than on possibility. Philosophy, said Aristotle, begins to wonder. So does education. . . .

There is a strong impulse in American education — curious in a country with such an ornery streak of antitraditionalism — to define achievement and excellence in terms of the acquisition of a historically validated body of knowledge, an authoritative list of books and allusions, a canon. We seek a certification of our national intelligence, indeed, our national virtue, in how diligently our children can display this central corpus of information. This need for certification tends to emerge most dramatically in our educational policy debates during times of real or imagined threat: economic hard times, political crises, sudden increases in immigration. Now is such a time, and it is reflected in a number of influential books and commission reports. E. D. Hirsch argues that a core national vocabulary, one oriented toward the English literate tradition — Alice in Wonderland to zeitgeist — will build a knowledge base that will foster the literacy of all Americans.[9] Diane Ravitch and Chester Finn call for a return to a traditional historical and literary curriculum: the valorous historical figures and the classical literature of the once-elite course of study. Allan Bloom, [former] Secretary of

Education William Bennett, Mortimer Adler and the Paideia Group, and a number of others have affirmed, each in their very different ways, the necessity of the Great Books: Plato and Aristotle and Sophocles, Dante and Shakespeare and Locke, Dickens and Mann and Faulkner. We can call this orientation to educational achievement the canonical orientation.

At times in our past, the call for a shoring up of or return to a canonical curriculum was explicitly elitist, was driven by a fear that the education of the select was being compromised. Today, though, the majority of the calls are provocatively framed in the language of democracy. They assail the mediocre and grinding curriculum frequently found in remedial and vocational education. They are disdainful of the patronizing perceptions of student ability that further restrict the already restricted academic life of disadvantaged youngsters. They point out that the canon — its language, conventions, and allusions — is central to the discourse of power, and to keep it from poor kids is to assure their disenfranchisement all the more. The books of the canon, claim the proposals, the Great Books, are a window onto a common core of experience and civic ideals. There is, then, a spiritual, civic, and cognitive heritage here, and *all* our children should receive it. . . . This is a forceful call. It promises a still center in a turning world.

I see great value in being challenged to think of the curriculum of the many in the terms we have traditionally reserved for the few. . . . Too many people are kept from the books of the canon, the Great Books, because of misjudgments about their potential. Those books eventually proved important to me, and, as best I know how, I invite my students to engage them. But once we grant the desirability of equal curricular treatment and begin to consider what this equally distributed curriculum would contain, problems arise: If the canon itself is the answer to our educational inequities, why has it historically invited few and denied many? Would the canonical orientation provide adequate guidance as to how a democratic curriculum should be constructed and how it should be taught? . . .

Those who study the way literature becomes canonized, how linguistic creations are included or excluded from a tradition, claim that the canonical curriculum students would most likely receive would not, as is claimed, offer a common core of American experience.[10] The canon has tended to push to the margin much of the literature of our nation: from American Indian songs and chants to immigrant fiction to working-class narratives. The institutional messages that students receive in the books they're issued and the classes they take are powerful and, as I've witnessed since my Voc. Ed. days, quickly internalized. And to revise these messages and redress past wrongs would involve more than adding some new books to the existing canon — the very reasons for linguistic and cultural exclusion would have to become a focus of study in order to make the canon act as a democratizing force. Unless this happens, the democratic intent of the reformers will be undercut by the content of the curriculum they propose.

And if we move beyond content to consider basic assumptions about teaching and learning, a further problem arises, one that involves the very nature of the canonical orientation itself. The canonical orientation encourages a narrowing of focus from learning to that which must be learned: It simplifies the dynamic tension between student and text and reduces the psychological and social dimensions of instruction. The student's personal history recedes as the what of the classroom is valorized over the how. Thus it is that the encounter of student and text is often portrayed by canonists as a transmission. Information, wisdom, virtue will pass from the book to the student if the student gives the book the time it merits, carefully traces its argument or narrative or lyrical progression. Intellectual, even spiritual, growth will *necessarily* result from an encounter with Roman mythology, *Othello,* and "I heard a Fly buzz — when I died —," with biographies and historical sagas and patriotic lore. Learning is stripped of confusion and discord. It is stripped, as well, of strong human connection. My own initiators to the canon — Jack MacFarland, Dr. Carothers, and the rest — knew there was more to their work than their mastery of a tradition. What mattered most, I see now, were the relationships they established with me, the guidance they provided when I felt inadequate or threatened. This mentoring was part of my entry into that solemn library of Western thought

— and even with such support, there were still times of confusion, anger, and fear. It is telling, I think, that once that rich social network slid away, once I was in graduate school in intense, solitary encounter with that tradition, I abandoned it for other sources of nurturance and knowledge.

The model of learning implicit in the canonical orientation seems, at times, more religious than cognitive or social: Truth resides in the printed texts, and if they are presented by someone who knows them well and respects them, that truth will be revealed. Of all the advocates of the canon, Mortimer Adler has given most attention to pedagogy — and his Paideia books contain valuable discussions of instruction, coaching, and questioning. But even here, and this is doubly true in the other manifestos, there is little acknowledgment that the material in the canon can be not only difficult but foreign, alienating, overwhelming.

We need an orientation to instruction that provides guidance on how to determine and honor the beliefs and stories, enthusiasms, and apprehensions that students reveal. How to build on them, and when they clash with our curriculum — as I saw so often in the Tutorial Center at UCLA — when they clash, how to encourage a discussion that will lead to reflection on what students bring and what they're currently confronting. Canonical lists imply canonical answers, but the manifestos offer little discussion of what to do when students fail. If students have been exposed to at least some elements of the canon before — as many have — why didn't it take? If they're encountering it for the first time and they're lost, how can we determine where they're located — and what do we do then?

Each member of a teacher's class, poor *or* advantaged, gives rise to endless decisions, day-to-day determinations about a child's reading and writing: decisions on how to tap strength, plumb confusion, foster growth. the richer your conception of learning and your understanding of its social and psychological dimensions, the more insightful and effective your judgments will be. . . .

To understand the nature and development of literacy we need to consider the social context in which it occurs — the political, economic, and cultural forces that encourage or inhibit it. The canonical orientation discourages deep analysis of the way these forces may be affecting performance. The canonists ask that schools transmit a coherent traditional knowledge to an ever-changing, frequently uprooted community. This discordance between message and audience is seldom examined. Although a ghetto child can rise on the lilt of a Homeric line — books *can* spark dreams — appeals to elevated texts can also divert attention from the conditions that keep a population from realizing its dreams. The literacy curriculum is being asked to do what our politics and our economics have failed to do: diminish differences in achievement, narrow our gaps, bring us together. Instead of analysis of the complex web of causes of poor performance, we are offered a faith in the unifying power of a body of knowledge, whose infusion will bring the rich and the poor, the longtime disaffected and the uprooted newcomers into cultural unanimity. If this vision is democratic, it is simplistically so, reductive, not an invitation for people truly to engage each other at the point where cultures and classes intersect.

I worry about the effects a canonical approach to education could have on cultural dialogue and transaction — on the involvement of an abandoned underclass and on the movement of immigrants . . . into our nation. A canonical uniformity promotes rigor and quality control; it can also squelch new thinking, diffuse the generative tension between the old and the new. It is significant that the canonical orientation is voiced with most force during times of challenge and uncertainty, for it promises the authority of tradition, the seeming stability of the past. But the authority is fictive, gained from a misreading of American cultural history. No period of that history was harmoniously stable; the invocation of a golden age is a mythologizing act. Democratic culture is, by definition, vibrant and dynamic, discomforting and unpredictable. It gives rise to apprehension; freedom is not always calming. And, yes, it can yield fragmentation, though often as not the source of fragmentation is intolerant misunderstanding of diverse traditions rather than the desire of members of those traditions to remain hermetically separate. A truly democrative vision of knowledge and social structure would honor this complexity. The vision might not be soothing, but it would provide guidance as to how to live and teach in a country made up of many cultural traditions.

We are in the middle of an extraordinary social experiment: the attempt to provide education for all members of a vast pluralistic democracy. To have any prayer of success, we'll need many conceptual blessings: A philosophy of language and literacy that affirms the diverse sources of linguistic competence and deepens our understanding of the ways class and culture blind us to the richness of those sources. A perspective on failure that lays open the logic of error. An orientation toward the interaction of poverty and ability that undercuts simple polarities, that enables us to see simultaneously the constraints poverty places on the play of mind and the actual mind at play within those constraints. We'll need a pedagogy that encourages us to step back and consider the threat of the standard classroom and that shows us, having stepped back, how to step forward to invite a student across the boundaries of that powerful room. Finally, we'll need a revised store of images of educational excellence, ones closer to egalitarian ideals — ones that embody the reward and turmoil of education in a democracy, that celebrate the plural, messy human reality of it. At heart, we'll need a guiding set of principles that do not encourage us to retreat from, but move us closer to, an understanding of the rich mix of speech and ritual and story that is America.

Notes

1Report of the Commission on the Humanities, *The Humanities in American Life* (Berkeley: U of California P, 1980) 2.
2The discussion of error and remediation is condensed from Mike Rose, "The Language of Exclusion: Writing Instruction at the University," *College English* 47 (April 1985): 341–59.
3James Berlin, *Writing Instruction in Nineteenth-Century American Colleges* (Carbondale: Southern Illinois UP, 1984) 73.
4Raymond Callahan, *Education and the Cult of Efficiency* (Chicago: U of Chicago P, 1962).
5W. S. Guiler, "Background Deficiencies," *Journal of Higher Education* 3 (1932): 371.
6William S. Gray, *Remedial Cases in Reading: Their Diagnosis and Treatment* (Chicago: U of Chicago P, 1922).
7Albert Lang, *Modern Methods in Written Examinations* (Boston: Houghton, 1930) 38.
8Robert Coles, in Sherry Kafka and Robert Coles, *I Will Always Stay Me: Writings of Migrant Children* (Austin: Texas Monthly Press, 1982), 134.
9E. D. Hirsch, *Cultural Literacy: What Every American Needs to Know* (Boston: Houghton, 1987); Diane Ravitch and Chester E. Finn, Jr., *What Do Our 17-Year-Olds Know?* (New York: Harper, 1987); Allan Bloom, *The Closing of the American Mind: How Higher Education Has Failed Democracy and Impoverished the Souls of Today's Students* (New York: Simon, 1987); William J. Bennett, *To Reclaim a Legacy* (Washington: Natl. Endowment for the Humanities, 1984); Mortimer J. Adler, *The Paideia Proposal* (New York: Colliers, 1982), *Paideia Problems and Possibilities* (New York: Macmillan, 1983), and *The Paideia Program* (New York: Macmillan, 1984).
10For a critical discussion of literary canon formation, see Paul Lauter, ed., *Reconstructing American Literature* (Old Westbury: Feminist, 1983).

Rose's Insights as a Resource for Your Teaching

1. In the synthesizing of personal narrative, research, teaching practice, and broad reading, Rose clearly models the importance to any professional of writing down the specific events, sudden insights, reflective speculations, and discouragements of practicing the profession. I haven't learned how Rose generated his text, but I would recommend that you use the dialectical journal or teaching portfolio to generate your texts.

2. In *Lives on the Boundary* Rose cites "stories" of his students to build his argument. Case studies are very persuasive data. For each writing course you teach, set yourself the writing task of keeping notes about three students that could be developed into case studies. Over the course of several semesters, you will discover that certain themes or intuitions about how you could more effectively teach will emerge as you reflect on the case studies and, by association, on your own learning and that of other students.

3. In *Lives on the Boundary* Rose identifies himself as one of the underprepared students whom education does not yet serve adequately. I think that many writing teachers begin as well-prepared and successful students who never had to struggle as fiercely with learning as many of their students. For this reason, it's critical that writing teachers begin and continue their work with very careful "listening" to their students and with interdisciplinary research and reading of philosophical perspectives and pedagogic strategies. Persist.

Rose's Insights as a Resource for the Writing Classroom

1. Students on the "boundaries" in your classroom may have less skill than mainstream students for "inventing the university," as Bartholomae describes movement from novice to academic initiate. Design journal entries and writing assignments that invite all students to reflect on the difficulties and successes they have in the courses they are taking besides the writing course. Use conferences, small-group discussion, or class discussion for writers to share their experiences and collaborate in "demystifying" the academic discourse community.

2. Students will have strong opinions about the canonical model of education. Organize discussion sessions followed by writings that move from personal reflection to analysis to a "What If" writing about what should be read by "educated persons" and why.

TESTING AND PORTFOLIO ASSESSMENT

One continuous task for writing instructors is responding to and evaluating student writing. The assessing that occurs within a composition course is connected to large-scale assessments mandated by national task forces, state legislatures, institutions, or writing faculty who evaluate curricula and services. Although some writing teachers disdain and keep themselves separate from any extra-classroom assessment, an increasing number of writing teachers use assessment experience and information to validate and enhance their own teaching.

Portfolio assessment, both within and outside writing classrooms, has become a very powerful evaluation tool for the student and for the writing instructor. Holistic evaluation of student writing, be it in portfolios or other writing samples, has dramatically increased the effectiveness of classroom instruction and teachers' responses to writers. The readings in this section will give you a preliminary perspective on an auxiliary professional activity of effective writing instructors.

RECONSIDERING THE LINKS BETWEEN TEACHING AND ASSESSING WRITING

Edward M. White

In the first chapter of Teaching and Assessing Writing, *Edward M. White explains why participation in extracurricular writing assessment is necessary for writing instructors. His discussion of the dual roles of "individualizing" and "socializing" writers can be connected to Elbow's discussion of "embracing contraries." In the 1992 text* Assigning, Responding,

Evaluating: A Writing Teacher's Guide, White develops more fully the themes he lays out in this excerpt.

Most of those who teach writing in America dislike and distrust testing. While this negative attitude stems in part from a general distrust of the use of numbers to measure people, a more important factor is the great gulf that now exists between the measurement and the teaching of writing. Many writing tests currently are imposed from outside the classroom, decided on by those unacquainted with either the students or the course of study, and scored in more or less mysterious ways. The widespread use of multiple-choice mechanics and usage tests trivializes reading and writing from the earliest grades through many university programs. In addition, test results are used routinely to support or suggest incompetence on the part of the students, the teachers, or both. It is no wonder that so many of those teaching in American classrooms, from first grade teachers wondering about the machinery that will bar some children from getting into second grade to college professors seeing their best students attempting to pass graduate record or law school entrance examinations, consider testing to be at best a necessary evil and at worst a destructive intrusion into the learning process. Teachers of writing in particular, charged in part with a concern for the creativity and individuality of students, normally consider testing to be a dirty word and an offensive action.

There is no point in denying that most testing of writing is poorly done, destructive to the goals of teaching, and improperly used. No sensible person could defend current practice, which has set up three hostile camps: the teachers, avoiding and undermining testing programs when they can, in the name of humane teaching; the public, with its general distrust of education, naively believing any number set out in the name of testing as if it revealed an unpleasant suspected truth; and test professionals, often aware of the uncertainty of their findings and unskilled in coping with more than routine number crunching and established item types, trying feebly to inform teachers and the public of technical issues with large political and economic impact. The present situation could hardly be worse.

Closing the Gap between Teaching and Testing

Since one major tenet of this book is that testing not only can be but should be a vital part of every writing teacher's professional equipment, this opening chapter confronts directly the almost unanimous opposition on the part of teachers to the testing of writing. Thus, I must say at the outset that the assessment concepts and procedures that are vital to the teaching of writing are very different from the confused, inefficient, and inappropriate testing that most writing teachers rightly condemn. When the testing of writing is done properly, it supports teaching both practically and conceptually, involves teachers in test planning and test design, and helps bring recent discoveries about the teaching of writing into the classroom.

It is not hard to see why most testing of writing is done poorly. Most teachers of writing know little or nothing about testing, and most specialists in testing know even less about the teaching and learning of writing. Furthermore, both groups of professionals suspect each other, and they confirm their suspicions by rarely communicating with those in a distant, slightly disreputable field. To be sure, not all of this distrust is unfounded. Writing teachers rightly believe that test specialists simplify writing and slight what is most important, while testing specialists rightly believe that teacher ignorance of testing and teacher arrogance about that ignorance lead to unfair treatment of students. Meanwhile, educational administrators and test directors face demands for test scores, program evaluation, and general accountability for resources, while the public wants some hard numbers to show that the schools and universities are doing their jobs. And so the testing goes on, as it must.

The gulf between teachers and test specialists becomes most apparent when people of good will try to bridge it. I have watched test consultants grow red-faced from frustration as they tried to explain the elementary statistics behind multiple-choice test construction to a friendly group of writing teachers who could not or would not understand; the routine and unexamined faith most writing teachers bring to essay testing, despite the poor design and unreliable grading it usually displays, drives test specialists wild. I have also watched a committee of distinguished composition faculty patiently (for the first few hours) try to educate a test consultant about writing; the consultant, typically, had such a narrow, blind commitment to multiple-choice testing that the committee voted to disband rather than continue to work with him. The usual result of these failed attempts at communication is to reinforce the prejudices that militate against the understanding that is so badly needed. Writing teachers typically show contempt for test specialists, whom they thus brush off as ignorant technicians; test consultants, instead of learning about the importance and possibilities of essay testing, spend their time and energy trying to manipulate the (usually mandatory) faculty committees, which they see as obstructing their task with meaningless and unmeasurable complications.

The peculiar irony of this unfortunate situation is that no one gives more test grades than writing teachers, even as they articulate their unwillingness to trust or even to learn about the fairly simple concepts of measurement that will make their job easier and their teaching more effective. In turn, the distrust generated by this attitude is returned by administrators as well as by test professionals, and it sometimes leads to the deliberate omission of teachers from programs designed to measure writing ability. The best hope for changing this situation rests with improved communication between teachers and test specialists and with greater understanding on all sides of the issues and concepts that underlie both perspectives on student writing.

This book is designed to support — from whatever part of the academy they may come — those who ask students to write in their classes or who become involved with programs that test writing ability at any of three different levels: the classroom, the campus (as in a placement or exit proficiency test), or the large-scale program that is multicampus, statewide, or national in scope. Of course, issues in measurement at these levels overlap. The same kinds of problems that may hamper national testing programs also tend to distort classroom teaching; put positively, better understanding of how to test writing at any level will improve classroom teaching at all levels. Furthermore, a teacher who knows how to use testing for more than mere grading in the classroom (to reduce writing anxiety, foster rewriting, develop positive attitudes toward the writing process, and so on) will be an informed and valuable member of any test committee; and a test specialist or educational administrator who understands the intimate relation of testing to teaching will be in demand at all levels of education.

In recent years, a very small cadre of writing teachers has developed some expertness in testing, and a handful of test professionals has come to understand the complexity of writing and writing measurement. A few school and university administrators have supported advanced testing and evaluation designs for writing programs and, in so doing, have gained an appreciation for the difficulties and rewards involved. Until that group grows larger, however, the testing of writing will continue to manifest the special problems that come from ignorance as well as the general problems that stem from the lack of communication endemic to academic programs in general.

The last decade or so has been enough changes in both the teaching and the testing of writing to suggest that the dismal picture I have been painting is ripe for change. Indeed, there already are signs that this change is beginning to take place. Such huge educational systems as the California State University, the City University of New York, and the Department of Higher Education of the State of New Jersey have instituted major testing programs in writing by bringing together professional test specialists, evaluators, and teachers. Just as encouraging are the widespread in-service workshops sponsored by the (San Francisco) Bay Area Writing Project — intense summer sessions that bring together teachers, professors, writing researchers, and those trained in testing. Furthermore, recent advances both in research in the teaching of writing and in the measurement of writing have led to new communication at the university research level between teachers and test specialists. More and more professionals are recognizing the need to bridge the gap that has led to the present situation.

Thus, the field of writing is particularly ready for the reconsideration of testing and its relation to the teaching of writing that this book proposes. Writing research (which at long last has developed significant findings for teachers) depends on measurement for validation of its findings, and the advances in testing chronicled in this volume have in fact allowed some of this writing research to occur. The proficiency testing movement, with its ubiquitous demand for certification of literacy at all levels from grade school through graduate school, has created an important cadre of English teachers who have made it their business to become specialists in testing — as a form of professional self-defense. Additional self-defense in measurement has become necessary as we have been asked to justify huge national and institutional expenditures on writing programs; outsiders using uninformed or (as one all-purpose evaluator puts it) "goal-free" evaluation will evaluate writing programs if writing teachers are unwilling or unable to participate in more responsible program evaluations. No sensible person in these academic hard times can object to the request that an expensive program show that it is producing some benefits; the only question to be asked is who is to evaluate writing programs and how.

These issues in measurement now lie at the door of those who teach writing, and by their presence they suggest that writing teachers can no longer afford the luxury of blind opposition to testing. However, it is always easy for teachers committed to the classroom to convince themselves that there are others to handle large professional issues, while their most essential task remains working with their own students. If measurement had no implications for the conduct of writing instruction, the testing issues in this book would remain of interest principally to specialists and concerned administrators, no matter how many exhortations to professional responsibility were included.

It is thus of primary importance that virtually all writing teachers who have become professionally involved in measurement have found their teaching changing profoundly. For example, consider the case of a college faculty member or a high school teacher who (usually unwillingly) finds himself or herself a member of an essay-testing team responsible for a multicampus writing assessment program. Since essay test development requires decisions about the kind of writing to be required, the committee needs to discuss such issues as the rhetorical mode or modes to be examined and what quality of writing might reasonably be expected to particular students under particular conditions; as the team considers many possible writing topics, rejecting most and choosing some for pre-testing, discussion about good and bad topics will occur; as the committee reviews the results of pre-testing and develops procedures for scoring the papers, discussion about reliable and fair grading must occur. Since these issues are of major importance to every writing class, the teacher who fails to see their application in his or her working life must have an extraordinary imperviousness to experiential learning.

When we speak of the opposition to testing on the part of writing teachers, we are not being strictly accurate. Their opposition is not to testing itself but to testing imposed by those outside the classroom, or, less charitably put, to less subjective evaluation than usually goes on. The great achievement of modern essay testing is that it allows the teacher enough subjectivity to deal with each student as an individual while at the same time reducing the partial, arbitrary, and whimsical nature of the grading of writing. In short, those who learn from the best testing procedures and carry those procedures back to their campuses and their classrooms have learned how to tame the beast. They can regain power over the testing of their students, since knowledge leads to power, and hence they can use this power for the benefit of their students and for the attainment of the best goals of education in reading and writing.

An even more compelling reason for writing teachers to consider an understanding of evaluation an indispensable part of their professional development concerns the strange paradox of revision: professional writers revise constantly, while naive and untrained writers, whose need for revision is much more severe, almost never revise. Routinely, teachers at all levels exhort, command, or require revision, but almost always in vain; the typical student paper is still written the night before it is due, and the typical student has absolutely no idea of the quality of the paper before (and often even after) the instructor has read it. Instructors spend endless hours meticulously marking papers in the belief that grading papers is the same as teaching writing, with irrepressible and unwarranted faith that conventional teacher comments on present papers will affect the writing of future papers.

When we look at this situation, in all its busy futility, the pressing need for teacher sophistication in evaluation becomes inescapable. Even serious students fail to revise, by and large, because they do not know how to evaluate their writing; since they see nothing to be changed (until the writing instructor uses the arcane and incomprehensible grading process), they see no need for revision, and hence they do not revise. Since the grading process normally remains not only mysterious (it is even written in quaint symbols) but irrational (one teacher praises the same things another teacher condemns), most students find revision futile: Who knows what the teacher really wants this time? So revision waits until after the teacher has commented, if revision occurs at all, and then the new work responds only minimally to teacher corrections, often making things worse rather than better.

Experience with and understanding of the best procedures in essay testing will allow the writing teacher to teach revision much more effectively. A teacher with awareness of issues in the creation of writing topics will make assignments with such clarity that the students will really know what is wanted; such a teacher will not hesitate to discuss the purpose and possibilities of these topics in class and will be ready with various "pre-writing" activities to help get students started. When papers or drafts of papers are turned in, such a teacher will prepare, or work with the class to prepare, a scoring guide that describes with some precision the differences between successful and unsuccessful papers; such a scoring guide allows the students to be part of the grading and responding process for one another's papers as well. Finally, the very openness of the grading process, with its positive tone (a typical scoring guide will caution readers to reward students for what is well done rather than merely punish them for what is not well done), encourages revision, since students learn to see the differences between the various qualities of writing and hence can begin to see what can be done to improve their work.

I am not suggesting that a magic formula called evaluation will easily transform the world of writing instruction. Nothing in the teaching of writing is that simple. Rather, I am saying that an understanding of some of the best procedures in the testing of writing not only will be important for those concerned with research and with student or program evaluation but also will be of substantial value for all writing teachers in their classes. It is time for teachers of writing at all levels to put aside their reflexive reaction against testing so that they can replace the inappropriate tests that still dominate the field with better, more supportive, more useful devices. It is time for us to learn from the recent advances in essay testing how to be better teachers of writing. We cannot consider ourselves fully professional until we do.

Defining, Teaching, and Measuring Basic Skills in Writing

Any discussion of the testing of writing needs to begin with a consideration of the subject itself and of ways of teaching and learning that subject. A theory of knowledge of the subject must precede any practice of testing that is to make coherent sense and that is to be useful to those teaching and learning; indeed, when theories of knowledge and of content are not taken into consideration, ill-considered tests can lead to a thoughtless curriculum as teachers wind up teaching to inappropriate tests.

This book is not directed to English teachers alone. Happily, at all levels of education, the teaching of writing at long last is going on across the curriculum, across the disciplines, across the various specializations; the measurement of writing ability calls for even wider participation — by all those teaching writing as well as various administrative and psychometric specialists. Nonetheless, most people connect the teaching of writing with the teaching of English (the discipline specifically devoted to reading and writing), and thus we need to begin our consideration of the writing curriculum and testing with a brief look at the discipline of English. Inappropriate testing has been destructive to the teaching of writing for the last two generations, during which such teaching traditionally has been entrusted to English teachers at all levels. One important reason for this destructive testing emerges from the contradictory purposes of the English curriculum as it has developed in America.

Multiple-choice usage testing has become so predominant as a means of testing writing that it has come to define the entire field of English for most of the population. Such testing often asks students to identify supposedly correct spelling, usage, or grammar out of context or to find errors in test-writer prose — sometimes technical errors on trivial matters that have little to do with communication or even with normal academic writing. But these are the tests that everyone remembers from school days and that serve to define the subject of English in the public mind. Every contemporary English teacher dreads the social moment when a stranger asks, "What do you do?" Those who confess the truth must confront the inevitable response, as the inquirer turns away with a scowl: "English was always my worst subject; I'd better watch what I say." New teachers, excited about English as a creative and even a revolutionary subject with great writers, great subjects, and great ideas, are puzzled or infuriated by such a response. I remember the murderous thoughts that crossed my mind after one of my daughters' boyfriends found out about my profession and asked, with genuine perplexity, "What kind of job is that for a grown man?" Why indeed should a grown person spend his or her days pointing out picky errors in other people's language to no useful purpose? Or, even more to the point, how can the grand subjects of reading and writing be rescued from the trivialization they have come to receive, usually in a well-motivated quest for "basic skills"?

It is important to understand the issues that have shaped the English curriculum if we are to make sense of the contradictions and confusions that make the teaching and testing of writing so difficult. Particularly in these days of proficiency testing of basic skills in English, a clear understanding of the contrasting and conflicting goals of English instruction is necessary if we are to define the term *basic skills* with clarity and then proceed to measure these skills responsibly. It is an inescapable fact that English is called upon to accomplish conflicting ends for a society with complex needs: English studies must both socialize and individualize students, despite the innate contradictions between these two goals.

English as a Socializing Discipline

The history of the American public high school helped set its basic tone and mission: to socialize and conventionalize students so that they will fit into a demanding, work-oriented society. The development of English as a discipline has been well chronicled by D. J. Palmer (1965), A. N. Applebee (1974), Richard Ohmann (1976), Alan Hollingsworth (1972) — to whose workshops and speeches the following discussion is particularly indebted — and others. It is a long and complex story, beginning with the dissenting academies in seventeenth-century England; the developing curriculum there showed a continuing concern for rhetorical and grammatical issues and at a late date was finally enriched by the addition of literature as an important study in its own right. Our concern here is not with the history in itself but only with the way that history has shaped current policies and goals.

When the citizens of Boston created a new kind of secondary school in 1821, it was designed to bring "the children of the poor and unfortunate elements of the community" into "the active life," that is, into the trades and into active citizenry but specifically not into the university. After some squabbling about names with the headmaster of the Boston Public Latin Grammar School (founded in 1635 to prepare university students), the new school came to be called the English High School. By 1870, the American high school, based on the Boston model, had appeared in most cities able to support public education. Its goals by that time had changed only slightly: Its mission in large part remained to prepare the children of the dispossessed and middle classes for business and the trades, for comfortable participation in ordinary social intercourse, and for enthusiastic spectatorship at patriotic and (increasingly) sports activities. Presently, the schools also prepare students for universities and make some gestures toward introduction to science, literature, languages, and the arts; that is, they have added some Boston Latin motifs into the Boston English curriculum.

A major part of schooling must be to socialize young people into their culture by teaching them its accepted truths, history, myths, rituals, crafts, and manners. This is not a surprising discovery, since education in all human societies traditionally has fulfilled this mission as its part in the transmission and preservation of culture. Furthermore, it should come as no surprise that English as an American school subject should be asked to play a major part in this socialization process. Manners are crucial to social standing and to social mobility, and linguistic etiquette is the most important of all manners in a highly verbal society.

When we look at the jobs assigned to English in its function as a socializing discipline, we find them affecting writing instruction at all levels. Grade school students first learn to write on the lines from left to right and then proceed to study spelling, vocabulary, and capitalization; the high school adolescent practices accepted punctuation and usage; the college student memorizes footnote style — all in the name of learning English. Do it the *right* way, we tell the student (quite properly, by the way) or you will be penalized. And the "right way" is defined very simply: It is the way it is done.

Think of spelling, for example, the archetypical socializing study, the darling of those who in the name of "standards" want education to focus on rote drill. The fact that Shakespeare spelled his name in an engaging variety of ways did not mean he was a bad speller; there was no such thing as a bad speller until much later when spelling began to mater. When printers began to normalize spelling, for their convenience, and when the written and spoken language diverged to the degree that simple phonetic spelling became impossible, spelling became (as it now is) an important social skill, comparable to knowing how to use knives and forks at table. Spelling is important — and important for English teachers to attend to — because manners are important for social mobility, and good spelling suggests good linguistic upbringing. Spelling is important not because it makes sense, or because it is good mental discipline, or because it has anything at all to do with thinking; spelling is important solely because people will think you are stupid if you fail to spell words the way everyone else spells words.

Spelling, or footnote style, or a dozen or so other matters that are part of the conventions of language, ought not to pose the theoretical problems for teachers that they often do. As long as we recognize that an important part of our job is to socialize students and that it is by no means the most important part of the job, we should be able to go about it with good will and good humor. It is not a sin to spell badly; it is a social indiscretion, rather like wearing torn jeans to the prom.

Of course, there are several problems with this socializing aspect of English discipline, and I want to look briefly at these problems. There are those who go to extremes on the matter, either ignoring the socializing skills entirely or (more usually) believing that those skills are all that should be taught; both of these extreme attitudes are simply unprofessional, wherever they appear, and are quite indefensible. Again, to consider English solely or principally as a socializing discipline implies a particular political and intellectual attitude toward education. It defines education as did the parent from Orange County who said, "We're paying you to *educate* our kids. Stop messing with their minds" — as rote training without intellectual content. And finally, the socializing skills, in English as in other areas, are not particularly intellectually challenging either to teach or to test, and so they become the easy way out for those prone to formula teaching and mechanical testing.

The socializing skills, then, are an accepted, appropriate, and necessary part of English at all levels. While they are neither the most important nor the only basic skills in the field, they form the code of linguistic behavior that allows more important matters to take place, and hence they need to be taught and tested. They are particularly valuable skills for students who are striving to move beyond the social level of their parents (since codes of behavior are learned at home), and all teachers should make plain the social value of these imitative skills without pretending that they have intellectual content. The particular danger of the socializing nature of English is that it is too often taken to be the major or even the only content of the field. Far too often, this relatively minor part of the discipline is defined as the basic skill of English, valued out of proportion, and tested in a rote fashion that demeans the field, the students, and the teachers.

There is, of course, no very clean break between the socializing skills of writing (or of behavior, for that matter) and substantive skills of expression. Some faults of sentence structure, such as fused sentences or comma splices, seem to be no more than careless breaches of linguistic etiquette; others, such as lack of clear predication or clarity of verb tenses, seem to reflect issues related to the deep structure of the sentence, the thought, or even the mind. The accuracy of vocabulary in expressing ideas is usually no trivial matter, although accidents of dialect or usage may be. As mere socialization shades into real substance, reasonable people will differ on the importance of this or that aspect of writing. But, unfortunately, the overall emphasis on the least significant aspects of writing in most so-called writing tests leaves no doubt that socialization, not writing, is what is being tested.

English as an Individualizing Discipline

While English must be seen in part as a socializing discipline, the major thrust of the modern English curriculum is directly contradictory to socialization. If the principal rule for socialization is to perform in conventional ways, the overriding motivation for good writing (or good reading, for that matter) is to think for oneself. We do not want creative spelling or punctuation, but we do want creative writing and thinking. We do not aim for new responses to the issue of subject-verb agreement, but we demand that students read and respond to literature or to political ideas or to issues in their lives for themselves.

The sharp contrast between these two aspects of English is often submerged in practice; since to be professionally responsible we must encourage both socialization and individualization, English instruction needs to contain and manage the innate contradiction. But we ought to be aware of the different kinds of demands the two aspects of English make on students: Spell and punctuate the way everyone else does, but do not simply tell me what everyone else thinks — you are required to present your own ideas, to have an individual response, to develop your own sense of identity through your reading and writing.

The tradition out of which this individualizing discipline emerges is ancient indeed: Classical rhetoric stressed invention, the discovery and elaboration of one's own thoughts, while the creation and reading of literature has always been so personal as to border on the revolutionary. The creation of a poem is a powerful political statement of nonconformity punishable by imprisonment or worse in many parts of the world; the transformation of marks on a page into meaning can only occur within a creative individual mind. The exiling of Ovid or Solzhenitsyn, the imprisonment of Defoe or Timerman, the deaths of Socrates or Mishima, the routine murders of writers by despots, and the underground circulation of writing under oppressive regimes all point to a vital and nonconformist tradition that is absolutely "basic" to the study of reading and writing. English as an American school subject nurtures the individualizing imagination through challenging reading and writing and supports the very foundations of political democracy by demanding independent thought and individual responses to ideas. While the socializing aspect of the discipline reduces behavior to more or less acceptable parts, the individualizing thrust treats people as units, as wholes greater than the sum of their behaviors.

Although it is unprofessional to ignore the conventionalizing nature of parts of the English curriculum, it is far more unprofessional to ignore the individualizing nature of the core of English. Basic skills in English ought never, at any level, to be defined in such a way as to omit or minimize the importance of the individualizing function of the discipline. These skills cannot be reserved for attention in college or even in high school. The writing teachers (and there are many) who deal only with "the naming of parts" in their classes in the belief that what they call grammar must precede thinking, reading, and writing are making a social decision about their function in society, not a pedagogical decision about teaching. The reading and writing of stories and poems, the exercise of the individualizing imagination, can and should be a part of the English curriculum from the first grade.

Both the teaching and the testing of English as an individualizing discipline are difficult and frequently unwelcome. It is easier to ask students to fill in workbooks than to assign writing projects; it is less time consuming (and hence less expensive) to correct rote exercises than it is to respond humanly to human expression. Many parents of schoolchildren value the socializing skills so highly that they question or resent teaching that fosters individualizing activities. It is difficult to ask students to think for themselves without getting into sensitive areas, such as sex, religion, or politics, and even the parents of college students become very uneasy if students are encouraged to question accepted truths in these areas. College students who have problems with writing think they need more of what they call grammar (usually collections of ill-formulated rules for supposedly correct writing) and are unhappy if asked to think for themselves and to write and revise papers. Teachers who encourage too much individuality or allow too much adventurous reading may find themselves known as troublemakers — and not only by timid administrators: Every English department has articulate members who believe in their hearts that departures from the socializing view of the discipline show grave failures in upholding academic standards.

The individualizing tradition generally holds sway in liberal arts programs at the college or university level, particularly where the tradition of teaching literature remains strong. However, when we move to "remedial" writing programs on these campuses, we often find a hard-core socializing program, sometimes using the same workbooks or programmed texts that have failed to work previously for the same students. As we move to the technical or business schools and then to the high schools, we find less and less individualizing (though always some) until we wind up in the grade schools, where only a few heroic teachers redeem the dry rote of the work sheets and the usage tests that make up the usual study of English.

Despite this unhappy picture, there are some faculty at all levels who keep insisting that basic skills in English must include reading (not merely decoding) and writing (not merely identifying errors). The basic skills of using the imagination and of comprehending complex meanings, of thinking for oneself and evaluating the thinking of others, of understanding oneself in relation to the world of experience and the world of ideas — these basic skills still assert their claims. The best teachers still respond to these claims, the best pedagogy still envisions students as whole people and not merely trainable parts, and the best tests engage students at the individual as well as the social level. . . .

References

Applebee, A. N. *Tradition and Reform in the Teaching of English: A History.* Urbana: NCTE, 1974.
Hollingsworth, Alan. "Beyond Literacy." Paper presented at the spring conference of the California State University Council, Sausalito, October 1972.

Ohmann, Richard. *English in America: A Radical View of the Profession.* New York: Oxford UP, 1976.

Palmer, D. J. *The Rise of English Studies.* New York: Oxford UP, 1965.

White's Insights as a Resource for Your Teaching

1. "Informal assessments" provide teachers with useful information about student performance and the practice of evaluating student writing. Arrange to work with a colleague who has taught the same writing course you teach and share a holistic reading of student papers. Read and rank the papers on a scale of most to least successful and then talk about what overall impression and features of a writing made you evaluate it as you did. From this conversation, you'll clarify your response and judgment and be able to write a "scoring guide" or end comments that specify why the paper succeeded and what to focus on in revision.

2. If you can join some local, regional, or national reading and scoring session, you will find your confidence in your "intuitive" and holistic judgment about the quality of the paper affirmed by the discussion that ensues during training for the scoring session.

White's Insights as a Resource for the Writing Classroom

1. White emphasizes that we must encourage both socialization and individualization within our teaching practice. If you simulate an essay exam by having students prepare readings for an in-class exam writing, you can follow up with a workshop. Ask students to read and rank a range of responses to a prompt and hold a class discussion on their assessments. The conversation will focus on both individual and social features of the writing. Explain how, in a real exam situation, you would grade and explain the awarding of that grade to a student.

2. It's only sensible and fair to share with students the criteria used for evaluation of their work. You can encourage them to use some self-assessment and to apply criteria for evaluation during drafting and revising. By demystifying the process of evaluation, you enable more writers to become autonomous learners.

BRINGING PRACTICE IN LINE WITH THEORY: USING PORTFOLIO GRADING IN THE COMPOSITION CLASSROOM

Jeffrey Sommers

Sommers emphasizes that portfolio grading in the composition classroom—an increasingly frequent teaching and learning option—presents a unique opportunity to connect the practice of responding to and evaluating student writing with an individual's beliefs about writing and about teaching writing. He demonstrates that a portfolio assignment encourages students to revise and helps them discover writing as learning.

Sommers argues that portfolio grading will aid both the learner and the instructor only if the reflective teaching practitioner identifies and works out appropriate answers to the hard questions that such an assessment practice prompts. He describes three portfolio models: representative sampling, holistic perspective, and developmental perspective. Sommers speculates about the interconnections among each model and assessment criteria, grading standards, student-instructor relationship in the writing classroom, and effects on paper load. The essay is one of twenty-three collected in Portfolios: Process and Product *edited by Belanoff and Dickson.*

Portfolio assessment in the composition classroom offers not a methodology but a framework for response. Rather than provide definitive answers to questions about grading criteria and standards, the relationship between teacher and student, and increased paper loads, the portfolio approach presents an opportunity for instructors to bring their practice in responding to student writing in line with their theories of composing and pedagogy. My essay proposes to take an exploratory look at how portfolio evaluation compels instructors to address a number of important, and long-lived, issues underlying response to student writing. When an instructor chooses to use a portfolio system, certain other decisions must inevitably follow, and it is the implications of these decisions that I propose to examine most closely.

As the writing process has become the focus of composition classes over the past three decades, it seems an almost natural evolution for portfolio evaluation to have entered the classroom. Emphasizing the importance of revision to the composing process — regardless of which theoretical view of composing one takes — ought to lead to a classroom practice that permits, even encourages, students to revise. While such revision can, of course, occur in a classroom in which the writing portfolio is not in use, the portfolio itself tends to encourage students to revise because it suggests that writing occurs over time, not in a single sitting, just as the portfolio itself grows over time and cannot be created in a single sitting. Elbow and Belanoff argue that a portfolio system evaluates student writing "in ways that better reflect the complexities of the writing process: with time for freewriting, planning, discussion with instructors and peers, revising, and copyediting. It lets students put these activities together in a way most productive for them" (14).

Additionally, the portfolio approach can help students discover that writing is indeed a form of learning. Janet Emig has argued that writing "provides [a] record of evolution of thought since writing is epigenetic as process-and-product" (128). Portfolios provide a record of that record. Emig also describes writing as "active, engaged, personal — notably, self-rhythmed" (128). The notion that writing occurs over time in response to the rhythms created by the individual writer — a notion that makes eminent sense when one considers that no two writers seem to work at precisely the same pace and that no two pieces of writing seem to take form at the same pace even for the same writer — is another excellent argument for using portfolios. The portfolio approach allows writers to assemble an *oeuvre* at their own pace, within the structure of the writing course and its assignments, of course. Nevertheless, the portfolio by its very nature suggests self-rhythm because some pieces will require more drafts than others, even if explicit deadlines are prompting their composition.

For good cause then have portfolio systems of evaluation become commonplace in composition classrooms. But with these portfolios also come serious issues about grading standards and criteria, about how teachers and students relate to one another, about how teachers handle increased paper loads. Before examining how these issues might be resolved, perhaps it is time to acknowledge that this essay has yet to define *portfolio*. I have deliberately avoided doing so for two reasons: first, *portfolio* is a familiar-enough term and not really all that mysterious, and thus what I have written so far should be comprehensible to my readers; second, no consensus exists about just what a portfolio is or should be, however familiar the concept may seem. In fact, two distinctly different models of portfolios exist, each compelling its adherents to address the central issues of response in very different theoretical ways.

The first model is described well by James E. Ford and Gregory Larkin, who use as an analogy an artist's portfolio. Each student's work is "collected, like the best representative work of an artist, into a 'portfolio' " (951). We are to see students in the role of free-lance commercial artists, approaching an art director at an advertising agency with a large portfolio case containing their "best representative work." Such a model is easily transferred into the writing classroom. Students in the writing course produce a certain number of written documents during the term, agreeing in advance that only a specified number of those documents will be graded by the instructor. Commercial artists would never compile a portfolio that consisted of every piece of work they had done and neither do the students; the idea is to select a representative sampling that shows the creators at their best.

This portfolio model most likely grows out of instructors' concern with grading criteria and standards. Ford and Larkin, as the title of their article suggests, came to the portfolio as a means of guaranteeing grading standards. Instructors are justified in upholding rigorous standards of excellence because their students have been able to revise their work and select their best writing for evaluation. As Ford and Larkin comment, "A student can 'blow' an occasional assignment without disastrous effect" (952), suggesting that the instructor is being eminently fair. Elbow and Belanoff, in the context of a programmatic portfolio-assessment project, make a similar argument, one equally applicable to the individual classroom. "By giving students a chance to be examined on their best writing — by giving them an opportunity for more help — we are also able to demand their best writing" (13). This portfolio system "encourages high standards from the start, thereby encouraging maximum development" (Burnham 137).

To Ford and Larkin, Burnham, and Elbow and Belanoff, a portfolio is a sampling of finished products selected by the student for evaluation. Although the instructor using this model may very well be concerned with the students' development as writers, as Burnham's remark indicates, essentially this portfolio model is grade driven and could be accurately labeled a *portfolio grading system*. It is grade driven because the rationale for using the portfolio framework grows out of an understanding that the student's written work will ultimately be evaluated.

However, portfolio grading, paradoxically, not only grows out of a concern for eroding standards, but also out of a concern for the overemphasis upon grades in writing courses. Christopher Burnham calls the students' "obsession" with grades a "major stumbling block" (125) to effective learning in the composition classroom and turns to portfolio grading as a means of mitigating the students' obsession with grades. Burnham concludes that the portfolio system "establishes a writing environment rather than a grading environment in the classroom" (137).

Thus, by addressing the issue of responding to the student's writing, Burnham wants to change the relationship between the student and the instructor. He wants to create a more facilitative role for the instructor, in accordance with suggestions about response from Donald Murray, Nancy Sommers, and Lil Brannon and C.H. Knoblauch. He not only wants to allow students to retain the rights to their own writing, he wants them to assume responsibility for their writing, asserting that portfolio grading "creates independent writers and learners" (136).

The question then of when and what to grade becomes quite significant. Although grading criteria must be established by instructors who employ portfolio grading, new criteria for grading the final drafts do not generally need to be developed. Presumably, instructors will bring to bear an already developed set of criteria for grading, applying these criteria rigorously to designated papers, thus protecting the integrity of their standards.[1] Nonetheless, a crucial question arises: when will student work receive a grade: at midterm, only at the end of the term, with each submission? Some instructors grade every draft and revision as students submit them, some grade only the revisions, some grade only papers designated as final drafts. In some portfolio-grading systems, the students select a specified number of final drafts at midterm and a second set at end of the term, while in other systems, all grading occurs at the end of the term.

Instructors using portfolio grading must decide when to offer grades. Grading every draft keeps the students informed, but, because even a temporary grade has an air of finality to many students simply because it is a grade, this policy may undercut the idea that each draft may potentially develop into a finished product. Grading revisions only may encourage the grade-obsessed student to revise if only to obtain a grade, thus introducing revision to some students who otherwise lack the motivation to revise, but also reinforcing the primacy of grades.

By deferring grades until the end of the term, instructors can extend the duration of the "writing environment" that Burnham hopes to substitute for the "grading environment" in the course. However, if students are indeed obsessed with grades, as he argues, then it seems likely that for a substantial number of students, or perhaps for all of the students to varying extents, there will always be a grading environment lurking beneath the writing environment of the course. If instructors respond effectively and frequently and confer with students individually, they can keep students informed of their approximate standing in the course, possibly deflecting their grade anxiety, but it is disingenuous to claim that portfolio grading removes grade obsession. If the portfolio ultimately produces an accumulation of individual grades, grade obsession cannot really be eliminated although it certainly can be reduced.

Yet a larger issue arises, an issue related to one's pedagogical assumptions about the significance of grades. Burnham discusses the portfolio system as a means of leading to student development, a development inevitably measured by the final grades earned by the student's portfolio. Inherent in this model is the idea that students can improve the writing, and thus the grade, by revising and selecting their best work. Inevitably, then, instructors using portfolio grading must address the issue of grade inflation. Although one of the motivating forces behind portfolio grading, as we have seen, is protecting grading standards, the system itself is designed to promote better writing by the students, and it stands to reason that many students are going to be submitting portfolios that consist of writing better than they might be able to produce in a classroom employing a traditional grading system. Will instructors raise the standards so high that even the improved writing in the portfolios falls into the usual grading curve? Or, and this seems much more likely, will the grades themselves on the whole be somewhat higher because of the portfolio approach despite higher standards? Should higher grades be of significant concern to instructors? Do higher grades mean "grade inflation"? What is the role of grades in writing courses? Portfolio grading compels instructors to consider these important questions.

Finally, portfolio grading presents problems to instructors in handling the paper load. Since most programs suggest or stipulate a certain number of assignments per term, instructors using the portfolio system must determine how they will count assignments. Will newly revised papers count as new assignments? By doing so, the instructor can keep the paper load from mushrooming. Let's focus on a course that requires seven papers in a semester (the situation at my institution), with the understanding that the portfolio will consist of four final drafts selected by the student. If instructors count revisions of papers 1 and 2 as papers 3 and 4, their paper load will be less because students will still only produce seven drafts for them to read. On the other hand, the students' options at the end of the term will be reduced by this method of counting; they will have to select four final drafts from only five different pieces in progress.

To ensure students the full choice of seven, however, instructors commit themselves to more responding. In our hypothetical case, they will read at least nine drafts, seven first drafts, and revisions of the first two papers. Thus a routine decision actually has important pedagogical implications.

Several methods of controlling the paper load do exist. One is to divide the term in half, asking students to produce two miniportfolios. At midterm, for instance, in the situation already described, students are required to submit two final drafts for grading out of the first four assigned papers. At the end of the term, students must select two of the final three assigned papers for grading. Thus the paper load is under greater control because the students cannot continue work on the first four papers after midterm. On the other hand, Burnham's desire to create a writing environment rather than a grading environment will be affected because grades will become of primary concern not once but twice during the term.

Another method for controlling the paper load is to limit the number of drafts students may write of individual papers. Without such a limit, some students will rewrite and resubmit papers almost weekly, adding greatly to the paper load; of course, one can argue that such students are developing as writers in an important way. Deadlines for revisions of papers can also be used to control the paper load since "real" writers always work under deadlines. They may revise and revise and revise, but ultimately they must conclude. Instructors may allow students to revise a given assignment as often as they wish but within a designated period of time. Another method of controlling the paper is to limit the number of revisions students may submit at one time or to designate specific times when revisions may be submitted. Late in the term, industrious students may have revisions of three or four different assignments ready to be submitted; some limit on the number they may hand in at one time can help instructors manage the course more effectively. Stipulating that revisions can be handed in only on certain days can allow instructors to plan their time for responding more efficiently.

Eventually, the end of the term arrives, and for many instructors using portfolio grading, the paper load explodes. Portfolios of four papers or more per student come in at the end of the term and must be graded quickly in order to submit final grades on time. Holistic grading can make the paper load manageable as instructors offer no comments but just a letter grade on each final draft. Grading portfolios at the end of the term undeniably requires more time than grading a single final exam or final paper would. However, mundane these questions of handling the paper load may seem, the answers one supplies affect the entire portfolio grading system because many of these decisions may influence the relationship between students and their instructors, and some may influence, or be influenced by, instructors' grading criteria and standards.

To sum up then, a portfolio grading system defines a portfolio as a sampling of students' finished writing selected by the students for evaluation. Portfolio grading offers instructors a means of keeping their grading standards high while employing their usual grading criteria, it presents one potential method for reducing students' obsession with grades and transforming the classroom environment into one more engaged with writing than grading, and it increases instructors' paper loads. Instructors' decisions about when to grade and how to manage the paper load raise complications because they affect the relationship between instructors and their students. Thus, teachers planning on implementing portfolio grading need to consider carefully how they will do so in a way that will keep their practice in line with their own theoretical assumptions about writing and about composition pedagogy.

The second, newer, portfolio system model I will call the "holistic portfolio." The holistic portfolio is a response to continued theorizing about the nature of the composing process. Louise Wetherbee Phelps argues that theories underlying teaching practices evolve toward greater depth, and she sketches a hierarchy of response models to student writing beginning with one she labels "evaluative attitude, closed text" (49). In this model, the instructor treats the student text as "self-contained, complete in itself. . . . a discrete discourse episode to be experienced more or less decontextually" (50). This concept of response to a text views reading as evaluation; instructors responding in this model may speak of "grading a stack of papers." The next response model described by Phelps is one she calls "formative attitude, evolving text" (51). Instructors read students' drafts as part of a process of evolution, thus entering into and influencing the students' composing process. In this model of response, instructors locate "learning largely in the actual composing process" (53).

Phelps describes a third model of response as "developmental attitude, portfolio of work": "Whereas the first group of teachers reads a 'stack' of papers and the second reads collected bits, scraps, and drafts of the composing process, the third reads a 'portfolio' of work by one student" (53). Phelps elaborates on two ways to work with portfolios, describing first the portfolio grading model we have already examined, which she dubs "the weak form." In this approach, she writes, "teachers continue to read and grade individual papers, attempting to help students perfect each one" (53). As Phelps has described the models of response, we can see that she has first described portfolio assessment used in a programmatic approach to large-scale decision making about student proficiency and placement. Her second model fairly accurately describes the portfolio-grading approach of Ford and Larkin and Burnham, elaborated upon somewhat in her depiction of "the weak form" of her third response model.

In the second method of using portfolios, Phelps also describes a different portfolio system. Some instructors employ portfolios because they wish to respond from a "*developmental* perspective." From this perspective, the student writing "blurs as an individual entity" and is treated as a sample "excerpted from a stream of writing stimulated by the writing class, part of the 'life text' each literate person continually produces" (53). Phelps concludes:

> The reader's function is [to read] through the text to the writer's developing cognitive, linguistic, and social capacities as they bear on writing activities. The set of a single writer's texts to which the reader has access, either literally or through memory, is the corpus from which the reader tries to construct a speculative profile of the writer's developmental history and current maturity. (53)

This definition of portfolio no longer serves as an analogy to the commercial artist's carefully assembled portfolio of a representative sampling of her best work. Instead it more closely resembles an archivist's collection of a writer's entire *oeuvre*. Instructors do not deal with selected writings but evaluate the entire output of the student writer. The implications of such a definition are quite different from those of the portfolio grading model defined by Ford and Larkin, Burnham, and Elbow and Belanoff.

While portfolio grading systems are driven by pedagogic concerns with fair grading as well as with composing process theory, the holistic portfolio system is primarily driven by a pedagogical concern with composing process theory. Although Knoblauch and Brannon's polemic *Rhetorical Traditions and the Teaching of Writing* does not discuss portfolio evaluation, its view of the composing process might very readily lead to it. Knoblauch and Brannon describe the "myth of improvement" that has stifled writing instruction by focusing on the kind of evaluation Phelps details in her first model of response (evaluative attitude, closed text). Knoblauch and Brannon suggest that "the most debilitating illusion associated with writing instruction is the belief that teachers can, or at least ought to be able to, control writers' maturation, causing it to occur as the explicit consequence of something they do or ought to do" (165). This illusion is reductionist, leading to a view of the writing course "in minimal functionalist terms" (165). This "myth of improvement" has produced a definition of teaching and curricular success that stresses "trivial but readily demonstrable short-term 'skill' acquisitions" and has led some teachers "to imagine it is fair to 'grade on improvement,' mistaking a willingness to follow orders for real development" (165).

While Knoblauch and Brannon's book remains controversial, their critique of "the myth of improvement" cogently articulates many instructors' reservations about grading practices based on the artificial academic calendar, a system that demands students learn at a given pace, defined by a ten-week quarter, a fourteen-week trimester, or a sixteen-week semester. Knoblauch and Brannon conclude by arguing that "symptoms of growth — the willingness to take risks, to profit from advice, to revise, to make recommendations to others — may appear quickly, even if improved *performance* takes longer" (169).

For instructors whose conception of the composing process is compatible with the developmental schemes underlying Knoblauch and Brannon's book and Phelp's third model of response, the holistic portfolio should have great appeal. It presents these instructors with difficult decisions, however, in the same areas that the portfolio grading system presented its practitioners: grading criteria and standards, the teacher-student relationship, and handling the paper load.

While upholding grading standards was the catalyst for portfolio grading, holistic portfolio systems appear to be less concerned with the notion of grading standards, at least in traditional terms. Because the holistic portfolio system does not focus instructors' attention on specific final drafts, it does present instructors with some major decisions about criteria for the final evaluation.

Several possibilities exist. Instructors may create a grading system that weights final drafts but also grades draft materials, notes, peer commentary, and so on. Counting the number of drafts or the variety of included material is a way to "grade" preliminary materials. However, any counting method might distort the course's emphasis on development by encouraging students to create "phony" drafts, drafts written after the fact simply to pad the portfolio (just as many of us used to compose outlines after completing high school term papers as a way of meeting a course requirement).

Another way to grade the final portfolio is more holistic, and thus probably "purer" in the sense that it avoids treating individual drafts as "collected bits, scraps, and drafts" and portfolios as part of "the life text" (Phelps 53). The instructor looks for "symptoms of growth," to borrow Knoblauch and Brannon's phrase — "the willingness to take risks, to profit from advice, to revise, to make recommendations to others." Those students who demonstrate the greatest growth receive the highest grades, assuming that the instructor has developed a scale that measures growth — no small assumption.

While the holistic portfolio can fit very nicely into a developmental view of the composing process, it presents great difficulties in fitting at all into a traditional academic grading system and poses serious questions for instructors about how they see their writing courses fitting into the academy. This method of evaluation works most readily in a pass/no pass grading situation, indeed is an argument for such a grading system. But pass/no pass writing courses are the exception rather than the rule. Unfortunately, neither Knoblauch and Brannon nor Phelps really addresses the issue of how to grade in a writing course that emphasizes a developmental perspective on writing. It is conceivable that an instructor holistically evaluating a set of portfolios could assign an entire class of industrious students grades of A, having developed grading criteria that emphasize "symptoms of growth"; such an instructor can have rigorous standards in that only those students who have made the effort and demonstrated the growth receive the A's. However, one suspects this instructor would face a one-to-one meeting with a concerned writing program administrator or department chair sometime after submitting the final grades.

Some compromise or accommodation must undoubtedly be made by instructors, perhaps along the lines discussed earlier of weighting final drafts. The important point to make here is that instructors should be aware of how the grading criteria they develop correlate with the theory underlying their use of portfolio evaluation.

Given the problematic nature of grading holistic portfolios, why would instructors adopt this model of the portfolio system? The holistic portfolio system offers distinct advantages in defining a healthy teacher-student relationship. Burnham's hopes of creating a writing environment rather than a grading environment are more readily realized in the holistic portfolio system. Because the final portfolio will not be graded in any traditional sense, because individual grades on drafts do not occur, in theory the classroom using the holistic portfolio can indeed become a writing environment, since there is no reason for it to become a grading environment, and the instructor can truly doff the evaluator's role and don instead the facilitator's role.

Burnham praises portfolio grading for encouraging students to assume responsibility for their learning; portfolio grading "creates independent writers and learners," he concludes (137). His point is that when students know that they can control their grades through extra effort in revising and through the selection process available to them prior to final evaluation, they become more responsible and more independent; in today's terminology, they become "empowered." However, the motivation comes from a concern with grades.

In the holistic portfolio system, the students are also afforded the opportunity to become more responsible, not for their grades so much as for their development. They can indeed become independent learners, independent of traditional grading obsessions as well. The teacher and student can become "co-writers," in Phelps's phrase. The emphasis in the course falls not on improving texts as a means of improving a grade but instead falls on developing as a writer, understanding that this development is more important than grades on individual texts.

Both models of portfolios, then, hope to free students of the tyranny of the grade. The portfolio grading system does so temporarily, but also readily accommodates the traditional institutional need for grades. The holistic portfolio system can indeed free students to become learners and writers for the duration of a writing course but only if instructors have resolved the essential conflict between their course and the institution's demand for traditionally meaningful grades.

In the final area of paper load, it seems most likely that the holistic portfolio system will produce a heavier paper load than the portfolio grading system will. Any schemes to limit students' output would likely conflict with the theoretical assumptions that lead to using the holistic portfolio system. Thus students' portfolios are likely to grow in length as well as in the hoped-for depth of development. At the end of the term, instructors must read not merely a specific number of selected final drafts, but entire portfolios, certainly a slower process. Periodic reading of the growing portfolios — which instructors taking such a developmental perspective will probably wish to do — may reduce the paper load at the end of the course since instructors can scan the familiar materials in the portfolio, but it will not significantly reduce the paper load so much as spread it out over the course of the term.

Instructors contemplating a portfolio system of either sort, or a hybrid version of the two models described, are faced with the need to answer some important questions for themselves before incorporating the system into their writing classes. Louise Weatherbee Phelps concludes her discussion by commenting that her depiction of response models represents an increasing growth on the part of instructors. She argues that "experience itself presses teachers toward increasingly generous and flexible conceptions of the text and the reading task" (59). If she is correct, as I think she is, then the movement in composition classrooms toward portfolio systems of one sort or another will accelerate as the emphasis on the composing process as central to writing courses continues.

As the profession continues to refine its thinking about composition pedagogy, portfolio systems seem destined to proliferate in use and grow in significance. The portfolio system of evaluation has tremendous advantages, which are described throughout the rest of this book, but it also requires great thought on the part of instructors because a portfolio system implemented in a scattershot manner may well undercut the goals of a writing course. The portfolio offers instructors wonderful opportunities to bring their teaching practice in line with their theoretical assumptions about writing and about teaching, but that convergence can only occur if instructors ask themselves the right — and the tough — questions and work out the answers that best provide what both instructors and students need in the writing course.

Note

[1] I am assuming that instructors themselves will grade the papers. Ford and Larkin describe a programmatic use of portfolio grading wherein the portfolios are graded by a team of graders not including the students' instructor. My interest in this essay, however, is in the issues faced by individual instructors who do not have the power to implement such grading practice but must conduct their own evaluations.

Works Cited

Belanoff, Pat, and Marcia Dickson, eds. *Portfolios: Process and Product*. Portsmouth: Boynton/Cook, 1991.

Brannon, Lil, and C. H. Knoblauch. "On Students' Rights to Their Own Texts: A Model of Teacher Response." *College Composition and Communication* 33 (1982): 157–66.

Burnham, Christopher. "Portfolio Evaluation: Room to Breathe and Grow." *Training the New Teacher of College Composition*. Ed. Charles Bridges. Urbana: NCTE, 1986.

Elbow, Peter, and Pat Belanoff. "State University of New York at Stony Brook Portfolio-based Evaluation Program." *New Methods in College Writing Programs*. Ed. Paul Connolly and Teresa Vilardi. New York: MLA, 1986. Reprinted in Belanoff and Dickson.

Emig, Janet. "Writing as a Mode of Learning." *College Composition and Communication* 28 (1977): 122–28.

Ford, James E., and Gregory Larkin. "The Portfolio System: An End to Backsliding Writing Standards." *College English* 39 (1978): 950–55.

Knoblauch, C.H., and Lil Brannon. *Rhetorical Traditions and the Teaching of Writing*. Portsmouth: Boynton/Cook, 1984.

Murray, Donald. "Teaching the Other Self: The Writer's First Reader." *College Composition and Communication* 33 (1982): 140–47.

Phelps, Louise Wetherbee. "Images of Student Writing: The Deep Structure of Teacher Response." *Writing and Response: Theory, Practice, and Research*. Ed. Chris M. Anson. Urbana: NCTE, 1989.

Sommers, Nancy. "Responding to Student Writing." *College Composition and Communication* 33 (1982): 148–56.

Sommers's Insights as a Resource for Your Teaching

1. Sommers emphasizes the serious inquiry a writing teacher should undertake before and while introducing portfolio grading in a writing classroom. If you've kept a reflective journal, scan it for passages where you've clarified your beliefs about the student-instructor relationship you desire and about assessment criteria and grading standards. Work out your portfolio policy from those stances.

2. Pat Belanoff and Peter Elbow have written collaboratively and frequently about what they learned from a portfolio-based evaluation program at the State University of New York at Stony Brook. They emphasize the collaborative learning and the feeling of community that result when writing instructors trade and evaluate student portfolios. To benefit most from using portfolio grading, work with one or two colleagues. Read the portfolios holistically, writing down general impressions and overall strengths and weaknesses. Then talk about how those features influence your responses and grading systems. Such conversation can help you clarify your teaching philosophy and gain confidence about your ways of responding to student writing.

3. The "teaching portfolio" cited throughout this ancillary is, of course, a "developmental portfolio." You will accrue the same benefits of ownership, empowerment, and autonomous learning from your teaching portfolio as can your students from their writing portfolios.

Sommers's Insights as a Resource for the Writing Classroom

1. It's possible to combine the representative and developmental portfolio models so that students can "own" the process and also become more able to identify the ways they have grown as writers. Negotiate with the class the minimum number of writing samples that should be submitted. Require that, for each submission and for the arrangement of the portfolio, students describe the entire process that led to the submitted writing, identify its strengths, and discuss why they view the work as "representative." Ask students to write a cover letter for the portfolio that applies shared criterion — such as an analysis of the "reflectiveness" or

"growth" of the writer as demonstrated by the portfolio. Ask for a discussion of goal setting for continuous growth as a writer and learner. Such self-assessment can lead even the most grade-conscious writers into some independence.

2. Invite class members to think about the writings they have peer-edited and offer advice to the writers about works they would recommend including in a portfolio.

3. Plan a conference or two with individual writers in which each can talk about the works and the decisions being made about submissions. Some students will be apprehensive about a portfolio assignment; some will dive in.

4. Encourage students to look at all they wrote during the term, including writing across the curriculum, in assessing their work and planning submissions.

WRITING ACROSS THE CURRICULUM

Concerns about a "decline" in students' writing and critical thinking abilities along with increased professional understanding of the composing process and of cognitive development have prompted experimentation with writing across the curriculum. More and more educational institutions are defining the teaching and fostering of writing as a professional responsibility shared by all members of the faculty and as the core of any curriculum.

From the title forward, *The Bedford Guide for College Writers* demonstrates that the writer's resources of recall, observation, reading, conversation, and imagination are tapped by thinkers in every corner of the university. The student and professional models, the copious examples of topics for writing assignments, and the "Applying What You Learn" sections reinforce the theory that writing is central to the intellectual (and personal) development of the apprentice scholar as well as the established scholar. The following essay provides a clear and optimistic overview of the groundswell called "writing across the curriculum."

WRITING ACROSS THE CURRICULUM: A BIBLIOGRAPHIC ESSAY

Patricia Bizzell and Bruce Herzberg

Patricia Bizzell and Bruce Herzberg pack an impressive amount of information and definition into a fairly concise essay. You can use this introduction in conversations with teaching colleagues and administrators across the campus. The bibliography provides a good starting point for your reading about this rapidly developing movement.

"Writing across the curriculum" has come to mean three things to writing teachers in America. It denotes, first, a theory of the function of writing in learning; second, a pedagogy to encourage particular uses of writing in learning; and third, a program that applies the pedagogy in a particular school. American interest in the theoretical, pedagogical, and institutional aspects of writing across the curriculum has been growing rapidly in recent years, in part as a response to perceived declines in students' writing ability. Harvey Wiener, president of the Council of Writing Program Administrators, estimates that there are now about four hundred college-level writing-across-the-curriculum programs.[1] Most American scholarship in the field is also recent, appearing after 1975.

The concept of writing across the curriculum was introduced in the 1960s by James Britton and his colleagues at the University of London Institute of Education. They studied language in secondary-level classrooms and found that most speaking, reading, and writing is used to convey information (Barnes et al.). In the London group's seminal work, *The Development of Writing Abilities* (11–18), Britton and his colleagues found that the overwhelming majority of student writing is "transactional," that is, writing used to convey information to a relatively distant and impersonal audience, usually the teacher in the role of examiner. Britton and his colleagues contrasted transactional writing with two other kinds, "poetic" and "expressive." Poetic writing allows the student to step back from the role of active participant in the world, to contemplate and speculate, and to share his or her thoughts with an intimate audience, for example, the teacher in the role of trusted adult. Expressive writing also allows students to explore ideas informally, but in expository modes such as the class journal rather than in fiction or poetry. (For summaries of the London group's work, see Applebee, "Writing"; Rosen; Shafer.)

The London group's studies in developmental psychology and the philosophy of language suggest that adolescents, like younger children, need to use language in personal, exploratory ways, with the support of a friendly audience, in order to learn (Britton). In other words, they need more opportunities for poetic and expressive writing. This need is particularly great for students whose social origins put them at a comparatively greater remove from school conventions of language use. Students need to be able to make connections in their own vernacular between school knowledge and their own interests and values before they can be expected to master transactional writing.

Out of this understanding of the function of the language in learning grew the London group's Writing across the Curriculum Project, headed by Nancy Martin. The Writing across the Curriculum Project published a series of pamphlets demonstrating, with many examples of expressive and poetic writing and talking, the academic benefits of allowing students to use language in the full range of ways. The pamphlets (*Information; Why Write?; Talking; Science; Options*) also suggest assignments for expressive and poetic writing in a variety of disciplines (see also Martin et al.).

A Language for Life, the report of the Bullock Commission, on which Britton served, advocates similar changes in language instruction across the curriculum. (See Brunetti.) This commission was appointed by then Secretary of State for Education and Science Margaret Thatcher to respond to Britain's version of the "back-to-basics" furor. Britton wrote the Bullock Report's chapters on early language development and collaborated on chapters dealing with writing instruction and language across the curriculum.

Britton and his colleagues were influenced by James Moffett's curriculum for *Teaching the Universe of Discourse* on the elementary and secondary levels, a curriculum recently detailed, with suggestions for college use, in Moffett's *Active Voice.* Moffett sorts language along a continuum from private, oral, concrete uses to public, written, abstract uses. Students will more easily master the full range of uses if they are encouraged to begin with those closest to their own speech. These beginning forms of language use are what Britton would call expressive — such as dialogues and letters — and poetic — such as plays and fictional autobiographies. Like Britton, Moffett does not aim to replace all transactional writing with expressive and poetic writing, but rather to help students feel comfortable with the full range of ways to use language to explore and communicate ideas.

Janet Emig was one of the first American theorists to make use of Britton's work. In *The Composing Processes of Twelfth Graders,* she revises Britton's classification of language uses. Her "reflexive" resembles his expressive, and her "extensive" resembles his transactional. Like Britton, she finds that when secondary-level students are given more opportunities to write reflexively, they engage in a more thoughtful writing process, write better and feel better about what they write, and learn more. Emig's argument for the importance of reflexive or expressive writing, however, differs from Britton's. In her seminal essay, "Writing as a Mode of Learning," Emig looks more to cognitive than to developmental psychology for evidence of the importance of all ways to use writing in learning. Whereas the London group emphasizes the continuity between speech and writing, Emig emphasizes the unique cognitive advantages conferred by writing. Writing requires imagining the audience and reinforces learning by involving hand, eye, and brain. The written text facilitates reflecting on and reformulating ideas. Writing thus becomes a central means to constitute and propagate knowledge.

Emig agrees with Britton that students must be given more opportunities to write reflexively (expressively) in all disciplines. Several studies have confirmed her finding that American students on the secondary and college levels do not have such opportunities now, because the great majority of the writing they do is transactional (Donlan; Tighe and Koziol; Eblen). The most comprehensive of these studies is Arthur N. Applebee's *Writing in the Secondary Schools: English and the Content Areas.* American interest in writing across the curriculum has been strengthened by the conjunction of findings that most student writing is transactional, and of widespread feelings that student writing ability is declining. Suspecting a causal relationship, many composition administrators have argued for a program to inform college faculty in all disciplines of the need for expressive and poetic writing, as well as the usual transactional assignments.

In addition to encouraging cross-disciplinary uses of expressive and poetic writing, some work on writing across the curriculum explores uses of language peculiar to the academy. The aim of this work is to reform freshman composition pedagogy as well as writing instruction in courses outside the English department. Elaine Maimon has argued that this new freshman composition pedagogy should teach academic discourse (*Instructor's Manual*). She explains that each academic discipline has its own way of making sense of experience, which is embodied in the discourse conventions of the discipline. Moreover, some discourse conventions are shared by all academic disciplines — that is, there is an academic discourse as well as disciplinary discourses. A. D. Van Nostrand argues that studying academic discourse teaches students how to find — or create — significant relationships between facts, rather than simply to report facts. The freshman composition course, where students learn what ways of relating facts are significant in the academy, is the place where they are initiated into academic discourse (Bizzell).

Writing program administrators have been eagerly exchanging ideas on how to implement the various aims of writing across the curriculum. A national network of writing-across-the-curriculum programs has been formed; several newsletters circulate. College-level writing-across-the-curriculum programs typically take one of two forms, Laurence Peters has found. One common kind of program is centered in an interdisciplinary freshman composition course. The other is centered in upper-level writing-intensive courses in various disciplines.

The most complete account of an interdisciplinary freshman composition course can be found in *Writing in the Arts and Sciences,* a textbook by Elaine Maimon and several of her colleagues from other departments at Beaver College. The book begins with the section "Writing to Learn," which discusses cross-disciplinary uses of expressive writing, heuristics, and informal academic writing, such as class notes and library work. The second major section, "Learning to Write," comprises chapters on discipline-specific discourse such as the humanities research paper, the social science case study, and the natural science laboratory report. A few other textbooks for writing across the curriculum have appeared, and more are likely to come out in the near future (Behrens; Bizzell and Herzberg). Another model for the interdisciplinary course has been developed by David Hamilton: students practice "serious parodies" of disciplinary discourse in order to grasp the underlying conceptual activities specific to each discipline. (See also Rose, "Remedial Writing.")

Writing-across-the-curriculum programs based in upper-level writing-intensive courses frequently stress the importance of expressive writing in all disciplines. Toby Fulwiler has shown how journals can be used both to explore academic content and to relate knowledge to one's own values ("Journals"). With Art Young, he has also edited a collection of essays on the teaching of poetic, expressive, and transactional writing in the Michigan Technological

University writing-across-the-curriculum program. On the other hand, in collections such as those edited by C. William Griffin (*Teaching Writing*) and by Christopher Thaiss, the assumption is not necessarily that expressive writing needs to be increased. Rather, teachers in all disciplines should use writing for learning in ways particularly useful in their disciplines. (See also Odell.)

Faculty development has become an important aspect of writing across the curriculum. Professors who have not been trained to teach writing, whether they teach literature or other academic disciplines, often have too narrow a notion of "good" writing as grammatically correct writing. If they do not see themselves as writers, experiencing the complexities of the composing process, they often do not appreciate students' need for guidance through this process. They may be reluctant to take on the extra work of teaching writing, or fear that it will take time away from essential course content. They may be wary of the writing program administrator's expanded influence in college affairs.

This need for faculty development has prompted much work on how to start a writing-across-the-curriculum program and conduct writing workshops for faculty from all disciplines. Elaine Maimon has given practical advice on coping with intracampus politics ("Cinderella"; "Writing"). Some workshops, such as those conducted by Anne Herrington and Ann Raimes, seek to sensitize faculty to the ways they are teaching academic discourse and to make their assignment design and essay evaluation more effective through discussion of examples from their own courses (see also Rose, "Faculty Talk"; Walvoord). Another kind of workshop aims to develop faculty's view of themselves as writers by asking them to write expressively and to critique each other's work. Toby Fulwiler has been an influential proponent of such workshops ("Showing"). (See also Bergman, "Inclusive Literacy"; Freisinger.)

This American work on pedagogical and institutional concerns has relied for its theoretical underpinnings on the scholarship by Britton — by far the most frequently cited authority — Emig, and Moffett. Their work has helped us to understand the function of writing in the intellectual development of the individual student. But Britton, Emig, and Moffett have done most of their work on the elementary and secondary level. We are only now beginning to realize that new American theoretical work in writing across the curriculum is needed, work which addresses concerns particular to American, college-level writing instruction. This new theoretical work is beginning to take shape around the question of whether all students should be required to learn academic discourse. Mina Shaughnessy has diagnosed basic writers' fundamental problem as ignorance of academic discourse conventions.

In exploring this question, theorists are reexamining the importance of expressive writing in writing-across-the-curriculum programs. Expressive writing plays a part in most programs. It can be regarded as one important stage in a writing process which will issue eventually in finished pieces of academic writing. But C. H. Knoblauch and Lil Brannon have argued that keeping up a student-teacher dialogue through expressive writing should be the main goal of writing across the curriculum, because it is through such dialogue that inquiry methods are learned. They see the teaching of academic discourse as drill in "formal shells," leading to nothing more than "grammar across the curriculum." They fear that students whose home languages are at a relatively greater remove from academic discourse will be unduly penalized by a policy which requires all students to master academic discourse. These students will spend so much time on superficial aspects of academic discourse, such as Standard English usage, that they will have little time left for substantive learning.

Other theorists argue that learning and discourse conventions cannot be separated in the academy. Students must be able eventually to use academic discourse if they are to master the full complexities of academic thinking. The notion of dialogue or conversation as a mode of learning here is redefined to mean not a face-to-face encounter, but a sustained communal enterprise. Charles Bazerman has explained that learning how to enter this ongoing conversation means learning how the academic community talks and writes about what it does. As

Elaine Maimon has argued, this is a matter of "Talking to Strangers" for students unfamiliar with the academic discourse community. But if students are not required to learn this discourse, they risk not participating fully in college intellectual life. To help them, we need more study of how this community develops and transmits its discourse conventions, a study in which scholars trained in literary criticism may be particularly well suited to engage (Maimon, "Maps and Genres").

Such study would help to return rhetoric to its eminent place in the curriculum. James Raymond has argued that rhetoric is the least reductive, most interdisciplinary methodology in the liberal arts. Taking a similar position, James Kinneavy has observed that increased attention to rhetoric helps faculty in all disciplines to communicate better with each other about the intellectual problems upon which they are working. They are thus better prepared to train their students not only to develop complex arguments within the disciplines but also to explain their areas of expertise cogently to a general audience. Kinneavy hopes that the spread of writing-across-the-curriculum programs will eventually revivify informed public discourse in our democracy, since citizens will be better able to sift evidence and evaluate debates on complex issues.

The study of "rhetoric across the curriculum," to coin a phrase, is becoming the study of how the academic community constitutes and legitimates its knowledge through its discourse. We are learning, as Kenneth Bruffee has shown, that knowledge is a "social entity," always collaboratively produced. From such study, too, we learn how other communities similarly constitute themselves in language. Because this is becoming the focus of rhetoric, literary critics have recently been studying it together with composition specialists. In one such fruitful exchange (Horner), eminent scholars agree that the establishment of English departments was justified by a false distinction between literary discourse and discourse that conveys information. This distinction leads to a separation between reading instruction, which focuses upon interpreting literary texts, and writing instruction, which focuses upon producing expository texts. Because this separation not only devalues composition studies but also impoverishes literary theory, it is now ending. A new kind of English department is emerging, united under a rhetorical paradigm, and well suited to study all kinds of discourse, not just fiction and poetry, and to foster rhetoric across the curriculum.

Bibliography

Applebee, Arthur N. "Writing across the Curriculum: The London Projects." *English Journal* 66 (1977): 81–85.
_____. *Writing in the Secondary School: English and the Content Areas.* Urbana: NCTE, 1981. Eighty-two percent of teachers surveyed agree that writing instruction is the responsibility of all faculty. But only 3 percent of lesson time is spent on writing of paragraph length or more. Very little attention is given to the writing process. Virtually all writing is informational (transactional), for an audience of teacher-as-examiner.
Barnes, Douglas, James Britton, and Harold Rosen. *Language, the Learner, and the School.* Harmondsworth: Penguin, 1969.
Bazerman, Charles. "A Relationship between Reading and Writing: The Conversation Model." *College English* 41 (1980): 656–61.
Behrens, Laurence. "Meditations, Reminiscences, Polemics: Composition Readers and the Service Course." *College English* 41 (1980): 561–70. Surveying composition readers, Behrens finds that almost all selections are meditations, reminiscences, or polemics. Most of the writing that students do in other courses, however, seeks to convey information, and students are better at conveying information than they are at writing meditations, reminiscences, and polemics. A new kind of reader is needed to "serve" students by teaching the kinds of writing they do in other courses.
Bergman, Charles A. "An Inclusive Literacy: U. S. Schools Are Teaching and Writing in All the Subject Disciplines." *AAHE Bulletin* (Dec. 1982): 3–5. Bergman argues for writing across the curriculum as a way of demystifying the conventions of academic discourse, and describes the "conversation experience" of faculty at his university after a workshop with Kenneth Bruffee in which they learned to see themselves as writers.

_____. "Writing across the Curriculum: An Annotated Bibliography." *AAHE Bulletin* (1983–84): 33–38. Bergman selects forty-one entries, citing some important theoretical works and a number of articles that describe writing-across-the-curriculum programs at specific schools.

Bizzell, Patricia. "College Composition: Initiation into the Academic Discourse Community." *Curriculum Inquiry* 12 (1982): 191–207. Bizzell argues that students' unequal distance from school discourse is a function of social class, that access to academic discourse is a prerequisite for social power, and that linguistically disenfranchised students can be helped by a writing-across-the-curriculum approach that seeks to demystify the conventions of academic discourse.

Bizzell, Patricia, and Bruce Herzberg. "Writing-across-the-Curriculum Textbooks: A Bibliographic Essay." *Rhetoric Review* 3 (Jan. 1985): 202–17.

Britton, James. *Language and Learning*. Harmondsworth: Penguin, 1970. Britton develops the theory that we construct our understanding of the world through language, an individual task shaped by social interaction.

Britton, James, et al. *The Development of Writing Abilities* (11–18). London: Macmillan Education, 1975; Urbana: NCTE, 1977.

Bruffee, Kenneth. "The Structure of Knowledge and the Future of Liberal Education." *Liberal Education,* 67 (1981): 177–86. We have assumed that knowledge is determined by external reality and should be attained by individual effort in a hierarchical educational system. But the work of Einstein, Heisenberg, and Gödel suggests that knowledge is created and promulgated through social activity. Hence education should be restructured for collaborative work, as in peer-tutoring workshops and writing-across-the-curriculum programs.

Brunetti, Gerald J. "The Bullock Report: Some Implications for American Teachers and Parents." *English Journal* 67 (1978): 58–64.

Bullock Commission. *A Language for Life*. London: HMSO, 1975.

Donlan, Dan. "Teaching Writing in the Content Areas: Eleven Hypotheses from a Teacher Survey." *Research in the Teaching of English* 8 (1974): 250–62.

Dunn, Robert F. "A Response to Two Views." *AAHE Bulletin* (Dec. 1982): 7–8.

Eblen, Charlene. "Writing across-the-Curriculum: A Survey of a University Faculty's Views and Classroom Practices." *Research in the Teaching of English* 17 (1983): 343–48.

Emig, Janet. *The Composing Processes of Twelfth Graders*. Urbana: NCTE, 1971.

_____. "Writing as a Mode of Learning." *College Composition and Communication* 28 (1977): 122–28. Rpt. in *The Writing Teacher's Sourcebook*. Ed. Gary Tate and E. P. J. Corbett. New York: Oxford UP, 1981. 69–78.

Freisinger, Randall R. "Cross-Disciplinary Writing Workshops: Theory and Practice." *College English* 42 (1980): 154–56, 161–66. Following Britton, Freisinger strongly defends the use of expressive writing in all disciplines, in spite of faculty resistance to this notion. He uses Piaget to argue that the absence of expressive writing retards cognitive development in college-age students.

Fulwiler, Toby. "Journals across the Disciplines." *English Journal* 69 (1980): 14–19. Fulwiler cites Britton and Emig on the need for expressive writing across the curriculum, and argues that journals have served this end well. He describes both the "academic journal," which focuses on course content, and the "personal journal," which focuses on ethical responses to course content.

_____. "Showing, Not Telling, at a Writing Workshop." *College English* 43 (1981): 55–63. A good account of Fulwiler's methods in faculty workshops. He details five strategies and recommends conducting the workshop like a retreat.

Fulwiler, Toby, and Art Young, ed. *Language Connections: Writing and Reading across the Curriculum*. Urbana: NCTE, 1982. Twelve essays from the Michigan Tech writing-across-the-curriculum program, written by professors of literature, rhetoric, and reading. Essays address the interdisciplinary teaching of poetic, expressive, and transactional writing. The book includes three essays on reading, two on peer critiquing, and a selected bibliography.

Griffin, C. Williams, ed. *Teaching Writing in All Disciplines*. San Francisco: Jossey-Bass, 1982. Ten essays on writing-across-the-curriculum theory and practice, including John C. Bean, Dean Drenk, and F. D. Lee, "Microtheme Strategies for Developing Cognitive Skills"; Toby Fulwiler, "Writing: An Act of Cognition"; Elaine Maimon, "Writing across the Curriculum: Past, Present, and Future"; Chris Thaiss, "The Virginia Consortium of Faculty Writing Programs: A Variety of Practices"; Barbara Fassler Walvoord and Hoke L. Smith, "Coaching the Process of Writing."

Hamilton, David. "Interdisciplinary Writing." *College English* 41 (1980): 780–90, 795–96. Hamilton describes the Iowa Institute on Writing for writing program administrators, which developed an interdisciplinary freshman composition course using "serious parodies" of discourse modes of various disciplines, with the aim of teaching transferable processes of conceptualization. The article also analyzes the limitations of other interdisciplinary writing courses, such as those that ask students to write about their areas of expertise for a lay audience.

Herrington, Anne J. "Writing to Learn: Writing across the Disciplines." *College English* 43 (1981): 379–87. Following a defense of writing across the curriculum that draws on the work of Emig and Lee Odell, Herrington describes her workshops to help faculty design writing-intensive courses in their own disciplines. She describes good assignments in economics, sociology, and psychology.

Horner, Winifred, ed. *Composition and Literature: Bridging the Gap.* Chicago: U of Chicago P, 1983. Twelve essays by eminent literary critics and composition specialists, including Wayne Booth, E. P. J. Corbett, E. D. Hirsch, Jr., Richard Lanham, Elaine Maimon, and J. Hillis Miller.

Kinneavy, James L. "Writing across the Curriculum." *ADE Bulletin*, 76 (1983): 14–21. Rpt. in *Profession 83*. Ed. Richard Brod and Phyllis Franklin. New York: MLA, 1983. 13–20.

Knoblauch, C. H., and Lil Brannon. "Writing as Learning through the Curriculum." *College English* 45 (1983): 465–74.

Maimon, Elaine. "Cinderella to Hercules: Demythologizing Writing across the Curriculum." *Journal of Basic Writing* 2 (1980): 3–11. Maimon describes and debunks several "myths" that obstruct writing-across-the-curriculum programs, such as the Myth of the Simple Rules, which leads misguided college deans to think that writing across the curriculum is simply a matter of enforcing a few grammar guidelines; the Myth of Cinderella, which casts writing teachers in a menial role; the Myth of Hercules, which envisions an effective program being launched by the writing program administrator alone; and more. This issue of *JBW* includes seven other essays on writing across the curriculum.

———. "Maps and Genres." *Composition and Literature: Bridging the Gap.* Ed. Winifred Horner. Chicago: U of Chicago P, 1983. 110–25.

———. "Talking to Strangers." *College Composition and Communication* 30 (1979): 364–69.

———. "Writing in All the Arts and Sciences: Getting Started and Gaining Momentum." *Writing Program Administration* 4 (1981): 9–13. Maimon discusses administrative problems of launching writing-across-the-curriculum programs; how to deal with resistance within the English department; general curriculum guidelines. This issue of *WPA* also includes Toby Fulwiler, "Writing across the Curriculum at Michigan Tech," an account of his successful faculty seminars there; and a response to both Fulwiler and Maimon by Ann Raimes.

———. *Instructor's Manual: Writing in the Arts and Sciences.* Cambridge: Winthrop, 1981.

Maimon, Elaine P., and Gerald L. Belcher, Gail W. Hearn, Barbara F. Nodine, Finbarr W. O'Connor. *Writing in the Arts and Sciences.* Cambridge: Winthrop, 1981.

Martin, Nancy, et al. *Writing and Learning across the Curriculum 11–16.* London: Ward Lock, 1976.

Moffett, James. *Active Voice: A Writing Program across the Curriculum.* Upper Montclair: Boynton/ Cook, 1981.

———. *Teaching the Universe of Discourse.* Boston: Houghton, 1969.

Odell, Lee. "The Process of Writing and the Process of Learning." *College Composition and Communication* 31 (1980): 42–50. In faculty writing workshops, Odell discovered that writing in different disciplines requires a wide variety of conceptual activities; the inability to perform them is the chief cause of bad student writing. Workshops should not, therefore, seek to persuade faculty to teach any one heuristic method. Elements from a few powerful heuristics, however, can be combined to provide an invention method useful across the disciplines.

Peters, Laurence. "Writing across the Curriculum: Across the U.S." *Writing to Learn: Essays and Reflections by College Teachers across the Curriculum.* Ed. Christopher Thaiss. Fairfax: George Mason U Faculty Writing Program, 1982. 4–19.

Raimes, Ann. "Writing and Learning across the Curriculum: The Experience of a Faculty Seminar." *College English* 41 (1980): 797–801. To attend a seminar led by Raimes and Charles Persky, faculty in several disciplines received released time during the semester so that they could work on writing assignments and use student writing from current courses as the principal "text." Discussions focussed on assignment design and essay evaluation.

Raymond, James C. "Rhetoric: The Methodology of the Humanities." *College English* 44 (1982): 778–83.

Rose, Mike. "Remedial Writing Courses: A Critique and a Proposal." *College English* 45 (1983): 109–28. Rose argues against the focus on personal writing common to many remedial composition programs, and for an interdisciplinary course that introduces developmental students immediately to college-level reading, writing, and thinking tasks.

———. "When Faculty Talk about Writing." *College English* 41 (1979): 272–79. A cross-disciplinary group of faculty, teaching assistants, and student counsellors met to discuss their perceptions of student writing problems and agreed on some action — give professional recognition for composition teaching and research; teach academic discourse in freshman composition; and move university-wide standards for evaluating writing beyond a narrow focus on grammar.

Rosen, Lois. "An Interview with James Britton, Tony Burgess, and Harold Rosen. Closeup: The Teaching of Writing in Great Britain." *English Journal* 67 (1978): 50–58.

Shafer, Robert E. "A British Proposal for Improving Literacy." *Educational Forum* 46 (1981): 81–96. Shafer summarizes work of Britton and his colleagues, giving particular attention to theory. He discusses Britton's spectator/participant distinction; the work of Barnes and Rosen on the chasm between academic discourse and the students' own language; the influence of Sapir, Kelly, and Vygotsky; and the relation between speaking and writing.

Shaughnessy, Mina. "Some Needed Research on Writing." *College Composition and Communication* 28 (1977): 317–21. Shaughnessy argues that basic writers are those "unskilled in the rituals and ways of winning arguments in academe." To help them, we need a taxonomy of academic discourse conventions.

Thaiss, Christopher, ed. *Writing to Learn: Essays and Reflections by College Teachers across the Curriculum*. Fairfax: George Mason U Faculty Writing Program, 1982. Sixteen essays by professors of accounting, education, English, finance, mathematics, nursing, physical education, and psychology. They argue for the value of writing across the curriculum while describing classroom ideas that have worked well.

Tighe, M. A., and S. M. Koziol, Jr. "Practices in the Teaching of Writing by Teachers of English, Social Studies, and Science." *English Education* 4 (1982): 76–85.

Van Nostrand, A. D. "Writing and the Generation of Knowledge." *Social Education* 43 (1979): 178–80. This article heads a special section, "Writing to Learn in Social Studies," edited by Barry K. Beyer and Anita Brostoff, and aimed at secondary-level teachers.

Walvoord, Barbara E. Fassler. *Helping Students Write Well: A Guide for Teachers in All Disciplines*. New York: MLA, 1982. A good book for faculty who have not yet thought about how they teach writing. Walvoord concentrates on ways to respond effectively to student writing above the developmental level. Many specific examples of assignments and student papers.

Writing across the Curriculum Project. *From Information to Understanding: What Children Do with New Ideas*. London: Ward Lock, 1973; Upper Montclair: Boynton/Cook, 1983.

_____. *Why Write?* London: Ward Lock, 1973; Upper Montclair: Boynton/Cook, 1983. Children should be encouraged to write about knowledge important to them, rather than forced to learn particular essay forms.

_____. *From Talking to Writing*. London: Ward Lock, 1973; Upper Montclair: Boynton/Cook, 1983. This pamphlet argues for expressive talk, but also argues that some kinds of thinking can only be accomplished in writing, because writing facilitates reflection and reformulation. Writing assignments should call on these unique powers rather than simply asking for a report on what has been learned.

_____. *Writing in Science: Papers from a Seminar with Science Teachers*. London: Ward Lock, 1973.

_____. *Keeping Options Open: Writing in the Humanities*. London: Ward Lock, 1973; Upper Montclair: Boynton/Cook, 1983.

Writing across the Curriculum as a Resource for Your Teaching

1. You'll find many practical suggestions for reinforcing the theory that writing is a mode of learning in *Teaching with* The Bedford Guide for College Writers: *Practical Suggestions*. Look particularly at the recommendations for teaching in Chapter 3, "Writing from Reading," Chapter 4, "Writing from Conversation," and Chapter 12, "Writing in Class."

2. Use recall to generate a personal list of instances when writing helped you learn to think and to speak appropriately in some discipline that was foreign to your experience. Use observation of your campus and teaching colleagues to generate a list of kinds of writing expected of all students. Use reading of course descriptions in your campus bulletin to draw up a list of learning situations where critical writing is expected. Interview department heads or academic deans about the institutional importance of writing as a mode of inquiry. Survey students to learn their experiences with writing in classes that aren't designated as writing courses. Imagine a course proposal that combines writing instruction with the "seven prin-

ciples of excellent undergraduate education." Then draft an argument for the introduction or improvement of writing across the curriculum on your campus. Keep a copy for your professional portfolio; send the other to appropriate academic officers and to the campus newspaper.

Writing across the Curriculum as a Resource for the Writing Classroom

1. Tap student recall, observation, reading, conversation, and imagining of significant writing experiences across the curriculum. Invite students to discuss the thinking strategies they use when they write inside and outside class. Encourage them to form a community of writers outside your classroom that can sustain them through their college careers. Refer them to the discussion in Chapter 19, "Strategies for Working with Other Writers."

2. Suggest that students conduct field research to analyze the strength of the writing-across-the-curriculum program on your campus. Use the advice about researching in groups that the authors of *The Bedford Guide* provide in *A Writer's Research Manual*.

3. Ask research groups to prepare oral presentations of their analyses of the campus writing-across-the-curriculum program in a public forum. Help them invite appropriate administrators and faculty leaders.

PART FOUR

ANNOTATED BIBLIOGRAPHY

Research into and reflection on the writing process and our process of nurturing writers have proliferated in the past two decades, and even doctoral programs are now offered in rhetoric and composition theory. Many resources are available to help you teach yourself more about teaching writing. I recommend a small library that you need on your shelf, and I list additional materials that will help you develop or improve your philosophy for teaching writing and strategies for doing so.

First, beg, borrow, or barter for these books until you can have your own copies.

Enos, Theresa, ed. *A Sourcebook for Basic Writing Teachers*. Manchester, NJ: McGraw, 1987. Thirty-nine essays extend the discussion of basic writing and complement the Wiener text. The collection focuses on the sociolinguistic dimensions of literacy and shows the range of contemporary research, theory, and practice, building upon the foundation laid by Mina Shaughnessy in *Errors and Expectations*.

Freire, Paulo. *Pedagogy of the Oppressed*. Trans. Myra Bergman Ramos. New York: Seabury, 1968. Freire argues that literacy empowers the individual and that through the process of "naming his world," a person becomes free. His discussion of learner and master-learner collaborating in dialogue and action provides a useful model for writing as process pedagogy.

Graves, Richard. *Rhetoric and Composition: A Sourcebook for Teachers and Writers*. 3rd ed. Upper Montclair: Boynton/Cook, 1990. Graves organized this sourcebook for writing teachers of all levels. The thirty-eight selections by well-known theorists and researchers document the energetic growth in the discipline of writing since 1963. Five chapters introduce the novice instructor to and update the veteran instructor about the growth and health of the scholarly discipline; practicing teachers' reports and "lore"; strategies to motivate student writers; questions about style; and "new perspectives, new horizons."

Irmscher, William F. *Teaching Expository Writing*. New York: Holt, 1979. The first text written for teachers of writing, this book poses the central questions every new teacher has. Irmscher writes from all the writer's resources: recall of his decades of teaching writing and his status as the "most senior" director of a composition program; humanistic observation of students as writers; conversation with writers and writing specialists; continuous reading in the discipline; and a lively imagination.

Lindemann, Erika. *A Rhetoric for Writing Teachers*. New York: Oxford UP, 1982. Lindemann does not supplant Irmscher but enriches the reading about teaching writing. Her text reports both theory and practice. I use both Irmscher and Lindemann as required texts in my course Teaching College Composition.

Shaughnessy, Mina P. *Errors and Expectations: A Guide for the Teacher of Basic Writing*. New York: Oxford UP, 1977. Shaughnessy was the first to demonstrate a respect for an understanding of the processes that "basic writers" experience. This landmark study helps clarify the philosophy of teaching basic writers and design curriculum and classroom practice to assist these writers to develop into mature writers.

Tate, Gary, and Edward P. J. Corbett, eds. *The Writing Teacher's Sourcebook*. New York: Oxford UP, 1981. You'll find many of the articles listed below in this collection. It's a good jumping-off point for your reading.

Wiener, Harvey S. *The Writing Room: A Resource Book for Teachers of English*. New York: Oxford UP, 1981. Like Irmscher and Lindemann, Wiener offers advice about teaching writing from day one. His focus is the basic writing classroom and his discussion is informed — like Shaughnessy's — by his classroom experiences in an open-doors writing program.

Second, write to Bedford Books of St. Martin's Press (29 Winchester Street, Boston, MA 02116) for a free copy of *The Bedford Bibliography for Teachers of Writing,* Third Edition (1991). The *Bibliography* lists and annotates the essential materials for writing teachers. It begins with a particularly helpful history of the rhetorical tradition and a description of the contemporary issues and theories of teaching composition. You need it in your library.

Third, you might sample some of these materials as you reflect on your process of teaching writing.

Philosophies and Pedagogies

Berlin, James. "Rhetoric and Ideology in the Writing Class." *College English* 50.5 (Sept. 1988): 477–94. Berlin describes three rhetorics and their ideological implications that show up most often in contemporary writing classrooms: cognitive psychology with Linda Flower as the "representative rhetorician"; expressionism, with Peter Elbow and Donald Murray; and socio-epistemic with Ira Shor.

Berthoff, Ann E. *Reclaiming the Imagination: Philosophical Perspectives for Writers and Teachers of Writers.* Upper Montclair: Boynton/Cook, 1983. Berthoff's theme of "reclaiming the imagination" reflects her philosophy and practice of encouraging writing as dialectical and reflective action.

Bruffee, Kenneth A. "Social Construction, Language, and the Authority of Knowledge: A Bibliographical Essay." *College English* 48 (Dec. 1986): 773–90. This introduction to social constructivist thought in literary criticism and history with its connections to composition studies lays out a foundation of a "socio-epistemic" approach to teaching writing. Bruffee provides a bibliography to help other writing teachers explore these philosophical underpinnings.

Hillocks, George, Jr. "What Works in Teaching Composition: A Meta-Analysis of Experimental Treatment Studies." *American Journal of Education* 93 (Nov. 1984): 133–70. Hillocks reviews experimental treatment studies of the teaching of composition over twenty years. While assessing the effectiveness of different modes and focuses of instruction, he found that a writing-as-process focus within an "environmental mode" edged ahead of other approaches to composition. His discussion of the implications of the research is especially useful.

Moffett, James. *Coming on Center: Essays in English Education.* Portsmouth, NH: Boynton/Cook, 1988. Moffett makes practical suggestions about ways to teach reading and writing in the current state of the art. His talks and essays range from writing as a process of "liberating inner speech" to connections among cognition, holistic learning, and collaboration to a pluralistic curriculum to improvement of English teaching.

——. *Teaching the Universe of Discourse.* Boston: Houghton, 1968. Although first published in 1968, this text continues to assist writing teachers with its encouragement and practical demonstrations of ways to prompt the development of communication skills. The text emphasizes the necessity of designing sequences of activities that correlate with both affective and cognitive growth of the student.

Myers, Greg. "Reality, Consensus, and Reform: Rhetoric of Composition Teaching." *College English* 48 (Feb. 1986): 154–74. Myers analyzes and raises questions about two teaching strategies: collaborative work in peer editing and case assignments based on some "real" writing situations.

Myers, Miles, and James Gray. *Theory and Practice in the Teaching of Composition.* Urbana: NCTE, 1983. The text has a double audience: it shows teachers how their strategies for teaching writing connect to and reflect an area of research, and it shows researchers that what teachers do intuitively can often be validated by research. The organization of readings by the teaching methods of processing, distancing, and modeling is especially useful.

Smith, Frank. "Myths of Writing." *Language Arts* 58.7 (Oct. 1981): 792–98. Smith describes and clarifies twenty-one misconceptions that students, faculty, and the public hold about what writing is, how it is learned, and who can teach it.

Responding to Student Writing

Cooper, Charles R., and Lee Odell, eds. *Evaluating Writing: Describing, Measuring, Judging.* Urbana: NCTE, 1977. With its comprehensive survey of ways teachers can describe writing and measure the growth of writing, this remains a useful sourcebook. The discussion of involving students in the evaluation of writing includes individual goal setting, self-evaluation, and peer evaluation. Multiple responses to multiple processes and features of the writing are implicitly recommended.

Hillocks, George, Jr. "The Interaction of Instruction, Teacher Comment, and Revision in Teaching the Composing Process." *Research in the Teaching of English* 16 (Oct. 1982): 261–82. An early study

ANNOTATED BIBLIOGRAPHY

of the effects of instructor response on student revision and attitudes toward writing. The article points out that helpful commentary or conference discussion promotes a writer's growth.

Odell, Lee. "Defining and Assessing Competence in Writing." *The Nature and Measurement of Competency in English*. Ed. Charles R. Cooper. Urbana: NCTE, 1981. Practical advice about clarifying what an instructor defines as writing competence along with descriptions of holistic and other assessment measures for both classroom and large-scale assessment.

White, Edward M. *Teaching and Assessing Writing*. San Francisco: Jossey-Bass, 1985. White argues skillfully that good teaching practice should inform assessment and that assessment is valuable to instructors. He demonstrates that the process of assessing and describing student writing clarifies and makes specific the responses of instructors to students.

Getting Started

Emig, Janet. *The Composing Processes of Twelfth Graders*. Urbana: NCTE, 1971. In this pioneer study of the processes students use to write, Emig identified two modes of composing: extensive and reflexive. Twelfth-grade writers began composing "extensively" because of class activities, but they composed "reflexively" because of actions they initiated. Emig concluded that the data demonstrated that major changes were needed in the way that writing was taught in secondary school.

Fulwiler, Toby. *The Journal Book*. Portsmouth, NH: Boynton/Cook, 1987. Forty-two essays discuss the use of journals for discovery and invention in writing classrooms and in other disciplines across the curriculum.

Rose, Mike. *When a Writer Can't Write: Studies in Writer's Block and Other Composing-Process Problems*. New York: Guilford, 1985. Eleven essays identify and analyze cognitive and affective dimensions of writing apprehension. The range of discussion emphasizes the effects of the environment and writing situations on the writer: novice writers, ESL writers, graduate students, and professional writers are all affected by writing apprehension at various times.

_____. *Writer's Block: The Cognitive Dimension*. Carbondale: Southern Illinois UP, 1984. This landmark book researching and analyzing writer's block emphasizes that a variety of cognitive difficulties are behind the problem. Case studies and the report of research results offer useful insights about ways to teach writing that will enable writers to get beyond blocks.

Rewriting

Bartholomae, David. "The Study of Error." *College Composition and Communication* 31 (Oct. 1980): 253–69. Bartholomae encourages a study of how students revise texts as they speak aloud about them. He connects the phenomenon to his definition of basic writing as a kind of writing produced as students learn the knowledge of a new discourse community.

Flower, Linda, John R. Hayes, Linda Carey, Karen Schriver, and James Stratman. "Detection, Diagnosis, and the Strategies of Revision." *College Composition and Communication* 37 (Feb. 1986): 16–55. This article, produced through collaborative research and writing, describes some of the important intellectual activities that underlie and affect the process of revision. The article presents a working model for revision, for identifying "problems," and for generating solutions.

Freedman, Sarah, ed. *The Acquisition of Written Language: Response and Revision*. Writing Research: Multidisciplinary Inquiries into the Nature of Writing Series. Norwood, NJ: Ablex, 1985. Governed by a definition of writing as both a form of language learning and an intellectual skill, this collection of essays focuses on three topics: the language of instruction and the means by which response and revision occur in educational settings; the use of computers for response to and revision of writing; and research on and theories about revision.

Harris, Muriel. "Composing Behaviors of One- and Multi-Draft Writers." *College English* 51 (Feb. 1989): 174–91. This study of eight experienced writers who described themselves as one-draft or multidraft writers provides useful materials for individualizing the processes of rewriting for students.

Maimon, Elaine. "Talking to Strangers." *College Composition and Communication* 30 (Dec. 1979): 364–69. This early article emphasizes that revision and peer evaluation of drafts can enhance student writers' understanding of how writers revise to meet the needs of the "reader as stranger."

Sudol, Ronald A., ed. *Revising: New Essays for Teachers of Writing*. Urbana: NCTE, 1982. Useful essays describing both the practice and the theory of revising strategies and processes.

255

Thinking Critically

Berthoff, Ann. "Is Teaching Still Possible? Writing, Meaning, and Higher Order Reasoning." *College English* 46.6 (Dec. 1984): 743–55. Berthoff surveys and evaluates models of cognitive development and their connections to positivist perspectives on language. She discusses alternative perspectives on language and learning that emphasize reading and writing as interpretation and as the making of meaning.

Elbow, Peter. "Teaching Thinking by Teaching Writing." *Change* 15.6 (Sept. 1983): 37–40. Elbow's argument that "first-order creative, intuitive thinking and second-order critical thinking" can and should be encouraged in writing instruction could be used for writing across the curriculum initiatives.

Flower, Linda, and John R. Hayes. "The Cognition of Discovery: Defining a Rhetorical Problem." *College Composition and Communication* 31.1 (Feb. 1980): 21–32. The researchers used protocol analysis to study the differences between writers engaged in problem-solving cognitive processes.

Karbach, Joan. "Using Toulmin's Model of Argumentation." *Journal of Teaching Writing* 6.1 (Spring 1987): 81–91. This article illustrates the use of Toulmin's three-part model of argumentation: data, warrant, and claim. While describing heuristic procedures, Karbach proposes this informal logic as a strategy for teaching inductive and deductive logic within any writing assignment.

Kneupper, Charles. "Argument: A Social Constructivist Perspective." *Journal of the American Forensic Association* 17.4 (Spring 1981): 183–89. A communication specialist analyzes argumentation theory from the perspective of social constructionism. He examines uses and connections between argument as structure and argument as process along with their socio-epistemic implications.

Lunsford, Andrea. "Cognitive Development and the Basic Writer." *College English* 41 (Sept. 1979): 39–46. After reviewing theories of cognitive development, Lunsford demonstrates that many basic writers operate below the stage of forming concepts and have difficulty in "decentering." She recommends strategies and writing assignments to help basic writers practice and acquire more complex cognitive skills.

_____. "The Content of Basic Writers' Essays." *College Composition and Communication* 31.3 (Oct. 1980): 278–90. Lunsford reports that three factors affect word choice and linguistic flexibility of basic writers: the level of writing skill they bring to a classroom, their stages of cognitive development, and their self-concepts.

Shor, Ira. *Critical Teaching and Everyday Life.* Boston: South End, 1980. Influenced by Paulo Freire's pedagogical theories, Shor emphasizes learning through dialogue. His analysis of education is inclusive: open admissions teaching of writing, traditional and nontraditional students and learning environments, elite and nonelite educational missions, and "liberatory" teaching modes that challenge social limits of thought and action and encourage cultural literacy. Cognitive skills are acquired and enhanced through collaborative problem solving and reflection leading to action.

Collaborative Learning

Bruffee, Kenneth A. "Collaborative Learning and the 'Conversation of Mankind.' " *College English* 46 (Nov. 1984): 635–52. Bruffee explains collaborative learning as "the conversation of mankind"; he emphasizes the social constructivist philosophy of Richard Rorty in his analysis and demonstration of the processes of negotiation and consensus in writing classrooms.

_____. "On Not Listening in order to Hear: Collaborative Learning and the Rewards of Classroom Research." *Journal of Basic Writing* 7 (Spring 1988): 3–12. Bruffee describes the history of his early work with collaborative learning and discusses how collaborative learning provides a wealth of information for classroom research.

_____. *A Short Course in Writing.* 3rd ed. Chicago: Scott, 1985. This textbook with prompts for creative and transactional writing can be used in classrooms or by an individual for self-teaching. Chapters 4 and 5 describe and argue for an autonomous writing class in which a number of writers meet regularly to react to the writing of group members.

Skon, Linda, David W. Johnson, and Roger T. Johnson. "Cooperative Peer Interaction versus Individual Competition and Individualistic Efforts: Effects on the Acquisition of Cognitive Reasoning Strategies." *Journal of Educational Psychology* 73 (1981): 83–92. The researchers compared the effects of cooperative, competitive, and individualistic goal structure on what students achieve and what higher-order cognitive reasoning strategies they learned. The results indicated that cooperative goal structures and the collaboration that ensued prompted higher achievement and more discovery of higher-order cognitive reasoning strategies.

Trimbur, John. "Consensus and Difference in Collaborative Learning." *College English* 51 (Oct. 1989): 602–17. Trimbur extends the conversation about Bruffee's writing on collaborative learning and responds to critical counterclaims by emphasizing the practical realities of collaborative learning.

Reading and Writing Connections

Berthoff, Ann. *Thinking, Writing: The Composing Imagination*. Portsmouth, NH: Heinemann, 1982. Berthoff focuses on the reading-writing relationship within a course organized around the central task of teaching composition. Insights and practical suggestions abound.

Bizzell, Patricia. "On the Possibility of a Unified Theory of Composition Theory and Literature." *Rhetoric Review* 4.2 (Jan. 1986): 174–80. Bizzell suggests that no unifying theory for composition and literature has emerged because of a lack of dominant theories in either discipline. She believes that such a theory can now be developed because of the similarity of current controversies in both fields.

Flower, Linda, and Christina Haas. "Rhetorical Reading Strategies and the Construction of Meaning." *College Composition and Communication* 39.2 (May 1988): 167–83. This article argues that writing instructors should help students move from an information-exchange perspective on reading to a more complex rhetorical process of constructing meaning.

Flower, Linda, and Thomas Hucking. "Reading for Points and Purposes." *Journal of Advanced Composition* 11.2 (Fall 1991): 347–62. By researching how undergraduate and graduate students use point-driven or purpose-driven reading strategies, the authors conclude that readers who use a point-driven strategy tend to stay at a less complex level of interpretation.

Newkirk, Thomas, ed. *Only Connect: Uniting Reading and Writing*. Upper Montclair: Boynton/Cook, 1986. The fifteen articles in this collection by major scholars in the discipline of "English" explore the relationships of reading and literary study to composition.

Scriven, Karen. "Composition as Content: Clarifying the Limits of Literature in the Writing Classroom." *Writing Instructor* 7.3/4 (Spring–Summer 1988): 115–21. Arguing for composition as a distinct discipline from literary studies, Scriven describes problems that can occur when instructors use literature in composition courses. She concludes that limited use of literature can strengthen student writing.

Smith, Frank. *Essays into Literacy*. Portsmouth, NH: Heinemann, 1983. Smith's theory about literacy as the ability to make use of all available possibilities of written language informs thirteen essays written over a ten-year period. The research into and reflection on elementary and secondary reading and writing experiences produced insights that transfer easily to discussion of college-level literacies.

Literacy, Diversity, and Multiculturalism

Heath, Shirley Brice. "An Annotated Bibliography on Multicultural Writing and Literacy Issues." *Quarterly of the National Writing Project and the Center for the Study of Writing and Literacy* 12.1 (Winter 1990): 22–24. This bibliography lists and annotates sixteen books and articles that focus on multicultural writing and literacy issues, including bilingual education, English as a second language, writing instruction, literacy, and multicultural education.

Herrington, Anne. "Basic Writing: Moving the Voices from the Margin to the Center." *Harvard Educational Review* 60.4 (Nov. 1990): 489–96. Herrington describes the redesign of a basic writing course to give voice to marginalized minority students. After a shift to reading works by mostly nonwhite authors, students were encouraged to reflect in writing on those readings and on their experiences of marginalization.

Raimes, Ann. "Language Proficiency, Writing Ability, and Composing Strategies: A Study of ESL College Student Writers." *Language Learning* 37.3 (Sept. 1987): 439–68. Raimes analyzed the writing strategies of ESL student writers from different levels of ESL instruction. She found that although both native and nonnative writers shared many strategies, ESL learners were less inhibited by attempts to correct their work.

Rose, Mike. *Lives on the Boundary: The Struggles and Achievements of America's Underprepared*. New York: Free, 1989. Through personal narrative and incisive analysis, Rose describes the underclass of students representing diverse cultures and subcultures who are considered underachieving, remedial, or illiterate. Rose speculates about the nature of literacy and liberal learning curricula that could empower these marginalized writers and learners.

Assessing Student Writing

Belanoff, Patricia, and Marcia Dickson, eds. *Portfolios: Process and Product*. Portsmouth, NH: Boynton/ Cook, 1991. In the first comprehensive collection of writings on using portfolios for classroom and portfolio assessment, the editors called for "practitioners' lore" and research. This is the book to start with when considering use of writing portfolios.

White, Edward M. *Assigning, Responding, Evaluating: A Writing Teacher's Guide*. New York: St. Martin's, 1992. For the "state of the art" in writing assessment, White surveys and evaluates the designs and applications of writing assessments and helps writing instructors use the information garnered through assessment to improve classroom instruction.

———. *Teaching and Assessing Writing*. San Francisco: Jossey-Bass, 1985. The publisher here is significant: in this first major discussion of the symbiosis of writing assessment and classroom teaching, the preeminent publisher of discourse in higher education agreed that this would be an important test. This should be the first book a new writing teacher uses to learn about contemporary research and practice in understanding, evaluating, and improving students' writing performance.

Yancey, Kathleen Blake, ed. *Portfolios in the Writing Classroom: An Introduction*. Urbana: NCTE, 1992. This collection focuses on the use of writing portfolios in secondary and higher education courses across the curriculum. The articles describe objectives and designs for the use of portfolios. Some theoretical discussion appears in assorted entries. Like most NCTE publications, this is a very useful introduction to the field.

Writing across the Curriculum

Fulwiler, Toby, and Art Young, eds. *Language Connections: Writing and Reading across the Curriculum*. Urbana: NCTE, 1982. This text, aimed at all college and university instructors, offers theoretical perspectives and practical activities to prompt writing as learning. The text encourages peer evaluation, conferences between instructors and students, and shared evaluation and includes a limited bibliography on cross-curricular language and learning.

Herrington, Anne. "Writing to Learn: Writing across the Disciplines." *College English* 43 (Apr. 1981): 379–87. This essay focuses on the design of writing assignments that can be connected to course objectives, whatever the discipline. Herrington encourages instructors to emphasize writing as discovery and learning in their responses to student writing.

Professional Development

Gotswami, Dixie, ed. *Reclaiming the Classroom: Teacher Research as an Agency of Change*. Upper Montclair: Boynton/Cook, 1987. This book of essays describes reasons for and methods of conducting research in the classroom. Its scope is impressive, both in variety of research projects and methodologies and in discussions of the effects on instructors and students. The editor has pulled together important — and often original — essays by the leading teacher-scholars in composition and rhetoric.

Myers, Miles. *The Teacher-Researcher: How to Study Writing in the Classroom*. Urbana: NCTE, 1985. An introduction to classroom writing assessment and research into writing processes, this book reviews procedures for teacher research and theoretical frameworks. It shows teachers — from kindergarten through college — ways to study writing in the classroom using specific examples of research.

New and Best-Selling Short Fiction Anthologies

THE SITUATION OF THE STORY
Short Fiction in Contemporary Perspective
Diana Young

■ innovative new short story anthology ■ 50 selections (35 of which appear in no other anthology of short fiction) arranged in 8 story groupings reflecting major concerns of contemporary literary theory ■ a unique mix of 24 little known, hard-to-find stories by well known writers, 16 stories by writers whose work is seldom reprinted, and 10 classic stories ■ unusual organization provides an apt setting for lesser known works and a fresh context for familiar ones ■ unobtrusiv apparatus includes chapter introductions which situate each story withi that chapter's topic and brief biographical footnotes that focus on each author's development as a writer

1993/paper/
pages/$19 net/
uctor's Manual

MAJOR WRITERS OF SHORT FICTION
Stories and Commentaries

Ann Charters, *University of Connecticut*

■ 40 major authors treated in depth ■ 93 short stories, including 54 rarely anthologized pieces and 39 frequently reprinted classics (here in fresh company) ■ 43 commentaries — at least one for each writer ■ biographical headnotes for each author ■ bibliographies of each writer's paperback short story collections ■ 4 appendices from *The Story and Its Writer,* Third Edition: history of the short story, elements of fiction, writing about short stories, and glossary of literary terms

1993/paper/
pages/$21 net/
uctor's Manual

THE STORY AND ITS WRITER
An Introduction to Short Fiction
Third Edition

Ann Charters, *University of Connecticut*

■ 115 stories by 100 writers ■ 59 commentaries by 55 writers and critics ■ more stories by women (47) and by contemporary American writers (34) than in any comparable anthology ■ 48 stories by international writers ■ 4 appendices: history of the short story, elements of fiction, writing about short stories, and glossary of literary terms ■ highly praised instructor's manual

90/paper/
ages/$21 net/
ctor's Manual

Bedford Books *of* St. Martin's Press
For exam copies, call 1-800-446-8923

ACKNOWLEDGMENTS

Linda Flower, "The Construction of Purpose in Writing and Reading," *College English,* September 1988. Copyright 1988 by the National Council of Teachers of English. Reprinted with permission. "Writer-Based Prose: A Cognitive Basis for Problems in Writing," *College English,* September 1979. Copyright 1979 by the National Council of Teachers of English. Reprinted with permission.

Muriel Harris, "Cultural Differences which Influence Writing." From *Teaching One to One: The Writing Conference,* pp. 87–94 (with notes). Copyright 1987 by the National Council of Teachers of English. Reprinted with permission.

Betsy S. Hilbert, "It Was a Dark and Nasty Night It Was a Dark and You Would Not Believe How Dark It Was a Hard Beginning," *College Composition and Communication,* February 1992. Copyright 1992 by the National Council of Teachers of English. Reprinted with permission.

Sondra Perl, "Understanding Composing," *College Composition and Communication,* December 1980. Copyright 1980 by the National Council of Teachers of English. Reprinted with permission.

Anthony R. Petrosky, "From Story to Essay: Reading and Writing," *College Composition and Communication,* February 1982. Copyright 1982 by the National Council of Teachers of English. Reprinted with permission.

Ann Raimes, "Out of the Woods: Emerging Traditions in the Teaching of Writing," by Ann Raimes, 1991, *TESOL Quarterly,* Vol. 25, No. 3, p. 407. Copyright 1991 by Teachers of English to Speakers of Other Languages, Inc. Reprinted by permission.

Mike Rose, "Crossing Boundaries." From *Lives on the Boundary: The Struggles and Achievements of America's Underprepared.* Edited with the permission of The Free Press, a Division of Macmillan, Inc., from *Lives on the Boundary* by Mike Rose. Copyright 1989 by Mike Rose.

Ira Shor, "Extraordinarily Re-Experiencing the Ordinary: Theory of Critical Teaching." From *Critical Teaching and Everyday Life,* pp. 96–113 (with notes). © 1980, 1987 by Ira Shor. All rights reserved.

Jeffrey Sommers, "Bringing Practice in Line with Theory: Using Portfolio Grading in the Composition Classroom." Reprinted with permission from Jeffrey Sommers. In *Portfolios: Process and Product,* edited by Pat Belanoff and Marcia Dickson (Boynton/Cook Publishers, Portsmouth, NH, 1991).

Nancy Sommers, "Responding to Student Writing," *College Composition and Communication,* May 1982. Copyright 1982 by the National Council of Teachers of English. Reprinted with permission. "Revision Strategies of Student Writers and Experienced Adult Writers," *College Composition and Communication,* December 1980. Copyright 1980 by the National Council of Teachers of English. Reprinted with permission.

Edward M. White, "Reconsidering the Links between Teaching and Assessing Writing." From *Teaching and Assessing Writing: Recent Advances in Understanding, Evaluating, and Improving Student Performance,* pp. 1–17. Copyright 1985 by Jossey-Bass Inc., Publishers. *Teaching and Assessing Writing* may by purchased from Jossey-Bass Inc., 350 Sansome Street, San Francisco, CA 94104. For ordering information, please call Customer Service at (415) 433-1767.

Harvey S. Wiener, "Collaborative Learning in the Classroom: A Guide to Evaluation," *College English,* January 1986. Copyright 1986 by the National Council of Teachers of English. Reprinted with permission.

CASE STUDIES IN CONTEMPORARY CRITICISM

Series Editor Ross C Murfin, *University of Miami*

■ highly-praised and widely-adopted series
■ each volume reprints an authoritative text of a classic literary work together with 5 critical essays representing 5 contemporary critical approaches ■ each critical essay has been especially written or edited for undergraduates and is preceded by an introduction (with bibliography) to that critical perspective
■ the work itself is preceded by an introduction providing important biographical and historical contexts and followed by a survey of critical responses since publication

FORTHCOMING TITLES

Gulliver's Travels, The House of Mirth, Great Expectations, The Turn of the Screw, The Dead

A PORTRAIT OF THE ARTIST AS A YOUNG MAN
James Joyce
edited by
R. B. Kershner,
University of Florida

December 1992/
paper/416 pages/
$6.00 net

Psychoanalytic Criticism: Sheldon Brivic
Reader-Response Criticism: Norman Holland
Feminist Criticism: Suzette Henke
Deconstruction: Cheryl Herr
The New Historicism: R. B. Kershner

FRANKENSTEIN
Mary Shelley
edited by
Johanna M. Smith,
University of Texas at Arlington

1992/paper/
358 pages/
$6 net

Reader-Response Criticism: Mary Lowe-Evans
Psychoanalytic Criticism: David Collings
Feminist Criticism: Johanna M. Smith
Marxist Criticism: Warren Montag
Cultural Criticism: Lee E. Heller

WUT[HERING] HEIG[HTS]
Emily [Brontë]
edit[ed by]
Lind[a]
Yale [University]

1992/paper/
467 pages/
$6 net

Psychoanalytic Criticism: [...]
Feminist Criticism: Marg[...]
Deconstruction: J. Hillis [...]
Marxist Criticism: Terry [...]
Cultural Criticism: Nanc[...]

THE AWAKENING
Kate Chopin
edited by
Nancy A. Walker,
Vanderbilt University

December 1992/
paper/320 pages/
$6.00 net

Feminist Criticism: Elaine Showalter
The New Historicism: Margit Stange
Psychoanalytic Criticism: Cynthia Griffin Wolff
Deconstruction: Patricia S. Yaeger
Reader-Response Criticism: Paula A. Treichler

HAMLET
William Shakespeare
edited by
Susanne L. Wofford,
University of Wisconsin, Madison

May 1993/
paper/352 pages/
$4.50 net (tentative)

Psychoanalytic Criticism: Janet Adelman
Marxist Criticism: Michael D. Bristol
Feminist Criticism: Elaine Showalter
Deconstruction: Marjorie Garber
The New Historicism: Karin S. Coddon

THE SCARLET LETTER
Nathaniel Hawthorne
edited by
Ross C Murfin,
University of Miami

1991/paper/
371 pages/
$6 net

Psychoanalytic Criticism: Joanne Feit Diehl
Reader-Response Criticism: David Leverenz
Feminist Criticism: Shari Benstock
Deconstruction: Michael Ragussis
The New Historicism: Sacvan Bercovitch

HE[ART OF] DA[RKNESS]
Jos[eph Conrad]
edit[ed by]
R[oss]
Un[iversity of Miami]

1989/paper/
270 pages/
$6 net

Psychoanalytic Criticis[m:] [...]
Reader-Response Criti[cism:] [...]
Feminist Criticism: Joh[...]
Deconstruction: J. Hilli[s...]
The New Historicism: [...]